# Chris Leadbetter, Stewart Wainwright and Alan Stinchcombe

## Cambridge IGCSE®

# Computer Studies

## Coursebook

**Completely Cambridge – Cambridge resources for Cambridge qualifications**

Cambridge University Press works closely with University of Cambridge International Examinations (CIE) as parts of the University of Cambridge. We enable thousands of students to pass their CIE Exams by providing comprehensive, high-quality, endorsed resources.

To find out more about CIE
visit www.cie.org.uk

To find out more about Cambridge University Press
visit www.cambridge.org/cie

# CAMBRIDGE
### UNIVERSITY PRESS

University Printing House, Cambridge CB2 8BS, United Kingdom

Cambridge University Press is part of the University of Cambridge.

It furthers the University's mission by disseminating knowledge in the pursuit of education, learning and research at the highest international levels of excellence.

Information on this title: education.cambridge.org

© Cambridge University Press 2011

First published 2011
8th printing 2015

Printed in the United Kingdom by Latimer Trend

*A catalogue record for this publication is available from the British Library*

ISBN 978-0-521-17063-5 Paperback with CD-ROM for Windows® and Mac®

® IGCSE is the registered trademark of University of Cambridge International Examinations

Cover image: Frank Muckenheim / Westend61 / Corbis

# Contents

## Part II: Uses and implications

## Part III: Problem solving with programs and logic gates

# Introduction

Welcome to the new, full-colour *Cambridge IGCSE Computer Studies*. Like its companion volume, *Cambridge IGCSE ICT*, this book has evolved from *IGCSE and O Level: Computer Studies and Information Technology*. While drawing on many of the topics in the parent book that are relevant to Computer Studies, this new text has been extensively revised and considerably enlarged, for two main reasons:

- to focus clearly on the *Cambridge Local Examinations Syndicate* IGCSE examination in Computer Studies (syllabus 0420) including the exam board's latest house style for presenting pseudocode and logic gates in exam papers;
- to update the content with recent developments in computer technology and its effects on our lives.

In making these changes, we have:

- ensured that explanations are as accessible as possible to students and included a Glossary at the end of the coursebook, which gives definitions for all the key terms presented in bold type in the text;
- included practical examples of the devices, processes and methods being explained;
- included brand-new short, self-assessment questions throughout the text;
- revised and updated the questions for individual work and class discussion;
- refreshed the design, making full use of colour and photographs where possible;
- created a brand-new CD-ROM, loaded with materials to improve your chances in the examination.

The coursebook is designed to help students studying for the *Cambridge Local Examinations Syndicate* IGCSE examination in Computer Studies (syllabus 0420). It provides support for: the compulsory question paper, Paper 1, syllabus Sections 1–5; the coursework, Paper 2; and the alternative to coursework question paper, Paper 3, syllabus Section 6. On the CD-ROM, we have supplied material for revision of the coursebook material

and further support with exemplar answers and our examiner's comments for tackling Papers 1, 2 and 3.

We have divided the coursebook into three parts: Part I deals with the theory of computer technology, Part II deals with applications of the technology and Part III deals with programming and logic gates. Each chapter begins with a list of learning objectives (headed 'When you have finished this chapter you will be able to:'), which is intended to provide a skeleton upon which to hang the detail provided in the text. Also, each chapter ends with a summary of the specific points that have been covered, which is intended to assist students when they revise, by providing a short overview of the contents to allow students to be confident in their grasp of the material.

Throughout each chapter, specific syllabus codes alongside subheadings show which sections of the syllabus are being addressed, as follows:

The text aims to encourage an active learning style and includes many self-assessment questions as well as varied longer-answer questions and tasks, while maintaining a structured approach to the learning process.

Self-assessment questions require short answers only, and are intended to allow students to check their understanding of the material as they move through the coursebook. Answers to these questions are provided at the end of the coursebook. The self-assessment questions are indicated in the text by a box with an icon like this:

Longer-answer questions are of two types. These questions are contained in a purple box labelled 'Questions', as follows:

Some questions are related directly to the requirements that students will find when they sit their examination. These questions are intended to stretch the students more than the SAQs do, and let them demonstrate their understanding of the concepts being taught. These questions are related to the text and are intended to form a starting point for activity in class or for individual work. They are indicated in the text by an icon like this:

Other questions are more broadly based and are intended to encourage the students to find out about a small area of the course, and are often suitable for classroom discussion as well as independent thinking. We find this type of work to be especially effective because it allows students to formulate their own answers – there is often no single right answer to the question. These questions are indicated with an icon like this:

Finally, there are extension questions and tasks. These include concepts, examples or thinking that fall beyond the strict boundaries of the syllabus. However, addressing these questions will nevertheless deepen students' understanding of and appreciation for the concepts being presented. Each of these pieces of work is meant as a starting point which may interest students, particularly the more able, and encourage them to do some independent enquiry into a topic.

**It must be stressed that this work is not an integral part of the syllabus requirements and can be omitted without prejudicing attainment in the examination.** These materials are contained in a green box, labelled 'Extension', like this:

The CD-ROM contains many categories of material:
- *Learning and revision guide*, with useful tips on study skills
- *Tackling the exam papers*, with useful tips on exam technique
- *Exemplar answers and comments for Paper 1*, with exemplar answers, fuller lists of how to get marks and comments indicating common pitfalls or giving some explanation of why certain answers are correct or how the marks are awarded
- *Answers to examination practice for Paper 3*, providing exemplar answers, fuller lists of how to get marks and comments for end-of-chapter *Examination practice for Paper 3* questions
- *Mock exam papers and mark schemes*, for both Paper 1 and 3
- *Guidance on the coursework (Paper 2)*
- *Guidance for Paper 3 (Alternative to coursework)*
- *Revision notes, Revision questions (with answers)* and *Revision tests* (with answers) to ensure that students' revision for Paper 1 goes smoothly

We hope that this resource is both useful and interesting to the reader, and helps them achieve a good grade in the *Cambridge Local Examinations Syndicate* IGCSE in Computer Studies.

Chris Leadbetter
Stewart Wainwright
Alan Stinchcombe

# Part I:
# Theoretical concepts

# 1 Generic application software

When you have finished this chapter, you will be able to:

- understand the difference between application and system software

- understand the use of graphical user interfaces

- identify typical features of, and uses for, various types of generic application software

- explain the use of tools for data-logging

- understand how generic application software may be customised by the use of macros

- appreciate the advantages and disadvantages of generic application software compared with bespoke software.

**4.1** A **computer** is an automatic, programmable, electronic data processing device. We refer to the physical parts of a computer as its **hardware**. Hardware includes the plastic and metal parts that you normally handle. It also includes the electronic components and storage devices within its case (see Chapter 3). **Software** refers to computer programs: sequences of instructions for the computer's processor that control everything that the computer does. Without software, a computer would be useless. The word software was invented as an opposite to hardware. It distinguishes the programs from a computer's hardware.

There are two types of software:

- **System software** consists of the programs and related data needed to manage the computer hardware. It provides a uniform environment in which application programs can run. It also provides tools for 'housekeeping' and monitoring tasks. This type of software is covered in detail in Chapters 4 and 5.

- **Application software** consists of the programs that allow us to use the computer to do something useful. Many, though by no means all, computers are general purpose. We use application software to apply them to a particular application or task. Such applications range from playing games to word processing to monitoring the condition of patients

in a hospital. We study these applications in more detail in Chapter 7. Sometimes people abbreviate 'application program' to 'application'. However, we need to be clear, in the context of smartphones, when we use the word 'application'. Are we talking about an application of a computer or about an application program that we can use for that purpose?

## Introduction

In this chapter, we look only at application software. It is not always obvious how to use software, so user documentation must be included to tell you how to use it (see Chapter 6). Nowadays, most documentation is available through a Help menu in the software as 'online' or 'on-screen' help. The software is often purchased in a box containing one or more CD-ROMs or DVD-ROMs. These optical discs store all the files for the main program, or suite of programs, and for any 'tools' (accessory programs) and help files.

The files are temporarily joined together and often compressed to save disc space. The single resulting file is in a format technically known as a 'software package'. So the software comes in a box and is formatted as a 'package'. This means that people often talk about software 'packages' or a specific application 'package', although not always in the technical sense.

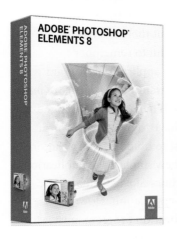

A utility program, called an 'installer', automatically installs the package. **Installation** means unpacking the software files and copying them onto the computer's internal storage device. They may also need further preparation for use.

If the software is intended for a range of similar problems, it may be called **generic application software** or 'productivity software'.

## What to consider

When studying application software there are two questions to bear in mind:
- what does the software do?
- what is the software used for?

The best way of answering these two questions is to use the software, as you will do in your practical lessons. It is to be hoped that you have used each of the different types of application software described here or, at least, seen them working.

Many application programs have the following features:
- managing files within *File: Open* or *Save As* dialogue boxes: creation, deletion, moving, copying, searching;
- working on multiple files simultaneously in separate windows;
- changing the magnification (or 'zoom level') of the work;
- scrolling through the work when it is too large to be completely displayed, using scroll bars or *Page Up* and *Page Down* keys;
- moving an insertion point or other selection using arrow keys;
- importing text and graphics from files (including photographs from a digital camera) or a scanner;
- insertion of automatic diagrams, charts and graphs;
- a wide range of embedded objects, such as text **formatting** options, including font name, style and size, and text alignment;
- tools for creating and editing drawings;
- editing content using insertion, deletion, cut-and-paste and copy-and-paste to avoid having to re-enter content; and find-and-replace for selective or global substitution of one word or phrase for another;
- multiple *Undo* and *Redo* commands;
- language tools such as checking spelling and grammar, a thesaurus and translation between languages;
- re-usable templates that specify the structure, formatting and standard content of a file;
- viewing a file as it will look when printed – 'what you see is what you get';
- macros that increase functionality by recording a sequence of commands or by writing code in a scripting language (see page 14), and which can be assigned to buttons or images;
- text and image hyperlinks to other locations in the same file or to an external file or web page;
- printing files.

Questions in exam papers are likely to give you a situation and ask what software should be used in such a situation. You will also be asked to justify your choice. Remember that when you are answering questions, you should not use the name of a particular brand of software but you should always give a type of software. So, 'Impress' or 'PowerPoint' would gain no marks; the correct answer would be 'a presentation application program'.

## Graphical user interface

The earliest software displayed only text on a screen. The majority of modern software for PCs and laptops has a graphical user interface (GUI – see Chapter 4). As we study the features and uses of different types of application program, you should note the extent to which they rely on the following features of their GUIs:

- windows that enable easy switching between different application programs or different files within the same application program;
- icons that give easy access to commands on toolbars without the use of text; dragging a file's icon onto an application window often opens the file;
- menus that give access to lists of commands;
- pointing devices, such as a mouse, that give an easy means of selecting text or objects by clicking or clicking-and-dragging and moving them by dragging-and-dropping.

### Importing and exporting data files

While working on a data file in an application program, it is often possible to bring the whole of another file into your work. This called **importing** a file. For example, in a word processing or desktop publishing program, you can usually import a text, word processing or graphics file directly into your work. You can also import it into your work as an **embedded object**. With this approach, you have a wider choice of file formats to import, including spreadsheets or presentations. You can edit an embedded file with all the facilities of an appropriate application program, without ever having to leave your word processing or desktop publishing program.

You can sometimes obtain automated assistance from an import 'wizard' simply by trying to open the file. You may need to select the relevant format or *All Files* option when doing so. If not, there may be a suitable option on the program's *File* or *Data* menu. The authors of this book wrote it using a word processing program and the publisher imported the word processing files into a desktop publishing program to lay it out and add the diagrams, photos and the various graphical features.

Normally, you save files in an application program using its default or 'native' file format, which preserves all the relevant data. However, it is sometimes necessary to save a version of your work in a different format that other software can read. This is called **exporting** a file. For example, some presentation software can export slides from the current presentation as graphics files or web pages. Obviously, not all the features of the original slide (such as animation) are likely to be preserved in such a different file format. You can usually find export facilities by selecting *Save As* or *Export* on a program's *File* menu.

## Word processing and desktop publishing programs

As you will see below, the features of these two types of software are very similar, but there is a basic difference which may be helpful to remember.

A **desktop publishing** (**DTP**) application program creates a publication file representing a *sequence of pages* containing *graphical objects*. If a user starts typing text, nothing will happen. They have to insert a graphical object called a 'text box' first to hold text and position it on a page. After creating a new single-page publication, they have to insert each additional page or batch of pages required.

A **word processing** application program creates a document file representing a *sequence or 'string' of text characters and formatting codes*. By default, keyboard input appears as text on the page and the user inserts any graphics 'inline', as if they were blocks of text. As the string gets longer, the program automatically creates additional pages onto which the content flows. The only control that the user has over the page on which particular content appears, apart from shrinking or enlarging the text, is to force that content onto the next page by inserting a 'page break'.

### Desktop publishing programs

Publishing means producing and distributing information beyond one's own organisation. For example, your class might produce a magazine for publication in and around your school. Nowadays, publishing applies not only to printed leaflets, newspapers and magazines, but also to electronic 'pages' for viewing on a computer screen, an e-reader, a mobile phone or similar device. It can also apply to multimedia 'movie files' for web pages, such as advertisements and games, and computer-aided learning files.

Features of DTP programs include:

- creation of a defined number of pages, each of which retains its own structure, but which may share common margin or grid guidelines, page orientation and paper size;
- creation of 'master pages', each of which acts as an underlay containing standard elements that can be applied to one or more of the publication's pages;
- complete control of the layout of text boxes, drawings, photos and other elements on each page;
- tools for creating and editing tables;
- a wide range of formatting options for graphics, including 'washout' for a watermark image, and text, such as drop capitals or rotation of text boxes (Figure 1.1);
- exporting as a text, web page or graphics file, or as a mail or email 'merge' with records from a database.

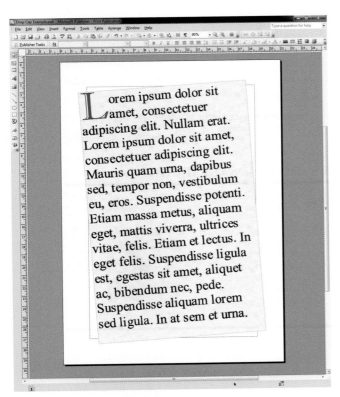

**Figure 1.1** A DTP document showing drop capital formatting and rotation of a text box.

The elements of a master page are visible but cannot be accidentally edited while editing one of the pages to which it has been applied. For example, a master page may add background colours, page borders and header and footer elements, such as logos or automatic page numbers. Different parts of a publication can use a different master page with different elements.

People use DTP programs to create publications such as newsletters and magazines that require complex layout, such as columns of text wrapped around graphics. They usually create the layout before the text is available, link the text boxes together and import the text later, usually from a word processing program. A publication's content has no sequence, other than the order of the pages. Text inserted in one text box cannot affect the content of any other text box, unless the user has linked them. In linked text boxes, text flows from one box into the next when the first is full. Similarly, material inserted on one page does not automatically overflow onto the next; a new page has to be created or text boxes need to be linked. The newsletter in Figure 1.2 was created with a DTP program.

## Word processing programs

Features of word processing programs include:

- creation of a sequence of content, with pages created automatically (or with manual page breaks and sections created with section breaks);
- headers and footers for each section that can hold standard text, graphics, automatic page numbering and a faint 'watermark' behind the document's text;
- margins, borders, paper size and page orientation (portrait or landscape) for each section;
- formatting of text as single or multiple columns;
- tools for creating and editing tables;
- document statistics, such as word count and readability scores;
- automated creation of a table of contents, numbered captions, cross-references, citations, bibliography and index;
- exporting as a text or web page file, or as a mail or email 'merge'.

People use word processing programs to produce letters, business documents, such as contracts and reports, and mail merges. They also use them to prepare text for publications such as magazines and books. Nowadays, a good word processing program will do many of the more graphics-oriented things that only DTP used to do. For example, it can re-format an inline graphic as a 'floating' graphic, so the user can make fine adjustments to its position and make text wrap around it.

**Volume 11, Number 3
February 2011**

NEWS LETTER

Trinity High School

# Success in IGCSEs at Trinity High School

The purpose of a newsletter is to provide specialised information to a targeted audience. Newsletters can be a great way to market your product or service, and also create credibility and build your organisation's identity among peers, members, employees or vendors.

First, determine the audience of the newsletter. This could be anyone who might benefit from the information it contains, for example, employees or people interested in purchasing a product or requesting your service.

You can compile a mailing list from business reply cards, customer information sheets, business cards collected at trade shows, or membership lists. You might consider purchasing a mailing list from a company.

If you explore a publisher catalogue, you will find many publications that match the style of your newsletter. Next, establish how much time and money you can spend on your newsletter. These factors will help determine how frequently you publish the newsletter and its length. It's recommended that you publish your newsletter at least quarterly so that it's considered a consistent source of information. Your customers or employees will look forward to its arrival.

Try to include interesting facts and figures, like a colourful pie chart for example.

The opening article in the newsletter should be one of the greatest significance and interest, in order to immediately capture your audience's attention.

## School dinners – no chips on menu?

This story can fit 75-125 words, so should be shorter and more snappy than the main article.

You should include catchy sub-headings for smaller articles. Though all headings should be interesting, the main heading at the top, the 'headline' is the most

important, and should be considered carefully.

In a few words, it should accurately represent the contents of the story and draw readers into the story. Developing the headline will help you keep the story focused.

Include photos and illustrations where you can.

### Inside this issue:

| | |
|---|---|
| Exams | 2 |
| Holidays | 3 |
| School trips | 4 |
| After-school club | 5 |
| Choir | 5 |
| Teacher's corner | 5 |
| Coming soon | 6 |

### Special points of interest:

- *Exam results.*
- *What's happening to school dinners?*
- *Where do we go on our next trip?*
- *More computers for our school.*

**Figure 1.2**   School newsletter showing text set in columns, headlines, a table and coloured images.

It can also create things automatically that would take a long time to do manually, such as producing and updating a table of contents whilst the document is being written (see Figure 1.3).

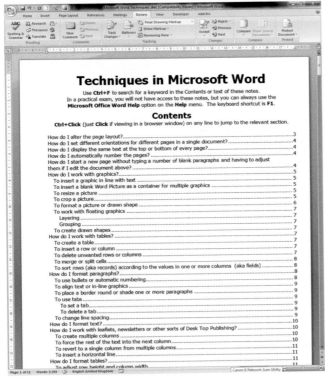

**Figure 1.3** A table of contents automatically produced for a multiple-page word-processed document.

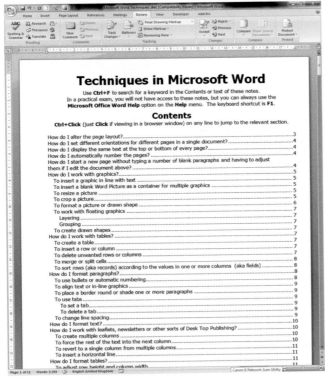

**SAQs**

1 Which type of application program would be appropriate for:

a a report with a contents list, headers and footers, chapter headings and footnotes?

b a three-fold, company brochure with logos for each division down the side of each fold and pictures and descriptions of each product across the fold?

## Spreadsheets

Spreadsheets take their name from the oversize sheets or double-page spreads of an accounting record book, ruled into rows and columns. The rectangle at the intersection of a row and column is known as a 'cell'.

Features of **spreadsheet programs** include:

- creation of a 'workbook' file consisting of one or more 'sheets', whose cells contain labels, numerical data or text data, or formulae;
- identification of cells by row number and column letter (or letters);
- sheet headers and footers that hold standard text, graphics and automatic page numbering for each *printed* page;
- margins, paper size and orientation for pages;
- importing data from a text file, a database or a table on a web page;
- data entry controls such as combo boxes, list boxes, spin buttons, scrollbars, check boxes and option buttons to speed up data input and help to validate the data;
- 'validation rules' for input data to check that an item falls within specified limits and, if not, produce an error message;
- calculations performed by formulae;
- replication of the contents of a cell;
- automated error checking: the program may warn the user when a formula in one cell is inconsistent with that in adjacent cells;
- formatting options for cells and their contents, including number formats such as decimal, currency, date and time; font name, style and size; text alignment and orientation;
- creation of graphs or charts from the spreadsheet's data, often using a chart wizard;
- exporting data as a text file or a web page.

In a formula, a reference to another cell can be entered by selecting the cell. All formulae (or 'formulas') are recalculated each time *any* cell is updated. A formula can contain one or more mathematical functions or functions for calculating statistics such as a sum, count, maximum, minimum, average or rank. For example:

- $= (A3 + C9) * 100$ adds the numerical contents of A3 and C9 and multiplies the result by 100.
- $= C8 \& " " \& D8$ joins (or 'concatenates') the text or number in C8, a single space and the text or number in D8.
- $= SUM(C2:C37)$ adds the numerical contents of the range of cells from C2 to C37, ignoring any non-numerical values in those cells. The formula $= C2 + C3 + \ldots + C37$ would find the same total, but

take a long time to construct, might contain errors and would return an error message if any cell were to contain text.

- `=IF(C6>200, C6*5%, "No Discount")` tests the logical condition `C6>200`, which is either TRUE or FALSE depending on the current value of cell C6. It uses the outcome to decide the value to be calculated, in this example, 5% of C6 if the condition is TRUE and 'No Discount' if it is FALSE.

The contents of a cell, whether data or a formula, can be replicated automatically. When the user positions the cursor over the cell's black handle at the bottom right-hand corner, the cursor becomes a skinny '+'. The user can then drag the handle across the required cells in the same row or column. This is especially useful with complex formulae copied to many cells. By default, the software helpfully adjusts all the column letters and row numbers (see Figure 1.4).

People use spreadsheet programs as follows:

- To perform repeatable financial, scientific and engineering calculations and display the results graphically. As a simple example, replication of formulae makes it easy to calculate the effect of compound interest on a loan or investment year-by-year, even if we have forgotten the details of the formula for directly calculating the future value.

- As 'what if?' tools for performing mathematical modelling of future events or simulation of existing technology or new designs that are too time-consuming, expensive or dangerous to test in reality. The same calculations are performed using alternative sets of data, known as 'scenarios'. For example, repeatedly crash-testing prototype cars under different conditions is very time-consuming and expensive. Similarly, exploring what might happen in a nuclear reactor under certain conditions is likely to be too dangerous. A test pilot wants to know that the performance of a prototype aircraft's design has been modelled mathematically before flying it for the first time.

- To create simple databases. As records are not recognised as such by the program, they can be held in either rows or columns.

Limitations of spreadsheets include:

- a limited number of cells – older software is limited to 65,536 rows and 256 columns, although the best software currently has 1,048,576 rows and 16,384 columns;

- lack of security – it is relatively difficult to control users' access to a spreadsheet so, for example, financial data are vulnerable to fraud;

- lack of 'concurrency' – usually only one user can work on a spreadsheet at any given time;

- lack of consistency – data can exist in multiple and mutually inconsistent versions.

## Databases

A database is a set of tables that hold information about related things. Chapter 2 discusses databases in more detail. **Database management system (DBMS) programs**, to give them their full title, are designed purely to manage databases. They do this more efficiently than spreadsheet programs, although they are less instinctive to learn.

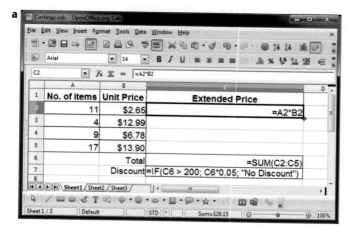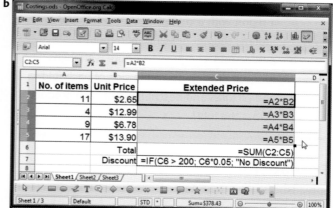

**Figure 1.4** Replication of the formula in cell C2. **a** 'Before' view – note the skinny '+' cursor positioned over the cell's handle. **b** 'After' view with the row numbers adjusted. The highlighted blue cells show where the drag occurred, i.e. downwards from cell C2.

Features of **database** programs include:

- creation of a database file consisting of one or more database objects: tables, queries, forms and reports;
- wizards that guide the user through the creation of queries, forms including a menu system or 'switchboard', and reports;
- importing data from a text file, a spreadsheet or a table on a web page;
- formatting options for forms, reports and their controls and contents, including font name, style and size, and text alignment;
- creation of graphs or charts from a table or query, often using a chart wizard;
- exporting a database object as a spreadsheet, a text file or a web page.

Tables store data and can display them in a 'datasheet' view (Figure 1.5). Each row of data represents a **record**, which is a set of data about one type of thing such as an individual person, object or transaction. Each column contains a data **field** (or attribute). A field holds a specific type of data about a characteristic of the subjects of the records. Each column must have a unique name. The type of data in a field is often text, but may also be numeric, date/time or other types.

| Atomic Number | Name | Group | Melting Point (°C) |
|---|---|---|---|
| 1 | Hydrogen | Non-Metal | -255.34 |
| 2 | Helium | Noble Gas | -272.2 |
| 3 | Lithium | Alkali Metal | 180.54 |
| 4 | Beryllium | Alkali Earth Metal | 1287 |
| 5 | Boron | Non-Metal | 2079 |
| 6 | Carbon | Non-Metal | 3825 |
| 7 | Nitrogen | Non-Metal | -209.86 |
| 8 | Oxygen | Non-Metal | -218.4 |
| 9 | Fluorine | Halogen | -219.62 |
| 10 | Neon | Noble Gas | -248.67 |
| 11 | Sodium | Alkali Metal | 97.81 |
| 12 | Magnesium | Alkali Earth Metal | 648.8 |
| 13 | Aluminum | Metal | 660.37 |
| 14 | Silicon | Non-Metal | 1410 |
| 15 | Phosphorus | Non-Metal | 44.1 |
| 16 | Sulphur | Non-Metal | 115.21 |
| 17 | Chlorine | Halogen | -100.98 |
| 18 | Argon | Noble Gas | -189.2 |
| 19 | Potassium | Alkali Metal | 63.25 |
| 20 | Calcium | Alkali Earth Metal | 839 |
| | | | 0 |

Record: 14 ◄ 21 of 21 ► ►I ►* No Filter Search

**Figure 1.5** Table of 20 chemical elements shown in a 'datasheet' view.

A **relational database** is a relatively complex but highly efficient type of database. It contains a table for each 'entity' (type of person, object or transaction) about which data are stored. The tables are linked by 'relationships', which consist of references in a field in one table to a unique identifying (or 'ID') field in another table. An important validation check (see Chapter 2), known as 'referential integrity', ensures that references can be made only to records that exist.

Queries retrieve information from tables (Figure 1.6). A query can sort, search according to criteria, calculate and combine records from two or more tables. A suitably experienced 'user-developer' can create their own queries and view their results in datasheet view, but most users only see query results through forms and reports. Other sorts of query can alter data.

**a**
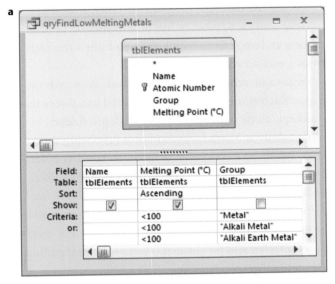

**b**
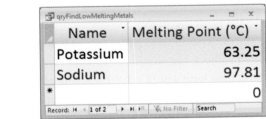

**Figure 1.6  a** A query in 'design' view, showing selection of certain fields and the sorting and search criteria for metals with melting points below 100°C. **b** Results of the query.

Forms are windows on a display screen through which the user can enter or edit data or view read-only information. A form often communicates with one or more tables through one or more queries. It further controls the user's view of the data. For example, it may display only one record at a time during data entry, which helps to reduce errors. A form usually has navigation buttons, to guide the user, and command buttons, which may restrict the commands that the user can issue.

Reports are the printed output from one or more queries. Forms are not usually printed. Although a report can be viewed on screen, this would be risky for an inexperienced user, as the report has no area for text instructions or command buttons for navigation back to a main menu. A report has headers and footers for standard text, graphics and automatic page numbering for both the report and its individual pages. A report's margins, paper size and page orientation can also be set. A report can be exported as a spreadsheet, a web page or a text file attachment to an email.

People use database programs to enter, store and retrieve records to provide useful information in printed reports and on screen, both locally and often remotely from a web server.

Years ago, schools used to keep student records on paper. Each student's details were stored in a folder that was kept, along with all the other students' folders, in filing cabinets. Nowadays your school probably stores your details on a computer. Why do we use computers for this? If a teacher wants details about student Raiza Saddiqi, the computer has to be turned on, the correct software has to be loaded and then information has to be entered so that the correct student is found. It used to be a lot faster, and far cheaper, just to look in the filing cabinet and get out her paper.

But would it have been quicker if the teacher had wanted details of all the students doing Computer Studies? The old system used paper lists of who was doing which subject, but would the teacher have had a copy? If not, how long would it have taken to get one? What if the teacher wanted to know which students were in room D3 on a Tuesday afternoon? What about obtaining a list of all students who attained a grade B or higher in their last exams?

Now the problems are getting immense. In the old system, someone would have to go through all the information and pick out the students who fit the criteria. This is possible but it takes a lot of time and is likely to contain mistakes. Database software on a computer is good at searching and sorting very quickly and accurately. Queries can be made on any

combination and value of fields in the database, allowing non-standard (or *ad hoc*) queries to be easily made.

Imagine a teacher in another building who needs to see Raiza's record. The teacher does not need to walk over to the administrative office and search for Raiza's record: they simply go to a computer and access it from where they are. For a school, a relational database may have tables for students, student enrolments on courses, courses, teachers and classrooms. So, for example, we would be able to associate a student with their maths teacher, the classroom used at a particular time for maths and the student's maths exam marks.

 **SAQs**

2   You are asked to suggest an application to manage a small library. You need to keep track of books, borrowers and borrowed books. What would you suggest and why?

**Questions**

1   Make a list of the advantages and disadvantages of the student records being stored on the school computer network, rather than being stored on paper in the administration office.

## Communication programs

A local area network (LAN) can provide communication services on a single site. However, the power of computer communications lies in the use of a wide area network (WAN). A large company may have its own private WAN for security reasons. Most organisations and individuals rely on the **Internet**, a global WAN consisting of many *inter*connected *net*works, containing servers. A **server** is a combination of computer and software that provides a service to other **client** computers or application programs.

Everyone has heard of the Internet and most of us have used it at one time or another. Once you have paid an **Internet service provider** (**ISP**) for Internet access, most communication services are available at no extra charge.

Most people's first experience of using a service provided over the Internet is using a web browser to view information from a web server, but it is important to understand that the **World Wide Web** (**WWW** or **Web**) is just one of many Internet services. The Web is the totality of all the websites stored on web servers. Each **website** consists of a collection of information stored as HTML or similar files, known as **web pages**. These files and related graphics, sound and video files are stored within a single directory (or folder) on a web server with an Internet address known as its **Uniform Resource Locator** (**URL**), such as http://www.number10.gov.uk. Apart from the services discussed here, we look at recent developments in the use of the Internet in Chapter 8.

We now need to turn our attention to the application programs that give us access to communication and information over the Internet.

## Fax

**Fax** is a pre-computer technology for sending images of documents over telephone lines. It has been successfully adapted for use by computers. Features of fax programs include:

- sending a scanned image of a printed document over a phone line to a recipient with a fax machine or suitably equipped computer;
- sending an image of an electronic file, usually by 'printing' the file with the fax program's virtual printer, or 'printer driver';
- receiving a transmitted fax and displaying or printing it.

Fax is a useful way of sending a letter or other document almost instantly to an organisation that has a fax machine but does not advertise an email address. It may not be a very secure way of communicating with an individual, as an organisation often has a single shared fax machine for receiving faxed documents.

## Telephony

The receptionist in a small organisation can use a switchboard program with a headset consisting of headphones and a microphone to answer conventional phone calls and transfer them to colleagues. Call management software performs a similar function in a multi-agent call centre and has management functions for monitoring performance.

## Voice over Internet Protocol

Voice over Internet Protocol (VoIP) technology enables calls to take place over the Internet rather than over communication circuits maintained by telephone companies. VoIP providers offer use of their VoIP servers and free VoIP software (Figure 1.7) to allow users to make free VoIP-to-VoIP calls using a microphone and loudspeakers or headphones. Providers charge for VoIP calls to landline or mobile phones and SMS text messages. Headphones eliminate the echoes that occur when a participant's voice is heard on loudspeakers by one or more participants and enters their microphones and returns to the first participant after a delay. Video communication is optional, using a video camera, known as a 'webcam', but a broadband Internet connection (see Chapter 7) is essential. A dial-up connection would not be able to transmit enough data quickly enough and the pictures and sound would break up.

**Figure 1.7**   The user interface of a VoIP video phone application program.

## Video-conferencing

Many organisations use video-phone calls as a cheap method of **video-conferencing**, in which several participants in different locations can have a discussion and see each other at the same time. Imagine a business with offices all over the world. Instead of flying all the participants to one place for a meeting they can stay where they are and hold a meeting electronically. This saves the time, monetary and environmental costs of travelling to meetings and accommodating people in hotels.

## Email

Many people first use electronic messages or **email** through a web application, such as *Hotmail* or *Yahoo! Mail*, known as 'webmail'. Often, they do not realise that email is an Internet service provided by mail servers, not web servers. Many people, especially at work, use an email client program such as *Microsoft Outlook* (Figure 1.8) to communicate directly with their email server, without using a web browser program. One of the advantages of doing so is that the user can compose messages with the full editing facilities of a word processor.

Features of email client programs include:

- Transmission of typed messages and attached files anywhere in the world to a recipient with an email address.
- Storage of names and email addresses of contacts in an 'address book' or 'contact list' (the user can select an address from the address book or from a list of matching addresses that appears as they start to type the name or address).

- Creation of an 'address group' (or 'distribution list'), which is a list of email addresses of contacts to whom the user wants to send the same messages.
- Sending a message simultaneously to one or more individuals or groups; this can be done by entering all email addresses into the 'To' field, or the 'Cc' or 'Bcc' fields. 'Cc' means 'carbon copy' and all recipients can see who else the message has been sent to. 'Bcc' means 'blind carbon copy' and none of the other recipients can see the email addresses in this field.
- Sending a message with a 'digital signature'; this is a cryptographic technique to ensure that the message comes from the true sender and has not been altered.
- Sending a message with encryption, to prevent anyone but the intended recipient receiving it.
- Sending a message with high or low priority.
- Replying to a message by using a *Reply* button, which automatically ensures that the reply is correctly addressed and includes a copy of the original message.

**Figure 1.8** An email received in an email client program.

- Forwarding a message to another recipient without having to re-type it.
- Exporting a message as a text file.

People use email client programs and web applications to send messages for both work and social purposes. They can do this on many devices, including computers, mobile phones and Wi-Fi-enabled devices, such as game consoles, MP3 or MP4 media players or PDAs. This provides much swifter exchange of information with less environmental impact than posting letters. It also avoids the expense of phone calls.

Although transmission typically takes only seconds, the message is sent via the sender's mail server to the recipient's mail server. Here it is stored until their email client program or webmail downloads it from the server and displays it. Therefore, recipients in different time zones do not have to be available simultaneously, as they would for a two-way or multi-way 'conference' phone call. Email can also help, together with other communication technologies, to save the time, monetary and environmental costs of travelling to meetings.

An obvious advantage of using a webmail service is that, even if you are not carrying a portable computer or email-enabled device with you, you can still access your email by visiting an Internet café anywhere in the world.

### Instant messaging

**Instant messaging** (**IM**) is a service provided by an instant messaging server, although the user's application program may be a web application.

Features of instant messaging programs include:
- sending typed messages between users whenever a character is typed or the *Enter/Return* key is pressed, depending on the application;
- display of the availability or other status of contacts on a contact list;
- multiple, simultaneous, two-way conversations;
- group conversations;
- optional telephony and video;
- export of a conversation as a text file.

People use IM programs and web applications on a similar range of devices and for similar purposes as email. The major difference is that even with only text,

users have more sense of a conversation, because they perceive communication as being instant or in 'real-time' (Figure 1.9).

**Figure 1.9** An instant messaging conversation.

## Web authoring software

In order to produce a website, we can use a simple text editor program to write HTML code for the content and to create **interactivity** on web pages. The code is written in a 'scripting language', which is a programming language that controls the behaviour of an existing program, in this case any web browser that will display the website. Interactivity means opportunities for someone using a website to interact with and change what is displayed.

A **web authoring program** allows a user to generate code for a web page automatically. A web authoring program is often described as 'web design' software, although it is used for *building* a website rather than designing it.

By default, the content of a web page is displayed in a web browser in the sequence in which it was written, so a web authoring program is more similar to a word processing program than to a DTP program.

Features of web authoring programs include:
- creation of a sequence of content, with importing of text and the full range of multimedia files;
- templates to which web pages may be attached to place common content in certain regions, rather like a master page in a DTP application;

- facilities for creating tables, formatting text and graphics, and editing text;
- interactivity for the user of a web browser, including hyperlinks and forms with text boxes, drop-down lists, check boxes, option buttons and command buttons;
- control of the layout of 'absolutely positioned' images or text boxes, similar to the control of floating graphics in a word processing program;
- language tools, such as checking spelling;
- visual transition effects for entry to, or exit from, a page;
- animation effects for absolutely positioned images or text boxes;
- previewing websites in the user's web browser;
- uploading (or 'publishing') of the finished website to a web server, use of which is usually rented from an ISP or 'web hosting' company.

## Web browsers

A web browser program enables a user to interactively access information, in the form of text and other media, from remote web servers.

Features of web browser programs include:
- requesting a web page by typing an address or using a previously stored list of 'bookmarks' or 'favourites';
- reception and display of web pages, including text contained in the page's source code and referenced multimedia files;
- reloading of the current resource with a refresh button;
- cancellation of the loading with a stop button;
- a status bar to display the progress of loading the resource, the address of a link when the pointing device's cursor moves over it, and the zoom status;
- prompting the user to save the requested file to disk if the browser cannot display it or if the web server sends a 'content disposition' that enforces saving rather than display, usually referred to as 'downloading';
- allowing the user to 'navigate' to another resource by clicking a pointing device on a hyperlink (or 'link');
- allowing the user to navigate or submit data to a web server by clicking on a button, whose appearance may change when the pointing device has its cursor over it (a 'mouseover effect') or is clicking it (a 'mousedown effect');

- a *Find* facility for searching within a web page;
- 'handing off' to another application program a request that the web browser cannot directly handle (for example, *mailto:* requests are usually passed to the user's default email program);
- handling a request from a web application, such as a photo-sharing website, to upload a file to a web server;
- supplementary navigation (see below);
- saving a web page or printing it on as many paper pages as are necessary.

When a resource is requested, the browser also requests multimedia files referred to within the source code of the web page. When the requested resource is a website, rather than a specific web page, the web server interprets this as a request for the site's default page.

A **hyperlink** (or 'link') is a reference to another point in a long page or to another resource. It causes the browser to display that other point in the page or to make a request for that other resource. The link may be in the form of text (often blue and underlined), an image (a hotspot), or one of several regions within an image acting as a menu (an image map).

As well as clicking a hyperlink, the user can navigate using supplementary methods:
- *Back* and *Forward* buttons to go back to the previous resource and forward again.
- The *Home* button to return to the user's specified 'home page', often a search engine.
- The search toolbar to input terms into a search engine.
- An 'accelerator', which may be displayed as a link in a 'context menu' by right-clicking selected text. The text is passed to a web application such as a search engine or mapping service (Figure 1.10).

## Search engines

A **search engine** is a web application that uses an extremely powerful computer with a very efficient procedure (or 'algorithm', see Chapter 9) to perform many simultaneous searches for different users for Internet resources. Search engines are available for different Internet services, although most people use one which searches web and File Transfer Protocol (FTP) servers.

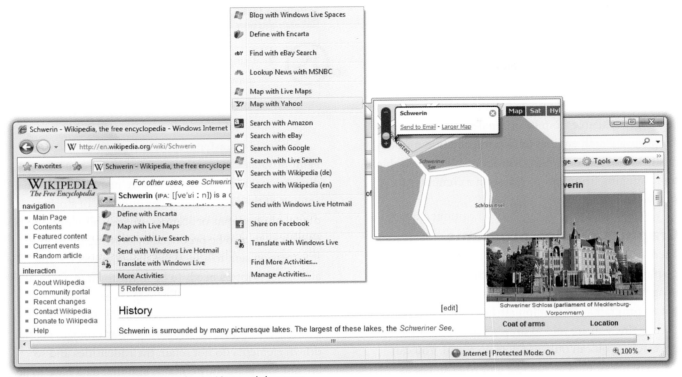

**Figure 1.10** A mapping service 'accelerator' in a web browser.

Unseen by users, the search engine's 'web-crawler' program is an automated browser that systematically explores the content of resources stored on these servers, updating its database (or 'index') with the content of each resource. The search engine may also store the number of links to the resource – it may use that information to establish the relevance of a resource, on the assumption that a resource to which many web pages have links is likely to be highly relevant to others.

Features of search engine web applications include:

- allowing a user to send a search request with search criteria (Figure 1.11) such as:
  - words, sometimes with suggestions supplied by the search engine as the user types;
  - phrases;
  - natural language, such as 'How can I learn to pilot a balloon?';
  - category of interest;
  - file type;
  - domain name;
  - size, type and colour of image;

- searching a database of many billions of resources in a few tenths of a second for web pages, images, videos, maps, news or products that match the user's search criteria;
- supplying a list of the first few search results ranked by relevance, together with the estimated number of results, often called 'hits'; the results usually consist of a title or image that is hyperlinked

**Figure 1.11** Entering search criteria into a search engine.

to the target resource and one or more text extracts indicating where the search criteria have been matched;

- supplying a stored copy of the resource (or 'cached page') that was indexed, even if the content has subsequently been updated or the whole page is no longer available from its original web server.

People use search engines to find information for both business and personal purposes about any conceivable topic, ranging from how to maintain a computer to spiritual guidance.

## Graphics editing programs

There are programs purely for viewing graphics, but a graphics application program is used to draw and edit images. There are two distinct sorts of graphics files and not all programs can manipulate both sorts.

Imagine you are told to draw a picture but there is a catch – you can only use dots on a grid. You can use as many colours as you like and you can use as many dots as you like, but the picture must be entirely dots. This is one way that a graphics program can draw pictures. Images drawn like this are known as **bitmap graphics** (or 'raster graphics'). The application program works by dividing the drawing area into lots of small squares called 'picture elements' (or 'pixels'). As the user moves a pointing device representing a pen, brush or spray can of a particular colour, the program shades in the selected pixels. Figure 1.12 shows a dog drawn using a bitmap, with only 30 squares and in monochrome (black and white). More squares and colours would mean that a better drawing could be made.

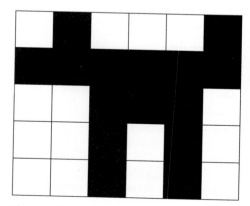

**Figure 1.12**  A bitmap image of a dog.

**Questions**

2  Using twice as many rows and columns, try to draw a better dog.

A bitmap or raster graphics file, such as Microsoft Paint produces, stores the resulting image as a two-dimensional array of numbers that 'map' the individual colours of the pixels. This is the only way of storing digital photographs or scanned images, although bitmap graphics can also be produced by drawing tools. The information sent to a monitor screen, projector and almost all printers needs to be in the form of a bitmap. A disadvantage is that as the image is enlarged, eventually the pixels become visible. This is known as 'pixellation' (Figure 1.13a). Other disadvantages are that drawn elements do not retain their identities and so are not independently editable and that data have to be stored for each one of possibly millions of pixels, in up to 16 million colours, so the file can be very large.

The other method of drawing pictures is known as **vector graphics**. A vector graphics file stores the drawn image as numbers that represent the properties of each **graphical object** that has been drawn. For example, these could include: the geometrical co-ordinates of the start and finish of a straight line or a rectangle, or a circle's centre co-ordinates and radius; line thickness; line colour; and fill colour. Each object remains independently editable. The file is usually much smaller than a bitmap graphics file with a similar appearance because relatively few numbers are required to recreate the drawn image. An example of a vector graphic is one you might draw using the drawing toolbar in Microsoft Word. When a vector graphics file is enlarged there is no pixellation (Figure 1.13b) because the properties of each graphical object are used to recalculate the larger bitmap required for the display or printer.

Features of graphics programs may include:

- drawing tools for lines, geometrical shapes and freeform objects;
- painting tools, such as brush, pencil and airbrush, for bitmaps only;
- input from specialised hardware, such as a pressure- and tilt-sensitive graphics tablet or a MIDI device;

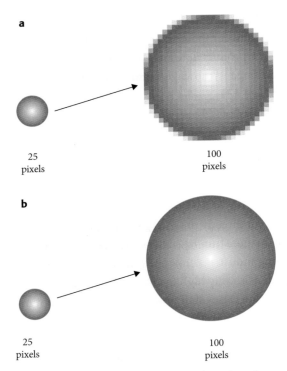

**a**

25
pixels

100
pixels

**b**

25
pixels

100
pixels

**Figure 1.13** A bitmap graphic cannot be enlarged without pixellation, unlike a vector graphic. **a** Bitmap graphic. **b** Vector graphic.

- separate layers to keep bitmap images editable, to facilitate hiding or locking part of the user's work while they work on other parts to prevent unintended editing or deletions;
- resize, rotate and flip tools;
- creation of animated graphics;
- exporting data in graphics file formats other than the program's native format, often with reversible or irreversible compression.

A bitmap image drawing program has additional features:

- selection tools including rectangle, rounded rectangle, ellipse, free and fuzzy;
- a foreground extraction tool to remove a figure from its background;
- a cropping tool for removing unwanted regions from the edges;
- adjustment and automatic correction of brightness, contrast and colour;
- photo enhancement using image transformation tools, such as shear and distortion correction, and photo retouching with 'red-eye' removal, healing and clone tools.

A vector graphics program treats freeform objects as a succession of smaller geometrical shapes.

Vector graphics can easily be saved in a bitmap format, but they cannot be changed back again. A bitmap image cannot easily be converted into a vector image though. An original photographed scene is not drawn as separate mouse strokes, so the number of graphical objects analysed by the conversion program becomes enormous. This means there may be no saving of storage space and therefore no benefit of converting to a vector for subsequent editing.

## CAD/CAM programs

In **computer-aided design** (**CAD**), a computer is used to help people design things. Computers are ideal instruments for design work, compared with pencil and paper, because changes to a design can be made without re-drawing the entire design. Also it is much easier to create three-dimensional (3-D) representations of a product in two dimensions using a computer. There are even free CAD applications that can be used to design 3-D models – try *Google SketchUp* (Figure 1.14).

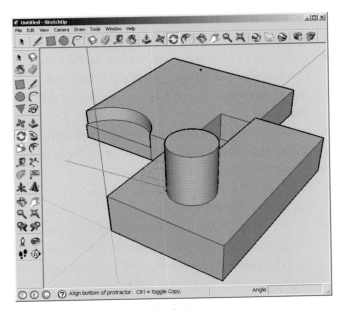

**Figure 1.14** A free CAD application program.

Features of CAD programs include:

- creation of 3-D design drawings using vector graphics, so that drawings can be resized or scaled with greater accuracy and without distortion or pixellation;

- importing existing drawings in PDF format or 3-D laser scan data of existing items requiring copying or renovation;
- standard objects such as nuts and bolts or electronic components can be stored in a library file and inserted as many times as required;
- surface, mesh and solid modelling tools;
- zooming in to work on fine detail;
- 2-D cross-sectional views with materials such as brick, concrete or timber indicated by 'hatching';
- 3-D views ranging from 'wire frame', with or without 'wires' representing hidden edges, to **rendering** (drawing surfaces) with light and shade and applying 'materials' to see the effects of different visual textures;
- multiple views available simultaneously (i.e. at the same time) and rotation to see views from all sides (Figure 1.15);
- 3-D navigation tools to 'walk' or 'fly' through a model to gain an impression of moving through it;
- stereoscopic display to enable a user to view a 3-D image;
- calculation of masses, surface areas and volumes to estimate the costs of materials, coatings and manufacture;
- performance of stress, strain, resonance, buckling, toppling and thermal analysis of the model and exporting of reports and videos to document the analyses;
- automatic optimisation of routing of conductive tracks on printed circuit boards or of cables or hoses within a vehicle engine compartment;
- validation of a design against the original requirement's specification;
- verification of design against design specification, engineering and safety standards; includes kinematic checking, using a simulation of moving parts in machines to check that they will not collide, or electronic circuit function testing using simulation to test its behaviour before a prototype is built;
- output directly to a 3-D printer for creating a 3-D model;
- exporting of files in PDF format or in a suitable format for computer-aided manufacture (CAM).

When the design has been finalised, it can sometimes be passed to computer-controlled machines, which can make the product automatically from the design. This second stage is known as **computer-aided manufacture** (**CAM**).

Features of CAM software include:
- creation of programs by specialist programmers or machinists to control CAM machinery;
- tools to manage planning of production, transportation, storage of raw materials, components and products;
- importing of data from CAD systems;
- output directly to CAM machinery.

Many manufacturers, such as the automotive and clothing industries, now use CAM systems because their consistently high quality, reliability and speed of production raises staff productivity and can minimise wastage of materials and energy consumption.

## Multimedia programs

We expect multimedia programs to be able to:
- import multiple types of electronic media files, including text, images, animated graphics and sound and video files;
- create transition and animation effects and interactivity (such as hyperlinks, hotspots, image maps, buttons and rollover effects).

### Multimedia authoring programs

A **multimedia authoring program** (or 'authoring tool'), such as Adobe Flash, can produce multimedia 'movie files' most often intended for viewing with a web browser. A web browser needs a multimedia player extension (or 'plug-in') to play these movie files. Some programs, such as Flash, are intended to have the interactivity of their output enhanced by programming in a scripting language, while others are intended for non-programmers.

Features of multimedia authoring programs include:
- 'frames' that hold successive appearances and positions of graphical objects in animations;
- layers to enable 'inbetweening' of graphical objects without interference from other graphical objects;
- creation of multimedia movie files (Figure 1.16) for web pages;
- creation of relatively powerful web applications, such as Rich Internet Applications (RIAs);

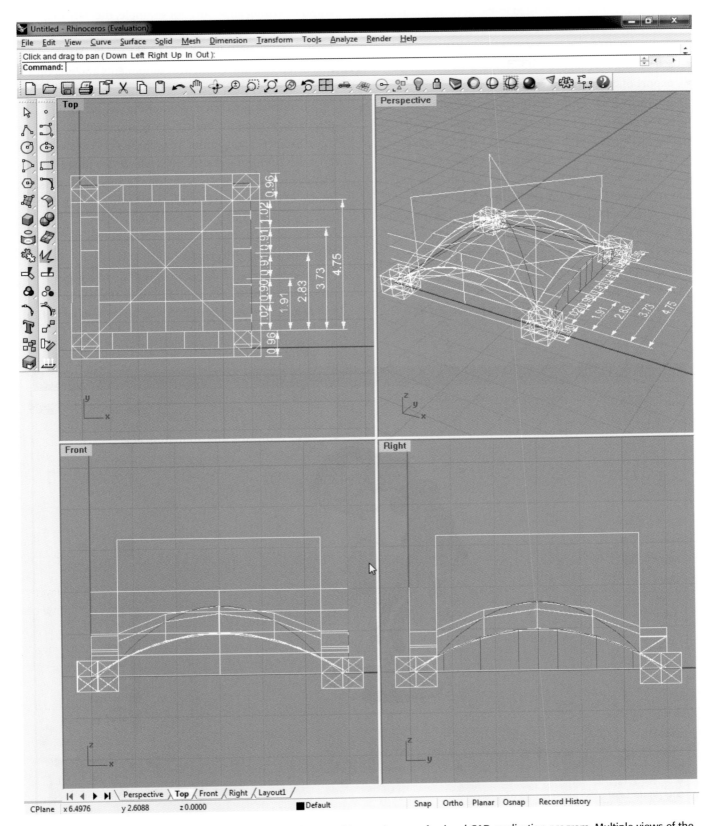

**Figure 1.15** A thin, brick, vaulted test structure designed by an architect using a professional CAD application program. Multiple views of the same object are shown together on one screen.

- creation of computer-assisted learning (CAL) activities (some authoring tools are able to produce modules that conform to e-learning content standards);
- a scripting language to extend interactivity;
- export of content as a website, presentation, interactive CD-ROM or computer program file.

**Inbetweening** is the process of automatically generating intermediate frames between two vector graphics of different positions, shapes or colours, to give an illusion of smooth change or movement. For example, the user may draw a cartoon car in a starting position at one side of the screen and then in its ending position at the other side of the screen. The computer will fill in sufficient frames between these two positions to make the car appear to move smoothly.

A scripting language may enable the use of pre-built functionality in a component (e.g. an option button)

without writing any code. For example, the user may assign a set 'behaviour' to one of the component's events (such as clicking it). It also allows the user to write code that can create and configure components and respond to (or 'handle') their events.

Web developers often use multimedia authoring programs to produce eye-catching, animated advertisements and games for web pages. They can even create entire websites from which downloading pictures is not so easy as selecting the *Save Picture As...* command. People have even made feature-length films using this software!

### Presentation programs

A presentation is a succession of multimedia pages. These pages are known as 'slides', by analogy with the transparent images inserted in succession into an optical

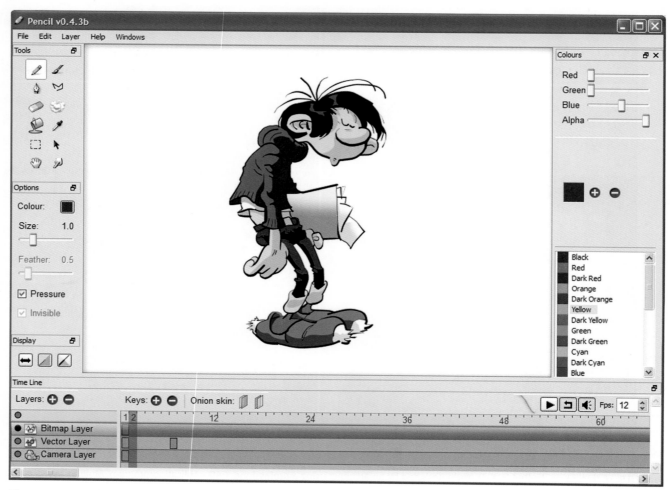

**Figure 1.16**   Creating an animated movie file in a multimedia authoring program.

slide projector. A **presentation progam** can be used to produce these slides.

Features of presentation programs include:

- creation of slides, layout of content and use of a 'master page', similar to the creation of pages in a DTP program but with the addition of multimedia;
- embedding multimedia content;
- animation of text and graphical objects on slides (Figure 1.17);
- transition effects between slides;
- interactivity in the form of hyperlinks and action buttons for navigation within the presentation and to external websites or programs;
- insertion of full-screen images, diagrams, charts and graphs;
- creation of CAL activities, using a scripting language to extend interactivity by writing code that can handle the events of data input controls such as text boxes, check boxes and option buttons;
- display of the slides as a 'slideshow' by the presentation program or a smaller 'viewer' program;
- exporting of a presentation as a non-editable slideshow, web page or outline text document;
- exporting of individual slides as graphics files;
- printing of slides in various formats: one slide per page, for a speaker with space for notes, or as a 'handout' with multiple slides per page.

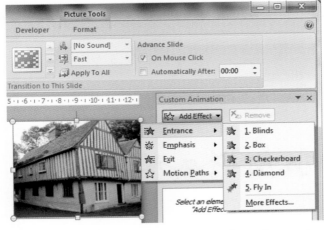

**Figure 1.17** An animation effect being applied to a photograph on a slide.

A user usually creates a presentation to display, using a multimedia projector, to a group of people. For example, a teacher might produce one for a class learning a new topic or a sales director might produce one for a group of potential customers. The presenter usually advances the slideshow from slide to slide, often using a remote control. Slideshows can also be set to run automatically without a presenter using pre-set timings in 'kiosk' mode.

Since presentation software resembles DTP software, some people use it to produce printed posters on extra-large slides. The term 'poster' has also crossed over into the idea of the electronic 'multimedia poster'.

## Questions

3 Many different types of media have been mentioned here. Two points need to be considered:
   a Is presentation software overused and are there occasions when the use of the software can hide the message that is being communicated?
   b What other media can be used to convey information? For each one try to answer the question, 'Is this a sensible use of the power of the computer?'

## SAQs

3 Which type of application program would be appropriate for a poster for a museum showing some of the exhibits, opening times and a sound interview with the curator?

## Data-logging

Data can be collected manually in many ways. Someone may conduct a survey by interview or questionnaire. Someone else may collect scientific data by repeated reading of one or more instruments and recording the measurements in a table. These data can later be entered into a computer program for analysis (processed to provide useful information). In Chapter 2, we study how data are sometimes fed straight into a computer, using automatic data capture.

For example, data from a temperature sensor may be used as part of an automated system to control a heating or air conditioning system.

**Data-logging** uses automatic data capture to record or 'log' data automatically for scientific, engineering and statistical purposes, usually at regular intervals of time. A desktop or laptop computer can be used directly for this purpose by connecting one or more suitable sensors to it via a suitable interface. However, it is more common to use a data logger, which is a computer dedicated to data-logging. For example, we may need to take readings from a temperature sensor over the course of a day to check how well an automated system is controlling temperature. In this case, the data do not need to be sent to a computer for display and analysis immediately; instead, we need a portable, battery-powered data logger (Figure 1.18) that we can leave in the room to capture and store the data at, say, 30-minute intervals.

Typically, a data logger stores its data in a format such as a comma-separated value (CSV) text file that a computer can download through a USB connection. This file can be imported into a spreadsheet or more specialised software for displaying the data and analysing them (Figure 1.19).

**Figure 1.18** A temperature data logger that stores 16,000 temperature readings at intervals between 10 seconds and 12 hours – note the USB plug for downloading data to a computer.

A smart device, such as a smartphone or media player, may contain accelerometer sensors or a Global Positioning System (GPS) receiver, a gyroscope. With an appropriate 'app' (a common abbreviation for applications used on smart devices), the device can log its location, speed, orientation and acceleration (Figure 1.20).

a

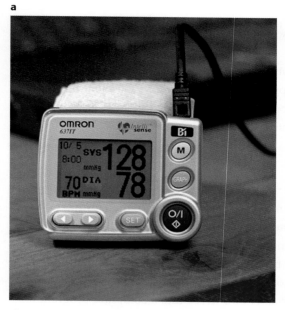

b

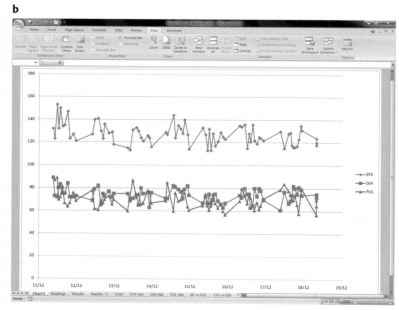

**Figure 1.19** **a** A blood pressure monitor connected to a laptop through a USB cable. **b** Graphs of the monitor's data produced in spreadsheet software.

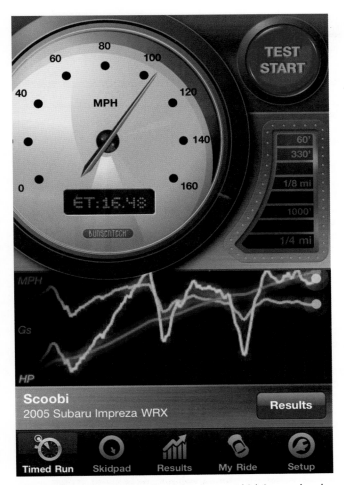

**Figure 1.20**  A smartphone 'app' that logs a vehicle's speed and acceleration.

You may have used data-logging for science experiments. For example, a data logger can be used to make automatic, regular measurements of temperature in an experiment. A data logger used in a school may have multiple input channels for sensors, software and a screen for displaying the data. It may create and display a graph of temperature change over time and send these data as files to a printer. If not, the data can be downloaded to a computer.

Data-loggers can gather data without human intervention for as long as required and at higher sampling rates than would be convenient or possible for a person. Oversampling can be used to make multiple measurements and automatically average the data to reduce the effect of random errors (or 'noise') in the signal. There is also less risk of missing any unusual data and no risk of making mistakes in reading instruments or writing down the measurements. Analysis can be performed as soon as the logging is complete and graphs or other output have been produced, which can be immediately.

We can also use data-logging software so that a computer records data about the behaviour of its own hardware and software, for example, its processor usage (Figure 1.21), network traffic, firewall intrusions or virus detection. In other words, to record data about the behaviour of its own hardware and software. A 'network analyser' is a program that intercepts and logs traffic passing over a network to which it is connected. Some software redraws a graph as new data become available.

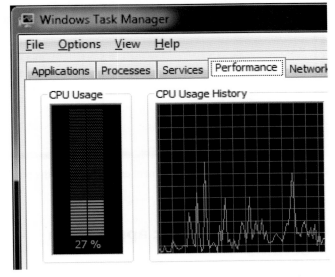

**Figure 1.21**  An operating system's Task Manager program logs and displays graphically the computer's processor (CPU) usage.

## Programming

We study programming in more detail in Chapters 10 and 11. Although program code can be written with a simple text editor program, it needs further software to compile, if required, and find errors in (or 'debug') it. For convenience, most programmers use a single program called an **integrated development environment** (**IDE**) for their chosen programming language to do these and other tasks (Figure 1.22).

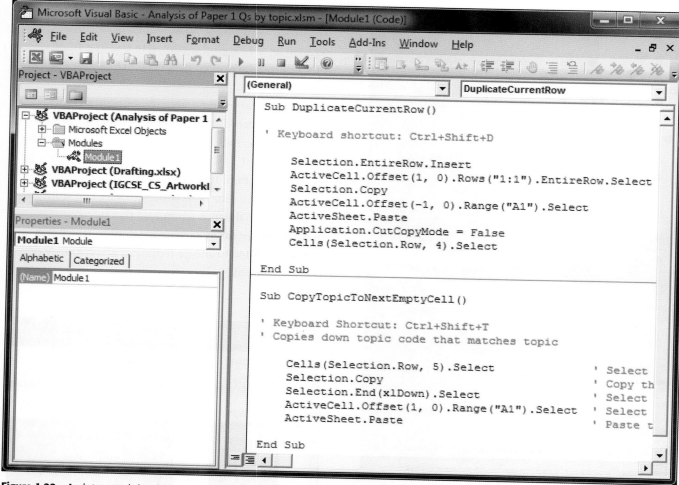

**Figure 1.22** An integrated development environment for the programming language Visual Basic for Applications (VBA).

## Customising generic application programs

A readily available, standard application program is often described as **off-the-shelf** software because it is a product that can be literally picked up off the shelf in a shop. Most computer users find that an off-the-shelf program is reasonably adequate for their needs. However, it is likely to have a few disadvantages. One of these may be that there are far more commands and options available than needed, which can slow the user down when they are trying to find the features that they do want. In a large organisation, this can have an important impact on training requirements and business efficiency.

Fortunately, an off-the-shelf generic application program can often have some of its menus and toolbars hidden. Also, some new menus or toolbars can be created with the essential requirements (Figure 1.23).

It may even be possible to substitute the organisation's logo and name for that of the program and set up input forms in the corporate colours. This is called **customising** the generic software because it is being altered to suit the needs of a particular customer.

A second disadvantage of generic software is that there may be no command for some processing that is repetitive, requires a long sequence of commands or involves several layers of menu or a particular option hidden away in a dialogue box. For example, you might want a quick and reliable method of inserting your organisation's logo and correctly formatted contact details in DTP documents. In this case, if the program has a scripting language, we may customise the software by creating a **macro**. A macro is a small piece of program code that can be run by clicking a toolbar button or pressing a keyboard shortcut (Figure 1.24).

**Figure 1.23** Macros assigned to toolbar buttons improve access to existing commands and provide some new ones.

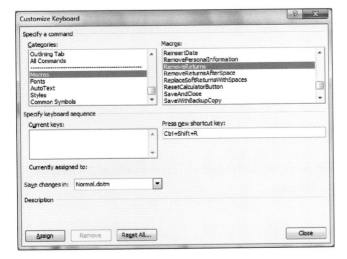

**Figure 1.24** Macros can also be assigned to shortcut key combinations.

You may have to write the macro, but in some application programs you can record a sequence of commands as a macro without needing to understand the details of its code. Trying to understand what the macro code means is quite a good way to learn how to write program code (see also Chapter 10). If an application has a macro capability, it is likely to have an IDE to let you annotate a macro with comments, edit it and write new ones (see Figure 1.22).

 **SAQs**

4   When using a word processor, you frequently have to remove multiple new lines where only one is required. You want to be able to do this easily throughout documents without manually deleting each one. How would you do it?

## Bespoke software

Sometimes it is necessary to have a piece of software specially written to solve a particular problem. Ideally, it will do exactly what is required. It is called **bespoke software** because it is designed to suit the needs of a particular client.

Both off-the-shelf and bespoke software have many potential advantages and disadvantages relative to each other. Off-the-shelf software's advantages are:

- it is immediately available;
- it is usually cheaper to buy because the development cost is shared by many users;
- it may have powerful features developed over many years;
- if it belongs to a suite (for example, Microsoft Office) it is likely to be able to exchange data and files easily with other members of the suite;
- it is well-tested by previous users;
- there is support available from experienced trainers and user groups.

Off-the-shelf software's disadvantages are:

- it may be overly complex and therefore difficult to learn;
- it is often a compromise between the different requirements of users;
- it may not fit an organisation's requirements and may require the organisation to adapt its business procedures to the software;
- if the user finds an error in the software, it is unlikely that it will be fixed rapidly since the software producer may be unresponsive or take a long time to conduct thorough testing.

Bespoke software's advantages are:

- it should match the organisation's requirements well, including operating reliably with the organisation's other software;

- it should operate more efficiently as it includes only the features required;
- it should be easier to learn and the developers of the software may be involved in training to meet the specific needs of staff members;
- it can be maintained reasonably promptly if errors need fixing, the organisation's requirements change or improvements in performance are needed;
- customer support is likely to be better with access to the software's designers.

All these advantages may help the customer to make long-term savings through increased efficiency that compensates for the much greater initial purchase cost.

Bespoke software's disadvantages are:
- it is much more expensive to purchase since the customer must pay for all the producer's development costs;
- its development time may be very long;
- its quality remains uncertain until it is used;
- it is likely to have more errors as it is not used by so many different people;
- its support and maintenance is very dependent on the producers of the software remaining in business;
- there are no other experienced trainers or user groups.

## Summary

- There are two types of software: system software controls the hardware of a computer, while application software allows the user to do something useful with the computer.
- There are many different types of application software for different purposes, each of which exploits various GUI facilities and possesses a combination of standard and application-specific features:
  - DTP;
  - word processing;
  - spreadsheet;
  - database;
  - communication;
  - web authoring;
  - web browser;
  - search engine;
  - graphics;
  - CAD/CAM;
  - multimedia authoring;
  - presentation;
  - data-logging;
  - programming.
- A macro is program code that can be written in a scripting language or recorded automatically.
- Generic application software may be customised to improve access to existing commands or to create new ones by the use of macros run by toolbar buttons or keyboard shortcuts.
- Off-the-shelf, generic software is readily available, relatively cheap to buy and well-tested. It can be tailored, to a certain extent, to the requirements of a purchaser. Its disadvantages are that it may be overly complex; it may not have exactly the facilities required; errors may not be fixed rapidly.
- Bespoke software is software specially written to solve a particular customer's problem. It is often very efficient, easy to learn and has good customer support and maintenance.

## Examination practice for Paper 1

### Exam Questions

1. You have been asked to produce a presentation on the social impact of computers on shop workers. What software features would you use to make your presentation interesting? **[2]**

   *Part of Question 3, Cambridge IGCSE Computer Studies 0420/01 Paper 11 May/June 2010*

2. The owners have decided to sell a shop and all its stock. They will produce a word-processed report to advertise the sale. Describe how the owners will create this report, which will contain text, data from the stock spreadsheets, pictures of the shop and some of its stock. **[3]**

   *Part of Question 12, Adapted from Cambridge IGCSE Computer Studies 0420/01 Paper 1 Oct/Nov 2008*

3. It was decided to link a computer to a scientific experiment so that all the results could be input directly and graphs produced automatically. Give **two** advantages of doing this. **[2]**

   *Part of Question 11, Adapted from Cambridge IGCSE Computer Studies 0420/01 Paper 1 May/June 2009*

### Exam-Style Questions

1. A company analyses its sales over a period of six months in a spreadsheet: **[2]**

| | A | B | C | D | E |
|---|---|---|---|---|---|
| 1 | Product Code | Number sold | Unit Selling Price ($) | Sales ($) | Average sales per month ($) |
| 2 | 100003 | 709 | 2.00 | 1418.00 | 236.33 |
| 3 | 100007 | 246 | 3.40 | 836.40 | 139.40 |
| 4 | 100011 | 5388 | 1.50 | 8082.00 | 1347.00 |
| 5 | 100023 | 344 | 4.00 | 1376.00 | 229.33 |
| 6 | 100025 | 768 | 3.50 | 2688.00 | 448.00 |
| 7 | 100067 | 3545 | 1.75 | 6203.75 | 1033.96 |
| 8 | 100071 | 964 | 2.50 | 2410.00 | 401.67 |
| 9 | Product averages | | 2.66 | 3287.74 | 547.96 |

(a) Draw a grid labelled with the column letters D and E and the row numbers 2 to 9 and complete it with the formulae needed to make the calculations. **[6]**

(b) The value of the data item in cell B7 was amended from 3549 to 3545. Which cells were automatically recalculated? **[2]**

→

**(c)** The company used the spreadsheet application to produce a graph of average sales per month against product code:

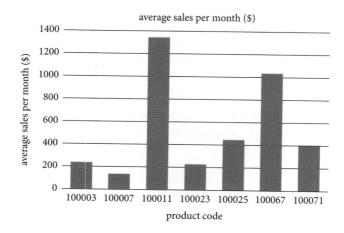

**(i)** Which cells were selected to produce this graph? [2]

**(ii)** How would the product average of the average sales per month of approximately $548 be added to the graph? [1]

2. The following is a database of information about some chemical elements:

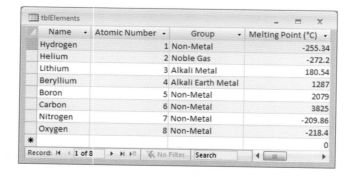

**(a)** List the values of **Atomic Number** for the records found by the following search condition:
(Group = 'Non-Metal') AND (Melting Point (°C) > 20) [2]

**(b)** Write a search condition to find all the elements that are not non-metals AND have a melting point below 400°C. [2]

**(c)** List the values of **Atomic Number** for the results of sorting the database in descending order of **Melting Point**. [2]

$\longrightarrow$

3. State **four** features commonly found in application programs. [4]

4. Explain what is meant by exporting a file from an application program. [2]

5. State **four** types of application program used for communication. [4]

6. State **two** types of visual effect that a web authoring program can *create*, rather than import, on a web page. [2]

7. Which output device could only receive from a computer-aided design (CAD) program? [1]

8. The publicity officer for an organisation frequently needs to insert the organisation's logo and contact details in various desktop publishing documents.

   (a) How might a macro be created to automate this? [1]

   (b) How could the macro be most conveniently run? [1]

9. State **three** possible advantages of 'off-the-shelf' generic application programs compared with specially written or 'bespoke' software. [3]

## Examination practice for Paper 3

To answer the following questions you will need to read the garage scenario provided in Appendix A (page 284).

It is proposed to customise either a spreadsheet program or a database management program.

1. State **three** different facilities of **each** type of software that would make it suitable for this application. For each facility, give an example of how it could be used. [6]

2. State **four** possible advantages of using a generic application program rather than purchasing bespoke software. [4]

**Comment**

Note that both questions require you to apply your knowledge to the scenario. Do not give a generic answer; make sure you apply the answer to the garage scenario.

# 2 Data

When you have finished this chapter, you will be able to:

**When you have finished this chapter, you will be able to:**

- explain the difference between data and information
- describe and select methods of data collection, encoding and preparation
- describe analogue-to-digital and digital-to-analogue conversion
- describe and select methods of automatic data capture
- explain why data need to be checked on input and describe and select validation and verification checks
- explain the ways in which records can be organised in a file and how this affects the time taken to process the file in different ways
- select appropriate file organisation and processing methods for a particular application
- describe methods of file maintenance
- explain the need for different data types and structures to hold data for a given problem.

## 4.2.1 Data and information

People tend to use the terms 'data' and 'information' to mean the same thing. In Computer Studies, we have to make a clear distinction between them. As we see in Chapter 3, data in a digital computer consist of binary numerical values. The word 'data' is a plural word and it may help to remember that its literal meaning in Latin is 'given things'. So **data** are the items we give to a computer as its input, which it holds and processes as binary numerical codes. These values represent things such as the denary numbers with which we are familiar, text characters, formatting codes, image pixels or sound samples.

Data may be encoded during collection or a programmer may have decided to ask the user to enter data in a coded form, such as 'M' for 'medium size', or to store the ID code '87' in a record when the user selects the country 'India' from a drop-down list.

The combination of human-readable codes, such as 'M' or '87', and binary numerical codes for them, such as 01001101 or 00000000000000000000000001010111,

makes computer data difficult to understand for anyone reading them.

Another way of thinking of data is as 'raw' text, numbers, ID codes or pixels. Without some processing and context, they lack any useful meaning. A single pixel is rarely very informative without the rest of the pixels in an image, and a graphics editing or viewing program to interpret and display them.

**Information** is the result of processing data to give them context and meaning and to make them understandable. For instance, '3' and 'L' are both data. They are obviously different from each other and they are also different from '6' and 'M', but they are meaningless without some description of what they represent. However, add '$' to the number to give '$3' and suddenly the '3' may mean something. Similarly, if someone tells you the letter is on a shirt, then 'L' probably means 'large' and 'M' means 'medium'. If we now state that football shirts cost $3 and they are of two sizes – large and medium – the data are now in context and become information.

1 If we were to put information about shirts into a table, what would the headings for this table be?

Information that is output from one system may become the data that are input into another system. For example, when you supply information to a program, it becomes the program's data. Of course, information can result from much more complex sorts of processing, such as searching, sorting and mathematical and statistical calculations.

## Data collection

**Data collection** is the process of gathering data ready for entry into a computer. Typically, this involves someone making a temporary record on paper, such as completing an application form or survey form. In the process, the data may have already been **encoded**. For example, customers may be asked the survey question 'How satisfied were you with the service you received today?' Instead of inviting a 'free text' response, the survey agent or questionnaire may ask customers to express their satisfaction on a scale of 1 to 4. Encoding data is a form of summarisation to remove unnecessary detail. It is important not to confuse encoding with encryption, in which data are scrambled in order to make them secret.

There are a number of advantages of encoding data like this. Everything each customer might have wanted to say has been 'compressed' by this encoding to a single digit. So these data are quicker to enter and require less memory and storage space. Since there are fewer characters to enter, there is less risk of making a mistake. It is very simple and rapid to process these data by counting each instance of the four possible response values to obtain their frequencies. The main disadvantages are:

- a scale of 1 to 4 may be too coarse to express fine differences between customers;
- unless the survey sheet also provides a free-response 'comment' box, important feedback from customers may be lost;

- there is a risk of annoying customers by the crudeness of the survey.

## Data preparation

Data are sometimes not in a suitable form to be entered into a computer. A simple example is a date of birth, which may be in any of the following formats:

- 18 November 2000;
- 18th November, 2000;
- 18th of November 2000;
- November 18th 2000;
- 18/11/00 (this is the UK style – day first);
- 11/18/00 (this is the US style – month first);
- 00/11/18 (this is the Australian style – year first).

How would you write down your date of birth?

Imagine that a question on a data collection form asked for the person's date of birth. The answer given would be likely to be in a different format depending on where the person was from. Before these data are input to a computer, they need to be **prepared** so that all the dates are in the same format, otherwise they cannot be processed reliably. A well-written data entry screen form would indicate the format to enter data (such as dd/mm/yyyy) to avoid any confusion.

Data preparation is also needed in data-logging or any system in which a sensor provides input data for a computer, such as input for monitoring or feedback from an actuator in a control system (see Chapter 5).

## Analogue-to-digital converters and digital-to-analogue converters

A sensor is a device that produces an electrical signal in response to a physical or chemical stimulus (see Chapter 3). Most physical and chemical changes occur smoothly over time. So the electrical signal from a sensor changes smoothly, rather than step-wise. For example, a temperature sensor may deliver an electrical voltage that varies smoothly between 0 V and 1.5 V as its temperature varies over the range of 0°C to 150°C. We call such a signal **analogue**, because it smoothly models even small changes in the stimulus.

Analogue computers exist for processing analogue signals, but they are uncommon. *IGCSE Computer Studies* focuses on digital computers, which cannot

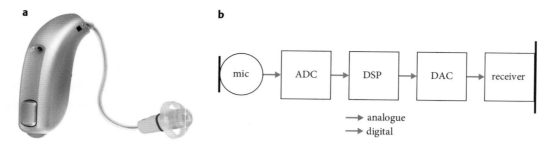

**Figure 2.1** **a** Digital hearing aid. **b** Simplified block diagram of the components of a digital hearing aid.

process analogue signals directly. As we said earlier, they need **digital data** consisting of binary numerical values. Therefore, a digital computer first needs to convert smoothly varying analogue signals into discretely varying or stepwise varying digital signals. We can connect an analogue signal to an input adapter in the computer. Here, a device called an **analogue-to-digital converter** (ADC) samples the analogue signal and converts it to a numerical value. Successive samples of the analogue signal become a sequence or 'stream' of digital data. This is called **digitisation**. So to prepare a sensor's analogue signal for processing by a computer, it is 'digitised' or converted into digital data by an ADC.

Although not really relevant to data preparation, we need to be aware of the opposite process of converting digital output from the computer into an analogue signal for an output device or actuator, using a **digital-to-analogue converter** (DAC).

It is possible that a control system might need digital processing of both the analogue input from a sensor providing feedback from an actuator and the analogue output to the actuator. However, an ADC and a DAC are also found working together in non-control systems such as a digital hearing aid (Figure 2.1). This uses a miniature computer called a digital signal processor (DSP), which provides adjustable digital filtering of audio signals that is more sophisticated than analogue processing circuitry can provide.

An ADC and a DAC are also found in a desktop computer's sound card. It converts a microphone's analogue signal into a digital input stream for recording or other processing and converts a digital output stream into electrical signals to drive headphones or loudspeakers.

## 4.2.1 Data capture and checking

We can distinguish the preparatory phase of data collection from **data capture**, in which the data actually enters the computer. Data capture can be divided into manual input methods and **automatic data capture**.

Manual input methods involve the user entering data by hand (or another part of the body) with a device such as a keyboard, keypad, mouse, touchpad, touch screens, joystick or remote control. Typing into a document and clicking on an icon are examples of manual input.

Automatic data capture involves using automated devices and methods for data input without human intervention. Typical examples of automatic data capture are:

- a barcode reader scanning a barcode in a shop or library;
- a data logger's sensor samples and stores the temperature of a room;

- an optical character reader (Figure 2.2) scanning the machine-readable portion of a cheque, passport or similar document and using optical character recognition (OCR) software to extract (or 'read') text characters from the scanned image; the text data are passed directly to the computer as if they had been typed on the keyboard.

**Figure 2.2**   An optical character reader for passports.

Manual and automatic input devices such as these are studied in greater detail in Chapter 3 and examples of how they are used are described in Chapter 7.

### Questions

1   Consider a questionnaire designed to find out what students think about their school uniform and how it can be improved. Think about the different ways that the students could be asked to respond to the questions:
   a   if their responses are going to be read and edited by a human so that they are suitable for entry into a computer;
   b   if their responses are going to be input direct to the computer either by using an on-screen questionnaire or using optical character recognition (see Chapter 3).

Whether automatic data capture is used or data are entered manually, errors can occur. It is important to minimise these errors to ensure that the data are as correct as possible. There is no point in spending a large amount of money on the most modern equipment and the best software if the wrong data are put into the system. As the acronym GIGO says: 'garbage in, garbage out'. There are two types of checking for correctness that can be performed when data are input to a system:
- data validation;
- data verification.

They sound very similar, but are rather different. Unfortunately, it is not always easy to categorise a method of checking, as it may have characteristics of both types.

### Data validation

In Computer Studies, **validation** means checking carried out by the computer to make sure that input data are within the limits of what a user might reasonably enter. Any value outside these limits is assumed to be a mistake. A program does this by checking that each input data item obeys a validation rule specified in the program or its customisation. If not, the program produces an error message, which tells the user that an error has occurred and, in a well-designed system, what they need to do about it. We can use a number of possible validation checks, sometimes in combination with each other.

### Type check

When the program expects to receive data of a particular type, it automatically rejects characters or symbols entered that are inconsistent with that type of data. For example, the characters '0' to '9' and '.' will be acceptable for a decimal number, but 'J' and '#' will not be. The programmer does not need to create any special rules for this.

### Range check

In a **range check**, the software checks that a numerical value is within a particular range of values. For example, the validation rule might be that a number must be greater than zero and less than or equal to 100. So −42 and 101 are both rejected.

### Limit check

A **limit check** is similar to a range check, but the rule involves only one limit. For example, a number might be limited to being greater than or equal to zero. This rejects any negative numbers. A useful validation check for a date of birth is that it must not be later (or, in terms of numerical code, greater) than today's date.

### Length check

In a **length check**, the software checks that the number of characters entered in a string is within specified limits. For example, we can use a length check to enforce a minimum of six characters when setting a password (Figure 2.3).

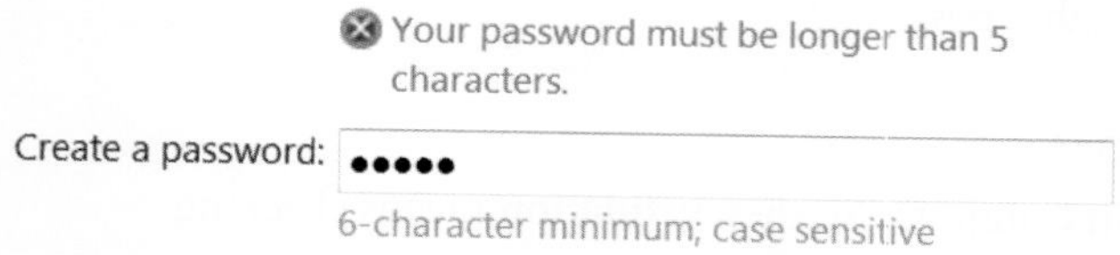

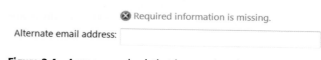

**Figure 2.3**  A length check that has produced an error message.

### Character check

In a **character check**, the software checks that a string of characters does not contain invalid characters or symbols. For example, when registering a birth, a parent is likely to be restricted to alphabetic characters for the baby's registered name. In this case, strings containing one or more numerals, punctuation marks or other symbols, such as 'K8' will be rejected. A username for an online service is unlikely to be so restricted.

### Format check

In a **format check** (or picture check), the software checks that a string of characters has the required pattern or 'format'. For example, an ID code may be required in the format 'LLL000000', meaning three letters followed by six digits. In this example, 'AB9423872' would be rejected because, although it has the right number of characters, it has one too few letters and one too many digits.

In a database management program, a format check for a field may be known as its *Input Mask* property to distinguish it from its *Format* property, which determines only how the field displays data items *after* entry.

It is a handy shortcut on a calculator or in a spreadsheet to be able to enter a decimal number without completing trailing zeros after the decimal point. However, in software used in banking it might be desirable to force the user to type *every* digit including, for example, the tens and units in currency. In this case, '$456', '$456.' and '$456.7' would all be rejected.

### Presence check

In a **presence check**, the software checks that essential data items have been entered when the current record is entered or 'submitted'.

For example, when applying for a service on a form on a web page you are usually required to supply certain minimum information, even if some fields remain optional. If you fail to supply the required information, clicking the *Submit* button, results in the form being re-displayed with error messages. For example, the word 'Required' may appear in red next to the relevant fields (Figure 2.4).

In a database management program, a presence check for a field may be enabled by setting the value of its *Required* property to True.

Required information is missing.

Alternate email address:

**Figure 2.4**  A presence check that has produced an error message.

### Consistency check

In a **consistency check** (or **cross field check**) the software checks that different fields in the same record correspond correctly. For example, if 'Ms' has been entered into the *Title* field, 'Female' must be entered into the *Gender* field.

### Check digit

Some codes are quite long and they are often represented by barcodes for reading by a barcode scanner. Even if the text is perfectly legible, a human can misread, omit a character, add an extra character, accidentally swap the order of characters (known as a 'transposition error') or make more complex errors. A scanner is likely to misread one or more characters if the barcode is smudged or on a label that has become wrinkled. In order to detect most, but not all, misread numerical codes, a check digit is included in the code. A check digit is an extra digit that is calculated from all the original digits in order to summarise them. The algorithm used for performing the calculation depends on the type of code, but relies on assigning a numerical 'weight' to each original digit that depends on its position in the number.

The ISBN-13 code (12 digits plus check digit) uniquely identifies books (Figure 2.5). It is printed with hyphens purely to help humans read it. The check digit can be used to detect three types of error reliably:

- two adjacent digits transposed, for example '3457' instead of '3547';
- an incorrect digit entered, for example '5675' instead of '5775';
- an omitted or extra digit, for example '687' or '68276' instead of '6827'.

The last digit is the check digit in an ISBN.

**Figure 2.5** A check digit in an ISBN-13 code, found on all recently published books.

The check digit for the ISBN 978–0–521–17063–? is calculated using the following steps (see the worked example):

1. Each digit of the code is given a 'weight'.
2. Each digit is multiplied by its weight and the products are added together.
3. The total is then divided by 10 using modulo-10 arithmetic, in which only whole numbers are used and only the remainder is retained; in other words, because modulo-10 arithmetic is used, only the last digit of the total is retained.
4. To make the sum of all the weighted digits, *including* the check digit, exactly divisible by ten, the check

digit is chosen to be zero if the result of Step 3 is zero and the difference between the remainder and 10 if the result of Step 3 is non-zero.

The complete ISBN becomes 978–0–521–17063–5, as in Figure 2.5.

**Worked example**

Calculating the check digit:

   Code:  9 7 8 0 5 2 1 1 7 0 6 3

**Step 1:** Weight: 1 3 1 3 1 3 1 3 1 3 1 3

**Step 2:** $9\times1 + 7\times3 + 8\times1 + 0\times3 + 5\times1 + 2\times3 + 1\times1$
$+ 1\times3 + 7\times1 + 0\times3 + 6\times1 + 3\times3$
$= (9 + 8 + 5 + 1 + 7 + 6) \times 1 + (7 + 0 + 2 + 1 + 0 + 3) \times 3$
$= 36 + 39$
$= 75$

**Step 3:** $75 \div 10 = 7$ remainder 5
or 75 modulo 10 = 5

**Step 4:** Result > 0, so check digit is $10 - 5 = 5$

When a code has been received by the scanner or entered into the computer, the received code can be validated by recalculating the check digit from the first 12 digits and comparing it with the received check digit. Because the check digit was chosen to make the sum of all the weighted digits exactly divisible by 10, it is quicker simply to calculate the sum of the weighted digits and check its divisibility. For example, the received ISBN code is checked in the following steps (see the worked example):

1. Each digit of the code, including the check digits, is given a 'weight'.
2. Each digit is multiplied by its weight and the products are added together.
3. The total is then divided by 10 using modulo-10 arithmetic, in which only whole numbers are used and only the remainder is retained.
4. The ISBN is valid if the result of Step 3 is zero.

## Worked example

Validation check of received ISBN code:

Code:   9 7 8 0 5 2 1 1 7 0 6 3 5

**Step 1:** Weight: 1 3 1 3 1 3 1 3 1 3 1 3 1

**Step 2:** $9\times1 + 7\times3 + 8\times1 + 0\times3 + 5\times1 + 2\times3 + 1\times1$

$\quad\quad + 1\times3 + 7\times1 + 0\times3 + 6\times1 + 3\times3 + 5\times1$

$= (9 + 8 + 5 + 1 + 7 + 6 + 5) \times 1$

$\quad + (7 + 0 + 2 + 1 + 0 + 3) \times 3$

$= 41 + 39$

$= 80$

**Step 3:** $80 \div 10 = 8$ remainder 0

or 80 modulo 10 = 0

**Step 4:** Result = 0, so the ISBN is valid

If the received code fails the validation check, there is definitely an error in the code. If it passes the check, the code is much less likely to contain an error. There is no guarantee: commonly used algorithms with a single check digit detect all errors involving only one digit but only about 90% of transposition errors.

## SAQs

2   The following ISBNs are received in error for 978–0–521–17063–5. Check whether the method used above for verifying ISBN-13 codes can detect each of the following errors:

a   978–**5**–0**2**1–17603–5

b   978–0–521–**7**7603–5

c   978–0–521–17603–**0**

## Data verification

A data item can pass validation checks but still be inaccurate due to a copying error. **Verification** means double-checking for accuracy when data are copied. For example, if a customer has written their date of birth as '18/11/00' on a data collection form and the input operator keys in '19/11/00', a copying or 'transcription' error has been made.

Copying errors by humans can be minimised by some form of double-checking:

- **Visual check** – a single operator reads through a whole record's data on the display screen, comparing each item with the original document to check for and correct any errors.
- **Double entry** – ideally, two operators enter the data, as two people are less likely to make the same error. The program compares the two inputs and only accepts them if they match. If they are not the same, the software can ask one operator to resolve the discrepancy or refer the source of the data for further investigation. Sometimes the same person is asked to perform double entry. For example, you may have been asked to perform double entry when setting up or changing a password (Figure 2.6). It would have been highly inconvenient if you had typed something other than what you thought you had!

**Figure 2.6** A double-entry verification check that has produced an error message.

The method that is used depends on the application and how important the accuracy of the data is. If the data are personal details of students in a school, errors are unlikely to have major consequences, so a visual check will be sufficient. If the data are customers' orders, errors are likely to annoy customers and possibly lose the organisation their future custom, so the extra expense of double entry may be justified.

Electronic copying errors during transmission across networks can be detected and, in some cases, even corrected by a number of methods. A **parity check** is a relatively simple check. An extra binary digit or 'bit' is added at an agreed position in each byte (see Chapter 3) before transmission. For **even parity**, the added **parity bit** is chosen to make the total number of 1s in the byte even. For **odd parity**, the parity bit is chosen to make the total number of 1s odd. For example, suppose that the sending and receiving devices are using *even* parity and the eight bits 11011110 are sent. When the bits 11001110 are received, the receiving device checks the parity and discovers that there is an *odd* number of 1s, so parity has been violated. The receiver registers that an error has occurred and can request re-transmission.

## Extension

1 If a single bit has changed during transmission, can a parity check identify which one has changed?
2 If two bits have changed during transmission, can a parity check detect the error? Can you spot another major disadvantage of using a parity check?

## Questions

2 Figure 2.6 contains a double-entry verification error message for password setting. Here is a similar message from the same website for password renewal. Discuss the advantages and disadvantages of each message.

Change your password

⊗ The new password and the confirmation password don't match. Please type the same password in both boxes.

*Type new password: ●●●●●●●●●●

Six-characters minimum; case sensitive

Password strength: Strong

*Retype new password: ●●●●●●●●●●

Notice that despite performing both validation and verification checks, it is still possible for an item of data to be entered inaccurately. For example, both entries during a verification check may suffer from the same transcription error. If the data item collected is accidentally or even deliberately inaccurate, no amount of care or checking at the data entry stage can correct it. Accidental data collection errors can only be detected by asking the person who supplied the data to visually check printed information from the system and amend

any errors that they spot. Organisations often do this at intervals to prompt their customers to supply updated information, such as changes of address or telephone number.

## Questions

3 Consider the different types of data that were collected when you surveyed students about their views on school uniform. If these data are going to be input to a computer, what measures could be taken to ensure that they were as accurate as they could be?

4 Think about the different pieces of information that your school holds about you. Try to find out what measures are taken to make sure that the data stored is as accurate as it can be.

### 4.2.2 File organisation and manipulation

In Chapter 1, we met the idea of a record and its fields or attributes. With a database management program, the software manages the storage of a database's objects, such as tables, queries, forms and reports, so a software developer does not have to be concerned with how the data are stored. However, we need to be aware of how records can be organised in a data storage file and how such a file can be processed and maintained.

Consider the set of data about students in a school as shown in Table 2.1. For simplicity, the table only shows records for four of the students in the school and only a small amount of data about each student. In reality, there may be more than a thousand students and each student may have tens of items of data held about them. We need to recognise that each *row* in this table represents a **record**. Each *column* represents a **field** within the records, which holds a specific type of data.

Each of the records in the table must be distinguishable from all the other records; we must be sure that we are looking at the data of the right student. In Table 2.1, everyone has a different name so it seems we could use the person's name to distinguish one record from another. But can we be sure that there is only one person in the school called Noah Amu or

**Table 2.1** Data about students in a school.

| IDNumber | Name | Gender | Form | Tutor |
|---|---|---|---|---|
| 18759 | Noah Amu | M | 4AD | Mr James |
| 36729 | Rose Thornton | F | 3JU | Mr Ali |
| 51734 | Liene Faizan | F | 6YD | Ms Sayer |
| 51736 | Omar Norton | M | 3JU | Mr Ali |

Rose Thornton? In our example, the *ID Number* is a field whose value we can make sure is unique for each record. Database management software can do this for us automatically. We call such a field containing unique identifiers the **record key**. It is also called the 'key field', 'primary key' or just the 'key'.

Now we have to consider storing this set of records as a data file. A **file** is a set of data or program items held in a named area of storage. A **serial file** (Figure 2.7a) stores records one after another in no particular order other than the one in which they are created. Its records can be read electronically (in no particular order) by reading the file from its beginning. Such a file can be stored on magnetic disk or a serial medium such as magnetic tape (see Chapter 3). On average, searching for a record that is present takes half the time to read the whole file. However, the lack of any order means that we have to read the *whole* file whenever we search for a record that turns out not to be present. A serial file is not a good choice for storing records other than those of transactions, which are recorded in the order in which they take place.

To avoid wasting so much time when seeking an absent record, the records need to be sorted and stored in a *sequence*, in order of record key value. This is called a **sequential file** (Figure 2.7b). Notice that the student records in Table 2.1 are in key order.

The sorting of records in a sequential file reduces the average seek time when seeking an absent record to half

the time to read the whole file. Once we pass its position in the sequence, we know that it is not present and can stop the search. This sort of file is perfectly satisfactory if most of the records need to be processed at a time, as when updating a sequential 'main file' (or 'master file') with data from a transaction file that is sorted into the same record key order. In our example, student records could be stored in a sequential file and updated at the end of the school year using a sorted transaction file listing the new school form for each student who is not leaving.

Other applications of this technique are:

- performing pay calculations and updating pay-to-date and tax-paid-to-date on a payroll file for the employees of an organisation, using a transaction file containing records of hours worked or bonus payments;
- updating a customer file when a utility company generates bills, using a sorted transaction file containing meter readings.

Searching for individual records for updating changed addresses, tax codes or bank account details takes a relatively long time, especially if the file is large.

Sorting is obviously essential for creating a sequential file and we meet one of a number of possible algorithms for sorting in Chapter 10.

It may also be necessary to merge two files. Merging two sequential files involves reading the two source files and writing a new merged file elsewhere on the disk.

a

| record 08 | record 13 | record 15 | record 21 | record 02 | record 06 | record 23 | record 07 | record 05 | record 16 |
|---|---|---|---|---|---|---|---|---|---|

b

| record 02 | record 05 | record 06 | record 07 | record 08 | record 13 | record 15 | record 16 | record 21 | record 23 |
|---|---|---|---|---|---|---|---|---|---|

**Figure 2.7** **a** A serial file. **b** A sequential file.

For example, having read the first record from each source file, we write the one with the lower record key value into the merged file. We then read another record from the same source file and if the record's key value does not exceed that of the current record in the other source file, we write it into the merged file and repeat the process. When we read a record with a key value that does exceed that of the current record in the other source file, we switch to reading records from the other source file. This repeats until we reach the end of both source files.

The most rapid access to a record chosen at random requires the storage of records in a **direct access file** (or **random file**). This sort of file can only be stored on a portion of a **magnetic disk**, which is a 'direct access' medium on which an individual record can be rapidly written or read, using an algorithm to generate the disk address from the record's key value. A very simple algorithm would be to use a numerical record key value as the disk address. If the record key values are too widely spaced, the disk address could be calculated (in denary arithmetic) as *key value modulo 1000*, which is equivalent to discarding all but the last three digits of the key value.

It is more complex to manage the growth of a direct access file, such as when merging two files into a much larger one, as it may be necessary to adjust the algorithm for converting a record key value to a disk address. However, a direct access file is highly suitable for any application requiring frequent access to records chosen at random. Applications that require random access include:

- using the username as the record key value to search for and check a user's password (stored in encrypted form) when they log in to a network;
- a seat booking system for a railway, airline or entertainment venue.

A direct access file is considerably slower than a sequential file for an application that requires all the records to be read from the file in key order.

## File maintenance

Any processing of a file that is not part of routine transaction processing (such as purchasing a concert ticket) or updating a main file (as in utility billing) is known as **file maintenance**.

File maintenance may involve:

- inserting a record;
- deleting a record;
- updating (or amending) a record.

If a new student arrives during the school year, we need to create (insert) a new record. If the file is sequential and the new student's record receives a record key value that is not last in the order, we need to rewrite the file by copying it to a new file to create space in which to insert the new record. Rewriting the file is not necessary if it is a direct access file.

If a student leaves the school during the school year, we need to remove their record (delete it) from the file.

If a student changes their address and the amended record occupies a different amount of storage from the original record, we need to rewrite the file by copying it to a new file. In another application, the amendment might be to an employee's tax code, a customer's bank account details or a product's price.

### Questions

5 How would a file be altered if a student left the school during the year? Think about how the update could be done if the file were:
  a sequential;
  b direct access.

6 A field in each record is the 'Age' of the student. What are the implications of this for updating the file? Is there a better solution?

7 A teacher gets married and changes his name. Explain how this could be updated in the file without a requirement to look at every record.

## 4.2.3 Data types

Application programs can only process and store data appropriately if the data items are given ('assigned') the correct **data type**. For example, software cannot perform arithmetic on the string of characters '3794' if they have been assigned the 'string' data type and it cannot process the third character ('9') independently of the others if they have been assigned the 'number' data type, although this can be done with string data.

The same keystrokes on the keyboard can represent different types of data in different contexts. All data entered using a keyboard are sent from the keyboard to the computer as numeric codes for the characters. A text or word processing program simply accepts the string of numerals '3794' as a string of characters, although a person reading it may interpret the string as a number.

However, a database or other program may be programmed or customised to accept the same string of numerals entered into a 'text box' as a number. When we press the *Enter* key, the software processes the string of characters to validate it as a string of numerals, possibly with a single decimal point. It then converts the string of characters into one of several types of number and holds the number in a suitably sized space in the computer's memory.

Our example student records in Table 2.1 have consistent sorts of data in each field. The *ID Number* field contains data items that are numeric codes, but not numbers. The *Name* field contains two (or possibly more) alphabetic names separated by spaces. The *Gender* field is a single alphabetic character that is either 'M' or 'F' and so on. Whether the records are stored as a table that is part of a database or as a file, the software is programmed or customised to assign a specific data type to each field. The main data types that we can assign to a field and how they might be used are described below.

### String data type

The **string** (or **text**) **data type** consists of a string, or sequence, of characters. A string can include the alphabetic letters ('A' to 'Z' and 'a' to 'z'), numerals ('0' to '9'), punctuation and other symbols, such as '@' or '#'. If a string is restricted to alphabetic letters and numerals only, we may call it an alphanumeric string, although this is not a separate data type. The majority of fields in many sorts of record have the string data type.

Strangely, some fields that are named 'number' are best given the string data type. For example, a telephone number is really a coded address for a telephone, not a number on which we ever want to perform arithmetic. To decide whether data are truly numeric, ask: 'Would the answer mean anything if two of these values were added together?' If the answer is 'No', the data should be given the string data type. If the answer is 'Yes', the data should be given a number data type. A telephone number may include an exchange name, an 'area code' in brackets, or spaces. Any of these could cause a 'number' to be rejected by the type check. Even if it were to be accepted, we would still be liable to lose leading zeros.

### Number (numeric) data type

A **number** (**numeric**) **data type** consists entirely of numerals ('0' to '9'), representing the digits of a number, and possibly a single decimal point. There are two main types of number (numeric) data:

- **integer**, which consists of a whole number such as −16 or 256913; it does not contain a decimal point;
- real or decimal, which consists of a number that has a decimal fraction part, such as 12.5 or 3.141592654; it is used for quantities such as a person's height, for example, 1.76 metres.

An integer number should always be given an integer data type, because the real data type takes up more storage space. If a database has a million records, using the real data type can result in a lot of wasted storage and memory space.

## Questions

8  Should you give an ID Number field a number (numeric) data type?

9  Investigate the 'character' data type. How does the character data type differ from the string data type?

10  A particular field holds integers. Another field holds the answer when some arithmetic is carried out on the integer field.
   a  What should the data type of the second field be?
   b  Investigate whether this answer changes for different types of arithmetic.

## SAQs

3  Do you think the value 78.123 would be accepted in the 'ID number' field? Give a reason.

## Currency data type

The **currency data type** consists of an amount of a specified currency whose value is usually displayed with a currency symbol, such as '$', and two decimal places. The internal representation is as an integer with digits reserved for hundredths of a penny, to reduce the errors otherwise caused by rounding off to the nearest penny in calculations.

## Date/time data type

The **date/time data type** consists of a real number representing a date alone, a time alone or a date and time. Values for each of these may be displayed in a variety of formats. A date is represented by a whole number of days from an arbitrary start date, usually somewhere around 1ˢᵗ January, 1900. For example, 1ˢᵗ January 2015 in Microsoft Excel is stored as 42,005.00 days. A time is represented by a fraction of a day; for example, 12 noon is stored as 0.50 day.

## Boolean data type

The **Boolean** (or Yes/No) data type consists of the values True or False. In some database software, these values are displayed by default as a ticked or un-ticked check box. They can also be displayed as True/False, Yes/No, On/Off or any other pair of values representing mutually exclusive alternatives, such as Member/Non-member, Female/Male, Paid/Unpaid.

## Arrays

A **data structure** is a more complex data type that consists of a number of data items of one or more data types. A record itself is a data structure, with its fields as the data items. An **array** is a data structure that consists of a number of data items of a *single* type. These data items are called the **elements** of the array.

A programmer can create an array by 'declaring a variable' (see Chapter 9) as an array structure with one or more dimensions to hold elements of a specified data type. This defines a uniquely named set of locations in memory, in which the array's elements are held. The programmer can refer to a particular element in the array variable by means of the array variable's name (or 'identifier') and one integer **index** (or 'subscript') for each dimension. The programming language determines the actual sequence in which the elements are held in memory. As a programmer, you can learn to write very efficient programs using these indexes (or 'indices') to manipulate the elements of an array. This is helpful when filling (or 'populating') the array with data, searching for a data item or generating output from its data.

A one-dimensional array is known as a 'linear list'. A two-dimensional array (Figure 2.8) is known as a 'table', with its two dimensions being thought of as the rows and columns of a table of data of a single data type. Although an array's dimensions have no inherent meaning, by convention, we think of the first subscript as the row number and the second subscript as the column number.

Let us consider the table in Figure 2.8, named `CapitalLookup`. It is used to look up the capital city for a country. Just six countries are shown in this example. `CapitalLookup[3, 2]` refers to the element whose value is 'El Djazaïr'.

## Questions

11 For each of the five named fields in Table 2.1:
   a State the data type that would be used, explaining your choice.
   b State the validation checks that you could use (apart from the type check).

12 Suggest extra fields that could be sensibly stored in the file that would be examples of the other data types mentioned.

13 A file is to be set up to store details of products that a supermarket has in stock. Decide which fields should be included in the file including the data type, justifying your choices. Choose which field should be used for the key, explaining why.

## SAQs

4 Answer these questions about the array in Figure 2.8:
   a How can we refer to the element whose value is 'Angola'?
   b To what does `CapitalLookup[1, 2]` refer?

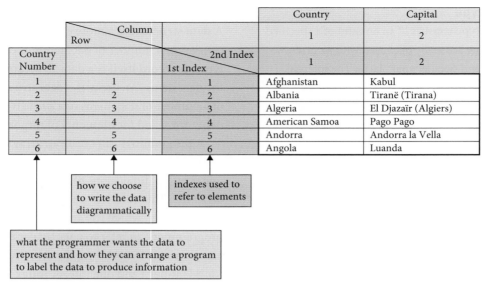

| Column | | | Country | Capital |
|---|---|---|---|---|
| Row | | | 1 | 2 |
| | | 2nd Index | | |
| Country Number | | 1st Index | 1 | 2 |
| 1 | 1 | 1 | Afghanistan | Kabul |
| 2 | 2 | 2 | Albania | Tiranë (Tirana) |
| 3 | 3 | 3 | Algeria | El Djazaïr (Algiers) |
| 4 | 4 | 4 | American Samoa | Pago Pago |
| 5 | 5 | 5 | Andorra | Andorra la Vella |
| 6 | 6 | 6 | Angola | Luanda |

how we choose to write the data diagrammatically

indexes used to refer to elements

what the programmer wants the data to represent and how they can arrange a program to label the data to produce information

**Figure 2.8**   A two-dimensional array of countries and their capitals, named `CapitalLookup`

## Summary

- Data are the raw facts and figures that we give to a computer as its input. They lack sufficient context and processing to have meaning.
- Information is the result of processing data to give them context and meaning.
- Data may need preparation after collection and before they are entered to ensure that they are in the correct format.
- Data are encoded to summarise them, so that they are quicker to enter and with fewer errors, occupy less memory and backing storage and are quicker to process.
- A sensor input signal that is analogue, or smoothly varying, needs conversion by an ADC into digital, or discretely varying, data.
- Digital output signals often need conversion by a DAC to analogue signals to provide smoothly varying output.
- Automatic data capture is the use of automated devices and methods for data input without human intervention.
- Inaccurate data are of little value, so their accuracy is checked by validation and verification.
- Validation checks ensure that the data entered are sensible and reasonable. Common checks are: range, length, character, format, presence, consistency and check digit.
- Verification checks ensure that data remain accurate when they are copied. Common checks are: visual, double entry and parity bit.
- A record is a set of data about an individual person, object or transaction, usually displayed in a row of a table. A data field holds a specific type of data about a characteristic of the items recorded, usually displayed in a column of a table.
- A record key field holds a unique identifier for each record. A set of records are stored together as a data file.
- Records within files can be organised in different ways:
  - A serial file stores records in chronological order, which is only useful for logging transactions.
  - A sequential file stores records in a logical order, that of their record key, which enables rapid updating of the whole file with data from a transaction file sorted in the same order. The specified file must be read from the beginning, which gives slow access to an individual record.
  - A direct access file allows rapid access to an individual record without reading any others. Updating of the whole file with data from a transaction file is slower.

$\longrightarrow$

*Summary continued …*

- File maintenance involves inserting, deleting and updating records.
- Different data types are identified so that a computer can store and process the data appropriately. Data types include string, numeric, currency, date, Boolean.
- Data structures are more complex data types. They include record and array structures.
- An array consists of a number of elements of a single data type. An array may have one or more dimensions. A program refers to an element using the array's identifier and an index number for each dimension. This approach enables efficient programs for filling an array, searching for a value in the array or generating output from its elements.

## Examination practice for Paper 1

### Exam Questions

1. Name **two** types of automatic data capture and give **one** application for each type named. [4]

   *Question 4, Cambridge IGCSE Computer Studies 0420/01 Paper 1 May/June 2008*

2. Examination results are stored in students' records as marks out of 100. Give **two** different validation checks that could be performed on students' marks. [2]

   *Part of Question 6, Cambridge IGCSE Computer Studies 0420/01 Paper 1 May/June 2008*

3. A screen has been developed to allow the input of data into the following fields: *name, sex, address, date of birth* and *examination results*.

   ```
   ┌──────────────────────────────────────────────────────────┐
   │                    Student Records                         │
   │                                                            │
   │   Student name: .......................... Sex: ........... │
   │   Student address: ....................................... │
   │   ........................................................ │
   │                                                            │
   │   Date of birth: ......... / ......... / .........         │
   │   Exam results: Subjects and Grades                        │
   │                                                            │
   └──────────────────────────────────────────────────────────┘
   ```

   (a) What is verification? [1]

   (b) Which fields should be verified? [2]

   *Parts of Question 7, Cambridge IGCSE Computer Studies 0420/01 Paper 12 May/June 2010*

   $\longrightarrow$

*Examination practice for Paper 1 continued ...*

## Exam-Style Questions

1. An online health information service uses a data entry form to input data about new clients.
   Name a suitable **different** validation check for each of the following fields:

   (a) Last Name, which may only have between 1 and 30 characters, which may only be alphabetic or a hyphen (-). [1]

   (b) Gender, which may only have the values 'F' or 'M'. [1]

   (c) Date of Birth, which cannot be earlier than today's date. [1]

   (d) Country of Residence, which must be stated and only have one of the 213 values in the service's database. [1]

2. (a) State **two** types of error that can be detected using a check digit. [2]

   (b) Calculate whether or not each of the following ISBN-13 numbers is valid. Show all your working.

      (i) 9780521728216 [3]

      (ii) 9780521165129 [3]

# 3 Hardware

**Hardware** means the physical parts of the computer. By contrast, software (see Chapter 1) refers to the computer programs that make the computer do something useful. An example of software is the **operating system (OS)**, which is a set of programs that manage the computer.

## 5.1.1 Main hardware components of a general-purpose computer

A **computer** is a programmable, electronic device. It receives input, stores data, processes data and produces output. A computer usually has a number of hardware components, which we can categorise into five types of device:

- an **input device** is used by the user to put data into the computer;
- a **processor** manipulates the data that the input device gives it;
- **internal memory** (also known as main memory) holds data and programs while the computer is on;
- **backing storage** stores data and programs while the computer is off;
- an **output device** reports results to the user or causes something to happen.

Figure 3.1 shows how the devices are linked. The arrows show the flow of data around the system.

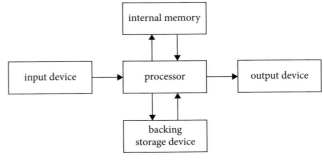

**Figure 3.1** The main components of a computer.

The processor was originally called the **central processing unit (CPU)**. It consisted of many sets of circuitry. Electronics engineers integrated all this circuitry into a single silicon 'chip'. It has become known as a **microprocessor**, often shortened to **processor**.

**Questions**

1 Figure 3.2 shows a personal computer (PC). List all the input and output devices that you can see. Can you think of any other input or output devices that are not shown in the picture?

**Figure 3.2** A personal computer.

## Extension

Investigate the use of other types of processor, for example, a microcontroller (see page 48), a digital signal processor (DSP) or a graphics processing unit (GPU).

## Computers and processing power

The power of a computer's processor determines what type of computer it is. Table 3.1 gives an overview of the types of computer.

### History of computer development

People have been building calculating devices for centuries but electronic computers only became possible in the 20th century. A brief history:

- **Early 1940s:** A team of code breakers invented Colossus to help decode messages sent by German military forces. Colossus worked far faster than humans but was very slow compared with modern computers. Colossus filled an entire room (Figure 3.3) and was very unreliable.
- **Late 1950s and 1960s:** Companies and universities began to purchase computers.
- **1970s:** Large organisations connected terminals to mainframe computers.

**Figure 3.3** The Colossus machine at Bletchley Park, UK, was one of the first electronic computers.

**Table 3.1** Classes of computer.

| Type of computer | Processor power | Example applications |
|---|---|---|
| Supercomputer | Extremely powerful | Used to process large sets of data in a short time: weather forecasting, molecular modelling, simulations of aircraft in flight or simulations of buildings in wind |
| Mainframe | Very powerful | Used by large organisations to provide central data storage and processing power to many users: running payroll processes and creating customer invoices |
| Personal computer (PC) or laptop | Powerful | Used by individuals to store and process data: word processing, spreadsheets, email, web browsing, playing music |
| Netbook, palmtop or personal digital assistant (PDA) | Moderately powerful | Used by individuals to store and process data while moving around: email, web browsing |

- **Late 1970s and 1980s:** Personal computers were developed.
- **1990s:** Portable computers (laptops and notebooks) became popular.

When computers were first developed, the process of using them was very long-winded. Users had to encode their programs and data onto punched cards or tape. The user then gave the cards or tape to another person, a 'computer operator'. The operator would run the program when the computer had time available and return the printed output to the user. If there was an error in the output, the user would have to recode the cards or tape and repeat the whole process!

## Types of computer

Organisations can link **terminals** to **mainframe computers** (Figure 3.4). A terminal has a keyboard for input and a monitor (see Figure 3.4 inset) for output. It does not have any data storage or processing power of its own. It simply sends the user's input to the computer and displays messages from the computer to the user. Many users can access the processing power of the mainframe at the same time, without the need for a computer operator or understanding of how the computer works. Many mainframe computers are still in use today, although a PC may be used as a terminal.

**Figure 3.4** A mainframe computer; the inset shows a built-in technician's terminal.

Most people today want their own computer. From their initial development, **microcomputers** or **personal computers** (PCs) were small enough and cheap enough

for an individual to have one on their own desk or at home (Figure 3.5). They have a disk for storing data and a processor to operate on the data. PCs can be large; they contain many components (such as sound cards, graphics cards and disk drives) and need a fan to keep the processor cool.

a

b

c

**Figure 3.5** Personal computers. **a** From the 1980s. **b** From the 1990s. **c** From 2010.

Portable computers (known as laptops or notebooks) have a built-in keyboard and screen (Figure 3.6) and are powered by a battery. A laptop is very portable but still has essentially the same facilities as a PC. The processor may have lower processing power than the processor in a PC and it is attached to an efficient 'heat sink'. The heat sink enables the processor to remain cool in operation and minimises the need to run a cooling fan. These features help to reduce the electrical power required and extend the endurance of the battery.

**Figure 3.6**   Laptop (left) and netbook (right) computers.

Palmtop computers were small enough to fit in the hand. They were cheap, portable computers that used less power. Modern versions of the palmtop with wireless or mobile network access are called netbooks. They are used mainly to access Internet services, such as the web and email.

An even smaller, less-powerful computer is the **personal digital assistant** (**PDA**) (Figure 3.7). A PDA does not have a keyboard. Instead, it uses a plastic stylus (shaped like a pen) to select commands or to input data on a touchscreen (see page 55), often by using a virtual keyboard on the screen. You can also write notes directly onto the screen, in your own handwriting. The PDA can convert your handwriting into typed text using optical character recognition (OCR) software (see page 60). A PDA runs basic versions of standard computer application programs. A PDA that includes a mobile phone is one form of **smartphone**.

**Figure 3.7**   A PDA – the stylus is used as a pointing device or to write text by hand.

## Questions

**2**   What are the advantages of a PDA compared with a paper notebook?

**3**   Since their invention, computers have become smaller in size and increased in processing power. What do you think will happen over the next ten years?

## Extension

Try to find out about computers from different eras. What were the sizes and processor powers of these machines? (Hint: see clock frequency on page 49.) To get started, go to http://oldcomputers.net/zx80.html.

Earlier in the chapter, you discovered that a microprocessor is a processor on a single chip. Because microprocessors are so small, it is possible for designers to embed a whole computer into appliances, such as washing machines, TVs, DVD players, cameras and burglar alarms. These computers are much simpler than a mainframe or a PC, of course. The design engineer usually uses a **microcontroller** (Figure 3.8). This combines the microprocessor with memory, backing storage and other circuitry, all in a single integrated circuit. It forms a tiny, but complete, computer-on-a-chip. These computers contain simple programs that allow the electronic appliances to perform in the way they do.

**Figure 3.8** A microcontroller in an 80-pin package.

**Questions**

4　Make a list of devices that contain a microprocessor (or microcontroller). What are the advantages of using a microprocessor? Are there any disadvantages?

A **supercomputer** (Figure 3.9) is an extremely powerful computer that may contain thousands of processors. The processors work in parallel with each other to achieve high processing power and

**Figure 3.9** NASA's supercomputer occupies many banks of equipment racks in a large room.

speed. Often the processors are standard, multi-core processors, such as those you would find in a PC. Supercomputers are used where a very large number of calculations must be made in a short time. Examples of use include weather forecasting, molecular modelling, simulations of aircraft in flight and simulations of buildings in wind.

### Measuring processor power

Processor power is usually measured in Millions of Instructions Per Second (MIPS). Supercomputer power is usually measured in much larger numbers of FLoating point Operations Per Second (FLOPS).

You are not expected to remember specific numbers. They vary greatly within classes of processor and classes of supercomputer. They also change over time.

**Extension**

Use the Web to find examples of each of the types of computer that we have considered.

A crude measure of processor power is the clock frequency, the number of electronic timing signals per second that is sent to the processor, measured in hertz (Hz). Try to find the clock frequency for each computer in your examples. You may need to enter **<name of computer> "clock speed"** into a search engine.

1 MHz (1 megahertz) = 1,000,000 Hz
1 GHz (1 gigahertz)  = 1000 MHz = 1,000,000,000 Hz

## Input devices and their uses

You will look at many different kinds of input device (Table 3.2) in this section. **Manual input devices** are used by people to capture data. **Automatic data capture** devices enable data to be entered without human intervention (involvement). We use them to enter large amounts of similar data. Sensors collect data automatically.

### Manual input devices
#### Keyboards and keypads

A user enters values and commands into a computer by pressing buttons (keys) on a keyboard. This section

**Table 3.2** Types of input device.

| Manual input devices | Devices and methods for automatic data capture | Sensors |
|---|---|---|
| • Keyboards <br> • Pointing devices (e.g. mouse, touchpad, touchscreen) <br> • Scanners <br> • Cameras (e.g. webcam, video camera) <br> • Microphones <br> • Musical keyboards <br> • Remote controls | • Optical Character Recognition (OCR) readers <br> • Optical Mark Recognition (OMR) readers <br> • Magnetic Ink Character Recognition (MICR) readers <br> • Barcode readers <br> • Radio-frequency identification (RFID) tag readers <br> • Magnetic stripe readers <br> • Smart card readers <br> • Biometric data capture devices (fingerprint readers, retina or iris scanners, microphones, cameras) | • Temperature <br> • Pressure <br> • Light <br> • Infrared <br> • Humidity <br> • Gas (e.g. oxygen, carbon dioxide, carbon monoxide, fuel) |

looks at standard keyboards, concept keyboards and numeric keypads.

On a standard keyboard, each key has a value (a letter, numeral, punctuation mark or other symbol) printed on it. When the user presses the key, it sends the computer a standard signal corresponding to the value on the key. Typically, a monitor displays what has been typed, to give immediate feedback to the user. Keyboards are used for typing anything, from an email to a book.

Users of English usually type on a QWERTY keyboard. It gets its name from the arrangement of letters on the top row of keys (Figure 3.10). This layout was originally used on a typewriter to prevent keys jamming when the user was typing rapidly. When computers became widespread, most users were familiar with using a typewriter and designers kept the QWERTY layout to avoid the need to re-train the users.

Keyboards have the advantages of using a simple, familiar, reliable technology. The disadvantages of keyboards are that they are slow compared with devices for automatic data capture. In public locations, they are prone to vandalism.

**SAQs**

1   What makes data input using a keyboard slow compared with other ways of inputting data?

**Figure 3.10** QWERTY keyboards. There are many different designs for QWERTY keyboards but they all follow the same letter pattern: Q-W-E-R-T-Y.

## Questions

5 A timber (wood) yard has a desk where customers order the wood that they need. The sales clerk has a QWERTY keyboard. Why would it be needed and what would it be used to input?

## Extension

• Investigate other layouts of keys on keyboards. For example, look at the Dvorak keyboard and keyboards designed for use with languages other than English.

• Find out about keyboards that have the QWERTY layout but are not rectangular (ergonomic keyboards). For example, look at the Kinesis keyboard.

A concept keyboard may consist of a rectangular grid of keys. The program designer decides the value or command that each key enters. A flat, flexible, overlay sheet covers the keyboard (Figure 3.11); it has a suitable picture, symbol or word printed for each key.

**Figure 3.11** An overlay sheet for the concept keyboard in a fast-food restaurant.

**Point of sale (POS)** computers often use a concept keyboard. It allows the user to enter products quickly, without having to remember or type codes. Groups of similar items can be colour-coded and the flat overlay is easy to clean. The concept keyboard can include letters and numbers, if required.

Young children and people with learning disabilities or other difficulties may have trouble using an ordinary keyboard. A concept keyboard, with its limited number of input values, may be helpful to such people.

Public information touchscreen systems (see page 55) often display a concept keyboard. Touching certain parts of the screen generates a command to display some relevant information.

## Questions

6 Find out about the use of concept keyboards in your school. Alternatively, find a shop (fast-food outlets are good places to start) that uses concept keyboards at the counter.
  a Why is this a good type of input device to use?
  b What outputs are generated by the inputs?

## ? SAQs

2 A concept keyboard is on the desk in the timber yard. It allows the user to input quantities and types of timber quickly.
  a What features will a keyboard used for this purpose have?
  b How can the concept keyboard allow the user to input addresses for delivery? Is this better than the QWERTY keyboard?

A numeric keypad is a rectangular block of keys with the numerals 0 to 9 and arithmetic operators (Figure 3.12). A keyboard usually has a numeric keypad for rapid entry of numbers. In some situations, a numeric keypad is provided without the rest of the keyboard.

We use numeric keypads to input:

• personal identification numbers (PINs) when we pay by bank card or withdraw cash from an automated teller machine (ATM);

**a**

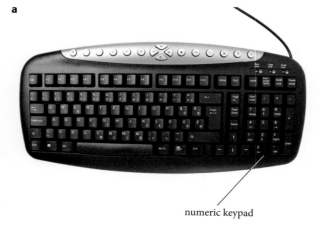

numeric keypad

**b**

numeric keypad

**Figure 3.12** Numeric keypads with different layouts: **a** on a QWERTY keyboard, **b** on a mobile phone.

- the combination for electronic locks on lockers, safes, rooms and buildings;
- numbers on telephones.

Numeric keypads are small, easy to use and independent of language. They are also easy to cover when you do not want anyone else to see what is being input. A disadvantage is that inputting other symbols is difficult. Even with 'predictive text', typing a text message on a mobile phone's numeric keypad is slower than using a keyboard.

*Pointing devices*

A mouse allows the user to point by moving the cursor in a graphical user interface (see Chapter 4) on a PC's screen. The user selects items by pressing ('clicking') switch buttons on the body of the mouse.

A mechanical mouse has a small ball underneath (Figure 3.13). As the mouse is moved around on a desk, the ball rolls over the flat surface. The mouse converts the rotations of the ball in two dimensions into digital signals that it sends to the computer. The operating system moves the cursor to match the mouse's movement. An optical mouse has no moving parts – it senses changes in reflected light as the mouse moves over the desk.

**a**       **b**

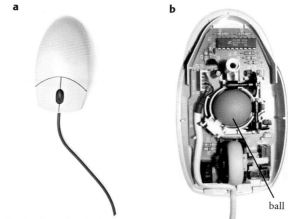

ball

**Figure 3.13** A mechanical mouse. **a** As seen from above, **b** as seen from below.

The advantages of using a mouse as a pointing device are that:

- it provides a fast method of input for commands;
- it feels natural (intuitive) to use because it involves pointing at things.

The disadvantages of using a mouse are that:

- it needs a flat surface on which to operate;
- it can be easily vandalised;
- some people find a mouse difficult to use, particularly if they have physical disabilities.

**8** There are other types of mouse apart from the mechanical one described here.

 **a** An optical mouse does not have a roller ball. Find out and explain the advantages of an optical mouse over a mechanical one.

 **b** A mouse does not always need a wire to connect it to the computer. Find out how a cordless mouse works and what advantages it has.

**9** If you need to select a toolbar icon, menu item or button displayed on a screen, the mouse needs to do more than just sense how it is being moved around. What other features are needed to let you select items using a mouse?

**SAQs**

**4** The computer used at the timber yard has a mouse. What sort of mouse would be sensible and what sort of input could it be used for?

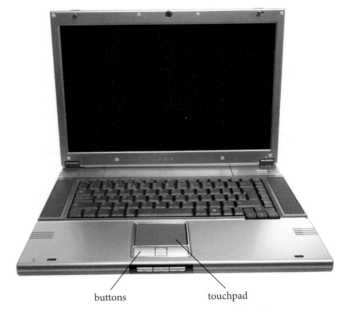

**Figure 3.14**   A laptop with buttons and a touchpad.

mouse, the user rolls the ball in a socket. Larger versions can be used for foot control by people with motor disabilities that affect their arms or hands.

A mouse is not always a suitable way to control the cursor. A laptop computer is designed to be self-contained and a mouse would have to be carried separately. A laptop is also designed not to need a desk, so there may be no surface on which to use a mouse. Laptops, therefore, usually have a touchpad (Figure 3.14), a smooth, touch-sensitive area next to the keyboard. It produces signals representing the motion of the user's finger.

Most touchpads have buttons that can be used like those on a mouse or the user can tap on the pad with a finger. A touchpad's advantages are the same as those for a mouse. An external touchpad used with a PC takes up less desk space than a mouse. A disadvantage is that the touchpad is very small relative to the laptop's screen.

A trackball is like an upside-down mechanical mouse (Figure 3.15). Rather than moving the whole

**Figure 3.15**   A trackball.

A trackball has the following advantages over a mouse:
- it is stationary and does not need a surface to move on;
- it can be built into an information kiosk and is not as likely to get damaged as a mouse;

- people may be able to use it even if they do not have the control necessary to use other pointing devices.

Disadvantages of a trackball are that:
- it can be difficult to use for applications needing fine control;
- rolling a ball is less like pointing.

**Questions**

10 The pointing devices discussed so far were designed for use with a GUI to select commands and manipulate data values on a screen. What other input device may be even more appropriate to use with a GUI?

**SAQs**

5 The owners of the timber yard have decided that a mouse is not an appropriate pointing device to use.
   a Explain why a mouse is not appropriate.
   b Assess touchpads and trackballs as input devices in this environment.

A **joystick** can act as a pointing device, by moving the cursor when the user rocks a lever connected to sensors. It can also provide input for an embedded computer, such as that of a motorised wheelchair (Figure 3.16). The user can give many different commands to the wheelchair with very little physical movement.

As a pointing device in a game, a joystick may control the movement of a vehicle or character. It may have buttons with specific uses, such as picking up an object or firing a weapon.

Some laptops have a miniature joystick, or 'thumbstick', in the middle of the keyboard. Some smartphones have a thumbstick in the keypad or keyboard.

Joysticks are the natural choice for using in applications such as:
- playing games;
- controlling fly-by-wire aircraft or flight simulation programs;
- controlling a motorised wheelchair.

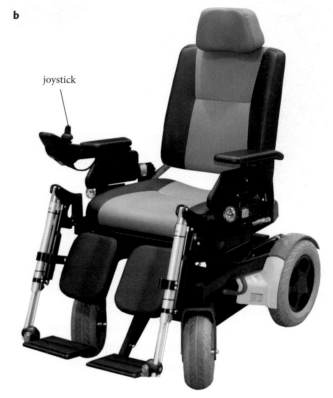

**Figure 3.16** Joysticks used for control. **a** In a computer game. **b** On an electric wheelchair.

The disadvantage of a joystick is that it may be more difficult to control fine movement than with a mouse.

**SAQs**

6 Describe a use for a joystick in a timber yard.

A touchscreen is a screen that is sensitive to the touch of a stylus or finger. Touchscreens range in size from smartphones and PDAs through tablet PCs (laptops with touchscreens) and PC monitors to interactive whiteboards. A touchscreen is very instinctive to use as a pointing device; the user literally points to the relevant part of the display, then touches an icon, menu option or button to select a command or to input data (Figure 3.17).

**Figure 3.17**   A touchscreen at a train station.

At a train station, the user touches the area of the ticket-machine screen on which the program displays the required type of ticket. The touchscreen sends a signal to the computer. The operating system works out the position of the touch and can interpret it as a mouse click. If a cursor is visible, it moves it to that point.

The operating system can also interpret movement of the point of contact as a drawing or dragging process. With suitable software, a user can draw directly on the computer's display. For example, a delivery courier may use a PDA's touchscreen to collect a signature on an electronic receipt.

Touchscreens are common in information kiosks or ticket machines because:
- they are difficult to vandalise;
- they can be made reasonably weatherproof and so can be placed in the open air, for example on a station platform;
- users need no previous knowledge of computers to be able to operate them.

A disadvantage is that people with disabilities can find them difficult to use.

**SAQs**

7   List the advantages and disadvantages of using touchscreens as input devices.

**Questions**

11   A system such as a ticket machine often uses a touchscreen as its input device. This is useful for limiting the number of options available to the user.
   a   List the uses of touchscreens you have seen. Try to decide what makes it sensible to use a touchscreen in each case.
   b   Most touchscreen applications have two areas of the screen reserved for important commands. Try to discover what they are and decide why they are important.

**Extension**

Find out about the use of touchscreens on devices such as mobile phones and portable game consoles such as the Nintendo DS.

A graphics tablet looks like a very large touchpad (Figure 3.18) but operates more like a touchscreen with a stylus. The operating system uses signals from the tablet to work out the position of the stylus on the tablet's surface and then moves the cursor to the corresponding point on the screen.

stylus

graphics tablet

**Figure 3.18**   A graphics tablet being used to draw.

A graphics tablet is highly suitable for creating original drawings and calligraphy (artistic handwriting). Some tablets can even detect how hard you are pressing or which way up the stylus is pointing, so you can 'rub out' mistakes. The user can trace a drawing that they have taped to the tablet. For plotting points precisely on an old design drawing, the user may use a 'puck' with cross-hairs instead of a stylus. A disadvantage is that it may be difficult to match the position and motion of the stylus on the tablet with those of the cursor on the screen.

A light pen (Figure 3.19) is a pointing device that can only be used directly on the screen of a cathode ray tube (CRT) monitor (see page 71). The display is created by a rapidly repeated scanning process. The light pen has a sensor in the tip that picks up the light from the screen. It produces an electronic signal whenever the display brightens. The computer's operating system uses the timing of this signal relative to the scanning process to calculate the position of the pen on the display.

**Figure 3.19** Using a light pen.

The advantages of a light pen are:
- it is instinctive to use – the user simply points to the relevant part of the display with the pen;
- with suitable software, the user can draw directly on the computer's display;
- it takes up little space.

The disadvantages are that it is not very accurate and it requires a cable to connect it to the computer, which makes it rather awkward.

Light pens are now rare, since graphics tablets and touchscreens are widely available.

## Image capture devices

A scanner creates a digital photograph of a paper document. It mechanically scans the illuminated surface of the document with a single row of hundreds of light sensors. Each sensor produces an analogue signal that depends on the intensity of the light it receives. The scanner's embedded computer repeatedly scans the signals from the sensors as they move across the document. The embedded computer then digitises the signals, processes them and sends them to the computer.

With a flatbed scanner (Figure 3.20), the user places the paper document on a flat sheet of glass, called the 'platen'. The document may be a drawing, a photograph or text.

**Figure 3.20** A flatbed scanner.

We can save the scanned data as an image file. This file can act as a backup copy of the paper document. It may even be appropriate to discard the paper document and keep only the electronic image. Many such electronic documents can be stored in a small physical space.

We can extract text from a scanned document using optical character recognition (OCR) software (see page 60). We can also extract data from a form using optical mark reading (OMR) software (see page 61).

 **SAQs**

8  What are the advantages of scanning a class photograph rather than having a printed copy?

A digital camera has a grid of light sensors (Figure 3.21) that pick up an optical image. The camera's embedded computer scans the analogue signals from the grid of sensors. It then digitises these data and displays them on a built-in monitor screen. A **pixel** (or **picture element**) is a single sample from a rectangular grid of samples in the final image. The more pixels there are, the more detailed the image is.

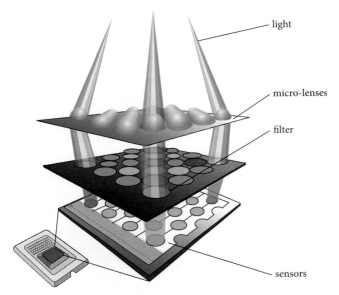

**Figure 3.21**  How a digital camera works.

When the user presses the shutter button (to take the photo), the shutter covering the lens opens so that light can enter the camera. The camera processes and stores the data as an image file in non-volatile memory (see page 86). The camera may contain built-in memory or it may save the image to a removable digital storage card (DSC). The user can transfer stored files to a computer through a cable or a wireless connection. The user can also insert a camera's storage card into a card reader connected to a computer.

Computer software can edit an image file's size or colour. It can also combine images. A stand-alone photo printer (see page 74) can print a photo directly from a digital camera. It usually has some basic software for image editing before printing.

The advantages of digital cameras over film cameras are:

- there is no repeated cost of purchasing and processing film;

- the display acts as a 'what you see is what you get' (WYSIWYG) viewfinder;
- there is no long delay for processing – the user can view the photo immediately and delete it if it is not good enough;
- it is easier and quicker to edit digital photos than film;
- a digital photo can easily be sent over a network or used in electronic documents.

A disadvantage of a digital camera is that it uses a lot of power, mainly to drive the display. This limits the endurance of its battery.

**Questions**

**12**  'The camera never lies' – is this true?

**13**  How does image editing affect people who appear in photographs? How does it affect people who view those photographs?

A digital video camera (Figure 3.22) captures a sequence of digital photos, typically at a rate of 30 images per second. The user can record the video sequence by saving these data as a video file. The file can include sound, known as the 'sound track'. The user can view the sequence of images, which gives the impression of motion.

Portable digital video cameras (known as 'camcorders') have facilities for recording files. Such a camera stores its files on magnetic tape, an optical disc, a hard disk or a non-volatile DSC. Many digital cameras and mobile phones can also record and replay short 'clips' of video. With suitable software, the user can edit a video file and publish the edited video on a website or DVD-R (see page 114).

Some digital video cameras have no recording facilities. A common example of such a camera is a webcam (Figure 3.23). It can feed its image sequence ('stream') to a computer. If needed, the computer can record the video stream as a file. A laptop may have a built-in webcam, just above the screen.

A webcam can provide live video while communicating over a broadband Internet connection. It can be used with both instant messaging and VoIP telephony software. Communicating by voice and video like this for business purposes is a form of video-conferencing.

**Figure 3.22** Digital video camera.

webcam

**Figure 3.23** Using a webcam.

The live video stream provided by a webcam can be used for a number of other purposes:
- displaying on a website – some webcams show street scenes, others show wildlife habitats;
- remote monitoring of the security of a building or of the welfare of an elderly person.

**? SAQs**

9  How might a timber yard use webcams to improve security inside and outside their building?

### Sound and music capture devices
A microphone converts sound vibrations into an analogue signal. We usually connect the microphone's signal to the computer's sound card with a cable. The sound card has an analogue-to-digital converter (ADC) that converts the microphone's input signal to a stream of digitised sound samples. Typically, each sample represents just 23 microseconds of the input signal and 44,100 of them are created every second! The user can record the microphone's signal by saving these data as a sound file. Users can edit recordings with suitable software. They can easily send a sound file over a network or use it in an electronic document such as a presentation or web page.

Speech recognition (or speech-to-text) software can recognise spoken words in a stream of sound data and convert them to text. If someone is unable to type words on a keyboard, speech recognition software enables them to convert their speech into text input (Figure 3.24).

**Figure 3.24** A microphone can be used with a speech-to-text program.

Someone with a hearing impairment can also use it to help them understand speech. A disadvantage is that speech recognition software can be unreliable.

## ? SAQs

10  Who is most likely to use a microphone and software to convert speech to text in the timber yard business?

## Questions

14  A microphone can provide input to a processor that controls a burglar alarm system in a car. The processor might be programmed to identify the sound of broken glass. This would work if someone broke a window in order to steal something, but what would happen if a bottle was smashed outside the car? How can the microphone–processor combination recognise that this is not damage to the car?

A **Musical Instrument Digital Interface** (**MIDI**) keyboard can provide input to a computer (Figure 3.25). It connects to a computer through a special MIDI interface. When a key is struck on the keyboard, the keyboard sends signals representing the start of a note of a particular pitch and volume, any changes in finger pressure while the key is down and the end of the note. These signals involve far fewer data than would result from recording the actual sound of the note.

The computer's MIDI software can record a performance on the MIDI keyboard by saving it as a file. One musician can perform on multiple MIDI instruments, edit the saved data together and play back the performance. The performer's musical ability still limits the quality of the recorded performance!

The MIDI protocol has become the industry standard for recording and editing performances on digital musical instruments.

## Extension

Investigate other types of MIDI device available and their features. A starting point would be to look at the Yamaha WX5, which allows synthetic wind instrument control.

### Remote controls

A remote control is a small, hand-held device with a relatively small number of labelled command buttons. It is used to operate equipment such as a TV, satellite or cable TV receiver, DVD player or home entertainment system (Figure 3.26). When a button is pressed, the remote control sends a coded infrared (IR) or radio signal to the equipment.

**Figure 3.25**  Using a music keyboard to input music via MIDI.

**Figure 3.26**  Using a remote control.

As people increasingly use PCs for home entertainment, manufacturers supply some PCs with remote controls.

An advantage is convenience; for example, you do not need to stand up to change TV channel. Disadvantages are that the signal may interfere with other equipment and an obstruction between the remote control and the equipment it controls may block the infrared signal.

## Devices and methods for automatic data capture

We have looked at manual input devices, which are used by people to capture data by hand. We now turn to devices and methods for automatic data capture without human involvement.

### OCR and OMR readers

Software can process data from a scanner to provide automatic data capture, especially if the scanner has an automatic sheet feeder.

**Optical character recognition** (OCR) software extracts text from the image data of a scanned document. OCR software compares the shape of each possible text character in the image data with templates for each character stored in the computer. When it recognises a character, it adds the character to its output data sequence (Figure 3.27).

**a**

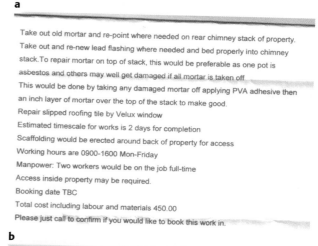

**b**

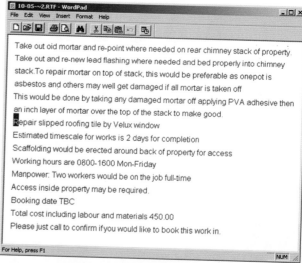

**Figure 3.27**   Using OCR software. **a** Scan of original text. **b** Resulting editable text.

The text can be sent to a word processor or other application and saved. It will occupy a much smaller file than the original image and is much quicker than re-typing the text from a paper document. It is also useful for people with visual impairments, who can scan a paper document and use text-to-speech software to read it out aloud. Postal services also use OCR software to read postal address codes in the automated sorting of mail.

One disadvantage is that the text produced is not always accurate, particularly if the original paper document is not printed or has smudged text.

Optical mark reading (OMR) software extracts response data from the image of a specially prepared data collection form. OMR software is only designed to detect the presence of marks in certain positions on the form. Unlike OCR software, it is not designed to detect characters.

OMR software can extract data such as answers to multiple-choice exam questions, survey results or votes in an election. For example, the correct answer to Question 1 in Figure 3.28 is E. The OMR software is programmed to detect the position of all the shaded regions on the paper. If a shaded region is detected in position E (and no other position) for Question 1, it will award a mark. Many school attendance registration systems and lottery entry forms use OMR for data input.

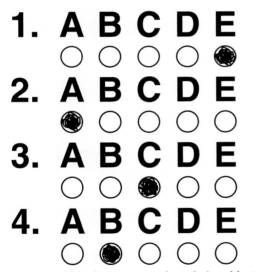

**Figure 3.28** A multiple-choice answer sheet designed for OMR.

The advantage of this method of input is that it is extremely fast and accurate because the coded data are so simple to detect. The disadvantages are that the forms can only be read accurately if they are properly lined up and also dirty marks on the paper might be misread as deliberately shaded regions.

*MICR reader*

**Magnetic ink character recognition (MICR)** uses software similar to OCR but it scans data for numerals and symbols printed in magnetic ink. The use of magnetic ink makes documents harder to forge (imitate dishonestly). It also increases the accuracy of recognising numerals and symbols even if they have been overprinted or obscured by visible marks.

MICR is used almost exclusively by bank cheque-processing systems for input of the pre-printed items (cheque number, bank sort code and account number) on the bottom of each cheque (Figure 3.29). This leaves only the amount to be keyed by an operator.

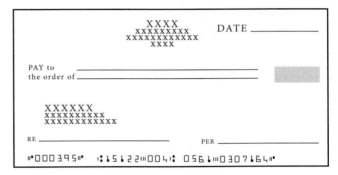

**Figure 3.29** The numbers on the bottom of a cheque are printed using magnetic ink so that they can be read by a magnetic scanner and MICR software.

The shapes of the MICR symbols and numerals were specially designed to be read with very high accuracy by machines. However, unlike a barcode (see page 62), their design also allows people to read the numbers.

 **SAQs**

11 Describe each of the following input methods. Give an application where each is used, justifying your choice in each case.
   a OCR
   b OMR
   c MICR

### Barcode reader

A **barcode** is a set of short parallel lines in contrasting colours (Figure 3.30), often black on a white background; the dark lines are thick, medium or thin. Barcodes are designed to be read accurately by machines. Barcodes are used to identify items of merchandise, resources, membership cards or documents.

**Figure 3.30** A laser wand scanning a barcode. The inset shows the sort of barcode commonly read at a store checkout.

Depending on the font used, the barcode symbols represent numeric digits or alphanumeric characters. The code is usually printed in a human-readable font underneath the bars, because the bars are not easily read by people.

A barcode reader is a combination of scanner hardware and software. Barcodes can be decoded by software working on image data from a document scanner. Store checkout (point-of-sale or POS) systems use a scanner wand or a laser scanner fixed to the operator's workstation. In these dedicated scanners, a suitable processor and decoding software are usually built in to the scanner. This enables the scanner to send a signal to the computer for each decoded character, re-encoded as if the character were being sent from a keyboard or keypad.

The barcode on merchandise almost always only represents an identification (ID) code identifying the product. Reading the barcode only tells us the manufacturer and product, not which instance of the product we are dealing with. Every similar item of merchandise (for example, every can of a particular brand of cola) carries the same barcode. At the checkout in a shop, the ID code is used to look up the description and price in a database. If the price changes, the database is updated and the new price is picked up automatically.

Advantages of using a barcode for data entry are that it is much faster than using a keyboard and more accurate than a person. A disadvantage is that the barcode can become difficult to read if it is obscured by marks.

### Extension

- Two barcode systems in commercial use are the European Article Number (EAN) and the Universal Product Code (UPC). Find out the difference between them. This exercise will give you an idea of how barcodes identify items of merchandise.
- A laser barcode scanner makes a beeping sound to tell the checkout operator that a valid code has been read. How does the scanner decide that the code is valid?

### RFID tag reader

A radio-frequency identification (RFID) tag reader reads an ID code from a small tag using short-range (or 'near field'), radio-frequency communication. The ID code is stored in non-volatile Read-Only Memory (ROM, see pages 79–80) with processing and radio circuitry on a 'smart tag' chip. The chip is less than 0.5 mm square – smaller than a grain of sand. The induction loop or 'antenna' can make the whole RFID tag (Figure 3.31) considerably larger than the chip – perhaps the size of a barcode.

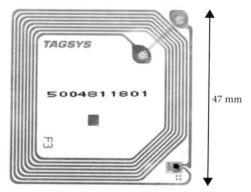

**Figure 3.31** A flexible RFID tag designed for use in books and magazines. Spot the chip!

The electronic product code (EPC) stored in the RFID tag has at least 96 bits (see page 63), so there are at least $2^{96}$ (about $8 \times 10^{28}$) possible codes. Of the 96 bits, 28 are reserved for identifying up to $2^{28}$ (about 268 million) managers of items, such as manufacturers. Another 24 bits are reserved for identifying up to $2^{24}$ (about 17 million) classes of items, such as products for each manager. Finally, 36 bits are reserved for serial numbers to identify up to $2^{36}$ (about 69 billion) instances of each item.

With such a large number of codes available, manufacturers can label as many products as they want with these uniquely numbered, small, contactless, machine-readable tags. You may wonder why identical cans of cola would each need their own serial number. After all, they are destined to be drunk and recycled maybe only days after production.

With RFID tags, we can reliably identify objects and track their movements past RFID tag readers. This enables manufacturers, distributors and retailers to track each tagged item automatically throughout the supply chain. Although the tag only stores the EPC, it can be associated with records in a stock control database. This can contain data about where and when the item was made, its 'sell by' date and where it should be delivered. This information can be updated as the item is detected by a tag reader at each stage of its journey.

Currently, only expensive products or whole pallets of identical goods are tagged. However, if supermarket suppliers were to supply goods with RFID tags, reader-enabled 'smart shelves' would be able to help supermarket staff to locate misplaced items. They could also inform supermarket staff which perishable items to remove when they reach their individual 'sell by' dates. At the checkout, RFID tag readers could scan items rapidly, ideally without the need to remove them from the trolley. At exits, readers could detect any items leaving the shop that had not been paid for.

Other applications of RFID technology include identifying:

- items of merchandise with bulky tags that can only be removed by a checkout operator and trigger an RFID alarm at the store exit, discouraging theft;
- library books and other resources, for lending and security purposes;
- vehicles, for parking and toll charges and for access through automated barriers (Figure 3.32);
- season tickets, for admission to car parks or sporting venues;
- hotel room keycards;
- documents within an organisation;
- pets and farm livestock;
- race competitors at timing points;
- baggage in airport baggage-handling systems.

The advantages of RFID technology are improved efficiency:

- of stock control;
- at the supermarket checkout;

**Figure 3.32** An RFID tag automatically identifies a bus to lower a barrier.

- of product recalls – a batch of suspect products can be traced to specific purchasers.

The disadvantages of RFID technology are:

- a tag costs more than a printed barcode;
- unauthorised persons may be able to read RFID tags within sealed packages in transit;
- 'data flooding' – each tag generating an event record whenever it is near a reader may create a flood of data that will require a lot of processing to produce useful information.

### Questions

**16** Imagine that you have bought clothes, accessories and portable electronic equipment that all contain RFID tags. Perhaps you already have! How would you know? They cannot easily be seen or removed because that would have reduced security in the shops where you bought them. Who could track your whereabouts as you go in and out of shops, places of learning, entertainment venues or on public transport wearing or carrying these items? What are the implications for your privacy? Can you shield the tags from readers with aluminium foil? Can you briefly 'cook' your jacket in a microwave oven to destroy its RFID tag?

### Magnetic stripe reader

On the back of debit and credit cards, library cards and hotel room keycards, you may see a brown, black or coloured **magnetic stripe** near the top. The stripe has three independent tracks that can be programmed to store different types of information. It can only store small amounts of data but this is sufficient for many purposes.

Consider a guest checking into a hotel. The receptionist uses a magnetic stripe writer connected to the hotel's computer system to write data onto the stripe on a keycard. The data includes a unique access code for the room. When the user puts the keycard into the magnetic stripe reader on the hotel room door, the code is read, and the door is unlocked (Figure 3.33).

**Figure 3.33** The magnetic stripe on the back of a hotel room keycard stores a code that unlocks the door.

Advantages of magnetic stripe cards are:
- if a keycard is lost there is no way of identifying which room it is coded to open (unlike a mechanical key, which is usually labelled with the room number);
- it is easy to write fresh data onto the stripe;
- it is not so serious if a guest leaves without returning the keycard, as the code ceases to be valid.

A disadvantage is that someone can read and copy or alter the data on the card with a magnetic stripe writer, which is easily available.

### Questions

**17** There is room for three sets of information on the stripe.
  **a** What other information might the hotel record on the card?
  **b** Is this reasonable or does it clash with the right to privacy of the customer?

**18** Some colleges issue cards to their students. The students use the cards to gain access to areas of the college.
  **a** What are the advantages to the college and to the individual students in doing this?
  **b** What disadvantages are there?
  **c** What other information might the college be able to learn from the use of these cards?

### Smart card reader

Debit and credit cards have always had a magnetic stripe on the back. This stores the card number and expiry date in order to make them machine-readable. It may also store an encrypted (secretly coded) version of the cardholder's secret PIN. It does not store monetary values or secret data such as the unencrypted PIN.

Unfortunately, it is relatively easy for criminals to copy or 'clone' cards. Many card issuers will no longer accept a signature to verify a card transaction. To make bank cards harder to clone, there is now an international standard for using **smart card** technology for card payments. In the UK, this is called **Chip and PIN**. A smart card has a microcontroller (a computer-on-a-chip) embedded in the plastic, behind the electrical contact pads (Figure 3.34).

When making a payment using a smart card, the user places the card in an input device called a smart card reader. The metal contact pads on the surface of the card connect the chip to the reader (Figure 3.35). The card reader communicates with the card's chip and uses cryptographic techniques to check that the card is authentic and has not expired. The embedded chip makes it much harder for a criminal to clone a card.

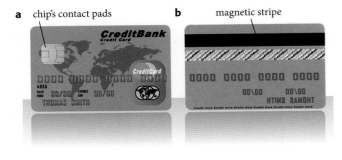

**a** chip's contact pads  **b** magnetic stripe

**c** chip

**Figure 3.34** A credit card. **a** The contact pads of the chip on the front. **b** The magnetic stripe on the back. **c** Cut open to show the chip.

**Figure 3.35** Using a smart card reader.

The user enters a four-digit personal identification number (PIN) code into a numeric keypad on the reader. The entered PIN is encrypted and checked against the encrypted PIN stored in the chip. Only if the two match is the payment authorised.

Smart card readers are mostly used when buying goods or services. They can also replace any other use of magnetic stripe technology, such as:

- access cards for buildings and computers;
- stored value cards, such as cards storing pre-paid amounts for public transport or telephone calls from payphones.

The improved security also allows smart card readers to be used with:

- cards storing e-cash (e-purses);
- cards storing the holder's medical records;

- driving licence cards storing personal information, licence type, digital photo, motoring offences and unpaid fines;
- ID cards storing biometric data.

For speed of use, a smart card reader is sometimes contactless, using similar radio technology to RFID (see page 62). For applications where security is not so important, the card may have non-volatile memory without a microprocessor.

The advantage of this technology is that cards are far more difficult to copy. The disadvantage is that people tend to be careless with their PIN; if it is shared or seen in use it can be used with the card if it is stolen.

### Biometric data capture devices

People's physical characteristics or behaviour, known as biometric data, can be used for the purposes of authentication. For example, someone may try to access a building by entering a user name or swiping a smart card to claim their identity. Instead of requiring the person to verify their identity by entering a password or PIN, the computer can capture their biometric data. The software only has to distinguish key features of the captured data and decide whether the data's pattern is a sufficiently good match with the biometric data pattern stored in the database record associated with that username or smart card.

Alternatively, for identification solely by the data captured, the software has to *recognise* the pattern. This means deciding whether the data pattern is a sufficiently good match with the pattern stored in *any* of the records in a database. If many people's records are stored in the database, this is a considerable amount of processing.

Things that you can carry (such as keys or ID badges) can be lost, stolen or duplicated; things you know (such as passwords) can be forgotten or shared. When they work reliably, biometric techniques have the potential to improve security when people gain access to facilities or even countries.

A **fingerprint reader** (Figure 3.36a) captures the print of a finger placed on it. The pattern-matching software must cope with an image that may be incomplete, rotated or distorted relative to the stored pattern.

A specialised camera, often using IR illumination, can capture an image of the retina or iris in a person's eye.

fingerprint reader

**Figure 3.36** **a** A mouse fitted with a fingerprint reader.
**b** A fingerprint captured by such a reader.

The pattern-matching software for the retina scanner or iris scanner must cope with an image that may be rotated or scaled by variation in the distance from eye to camera.

A microphone can be used to capture an audio recording of a person's voice from which a frequency–time pattern can be distinguished (Figure 3.37). The pattern-matching software must cope with a recording that may vary in loudness or be distorted by a blocked nose or hoarseness. Biometric matching software trying to match this 'voiceprint' also has to cope with mimicry of a person's voice. Speech recognition is another application for analysing voice data.

A camera can be used to capture an image of a person's face. The pattern-matching software must cope

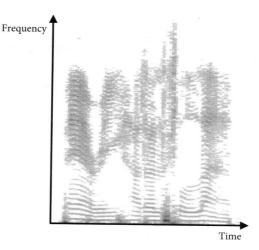

Frequency

Time

**Figure 3.37** A spectrogram – a graphical representation of a frequency–time pattern.

with an image that can be changed in many ways. The distance from face to camera and the brightness and colour of the lighting may be different. The person may also have a different facial expression; have a spot, a cut or a bruise; be wearing different make-up; have shaved or not, and so on.

A stream of image data from a video camera can be input to a video content analysis (VCA) program, which may perform the following traffic control, security or surveillance functions:

- automatic vehicle-number-plate recognition;
- motion detection;
- object detection;
- object tracking.

**5.1.3  Sensors**

A **sensor** is a device that produces an electrical signal in response to a stimulus. The stimulus may be physical (such as temperature or light level) or chemical (such as acidity or the presence of a gas). As we have seen, sensors are important components in input devices, such as scanners. They can produce a stream of input data automatically, without action by a person. We can use the data for measurement, monitoring, control and audio or video recording.

A microswitch (Figure 3.38a) is operated by mechanical contact. It is a very simple, cheap and useful sensor. It has just two states, open and closed, and can provide digital input data directly to a computer.

A similar sensor is a reed switch, which is operated by the presence of a small magnet (Figure 3.38b). There is no need for mechanical contact.

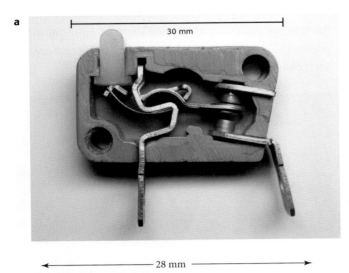

**Figure 3.38  a** An internal view of a microswitch. **b** A reed switch.

These and other types of switch-based sensor can supply input data to a control program. For example, a switch can send data about the position of a door or its latch to the control program of a burglar alarm. Similarly, a switch can prevent a user from turning on a microwave oven with its door open and prevent a lift door from opening until the lift has reached a floor. A switch can act as a 'limit switch' for a motorised valve or detect a paper jam or other fault in a printer.

The snap-action of a switch is step-wise. However, as discussed in Chapter 2, most sensors produce smoothly varying analogue signals. A sensor's analogue signal needs to be digitised or converted into digital data by an analogue-to-digital converter (ADC). Sometimes sensors have an ADC built in.

### Temperature sensor

A temperature sensor produces a signal that depends on the temperature of its surroundings. The computer processes the digitised signal to display a measurement or to control an appliance.

For example, think about running an automatic washing machine equipped with a microcontroller

(Figure 3.39). Its program uses input from a microswitch to check that the door is shut and opens a water valve to fill the drum. When a pressure sensor detects that the drum is full, the water valve is closed. The program uses input from a temperature sensor in the drum to check

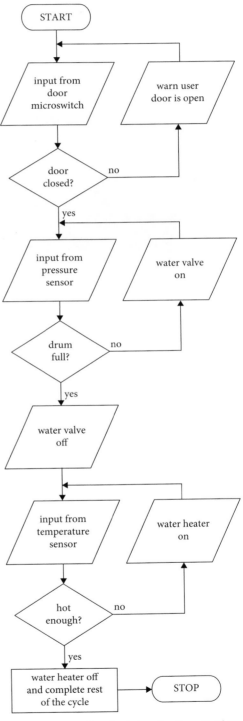

**Figure 3.39**  A program flowchart showing the use of sensors in a washing machine.

whether the water is hot enough. If not, it turns the water heater on. When the temperature sensor detects that the water is hot enough, it turns the water heater off and completes the rest of the wash cycle.

We can use temperature sensors in many other applications including:

- electronic thermometers;
- controlling heating systems in buildings, including horticultural greenhouses (Figure 3.40) and chemical reaction vessels.

**Figure 3.40** Temperature sensors are used in the automated system that controls temperature in a greenhouse.

 **SAQs**

12 Explain what is wrong with the following information:

A thermometer is used to control the temperature in a fish tank. The thermometer measures the temperature and decides whether it needs to turn on the heater to warm the water. A thermometer is used because a temperature sensor is electrical and cannot be used in water.

### Pressure sensor

A pressure sensor produces a signal that depends on the pressure to which it is exposed. An automatic blood pressure monitor (Figure 3.41) has a microcontroller, an air pump and an arm or wrist cuff whose pressure is sensed by a pressure sensor. The control program runs the pump to inflate the cuff until a pressure oscillation (the pulse) is first detected and shortly afterwards stops when the blood flow is cut off. The control program then opens a valve to allow air to escape slowly. The pressure at which the pulse is just detected is recorded

as the upper pressure. The pressure at which the pulse is no longer detected is recorded as the lower pressure. The control program performs some calculations on the upper and lower pressures to give better estimates of the true systolic (maximum) and diastolic (minimum) pressures. These results and the average pulse rate are then displayed on an LCD screen.

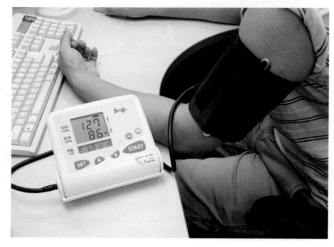

**Figure 3.41** A blood pressure monitor contains a pressure sensor.

We can use pressure sensors in many other applications. For example, pressure sensors can provide feedback to a robot's control program of the pressure with which its hand grips an object or monitor. Pressure sensors can also control the pressure of gases or liquids in a chemical reaction vessel.

### Light sensor

A light sensor produces a signal that depends on the level of light falling on it. We can use a light sensor in a car for input to an automated system that controls the headlights. The system's program can switch the headlights on whenever daylight falls below a certain level.

We can also use light sensors in more complex applications. A robotic truck may be required to follow a white line painted on a dark floor to mark its route through a factory (Figure 3.42). Left-hand and right-hand sensors spaced a line's width apart near the ground can provide input to the automated system steering the truck. If it drifts too far to the left, the left sensor will be more dimly lit than the right sensor; if it drifts too far to the right, the right sensor will be more dimly lit. The 'line-following' control program can use these differences to steer the truck back onto the line.

**Figure 3.42** These robot trucks use a light sensor to follow a route through the factory.

## Questions

19 Some school geography departments record the weather using an automatic weather station. How could temperature, pressure and light sensors be used to record the weather? Find out if your school has a weather station like this.

### Infrared sensor

An infrared (IR) sensor produces a signal that depends on the level of invisible IR radiation falling on it. All objects (unless they are extremely cold) emit significant IR radiation. A person's skin is at a different (usually higher!) temperature than their surroundings. We can use a simple camera consisting of a lens and a grid of IR sensors to form a detector for a person. This is called 'passive infrared' (PIR) technology because it relies on humans invisibly 'glowing' infrared. There is no need for any extra illumination of the scene. We can use PIR movement detectors to provide input to burglar alarm systems.

Higher-quality IR cameras, with grids of many more sensors, can photograph the IR radiation from hot spots on people's skin, poorly insulated buildings, the Earth's surface, oceans and cloud cover observed from satellites. Since people can only view displays of visible light, such photography uses 'false colour'. For example, in Figure 3.43, cooler temperatures are shown as lighter greyscale tones and warmer temperatures are shown as darker tones.

Of course, we can also use a simpler IR sensor with an IR beam generated artificially, usually by an IR light emitting diode (LED). For example, an intruder walking through an invisible beam of IR will reduce the response of a sensor at the far side of the room. An automated burglar alarm system can use this change in input signal to switch on the alarm. An IR sensor in a TV or similar

**Figure 3.43** A composite satellite infrared photograph of the Earth © Met Office.

appliance receives coded signals from a remote control. The appliance's control program decodes the signal. It then performs the command that the code represents.

### Humidity sensor

A humidity sensor produces a signal that depends on the concentration of water vapour in the atmosphere. A similar device for use in soil is called a moisture sensor (Figure 3.44).

**Figure 3.44** A soil moisture sensor in use.

If an irrigation system is controlled by a clock, the soil is watered at set times even when it is already moist enough. A moisture sensor can control an irrigation system more efficiently. A sensor-enabled, 'smart' irrigation controller only waters when the soil is dry. It can even be programmed to alter the minimum moisture level depending on the expected growth stage of a specific crop. This helps a farmer to grow more of a crop, of higher quality, using less water. In some parts of the world, installing a smart irrigation system is a legal requirement when building a new house. It may also be required in order to qualify for a lower price for water supply.

We can use humidity or moisture sensors in many other applications including:

- controlling a heating, ventilating and air conditioning (HVAC) system in a library or museum to prevent excessive humidity in the air (and reduce the risk of mould damaging books or artefacts);
- maintaining sufficient humidity in the air in a greenhouse (humidity can be raised by opening a valve to spray a mist of water);
- measuring humidity for meteorological records and forecasting in a weather station.

### Gas sensor

A gas sensor produces a signal depending on the concentration of a particular gas or vapour. We can use a sensor for an inflammable gas to monitor the atmosphere (Figure 3.45a) and sound an alarm if there is a leakage of, for example, liquid propane gas (LPG) that could cause an explosion.

In a vehicle engine, a sensor for oxygen (Figure 3.45b) is often known as a lambda sensor. An engine management computer receives the sensor's signal and uses it to adjust the air–fuel ratio to optimise the amount of oxygen in the exhaust gases. This improves fuel efficiency and reduces pollution by unburned fuel, carbon monoxide (CO) or mono-nitrogen oxides (NO).

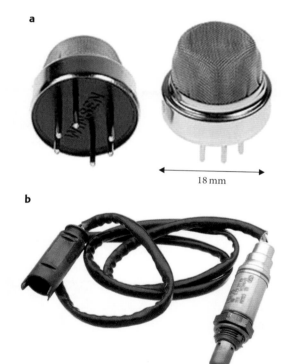

**Figure 3.45** Gas sensors. **a** An LPG sensor. **b** An oxygen sensor for a vehicle engine.

We can use gas sensors in other applications including:

- in a breathalyser, which measures the concentration of alcohol vapour in a sample of breath and estimates the concentration of alcohol in the blood;
- process control in the chemical industry;
- environmental monitoring of air pollution, particularly in urban areas where traffic congestion is heavy, or of oxygen dissolved in river water.

The advantages of using sensors (rather than people) to collect data are:

- they can collect data far more frequently than a person;
- they are more reliable than a person, who may forget to take readings;
- they are more accurate than a person, who may misread the signal;
- they can collect data from places where it is not possible for a person to go, such as inside a chemical or nuclear reaction vessel.

Disadvantages of using sensors are that they may need a power source to work and may need regular calibration to check their accuracy.

## Output devices and their uses

You will look at different kinds of output device in this section: monitors, printers and plotters, loudspeakers and actuators.

### Monitors

A monitor is an output device that displays information from a computer on a screen. The advantages of a monitor are that the output is immediate and visual. The disadvantage is that it does not last; when the display changes, the previous output is lost.

There are two main types of monitor screen:

- cathode ray tube (CRT);
- liquid crystal display (LCD).

CRT monitors are older and bulkier, being about as deep as they are wide (Figure 3.46). To 'paint' the display, an 'electron gun' fires a beam of electrons from the rear of the CRT. Electromagnets deflect the beam so that it scans the light-emitting coating behind the glass screen. To avoid the user seeing flicker, the beam completes between 60 and 100 scans of the whole screen per second.

A computer has an output adapter called a graphics card. The graphics card has a digital-to-analogue converter (DAC) to produce an analogue output signal. The CRT uses this signal to modulate (vary the strength of) the electron beam.

Advantages of CRT monitors are:

- they are relatively cheap;
- the image can be viewed from a wide range of angles;
- they can display a very wide range of colour and brightness.

CRT monitor

LCD monitor

**Figure 3.46** These screens have the same display area, but the LCD monitor is much thinner and lighter than the CRT monitor.

Disadvantages of CRT monitors are:

- they are bulky and difficult to fit on a desk;
- they are heavy and difficult to mount on a wall;
- there is quite a lot of reflection of ambient light from the glass screen.

An LCD monitor (see Figure 3.46) does not use a beam of electrons. Instead, its relatively thin screen has a 'backlight' behind a grid of tiny liquid crystal pixels. A computer graphics card can supply a stream of digital data to the LCD monitor. The digital-to-analogue converter (DAC) in the monitor's control circuitry converts the digital data from the graphics card into a stream of analogue signals. The monitor's control program electronically scans all the pixels. As it does so, row-by-row, it delivers an individual analogue signal to each pixel. The analogue signal controls how much light of a certain colour the pixel allows through from the backlight. The screen display is formed by the light shining through the grid of thousands or even millions of pixels. Each pixel can store its analogue signal for a relatively long time so there is no tendency for the display to flicker. The scan only needs to be repeated often enough for each frame of animated graphics or video to display properly.

### Extension

Investigate the different ways in which monitors generate displays on their screens. A starting point might be the names of the two types of monitor, 'cathode ray tube' and 'liquid crystal display'. How do they generate colour displays?

Advantages of LCD monitors are:
- they are small and easy to fit on a desk;
- they are light and easy to mount on a wall;
- they are compact enough to fit to laptops, PDAs, media players and mobile phones;
- there is relatively little reflection of ambient light from the screen;
- the stability of the display and absence of flicker make for more comfortable viewing.

For these reasons, LCD monitors have almost completely superseded CRT monitors. Disadvantages of LCD monitors are:
- the image can only be viewed from a relatively narrow range of angles;
- they can display a relatively limited range of colour and brightness;
- manufacturing defects can cause permanently lit or unlit pixels.

A multimedia projector is an output device similar to an LCD monitor. However, it uses lenses to project intense light through its grid of LCD pixels to form an image on a distant surface (Figure 3.47). Ideally, this surface should be a white projector screen or whiteboard. The projector is described as 'multimedia' because it contains low-power loudspeakers to cater for the audio output from the computer. These are only useful with a small audience.

A multimedia projector can also project the output from a TV or DVD player. We can therefore use a projector to screen televised sporting events in clubs or to create a 'home cinema'.

Advantages of a multimedia projector are that it can be used with a much larger audience than a monitor.

**Figure 3.47** Using a ceiling-mounted multimedia projector.

Disadvantages are that it is relatively expensive and has a fragile bulb, which can easily be damaged if the projector is moved while it is still hot.

### Questions

 20 How does a projector show black? What effect does this have on other colours?

 21 What is the effect on a projector of a bright summer day?

 22 Projectors and monitors have different resolutions. Find out about resolution. What resolutions are appropriate for different applications?

### Printers and plotters

Printers and plotters are output devices that print characters and graphics on paper or other materials. In this section, you learn about three types of printer: laser printers, inkjet printers and dot matrix printers (Figure 3.48).

A black and white laser printer uses a laser scanning a drum to print with powdered ink, known as toner (Figure 3.49). The printer places an even, negative, static charge on a photoconductive drum. It scans a very narrow laser beam across the surface of the rotating drum. The laser beam causes the negative charge to leak away wherever it shines on the drum. The drum revolves past a supply of toner which is also charged negatively. The toner

a

b

c

**Figure 3.48** Different types of printer. **a** Laser printer. **b** Inkjet printer. **c** Dot matrix printer.

is attracted onto those regions of the drum's surface where no charge remains. Toner particles are repelled by those regions that remain charged because they were *not* lit by the laser's beam. The printer rapidly switches the beam on and off to draw the required pattern of output.

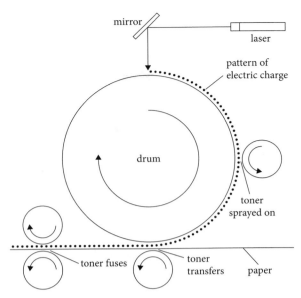

**Figure 3.49** How a laser printer works.

A roller presses a sheet of paper against the rotating drum and the toner particles transfer to the paper. Another roller presses the paper against a heated 'fuser' roller. The heated toner melts and bonds to the paper, producing a printed copy. If there are four drums with four different colours of toner, the printer can print in colour.

The main advantages of laser printers are the high **resolution** (detail) and rate of their output. Also, the toner is not water-soluble, so the ink does not run if prints get damp. These features make laser printers suitable for professional use.

Disadvantages of laser printers are:
- the reproduction of colour may not be so precise as with an inkjet printer;
- laser printers are usually expensive to buy, although the cost of toner per print tends to be lower;
- toner is toxic, so cartridges must be carefully disposed of after use.

An inkjet printer uses a printhead to propel differently sized droplets of ink, measuring just picolitres, from a number of fine nozzles onto a sheet of paper. The printhead scans from side to side on a stabiliser bar and rollers feed the paper forward (Figure 3.50).

The main advantages of inkjet printers are:
- the relatively high resolution;
- the good reproduction of colour;
- the low purchase cost.

They are also physically small and light, which makes inkjet printers suitable for home use.

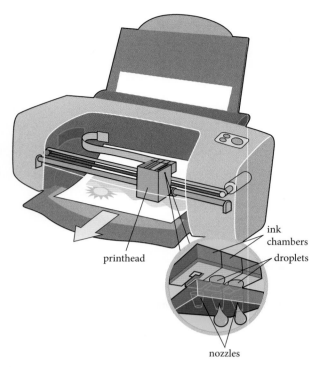

printhead

ink chambers

droplets

nozzles

**Figure 3.50** How an inkjet printer works. Ink is squirted out of differently coloured nozzles. A stepper motor moves the paper, and the printhead with nozzle scans across.

Disadvantages of inkjet printers are:
- the slow rate of printing, although this may not be a problem for small office and home office (SOHO) use;
- the relatively high cost of ink per print;
- the water-soluble ink, which runs if prints get damp.

A photo printer is a printer that produces prints of similar quality to those from photographic film. On suitable paper, it prints with a similar range of colours and resolution. It often uses inkjet technology, but with five or six inks rather than the usual four for a colour printer.

**Extension**

The next generation of printers are 3-D printers, used in 'rapid prototyping'. Some use inkjet technology to print alternating layers of adhesive and fine powder, or successive layers of ultraviolet-curable photopolymer or molten thermoplastic. Others use lasers to fuse granules of plastic, metal, ceramic or glass, scanning within a bed of granules. Investigate 3-D printers. Starting points might be the websites for RepRap (http://www.reprap.co.uk) or CandyFab (http://candyfab.org).

A dot matrix printer uses a printhead consisting of a vertical column of printing pins to tap an inked ribbon against the paper (Figure 3.51). The printhead scans from side to side on a stabiliser bar. Electromagnets operate the pins to produce characters by printing a pattern of small dots in a grid pattern (Figure 3.52). Toothed 'tractor feed' rollers feed the paper forward.

The relatively small number of dots in the grid pattern limits output to simple characters or very crude graphics. It can produce near-letter quality (NLQ) by printing a line twice with a small vertical shift of the printhead. If four differently coloured ribbons are used, the printer can print in colour.

A dot matrix printer can also produce multiple copies simultaneously on multi-part stationery, because of the impact of the pins against the ribbon and paper. The stationery has a plain sheet on top with differently coloured, self-carbonising sheets beneath.

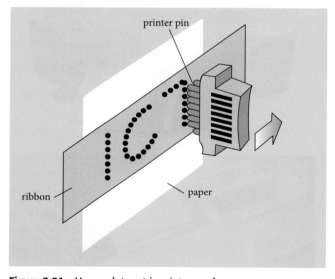

printer pin

ribbon

paper

**Figure 3.51** How a dot matrix printer works.

$5 \times 7$ matrix of dots just visible

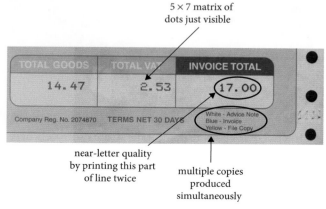

| TOTAL GOODS | TOTAL VAT | INVOICE TOTAL |
|---|---|---|
| 14.47 | 2.53 | 17.00 |

Company Reg. No. 2074870    TERMS NET 30 DAYS

White - Advice Note
Blue - Invoice
Yellow - File Copy

near-letter quality by printing this part of line twice

multiple copies produced simultaneously

**Figure 3.52** Detail from an invoice showing the grid pattern produced by a dot matrix printer.

The main advantage of a dot matrix printer is that it is robust; it is less likely to go wrong in dirty environments, such as factories and vehicle workshops. Also, its ability to print on multi-part stationery makes it useful if more than one copy of a document is needed.

Disadvantages of dot matrix printers are:

- low resolution;
- noisy because of repeated impact of pins;
- relatively low rate of printing.

A plotter can only print line-art, such as shapes stored as vector graphics (known as 'graphical objects') and text characters. Instead of scanning the surface of the paper, a plotter uses one or more pens to draw continuous curves or lines. As it draws a series of graphical objects, a pen may criss-cross the page many times. A plotter cannot shade a region but can draw hatching – a number of close, regular lines. Design engineers and architects produce vector graphics files using computer-aided design (CAD) software.

A flatbed plotter (Figure 3.53a) has the paper lying flat under the pen. The pen travels across the paper on one stabiliser bar, which itself travels along the paper on two other stabiliser bars. This type of plotter takes up a lot of space. In a drum plotter (Figure 3.53b), the paper hangs over a drum that rotates to move the paper under the pen in one direction, while the pen itself moves on a stabiliser bar at right angles to the paper's motion. Both motions can take place at the same time to draw curves and diagonal lines. This type of plotter takes up relatively little space.

Plotters could print sharper, more precise drawings than early versions of other types of printer but they are now rare. They have been superseded by high-resolution inkjet printers, although the drum type used for large paper sizes is still known as a 'plotter'. Genuine plotters are only made now as sign-cutting devices. These perform precision cutting of graphics printed by inkjet printers, for example, to produce shaped stickers and window signs.

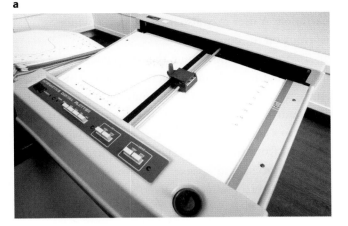

**Figure 3.53** Two types of plotter. **a** Flatbed plotter – note the red pen. **b** Drum plotter with 3 litre ink cartridges.

 **Questions**

**23** Printers can print on many materials other than paper. Investigate the use of other materials and the problems that might occur because of their use. Here are two suggestions to get you started.

**a** How can a street vendor at a tourist attraction print your photograph, with the attraction in the background, on a tee-shirt.

**b** How can the graphics on the side of a business van be produced?

**? SAQs**

**13** Describe each of the following print devices. Give an application where each may be used, justifying your choices.

**a** Dot matrix printer

**b** Inkjet printer

**c** Laser printer

**d** Plotter

## Loudspeakers

Many computer programs are designed to provide sound output. Any truly multimedia presentation needs sound output, which can be the soundtrack recorded by a video camera or a separately recorded narration. A user may also listen to music while working on the computer.

To provide sound output, the computer's sound card has a digital-to-analogue converter (DAC) to produce an analogue output signal. The computer also needs at least one loudspeaker (Figure 3.54). This is an electromagnet linked to a conical diaphragm that produces vibrations of the air from an electrical signal. The word loudspeaker is often shortened to 'speaker' and two of them are used to provide stereophonic (or 'stereo') sound.

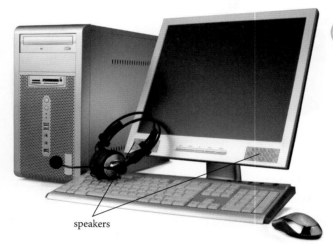

**Figure 3.54** Computer loudspeakers in a multimedia system. Note that the speakers are integrated into the monitor.

People with visual impairments may have difficulty viewing a screen. Text-to-speech software (known as 'screen readers') produces speech sounds (synthesises speech) from text on the screen or an image's pop-up title on a web page. Speakers allow the user to listen to what is shown on the screen.

Headphones are a version of speakers for personal use. They are often used in environments where other people should not hear the sounds produced. This might be because it would disturb their concentration or because the output is confidential.

Speakers would be used for a sales presentation to a group of customers. Headphones would be used in a classroom where each student is engaged on different work and the noise from many different speakers would be distracting.

Speakers and headphones, as output devices, naturally pair up with microphones, as input devices, as they all deal with sound.

**Questions**

**24** Microphones aid data input and speakers provide information output for people with visual impairments.
**a** Which other input and output devices are designed for use by people with visual impairments?
**b** Which devices are specifically designed to help people with other disabilities?

### 5.1.3 Actuators

An **actuator** can affect the real world without the user being involved. It is an output device but it does not always provide output directly to the user. It can change some physical value in response to a signal from an automated system or control system.

Actuators naturally pair up with sensors, which are input devices that automatically collect data. Sensors can provide feedback to the control program about the effects of its actuators. You will look at many examples of automated system and monitoring and control system applications in Chapter 7.

Consider how a program for controlling an irrigation system can turn on the water supply when the soil gets too dry. The control program can produce an electrical output signal, but this cannot open a supply valve directly. The output signal must be sent to an actuator that can operate the valve. A suitable actuator for an irrigation valve is a motor or an electromagnet called a solenoid. This is often built into the valve (Figure 3.55).

**Figure 3.55** Three solenoid-controlled irrigation valves in an underground box.

Light bulbs and LEDs are used to illuminate. Automated systems use light bulbs to provide artificial light in a greenhouse for forcing plant growth, to illuminate a control panel, room or stage, or to display a lightshow. Systems can also use light bulbs or LEDs as indicators of the status of equipment, including warning of faults (Figure 3.56).

**Figure 3.56** Light bulbs and LEDs in a car instrument cluster.

An electrical heater is an actuator that supplies heat. Automated systems use heaters for industrial processes and for heating buildings and greenhouses. They also use heat pumps that provide cooling for food stored in refrigerators and air conditioning systems in buildings.

A computer needs an extra actuator to switch on and off the electricity supply to a mains-driven actuator, such as a heater. This type of electrical-switching actuator is called a relay or contactor (Figure 3.57). Some relays are solid state to avoid wear on the switch contacts.

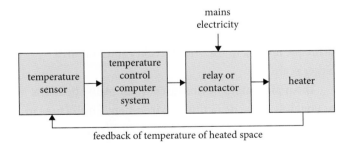

**Figure 3.57** A contactor and a mains-powered heater form the combined actuator in a heating system.

An electric motor (Figure 3.58) is an actuator that provides rotary or linear movement. Automated systems use motors to rotate microwave oven turntables; washing machine drums; hard disk drives in computers; optical discs in computers and CD and DVD players;

feed rollers and drums in printers; fans in heating, ventilating and air conditioning systems; and drills and lathe spindles in industrial robots, known as 'computer numerical controlled' (CNC) machines.

**Figure 3.58** An electric motor.

A motorised pump forms an actuator that moves gases or liquids (Figure 3.59). Automated systems use pumps to move water in dishwashers, washing machines and water-filled heating systems; refrigerant in heat pumps; and gases and liquids in industrial processes. An automatic blood pressure monitor uses an air pump to inflate its cuff. A motorised fan is a low-pressure pump for gases.

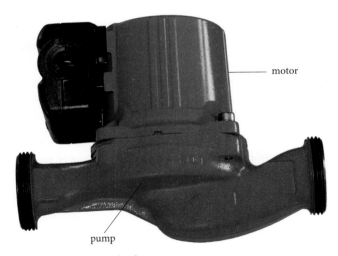

**Figure 3.59** A motorised pump.

A buzzer is an audio signalling device that makes a rasping sound (Figure 3.60). Automated systems use buzzers or similar actuators (such as bells, beepers or sirens) to indicate an event to the user. For example, when a microwave oven finishes heating, it can sound a beeper; when a fire alarm system detects a fire, it can sound a siren.

**Figure 3.60** An electric buzzer.

## Case study: sensors and actuators working together

Throughout this chapter, input and output devices have been mentioned as working together. For example, the input resulting from a mouse's movement causes a change in the display on a monitor screen. This section looks in more detail at an example where sensors and actuators work together – the operation of a washing machine.

1. The user switches on the machine.
2. The control program 'reads' the input signal from the microswitch in the door catch.
3. If the door is not properly shut, the control program may indicate the problem by sending output signals to a labelled LED or a buzzer.
4. If the door is shut, the control program sends an output signal to a relay and solenoid-controlled valve to let hot water in.
5. The control program repeatedly reads the signals from the water temperature sensor in the drum.
   a. If the temperature is too high, the program can send an output signal to another relay and solenoid-controlled valve to let cold water in.
   b. If the temperature is too low, the program sends an output signal to the heater's relay to turn it on until the temperature becomes high enough again.
6. The control program sends output signals to a relay to rotate the drum's motor.
7. When the wash programme is complete, the control program sends an output signal to the pump relay. The program usually runs the pump for a set time as there is no sensor to detect that all the waste water has left the drum.
8. The control program can indicate that the wash programme is complete by sending an output signal to a labelled LED.

**Questions**

25 The case study on page 78 shows how a control application uses sensors and actuators. A number of stages have been left out. Identify the other stages that allow the machine to do the wash properly. How can the control program use sensors and actuators in these other stages? It may help your understanding if you draw the stages as a flowchart as in Figure 3.39.

## Specialised input and output devices

Some input and output devices are in general use, while others are used for particular applications. We have looked at special input and output methods that assist people with disabilities. We have also looked at the use of sensors and actuators for automated control of washing machines. Another area in which we need special types of input and output device is virtual reality (VR) software (see Chapter 7). VR software creates a computer-generated, stereoscopic, 3-D view of an environment. It can give the user the illusion of moving within that environment.

VR input devices include a wired glove (or 'data glove', although this is actually a brand name). The user wears the glove, which contains sensors that detect the movements of the user's hand and fingers. Input data from the glove is processed to copy the hand's movements in the virtual environment. The same principle applies to the virtual reality suit, but on a larger scale.

The main output devices are virtual reality headsets or goggles. These depict the environment for the user in stereoscopic 3-D images and, with a headset, in stereo sound. An actuator can also release an odour from a capsule. Vibration actuators for wired gloves or VR suits can provide haptic (tactile) feedback. For example, if the user picks up a virtual artefact, it feels for the user as if they have it in their hand (Figure 3.61).

We can also project images of the virtual environment onto a room's walls. In this case, the user does not need to wear a headset or goggles to receive the panoramic visual

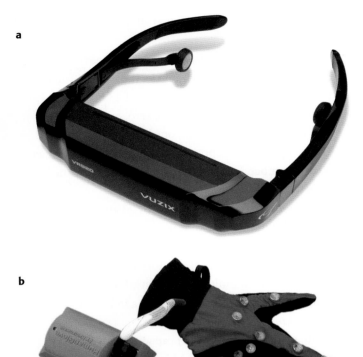

**a**

**b**

**Figure 3.61** Virtual reality hardware. **a** Goggles with headphones. **b** Wired gloves.

output. Such a room is known as a Cave Automatic Virtual Environment (CAVE). An example of this is the flight simulation system used to train pilots (see Chapter 7).

**Questions**

26 Find out about different forms of virtual reality. You may find these websites good starting places: http://www.vrealities.com; http://www.sciencedaily.com/news/computers_math/virtual_reality; http://www.nintendo.com/wii.

## (5.1.2) Internal memory and storage devices and their uses

A computer needs devices to keep the data that it processes. It holds the data that it is processing in rapid-access **internal memory** (also known as main memory).

After processing, it stores the data for future use in slower-access **backing storage**.

### Internal memory

The processor uses **internal memory** to hold:
- the program instructions that it is executing;
- the data in use;
- the results of processing the data.

It is the only data repository that the processor can access directly. This is reflected by another of its names: **immediate access store (IAS)**.

Modern types of internal memory are electronic and made as integrated circuits or chips, known as **random access memory (RAM)**. The name indicates that the processor can access the memory's data in any order needed by the program. This direct, electronic access ensures that the processor has extremely rapid access to the data.

With a RAM chip, the processor can read, or copy out, existing data from memory locations. It can also write, or copy in, new data into memory locations. So, with RAM, the processor can modify data from files and has 'workspace' for holding temporary results.

RAM chips hold data that are **volatile**. Volatile means that when we switch off the computer, the data are lost from the RAM. This is why we lose any work that we have not saved and have to 're-launch' programs and 're-open' data files when we switch a computer back on. RAM chips are usually installed in computers as plug-in, printed-circuit modules each carrying a number of chips and currently with a total capacity of 1 or 2 GB.

A special type of internal memory is called read-only memory (ROM). ROM shares the rapid, direct and random access characteristics of RAM. However, ROM differs from RAM because the data it holds are **non-volatile**. Once data have been written into a ROM chip during manufacture, they cannot be changed. The processor cannot write data to a ROM chip, it can only read existing data. The processor cannot modify existing data in ROM and cannot use it as workspace for holding temporary results. ROM is only suitable for holding unchanging ('lookup') data.

If a computer contained only volatile RAM, the processor would have no access to an operating system when we turned it on. It would read garbage from its RAM chips instead of valid program instructions. ROM provides a solution to this problem: it stores a small start-up program at the processor's default starting location. The start-up program instructs the processor to read a larger program from ROM into RAM and then switch to executing that program in RAM. In some cases, ROM holds the whole of a simple operating system or control program for an automated system. Such software stored in ROM is known as **firmware** because of its storage in hardware.

In general-purpose computers such as PCs, we need far more RAM than ROM because we work with very large programs and data files. However, in embedded computers such as the microcontroller in a washing machine, the ROM needs to hold the whole of the control program. It aslo holds any unchanging ('lookup') data, such as the temperatures, times and number of rinses for the various wash programmes. The RAM may only need to be very small, because relatively few data are processed.

Two words of warning:
- do not confuse internal memory ROM with a CD-ROM or DVD-ROM;
- do not confuse internal memory with backing storage (Figure 3.62).

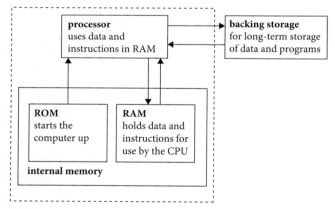

**Figure 3.62**  Internal memory and storage.

## Measuring the size of memory

Computers do not directly process and store data such as 'B', 'hello' or the number 23. Almost all digital computers work with electronic circuitry that has only two states, which we often represent as 0 and 1. This means that a computer stores and processes all data using binary number equivalents.

Binary numbers consist of digits. A **b**inary dig**it** is called a **bit**. Each bit can only take the values '0' and '1'. For example, the binary equivalent of 23 is 00010111. We must read this as 'zero, zero, zero, one, zero, one, one, one', not 'ten thousand, one hundred and eleven'! The computer also represents each character in text as a binary number. For example, a binary code for the letter 'B' is the eight-bit number 01000010.

Notice that the binary codes for 23 and 'B' were given as eight-bit numbers with leading zeroes. The reason for this is that a group of eight bits, called a **byte**, is the unit of data held in an internal memory location. A processor processes data in multiples of a byte: 8-bit, 16-bit, 32-bit or 64-bit. Backing storage holds data in blocks of 512 or 4096 bytes.

Internal memory (RAM) capacity is measured in bytes. Generally, a larger RAM capacity is better. It allows a larger quantity of programs and data files to be in RAM simultaneously. This avoids the operating system temporarily having to swap blocks of programs or data from RAM into backing storage to make room for other portions of programs or data. The effect of this is that software runs faster. Current PCs have RAM capacities of a few gigabytes.

The size of both internal memory and backing storage is usually measured in kilobytes (kB), megabytes (MB), gigabytes (GB) or terabytes (TB). However, internal memory is manufactured with numbers of bytes that are powers of two. The use of the denary prefixes kilo-, mega- and giga-, which refer to powers of ten, is actually incorrect. These prefixes are widely used simply because people are familiar with them. The correct **bi**nary prefixes, which refer to powers of two, are ki**bi**-, me**bi**-, gi**bi**- and te**bi**-. For example, USB flash drives (see page 86) are currently sold with capacities of one, two, four, eight, 16 or more gibibytes.

However, designers of hard disks produce byte capacities that are not powers of two. So the use of the denary prefixes is completely appropriate for hard disks. Besides, using prefixes with slightly smaller values enables makers to attach slightly bigger numerical sizes to their products! Table 3.3 shows how the two sets of prefixes relate to each other.

**Table 3.3** Prefixes for denoting the size of internal memory (binary) and hard disk storage (denary).

| Binary prefix and abbreviation | Value of binary prefix | Denary prefix and abbreviation | Value of denary prefix |
|---|---|---|---|
| kibibyte (KiB) | $2^{10} =$ 1,024 | kilobyte (kB) | 1,000 |
| mebibyte (MiB) | $2^{20} =$ 1,048,576 | megabyte (MB) | 1,000,000 |
| gibibyte (GiB) | $2^{30} =$ 1,073,741,824 | gigabyte (GB) | 1,000,000,000 |
| tebibyte (TiB) | $2^{40} =$ 1,099,511,627,776 | terabyte (TB) | 1,000,000,000,000 |
| pebibyte (PiB) | $2^{50} =$ 1,125,899,906,842,624 | petabyte (PB) | 1,000,000,000,000,000 |

## Worked example

Suppose that we need to calculate the capacity required for a Digital Storage Card (DSC) to store 15 minutes of video at 25 images per second and 500 kB per image.

We can calculate the capacity as follows:
Number of images to be stored
$= 15 \times 60 \times 25 = 22{,}500$
∴ Storage capacity required
$= 22{,}500 \times 500\,\text{kB} = 11{,}250{,}000\,\text{kB}$
If we assume that 500 kB means 500 KiB, this is
11,250,000 / 1,048,576 = 10.73 GiB.

However, if we assume that 500 kB means 500 000 B, this is 11,250,000 / 1,000,000 = 11.25 GB.

## SAQs

14 Complete the following sentences by using the correct words from this list: memory, megabytes, eight, gigabytes.
  a A school computer has 3 ......... of RAM.
  b A byte is a unit of computer ......... and it consists of ......... bits.

15 Put the following in order of size, smallest first:
   1 terabyte, 2048 kB, 1.2 GB, 16 bits, 1.5 MB

## Questions

27 Find out the RAM capacities of some computers. Try starting with computers that are used in school and any others you may have access to. (Hint: look at the properties associated with My Computer.) Is the RAM capacity of the computer used for school administration different from that of computers available in the classroom? If so, why might this be? Try looking at some adverts for computers and compare the sizes of the memories. To start you off, try this website http://www.dell.co.uk.

## Extension

Why is internal memory manufactured with numbers of bytes that are powers of two?

### Backing storage

**Backing storage** (also known as **auxiliary storage**) stores programs and data for future use. In order to store data while the electricity is switched off or unavailable, storage must be non-volatile. Access to backing storage is slower than access to internal memory but this is an acceptable penalty to pay for much lower cost and non-volatility. Operating system and program files are loaded into RAM from backing storage when required for execution. Data are stored on the hard disk and then sent to the computer's memory when they need to be used.

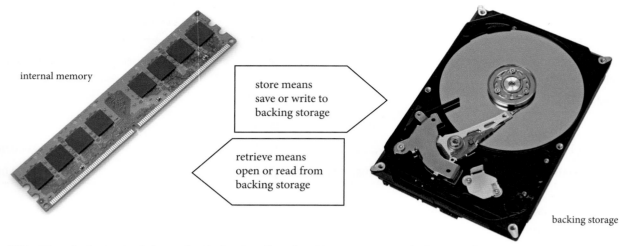

internal memory

store means
save or write to
backing storage

retrieve means
open or read from
backing storage

backing storage

**Figure 3.63**   Ways of referring to storing and retrieving data. Note that the processor controls these transfers.

It is important to distinguish between a storage device and a storage medium. The storage device is the machine that stores the data; the **storage medium** (plural: media) is the material on which the device stores data. For example, a hard disk drive is a device but the set of platters inside it forms the medium. This distinction is even more important when we look at devices whose media are removable.

There are three different types of backing storage device:

- A **magnetic storage device** stores data magnetically on a medium that moves past a read/write head. The head writes by magnetising short regions along a track on the surface of the medium to represent the binary values 0 and 1. The head reads data from a track by detecting the presence of a change or the absence of a possible change in magnetisation between successive regions.
- An **optical storage device** stores data on a read-only medium as tiny 'pits' pressed into the flat surface. It stores data on a recordable medium as similar-sized regions of a dye layer heated by a laser and on a rewritable medium as regions of a metal layer heated by a laser. The media can be read by shining a laser less intensely onto the disc and detecting the intensity of light reflected from successive regions.
- **Solid-state storage devices** are different from the other two because, like internal memory, they are electronic and are made as integrated circuits or chips. The chip is the medium and there is little separate drive reading from, and writing to, it.

When a file is saved (Figure 3.63), the data are stored in (or written to) the backing storage medium from RAM. When a file is opened data are retrieved (or read) from the backing storage medium to RAM.

### Magnetic storage media

A **hard disk** (Figure 3.64) is the main storage medium on most computers from laptops and PCs upwards. It was originally described as 'hard' to distinguish it from a removable type of disk made of flexible material. The **hard disk drive** (**HDD**) is usually mounted internally in a PC, although external versions are also available that connect to the computer by a different type of interface, such as USB.

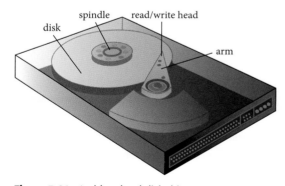

spindle    read/write head
disk
arm

**Figure 3.64**   Inside a hard disk drive.

The set of disk platters that form the medium is fixed in the HDD and cannot be removed by the user. An external HDD that connects through a USB port, for example, can be removed by the user, for security purposes. Some complete hard disk drives are internally mounted but can be removed.

A fixed hard disk is the predominant storage medium because:

- it can store large amounts of data – currently over 1 terabyte;
- access to the data is faster than for optical discs – the platters can be driven faster because they are securely attached to their drive spindle in a dust-free enclosure;
- there is no limit to the number of times it can rewrite data.

A disadvantage of a hard disk is that it is vulnerable to mechanical shocks, especially if its hard disk drive is part of a laptop computer that the user drops. To protect the data stored on a hard disk, the user should make regular backup copies to another medium.

Hard disks are used to store three types of data:

- the computer's operating system files;
- application program files;
- the user's data files, including the user's own work and files that that they have downloaded from Internet servers.

The operating system's file system maintains a directory file for each folder on each storage drive. When the user or a program issues a command to open a named file in a named folder, the file system uses the relevant directory file to look up the address of the location of the start of the file. On a hard disk, the file's disk address consists of identifiers in the directory file for the track, the head (as there is one for each surface of each platter) and the start of the first cluster of contiguous sectors. The file system also maintains a list of the clusters that the file occupies, when there is more than one.

A hard disk is a **direct access medium**, because the read/write head can travel straight to the correct track on the surface of the medium. The disk revolves rapidly and usually continuously, so it takes very little time for the start of the correct sector to pass the read/write head. There is no need to read all the disk's contents between the current sector and the sector to be accessed. This enables rapid access to data and program files.

HDDs have replaced magnetic tape for domestic video recording because of increased storage capacity, faster data access and reductions in the cost per unit of data stored. Some current digital video recorders can record one or more television programmes and simultaneously play back a previous recording, or even an earlier part of a current recording. This depends on the HDD's data transfer rate (the rate of reading the data) being much higher than the recording data rate. Special software provides apparently simultaneous dual-access to the HDD. It creates data buffers in internal memory. It uses the stream of programme data to continuously write to the recording buffer and continuously reads from the playback buffer to produce a stream of data for the TV to display. It rapidly uses the HDD alternately to write data from the recording buffer to the end of the recording file and to read data from the previous recording's file into the playback buffer.

Miniature HDDs are also used for high-capacity storage in portable media players. The low cost of HDD storage has made it possible for providers to offer free use of Web services such as search engines with massive databases, multi-gigabyte email and file storage, and video sharing.

A portable hard disk drive (Figure 3.65) is a small, external HDD. Some are lightweight and pocket-sized, which make them highly portable. They can be useful for transferring large quantities of data when there is no suitable access to a network. If used as a backup device, a portable HDD can easily be removed from the premises as a safeguard against loss through fire or theft.

**Figure 3.65** A portable hard disk drive with USB cable.

A small, removable HDD may even form part of a portable recording device such as a camcorder. This enables extra storage devices to be used for recording and the transfer of large quantities of data from the recording device to a computer. It costs rather more per unit of data stored than an internal HDD.

 **SAQs**

16 How does a computer find a particular file stored on a hard disk?

A **magnetic tape** stores data in a similar way to a magnetic disk. A tape drive has a read/write head similar to that in an HDD and the tape is driven past it. The major difference is that the data files are stored on a single track along the length of a reel of magnetisable tape contained in a removable cartridge (Figure 3.66). A magnetic tape is a **serial access medium**. Serial access means that the data files are written, and must be read, one after another. Often the order is chronological, as files are added to the end. The drive cannot jump along the tape to a distant file: it has to wind the tape through until the distant file is reached. There is often a delay of tens of seconds before the tape drive can read a file at a distant position on the tape. This results in relatively slow access, on average, to a specific file.

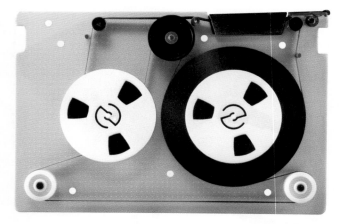

**Figure 3.66** The inside of a data cartridge showing the magnetic tape.

Magnetic tape is a useful storage medium where there is a need to store large quantities of data (currently up to 1 TB) and where the speed of access is not important. For example, a tape drive is good for storing

a backup, or archive, copy of data files from a hard disk. A tape cartridge is cheaper than a hard disk and is removable so that a backup copy can easily be removed from the premises for security.

**Questions**

 28 Which type of storage device will be used by a large organisation with large volumes of data where speed of access is not important? What kind of data access is available?

### Optical storage media

An optical disc is a direct access medium (Figure 3.67). The compact disc (CD) was the first optical disc format for storing digital data used with PCs. It can store 700 MB of data. The format was first developed for the distribution of sound recordings of up to 80 minutes by the music industry. However, the capacity is too small for a full-length movie.

For larger storage capacity, it is necessary to use the more recent digital versatile disc (DVD) format. The basic format of DVD can store 4.7 GB (or 4.4 GiB) of data. There are also various dual-layer and double-sided formats. These can store up to 17.1 GB (or 15.9 GiB).

Both CD drives and DVD drives use a laser to read and to write the data, but a DVD drive uses a more precise laser. Therefore, the data regions on a DVD can be smaller and more data can fit on the disc.

**Figure 3.67** Left to right: CD, DVD and Blu-ray™. They look similar but hold very different amounts of data. Also, some types can be written to (recorded on) once or multiple times whereas others cannot.

Throughout this section, it is vital to distinguish between discs that can be written to and those that cannot. A good principle is never to refer to 'CD' or 'DVD' on their own; they should always have some letters after them to say what type they are. The main types are as follows:

- ROM stands for 'Read-Only Memory' – these discs cannot be written to, only read from;
- R stands for 'Recordable' – these discs can be written to just once and then can only be read from;
- RW stands for 'ReWritable' – these discs can be written to and recorded on multiple times.

So, what can we use the different types of optical storage media for?

CD-ROM and DVD-ROM discs cannot be written to. This means that the contents of the CD or DVD can never be changed. This is a big advantage if the contents need to be protected from being corrupted. Examples include using them for the distribution of music, movies, software and data files such as encyclopaedias. These media are quite hard to damage and are likely to be durable compared with CD-R and DVD-R discs. Their data cannot be accidentally changed. These discs store large quantities of data and are fairly cheap. The only disadvantage is that we cannot change the contents of these discs.

CD-R and DVD-R discs can be written to once but after that the contents cannot be changed. They can be used to store music or movies of our choice, or to make archive copies of documents. Advantages of these media are that, like optical ROM discs, they are robust and have large capacities. Also, the user can write what they want onto them and then the files are tamper-proof. Disadvantages are that they are more expensive than optical ROM discs, they can be used only once and not all CD/DVD devices (especially audio CD players) can play them. Also, they are expensive media for making regular backup copies of files, because they cannot be re-used for a later backup. They may have shorter lives than other types of optical media because the dye layer may degrade over time.

CD-RW and DVD-RW discs are robust, have large capacities and can be used over and over again, which makes them ideal media for making regular backups of the files stored on a computer. They are also removable for security purposes. Their re-usability is useful for making temporary copies of data files that we want to move from one computer to another (using the so-called 'foot network'), perhaps taking work to school that you have done on a computer at home.

A DVD-RAM disc is very like a DVD-RW disc but the data are stored in a different way on the surface of the disc. The effect of this is that the medium can be rewritten far more times than a DVD-RW and access to small data files is faster. In some digital video recorders with removable DVD-RAM storage, reading and writing can occur at the same time, as with an HDD.

Blu-ray discs (officially BD, but also BR) have much larger storage capacities (from 25 to hundreds of GB) than other optical storage media and BD drives support a higher rate of data transfer. These two advantages mean that it is now possible to record and play back hours of high-definition (HD) video. Some computer games also benefit from this medium. ROM, recordable and rewritable versions of the medium exist. The disadvantage is the cost, which is much higher than that of the corresponding types of DVD media.

 **SAQs**

17 Is it a good idea for a small company to use DVD-Rs for backing up every day? Give a reason for your answer.

**Questions**

 29 Name eight different types of optical storage.

 30 Explain the difference between the ROM, R and RW descriptions. When would each be used?

**Extension**

The difference between DVD and Blu-ray devices is in the type of laser used. Different lasers use different parts of the spectrum of light. The shorter the wavelength used, the more data can be squeezed onto the disc surface. Investigate this and explain why this type of disc is called 'Blu-ray'.

### Solid-state storage media

Solid-state storage devices are electronic and made as integrated circuits or chips (Figure 3.68). The chip is the medium and there is little or no separate drive reading from it and writing to it. The currently predominant technology is flash memory, which, like ROM, holds data that are non-volatile but can be erased and rewritten in large blocks, maybe tens of thousands of times. We often refer to this as **non-volatile memory**.

Like other integrated circuit devices, flash memory tends to obey Moore's Law, with chip capacity doubling approximately every two years. This has enabled increasingly large storage capacities to be fitted to portable devices such as media (MP3/MP4) players, camcorders and mobile phones. Cameras could not be included in mobile phones until the large storage capacities required by still images and video were available.

**Figure 3.68** Solid-state storage.

A **USB flash drive** (also called a memory stick or a pen drive) is small, can hold several gibibytes of data, has minimal drive electronics and a built-in USB plug. Flash drives are useful for storing data and software that needs to be transported from one computer to another. They can also be used for storing backup copies of important files.

Flash memory chips are used as fixed storage in PDAs, mobile phones, cameras and some portable MP3/MP4 players.

Digital storage cards (DSCs) are used as removable storage for PDAs, mobile phones, cameras, camcorders and audio recorders. They are flat, very small cards that slot into a DSC card reader/writer, which is often included as a port in a PC or laptop. High-capacity (HC) versions of some types of DSC are intended for use with cameras or camcorders, especially high-definition (HD) camcorders.

Solid-state storage devices have a number of general advantages. They are extremely small and portable and can store large quantities of data. Many can connect directly to a computer port. In some cases, solid-state drives (SSDs) have data transfer rates that are at least as high as those for HDDs. They have no moving parts, which makes them more robust than disk media, with no noise and lower power consumption. For these reasons, flash-based SSDs are increasingly being used as alternatives to HDDs as the main storage medium, especially in netbooks, laptops and battlefield computers.

They have two main disadvantages:
- they are more expensive per unit of data stored than other forms of backing storage;
- Flash-based devices have a relatively limited number of write cycles.

### Comparing storage media

While the advantages and disadvantages of each type of storage medium are listed above, it can also be useful to compare them using five particular characteristics (see Table 3.4):
- volume of data held (storage capacity);
- rate (often called 'speed') of data access;
- portability – this is based on size, weight and how easy it is to remove the medium from the computer;
- robustness – how easy it is to damage the medium or device, and whether it is easy to lose the contents;
- cost.

It is not possible to state the numerical storage capacity for each type of device for two reasons:
- The media may be removable and are often available in a range of different sizes and types. For example, the amount of storage on a magnetic tape depends on how long the tape is and the particular tape technology used.
- The capacities are rapidly increasing, so by the time you read this book they are likely to have changed.

The cost considered here is the initial cost of buying a device. Devices incur other costs, such as the cost of the media to put into the device and the time taken by an employee to do something. For example, a full backup of a large system may require a large number of CD-RWs and someone to sit and change the discs as they are filled. A portable HDD would be more expensive to buy but it might be cheaper in the long term as the whole backup would fit onto the drive, so no additional media would be required and no-one would have to be paid to watch the backup.

One comparison of the cost of storage devices is the cost for each gibibyte or gigabyte of data stored. The table does not include this cost because it is so variable. The important thing is to be aware that there is more to 'cost' than the price of the device.

Because of these and similar issues, there are no actual values given in the table. However, barring any technological breakthroughs, the pattern should remain the same.

**Table 3.4** Comparing storage media and devices.

| Medium or device | Storage capacity | Rate of data access | Portability | Robustness | Cost |
|---|---|---|---|---|---|
| Internal hard disk drives | Very large | Fast | Not portable | Very fragile if dropped | Expensive |
| Portable hard disk drives | Very large | Fast | Less portable because of size | Robust but can lose data if wrongly used | Expensive |
| Magnetic tapes | Very large | Slow | Less portable because of size | Robust but can lose data if wrongly used | Expensive |
| Memory sticks and pen drives | Large | Very fast | Very portable | Robust but lose data if wrongly used | Medium |
| Digital storage cards | Large | Very fast | Very portable | Robust but can lose data if wrongly used | Medium |
| Blu-ray discs | Large | Fast | Very portable | Robust but can be damaged | Cheap |
| BD-RE (rewritable Blu-ray) | Large | Fast | Very portable | Robust but can lose data if wrongly used | Cheap |
| DVD-ROM | Large | Fast | Very portable | Robust but can be damaged | Cheap |
| DVD-R | Large | Fast | Very portable | Robust but can be damaged | Cheap |
| DVD-RW | Large | Fast | Very portable | Robust but can lose data if wrongly used | Cheap |
| DVD-RAM | Large | Fast | Very portable | Robust but can lose data if wrongly used | Medium |
| CD-ROM | Limited | Fast | Very portable | Robust but can be damaged | Cheap |
| CD-R | Limited | Fast | Very portable | Robust but can be damaged | Cheap |
| CD-RW | Limited | Fast | Very portable | Robust but can lose data if wrongly used | Cheap |

## SAQs

**18** Manufacturers are producing netbook computers with no hard disk drive but a reasonable amount of solid-state storage. Can you think of two advantages?

## Questions

**31** Make a list of the storage devices that you use at home and at school. What do you use them for? List the individual advantages and disadvantages that are important for your uses. Do you use any types of storage that are not mentioned in Table 3.4?

**32** One type of storage device that is not described here is a MiniDisc. Find out how a MiniDisc works. What is it used for? What are the advantages and disadvantages of using MiniDiscs?

**33** Try to look into the future. What sorts of storage device might there be in 10 years' time? Will we have memory chips implanted beneath our skin so that if we get taken to hospital a reader can display our full medical histories? What other things could a form of storage like this be used for?

## Extension

Find out about other types of storage. What is 'Racetrack Memory' storage? What would it be used for?

## 5.1.3 Mobile phones

Mobile phones are described in greater detail in Chapter 7. They have embedded processors usually dedicated to managing a range of recording, playback, communication and storage facilities. It is claimed that more processors are now sold as components in mobile phones than in PCs. In some parts of the world, people are more likely to access the Internet through a mobile phone than with a computer.

A mobile phone's input, processing, storage, output and communication facilities include or may include:

- access over a cellular network:
  - microphone input, processing of speech and output devices for digital telephony;
  - receiving SMS text messages;
  - multimedia messaging, sending and receiving photos and video clips;
  - connecting to the Internet for email or Web browsing, or linking a portable computer to the Internet;
- recording photos and video clips with a built-in camera;
- audio recording;
- storing messages, contacts, photos, video and music;
- displaying messages, photos and video;
- playing music;
- running game programs;
- receiving broadcast radio;
- global positioning system (GPS) reception for navigation and information about local facilities;
- Bluetooth, USB or removable DSC data transfer to or from a computer.

Smartphones have more flexible operating systems that can run more advanced application programs.

## Questions

**34** What other forms of input and output are available to the user of a mobile phone? How do they work?

**35** What else can a mobile phone be used for?

**36** 'A mobile phone is a small and powerful computer that has a full set of peripheral devices.' Do you agree with this statement? Support your answer by comparing the features of a mobile phone with those of a PC.

## Summary

- The main hardware components of a computer are input and output devices, a processor, internal memory and backing storage.
- Computers range in power from supercomputer, through mainframe, PC or laptop to netbook, palmtop or PDA.
- Examples of manual input devices are keyboards, pointing devices, scanners, cameras, microphones, MIDI keyboards and remote controls.
- Examples of devices and methods for automatic data capture are OCR, OMR, MICR, barcode readers, RFID tag readers, magnetic stripe readers, smart card readers and biometric data capture using fingerprint reader, retina or iris scanner, microphone or camera.
- Examples of sensors are those for temperature, pressure, light, IR, humidity and gases.
- Analogue-to-digital converters convert analogue data from sensors into a stream of digital data.
- Examples of output devices are monitor screens, multimedia projectors, printers and plotters, loudspeakers and actuators.
- Computers use actuators, such as a light bulb or LED, heater, solenoid, motor, pump or buzzer, to make a physical change.
- Computers use sensors and actuators together to do useful tasks, such as controlling a washing machine or providing a virtual reality experience.
- A computer holds programs and data in limited-capacity, rapid-access, internal memory during processing and in larger-capacity, slower-access, backing storage to keep them for future use.
- Internal memory consists of volatile, read-write RAM and non-volatile, read-only ROM.
- RAM holds the programs and data currently being processed.
- ROM holds a program that starts a large operating system or the whole of a simple operating system or control program for an automated system.
- Backing storage has to be non-volatile and includes magnetic media, such as hard disks and magnetic tape; optical media, such as CDs, DVDs and Blu-ray discs; and solid-state media, such as flash-based memory sticks and digital storage cards.
- Different storage media have different characteristics that make them suitable for particular applications.
- A mobile phone is an example of an embedded computer system; some phones have a wide range of input, processing, storage, output and communication facilities.

## Examination practice for Paper 1

### Exam Questions

1. State **two** desirable properties of processors found in laptop computers.
   Explain why the selected property is desirable. [4]

   *Question 1, Cambridge IGCSE Computer Studies 0420/01 Paper 1 Specimen for 2011*

2. (a) Describe **two** special devices that are used for man–machine interaction in virtual reality systems. [2]
   (b) Give **two** examples of typical output from a virtual reality system. [2]

   *Parts of Question 16, Cambridge IGCSE Computer Studies 0420/01 Paper 1 Oct/Nov 2008*

$\longrightarrow$

3. A CCTV camera system has a 400 gigabyte hard disk. Each image's size is 400 kilobytes (0.4 megabyte).

   (a) How many images can be stored before the hard disk is full? [1]

   (b) Once the hard disk is full, how can the system ensure that the stored images are not lost and new images can be stored? [1]

   *Adapted from Part of Question 12, Cambridge IGCSE Computer Studies 0420/01 Paper 1 Oct/Nov 2009*

4. A supermarket has decided to fit sensors at the shop entrance to count people coming in and leaving.

   (a) What type of sensor would be suitable to detect people? [1]

   (b) How could the supermarket use the information obtained from these sensors? [2]

   *Parts of Question 8, Cambridge IGCSE Computer Studies 0420/01 Paper 1 Oct/Nov 2009*

## Exam-Style Questions

1. Name **three** devices used for automatic data capture.
   For each one, give an example of an application. [3]

2. (a) Give **two** advantages of using a concept keyboard in a restaurant. [2]

   (b) Give another **two** examples of applications for a concept keyboard. [2]

3. State **two** advantages of a laser printer as an output device. [2]

4. The following memory and storage devices are all used in a typical personal computer. For each device, state whether it is necessary or merely desirable for a computer to have the device, what purpose it is used for and what characteristic makes it particularly useful for that purpose:

   (a) Hard disk drive [3]

   (b) RAM [3]

   (c) ROM [3]

   (d) DVD-RW drive [3]

5. A school maintains a database of 500 current students. Each student record consists of approximately 5 megabytes of data.

   (a) How much RAM capacity is occupied if the whole database is held in internal memory? [1]

   (b) What must the database administrator do to prevent the size of the database growing when new students enrol at the start of the year? [1]

6. A digital video recorder can record a TV programme on a hard disk drive (HDD) and simultaneously play back a previous recording. How is it possible to write to and read from the HDD at the same time? [2]

7. Many automated systems are controlled by embedded microcontrollers, sensors and actuators. Name **two** different applications for such automated systems. For each system, describe **one** appropriate sensor and **one** actuator whose effect can be detected by the sensor. [6]

8. Many mobile phones have high-quality digital cameras for still and video photography.

   (a) Apart from the miniature camera electronics and optics, what other technological development has made this feasible? [1]

   (b) Describe **two** ways of transferring a photo from the phone to a PC. [2]

## Examination practice for Paper 3

To answer the following question you will need to read the garage scenario provided in Appendix A (page 284).

1. State **two** items of hardware, other than a computer, that would be suitable for this application. Justify your choice for each item. [4]

*Question (c), Cambridge IGCSE Computer Studies 0420/01 Paper 3 Specimen for 2011*

**Comment**

Notice that there are 4 marks awarded for stating two items of hardware. You would get 1 mark for each appropriate item of hardware, then 1 mark for every suitable justification for each piece of hardware. Any hardware item can be chosen so long as you can explain why it is suitable for the particular scenario.

# Systems and communications

**When you have finished this chapter, you will be able to:**

- explain the need for an operating system and list its functions
- distinguish between the main types of operating system
- explain a user interface and describe two types
- explain how folders are structured and how folders and files can be managed
- describe how the operating system communicates with peripheral devices and maintains data integrity.

## Operating systems

In Chapter 1, we studied the use of application software for various productive and recreational tasks. An operating system (sometimes shortened to OS) is one type of system software. An operating system manages all of the computer's hardware and all the other programs. It acts as a layer of software between application programs and the computer's hardware and provides an interface through which a user can run an application program. As the application program runs, it commonly interrupts the operating system, requesting it to provide input, output or other services. In return, the operating system frequently interrupts application programs to report progress or deliver data from input devices.

A major benefit of an operating system is that it provides a uniform user interface and a uniform environment in which application programs can run. For example, you may upgrade a computer's RAM, hoping to improve the computer's performance. Afterwards you experience broadly the same 'look-and-feel' and you do not have to rewrite all your application programs to benefit from the increased amount of RAM.

When computers were first invented, there were no operating systems. This meant that if a programmer wanted to write a simple program to add two numbers together, they had to program the details of receiving numerical codes for the two numbers from an input device, adding the numbers and then sending the correct numerical code for the result to an output device.

This was a very unsatisfactory state of affairs. Even a simple program took a long time to write because of the need to program the communication with the input and output devices. Soon, people started to write sets of programs to tell the computer how to do some of the standard, repeatable operations. These programs were the very first operating systems. Over the years, they have developed into the highly complex systems that we take for granted today. Even 'smart' mobile phones have an operating system, which means that they are very flexible and the user can install 'apps' of their choice.

However, not all computers need an operating system. An automated system such as a household appliance that is microprocessor-controlled, like a washing machine or a digital camera, has a single control program performing a single task with a fixed set of input and output hardware. An operating system would unnecessarily raise the development and manufacturing costs.

### Loading an operating system

An operating system may consist of quite a lot of software, so that fitting it all into non-volatile, but rewritable, memory such as flash memory can pose a problem. When a user switches on a laptop, desktop or a more powerful computer, it usually has no operating system in internal memory ready to run and manage the computer. From the earliest days of computing, when nothing like flash memory existed, this has posed a conundrum: a computer cannot run without software but it must be running before it can load an operating system. The answer is to provide a small program that can at least *start* the process of loading the operating system. In the early days, every time that the computer was re-started, someone had to do this manually by setting hardware switches, as shown in Figure 4.1.

**Figure 4.1** Part of the 'dead start' panel on a CDC-6600 mainframe computer of the 1960s. Note the $2^n$ labels at the top of the columns.

Nowadays, computers automatically run a small firmware program to start the process of loading the operating system into RAM, ready to take control. In a PC or laptop, this firmware is stored in flash memory. The first firmware program performs a 'power-on self-test' (POST). The purpose of POSTing is to prevent the computer from starting to run in an unusable state. It checks the integrity of the firmware, what external devices are connected and the size of internal memory. Then it identifies the most promising disk drive from which to load an operating system. Firmware often also performs similar POSTing in an automated system without an operating system.

The second firmware program, called the 'boot loader', then loads the first, tiny portion of the operating system into RAM from a hard disk or CD. This portion of the operating system can, in turn, load the rest of the operating system software and associated data into RAM. This process, in which the operating system loads itself and then takes control of the computer, is known as 'bootstrapping', since it appears to be about as impossible as pulling oneself up by pulling one's own shoelaces! You may also have heard people refer to starting a computer as 'booting' it.

## Functions of an operating system

The operating system is a set of programs and related data files that controls the operation of the computer. The main functions of a computer's operating system are to:

- complete its own loading into RAM when the computer is started up;
- manage user accounts and security using one or more usernames and passwords;
- provide an interface for the user that allows the user to:
  - run application programs;
  - manage files in backing storage;
  - read and respond to error messages;
- control application programs – loading them into internal memory and allocating processor time;
- manage the processor's time;
- manage the allocation of internal memory;
- control **peripheral devices** – input devices such as keyboards, output devices such as printers and backing storage such as hard disk drives;
- provide 'spooling' – temporary storage of input or output data in a queue on hard disk (originally tape), to allow application programs to proceed with other tasks while peripherals such as printers operate relatively slowly;
- manage interrupt signals to the processor;
- perform 'housekeeping tasks', such as defragmenting a drive or file indexing.

## SAQs

1 Suppose that you switch your PC off and install some more memory and a new disk. How do you think the computer finds out about these and what will it do with them?

## Questions

1 Try to make a list of things that the operating system has to do when the computer is being used. Does it make any difference what the computer is being used for?

2 Describe the operating system that you use on the computers at school. What does the screen look like before you start any application software? What is it called? Why did the school choose this operating system? If you have a computer at home or know someone who uses a computer at work, is the operating system different from the one at school? If so, in what ways?

## 5.2.1 Types of operating system

Different types of operating system support one or more types of processing by application programs and of access by users. We consider the nature of these types of operating system here and study the types of computer system that they support in more detail in Chapter 5.

### Batch operating system

The nature of batch processing is that a batch of data is prepared, validated, often verified by double entry, and entered into a transaction file before any processing takes place. This enables an application program to process the batch very efficiently, without delays caused by waiting for a user to enter data. The processing runs to completion without any intervention from an operator, unless an error occurs, such as a printer running out of paper. The owner of the job receives

output in the form of updated files or printer output. This enables processing to take place at night or over holidays, when a powerful computer might otherwise be idle, making more efficient use of a valuable resource.

A **batch operating system** is dedicated to managing a succession of batch 'jobs', packages of work, each consisting of a program and a batch of data. The batch operating system allows an operator to specify the following information for each job:

- the owner;
- programs;
- data files;
- the priority (its importance in any queuing);
- a maximum allowance of processor time, memory and printing lines;
- actions to be taken in case of program error.

The operating system places each job in a queue at a position based on the order in which it was submitted and its priority. When one job has completed, the operating system immediately runs the next job in the queue (Figure 4.2).

Batch processing is extremely useful when the program is thoroughly tested and the data are properly prepared and entered. It is less useful when the data are unreliable. Since all the input is prepared before the program processes it as a batch, it cannot be modified in the light of the program's output while the program is running. It is rather like having to listen to a whole speech before being able to make a comment or ask a question.

All the other sorts of operating system that we study are **interactive** (Figure 4.3); they support programs in which some sort of output is available as soon as a data item has been entered. This allows the user's input to depend on earlier output, for example, spotting a typographical error (or 'typo') on the screen and correcting it. This is far more like a conversation and is better suited to many sorts of work and recreational tasks.

Even when the operating system is interactive, some tasks are designed to run as batch processes. For example, on a PC or laptop, housekeeping tasks are usually batch processes. They are often scheduled to run automatically without necessarily alerting the user, or 'in the background'. Examples of such batch processes are virus scanning of a folder or whole disk drive,

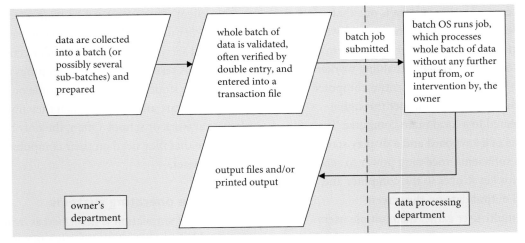

**Figure 4.2** Submission of a job to a batch processing operating system.

defragmenting a drive, file indexing, archiving of old emails and data backup.

In most interactive operating systems, the user can also execute tasks in batch mode by running a 'batch file' or 'shell script', a list of commands that will execute one or more tasks non-interactively.

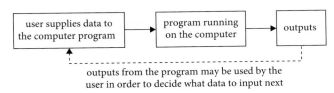

**Figure 4.3** Interactive processing.

## Multi-tasking operating system

Until the late 1980s, most personal computers could only run one program at a time. Imagine how frustrating it was for a user to have to copy material from a spreadsheet, then exit from the spreadsheet program to run a word processor and paste the copied material into a document, then exit from the word processor in order to run the spreadsheet program again and resume work on the spreadsheet.

A typical modern operating system for any sort of general-purpose computer is a **multi-tasking operating system**, which can simultaneously run several operating system processes and services and also more than one application program. The user can actively work on one program, while others continue to run in the background. Even if an interactive application program

is idle while the user is not actively working on it, the program and any open documents are instantly available to the user by switching to the required program using a pointing device or keystrokes.

For example, you may be writing an essay for school using a word processor. You decide that you would like to include some illustrations from the Web. So you run a web browser and switch between the browser and the word processor using a keyboard shortcut such as *Alt+Tab*, as you copy-and-paste. Meanwhile, you may have music playing from a CD that you placed in the DVD drive. You are expecting an email from a friend, so email software may be running in the background, which can alert you when a message arrives.

On any computer that has only a single processor, only one program can actually run at any instant, but the operating system creates an illusion of simultaneous running by sharing processing time between the programs.

## Multi-access operating system

A multi-access system allows more than one user to use the same computer at the same time. This is similar to two friends having a race on a computer car racing game using separate games consoles. The computer responds to input from both games consoles and gives a visual representation of a simulation of both the cars' movements. It is able to do this so quickly that neither player is aware that they are sharing the computer's processing time.

A **multi-access operating system** is one that permits multiple users to log in to the same powerful computer. The need for such an operating system arose before the days of PCs, as a way of enabling workers in organisations to share the use of a central computer. Each user interacts with the computer through a 'terminal' connected to a local main computer. The terminal consists of a keyboard and a display screen. It only contains sufficient processing power to send numeric codes for keystrokes to the computer and to display received output data on the screen.

As with the multi-user game, the multiple users are actually sharing the computer's processing time. In this case, the operating system is responsible for sharing processing time between the users. Each user experiences having all of the computer's resources available. If the operating system becomes very busy, there may be significant delays before the computer responds to their input. Terminals are relatively cheap and easy to maintain, but a failure of the central computer brings computer-based work to a halt!

The diagram in Figure 4.4 may look like a computer network, but it is important to remember that the terminals do not have their own processors and are therefore *not* computers, although a computer can run a program to operate as (or 'emulate') a terminal.

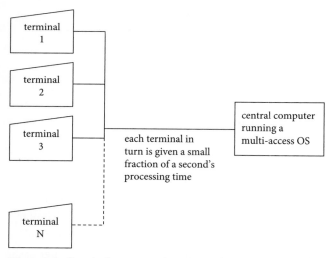

**Figure 4.4** Terminals connected to a central computer running a multi-access operating system.

Computers running different brands of operating system, with a limited set of application programs, or with minimal peripherals and operating system

('thin client' computers) can be connected through a computer network (described in Chapter 5) to a 'terminal server' that provides similar central computer facilities. A terminal server is sometimes used to give workers or students access from home or other locations to the software and data to which they normally have access at work or school. Often, the only application software that they need on their computer is a web browser.

## Real-time operating systems

A computer simulation is described as 'real-time' if its output keeps pace with the real-world process that it is simulating. Similarly, a **real-time operating system** is one that supports application programs that can process input within a guaranteed maximum time to produce the output required to keep pace with the user's needs for information or control. The maximum time may vary between microseconds and seconds.

A **real-time transaction processing operating system** supports application software for processing transactions, such as booking entertainment tickets or recording retail sales, as they occur. The maximum response time needs to be in the range of seconds.

If a movie theatre sells tickets for unreserved seating through its website (Figure 4.5), customers expect a response within seconds to their request for tickets for a particular screening. The operating system must also enable the application program to update the total number of tickets sold sufficiently rapidly to prevent the maximum number of tickets being exceeded. If individual seats can be booked, once a seat has been booked, it needs to be recorded immediately as 'unavailable' to avoid a double booking. Data files must be updated in real-time, so that customers or agents have access to completely up-to-date information.

A real-time process control application program is created to control a physical or chemical process. It does so by continuously monitoring conditions and processing set-point data (what the user is demanding) and sensor feedback data (responses to physical or chemical conditions resulting from the process). The data are processed to make decisions about, and calculations of, the output required to one or more actuators such as motorised valves or pumps.

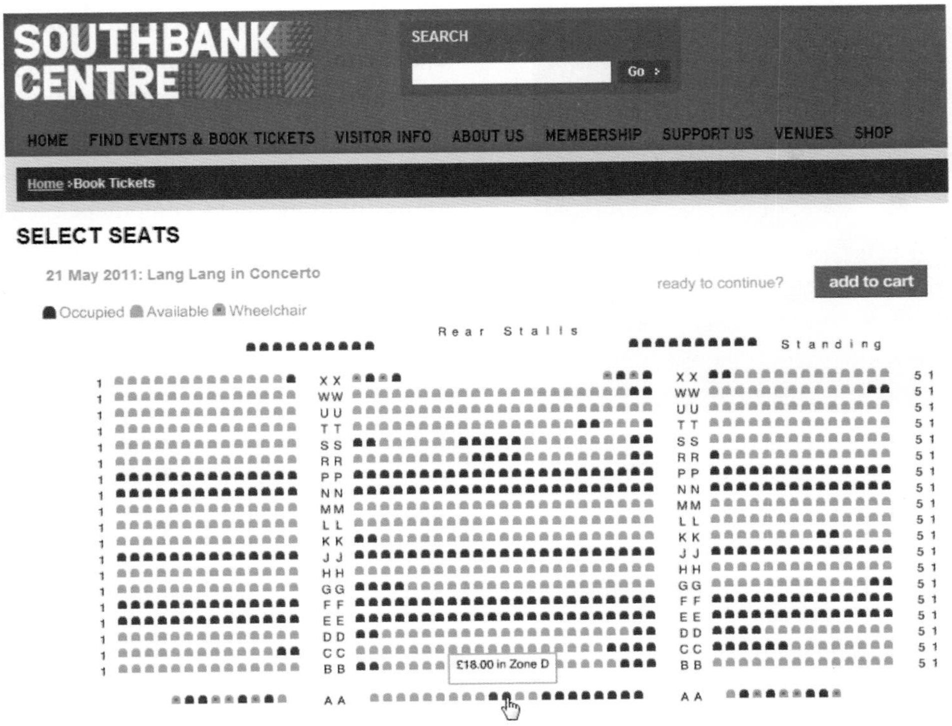

## SOUTHBANK CENTRE

SEARCH [ ] Go >

HOME   FIND EVENTS & BOOK TICKETS   VISITOR INFO   ABOUT US   MEMBERSHIP   SUPPORT US   VENUES   SHOP

Home >Book Tickets

### SELECT SEATS

21 May 2011: Lang Lang in Concerto

ready to continue?   [ add to cart ]

■ Occupied ■ Available ■ Wheelchair

Rear Stalls                    Standing

£18.00 in Zone D

**Figure 4.5**   A website seat booking system needs a real-time transaction processing operating system.

For example, a real-time process control program could be used to control the temperature in a chemical reaction in a chemical plant. It is a continuous, time-sensitive monitoring process. Input data must be processed sufficiently frequently and rapidly, otherwise the reaction may get out of control. A **real-time process control operating system** supports one or more such process control application programs (Figure 4.6).

Only sufficiently frequent sampling and rapid processing of these data can guarantee the production of output data for actuators in time to control the process effectively. The operating system has to be able to cope

**Figure 4.6**   A real-time process control operating system is likely to be used in an oil refinery.

with the unpredictable timing of events, which may take place simultaneously. The maximum response time often has to be in the range of microseconds to milliseconds.

Many real-time operating systems operate in safety-critical roles, such as a 'fly-by-wire' flight control system for an aircraft or a control system for an oil refinery or nuclear power station. Such systems need to maintain fault-tolerance through 'redundancy'. The operating system and hardware run well below their capacity for most of the time, to be able to cope with extreme situations. Hardware is duplicated so that there are replacements ready to run in the case of damage or failure.

For example, in the fly-by-wire flight control system for the Airbus A320 family of passenger airliners (Figure 4.7):

- Four control and monitoring computers are located in different parts of the aircraft, although one is sufficient to control the aircraft.
- Two of the computers were designed and are made by one manufacturer and the other two by a different manufacturer. This makes the overall system tolerant of a design or manufacturing fault in any computer's hardware or software.

**Figure 4.7** An Airbus 320 airliner has four computers to make its flight control system fault-tolerant.

2 Suppose that a microcontroller-based engine control unit, code-named Computer X, stores several hundred megabytes of input and output data during each test run of a prototype car. The data is supplied by 20 sensors.

After each test run, the data are downloaded to a powerful computer, Computer Y, at the manufacturer's design centre. Computer Y runs a program that performs very detailed analysis of the test data and produces graphs and statistics for design engineers without any user input. Computer Y is kept very busy by a steady stream of requests for data processing from different teams of engineers, so it needs to run very efficiently.

What types of operating system would be needed for Computer X and Computer Y?

### Network operating system

A **network operating system** manages communication between computers and peripherals equipped with a 'network interface card' (or NIC) and connected to a network (see Chapter 5). Each computer connected to the network needs a network operating system.

Most operating systems for laptops and PCs for small office and home use have built-in support for 'peer-to-peer' networking. This allows the computers to simply share resources such as specific folders of data, peripherals such as printers, and Internet access. Other families of operating system support server-based networks. These have a 'server' computer, running a 'server operating system', which controls access to the network and provides access to the network's resources for one or more 'client' computers, each running a 'client operating system' (Figure 4.8).

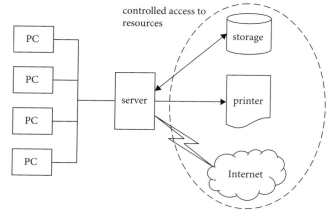

**Figure 4.8** PCs gaining access to resources on a server-based local area network.

3 Is this beginning to look like your computer system in school? Discuss the system in school with your teacher or with the technician. Do you have a local area network of computers? Can you use your school software and data from a remote computer? Does the school's computer system have any unusual features?

## 5.2.2 User interface

A **user interface**, or 'human–computer interface' (HCI), consists of all the hardware and software through which a user provides input to a computer or receives information from it. We need to remember that the term 'computer' does not only refer to laptops and PCs running application software for a wide range of work-related and recreational purposes. It also includes other computers, including embedded computers in equipment ranging from a digital camera to a nuclear power station.

We study the command line interface and graphical user interface.

## Command line interface

For several decades, a **command line interface** (**CLI**) was the only type of user interface available. Screen output was restricted to text without graphics or graphics without text. It was quite difficult to use a computer because a CLI has no permanently available menus. It relies on the user accurately remembering and entering commands, using only the keyboard for input. The user has to:

- remember what commands are available and the rules (or 'syntax') for constructing a valid command;
- type commands accurately – some errors can have drastic unintended effects, such as reformatting a hard disk containing all of a user's software and data.

However, a CLI can be very useful for an expert, such as a network administrator, because it enables them to work rapidly and access a very wide range of commands. Figure 4.9 shows an example of a CLI being used to display the configuration of the computer's network connections. A flashing underscore after the '>' symbol is the 'command prompt' at which the user types a command. The example shows a piece of system software, but application software is also similarly restricted to displaying text without graphics.

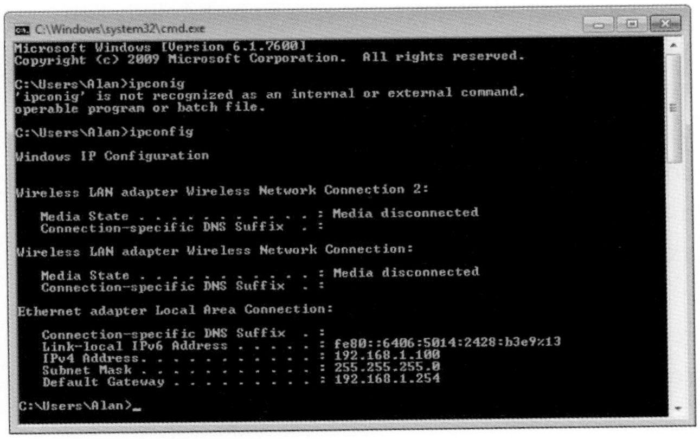

**Figure 4.9** A command line interface.

## Graphical user interface

A **graphical user interface** (**GUI**) is the type of interface that most modern computers offer. It is called 'graphical' because it displays graphics as well as text (Figure 4.10). As well as helping the presentation of information, this helps to make software easier for users to understand and to make computers more 'user-friendly'.

We briefly mentioned some commonly occurring features of a GUI when studying application programs in Chapter 1. They are summarised by the acronym 'WIMP':

- **windows**:
  - a multi-tasking operating system with a GUI usually displays each task in a separate window;
  - each window is a rectangular region of the screen through which we can view a running program, a document or a dialogue box;
  - clicking a mouse or other pointing device's button on an application program window is an intuitive way to switch to working on a different task, automatically bringing its window in front of other windows;
- **icons** (Figure 4.11):
  - a small, pictorial symbol, sometimes with text, that represents a command, a file or a shortcut to a program, file or Web resource;
  - an icon can be selected or 'clicked' by operating a button on a mouse or other pointing device;
  - an icon may be available on a permanently visible menu called a 'toolbar' or on a drop-down list;
  - dragging a file icon onto a suitable application program icon or window often opens the file in that application;
- **menus**:
  - a command menu displays a drop-down list of text options or a tabbed toolbar of command options depicted by icons;
  - commands may themselves give access to sub-menus;
  - a secondary mouse button may give access to a context-sensitive menu, which makes available commands used frequently with the type of resource that is currently selected;
- **pointing devices**:
  - a mouse or other pointing device positions a graphical cursor on the display screen;
  - the appearance of the cursor depends on its position relative to selected text or objects;
  - clicking the pointing device's button provides an intuitive means of selecting a window, an icon or a menu command;

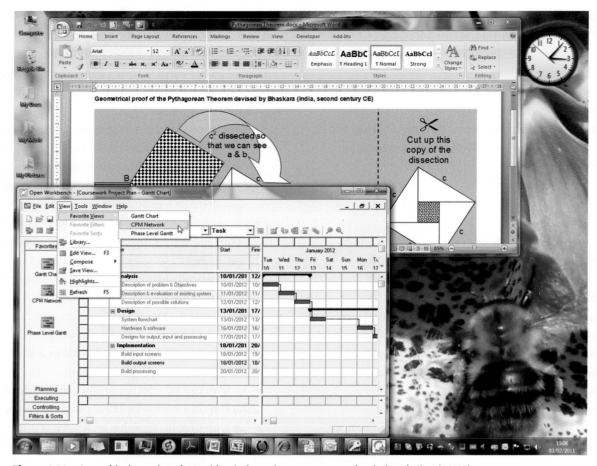

**Figure 4.10** A graphical user interface with windows, icons, menus and pointing device (WIMP).

New

Open

Convert

Save

Save As

Print

**Figure 4.11** Standard icons in a GUI.

– the device can select text or objects within an application window by clicking-and-dragging and move them by drag-and-drop.

Icons provide easy access to commands without relying on text. However, changes in technology can make an icon rather difficult to associate with a command. For example, in 2005, almost every computer user knew what a floppy disk looked like. New computers are not equipped with floppy disk drives, but a *Save* icon still depicts a floppy disk: . How do you explain that to a small child?

A GUI is very user-friendly because it is easier to recognise commands in a menu or toolbar than to remember them without any prompting.

**Questions**

4 Describe the types of interface that you use on your school system and that the technician or your teacher uses to maintain the system.

## File management

Each saved program or set of data, whether it is
something that you have created yourself or imported
from another source, is a **file**. There may be many
thousands or even millions of user files stored on one or
more hard disk drives and they need organising so that
they can be easily located.

We use a **folder** to organise files on backing storage
in a structured way. We can think of a folder as a
virtual container provided by the operating system's
**file manager**. It appears as a window in which the user
can see a list of the related files or even other related
folders stored within it. A folder within another folder is
called a **sub-folder** and can contain its own related files
and sub-sub-folders.

The operating system stores an index of the contents
of each storage drive, known as the drive's root directory.
As well as listing any files contained at the root of the
drive, this directory includes references to folders
within the drive. Each of these folders has its own

**file directory**, which in turn refers to any sub-folders
within it. Each sub-folder has its own **sub-directory**.
Since a directory is so closely identified with the folder
whose contents it lists, the two terms tend to be used
interchangeably.

An operating system with a GUI often includes
a navigational file manager. This typically displays
the hierarchical 'tree' structure of the file system in
the left pane and the current directory in the right
pane (Figure 4.12).

It is important for users to be able to manage the files
that they own. The operating system normally provides
facilities for this as part of the file manager, although
'utility' programs are also available. Facilities include:

- **List** – Opening a storage drive or folder lists the files
  and sub-folders it contains. It can display the name,
  size, type, date created and modified, and other
  details. The user can sort the list by any of the fields
  displayed. The user can re-name a file or sub-folder,
  create a new file or folder and search by file name
  and content.
- **Move** – If a user has stored a file or folder in the
  wrong place or wants to reorganise the folders, the
  user can use cut-and-paste commands to move them.
  The user can also drag files between two folders
  within the same drive.

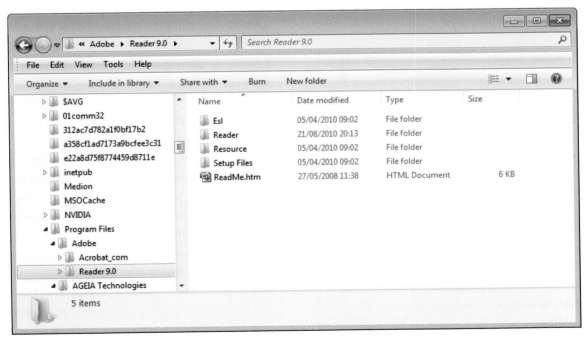

**Figure 4.12**  A navigational file manager.

- **Copy** – The user can copy files or folders from one place to another. This is very useful for making a backup copy of a file in case the original gets damaged or accidentally deleted. The user can use copy-and-paste commands or may be able to drag contents between different drives.
- **Print** – Printing a file opens a print dialogue within an appropriate application.

## 5.2.4 Peripheral device control

### Buffers

An operating system is often able to pass input data to an application program far faster than an input device can supply it. Similarly, it can often supply the application program's output data far faster than an output device can accept it. To compensate for the difference in rates of data processing and allow the processor to perform other tasks while waiting to receive or send data, system software called a device driver manages the transfer. This driver uses an area of memory to hold data temporarily. Such an area in memory is called a **buffer**.

For example, a computer's printer driver creates a printer buffer in memory to hold data for the printer when the printer is busy. The printer driver transfers output data to the buffer. It then waits until the printer has finished processing previous data or the user has attended to an error message (such as 'out of paper') before transferring the new data.

### Polling of peripherals

Peripheral devices cannot control the transmission of data to and from the computer. Only a running program can do that. So how does a peripheral device attract the operating system's attention to signal that it is ready to send data to a device driver's buffer or that it has finished receiving data from such a buffer? For example, the printer may need to signal to the computer's printer driver that it has successfully received the data sent to it and is ready for more, or that it has run out of paper or ink.

One method is for the operating system to be responsible for checking for communication from peripheral devices by periodically interrogating each peripheral device in turn to discover its status. This is known as **polling**.

Imagine a robot truck (see Figure 3.42, page 69) that has a number of sensors for obstructions. If a sensor spots an obstruction in front of it as the truck moves across a factory floor, it must alert the operating system. Although the operating system may be busy with other tasks, it is programmed to poll the sensors sufficiently frequently that there is little chance of the robot hitting the obstruction before the operating system checks the data from the relevant sensor. The disadvantage of this method is that the operating system has to devote significant processing time to polling all the peripheral devices, even when the devices are not active. A system in which a peripheral device waits to be asked whether it needs the attention of the operating system is called a **polling system**.

### Peripherals interrupting the operating system

To reduce the amount of time the operating system spends polling, processors were designed to accept a separate type of signal called an 'interrupt'. An **interrupt** is a signal sent from a peripheral device (hardware) or program (software) to the processor to indicate that the sender needs attention. This leaves the operating system entirely free to process other tasks until its attention is needed. A system in which a peripheral device signals that it needs the attention of the operating system is called an interrupt system.

A processor usually has relatively few hardware interrupt inputs with different priorities. Before fetching each machine code instruction (see Chapter 10) from internal memory, the processor checks an area of memory within the processor called its 'interrupt register' to see whether any interrupts are waiting to be serviced.

One way of allowing a number of peripheral devices to share these interrupt inputs is for the processor to respond to an interrupt signal by polling the peripheral devices. This wastes a certain amount of time polling, but now polling only occurs when a peripheral is known to need attention. Another system for responding to interrupts is known as 'vectored interrupt', in which a peripheral device supplies an internal memory address called a 'vector'. The vector contains the start address of the appropriate interrupt handler program code.

An obstruction sensor in our robot truck would need to generate a high priority interrupt to ensure that its input data are handled quickly to avoid hitting obstructions. Interrupts with high priority can be handled extremely rapidly. For example, if a peripheral device monitoring the power supply voltage detects a sudden drop indicating that a power failure is starting to occur, it can interrupt the processor to request saving the state of all the running programs to disk before the power supply is actually lost. If this succeeds, when the user re-starts the computer, the saved data enable the computer's operating system to resume operation with the running programs in the same state that they were in before the power failure. An 'uninterruptible power supply' similarly uses a microcontroller to rapidly switch from mains to battery power to continue to run a computer for long enough that it can be shut down using the normal procedure.

We said earlier that programs can also generate interrupts. An application program can use a software interrupt to request a service from the operating system. The sort of service an application requires would include opening a file from a disk drive or exiting the application. This is known as a 'system call'. Sending the interrupt to the operating system to request a service passes control back to the operating system. Since the operating system passed control to the application program in the first place, in effect, the application has interrupted itself to fulfil the user's request.

## Questions

5 A burglar alarm system is set up with a number of sensors around a large factory complex. Discuss the advantages and disadvantages of using a polling system or an interrupt system for computer control of the sensors and burglar alarm.

### Handshaking

In many cultures, people use a handshake as a physical gesture or 'body language' to indicate that they are ready to start communication or that they are ending communication with each other. We often use words such as 'Hello' and 'Goodbye' as the verbal equivalent.

Computers need to do similar things, sometimes to negotiate the rules or 'protocol' that they will use to communicate for the rest of the session. For example, they have to find a data transfer rate that is acceptable to both computers and to decide whether odd or even parity will be used. A computer also often needs to control the flow of data over a network with another computer or between the computer and a peripheral device such as printer. 'Flow control' is necessary to prevent a delay in processing data at the receiving end resulting in lost data or an irretrievable breakdown in communication.

A computer's **handshaking** may involve sending electronic signals as special codes down the normal data channel or, in some cases, sending extra signals down a separate hardware wire in a short cable.

As an example, we look at how a computer's printer driver program sends data to a printer over a USB connection. To start the transmission of a data packet (a bundle of up to 512 bytes), the computer's 'USB host controller' sends a relatively small OUT 'token packet' to the printer. This informs the printer that the computer is ready to send data. The 'handshake packet' from the printer replies with one of the following options:

- successful reception (ACK, short for 'Acknowledged');
- the printer's buffer is not yet empty because it is still processing a previous data packet (NAK, short for 'Not Acknowledged');
- the printer has encountered an error (STALL).

The complete process for transmitting one data packet looks like this:

1. The printer driver program fills the print buffer and requests the host controller to send the data to the printer.
2. The host controller sends an OUT token packet immediately followed by a data packet to the printer. Although the OUT packet is not technically a handshake packet, it marks the beginning of a handshaking flow control process.
3. The printer's USB hardware sends an ACK handshake packet to inform the host controller that it has successfully received the data packet in its input buffer.
4. The printer's USB hardware generates an interrupt signal to the printer's microcontroller.
5. The printer's firmware handles the interrupt by reading and processing the contents of its input buffer.

The steps above are repeated, possibly thousands of times, until the host controller generates a hardware interrupt to the computer's operating system to signal that the data transfer requested by the printer driver is complete.

## Checksum

When data are transferred to and from peripherals and over networks, they are vulnerable to signalling errors. It is therefore important to check that they have not been corrupted. In other words, we ensure that their 'integrity' (their completeness and correctness) has been preserved (see Chapter 8).

A **checksum** is a way of summarising a block of data such as a USB or network data packet (Figure 4.13). At its simplest, it consists of the arithmetical sum of all the numerical values of all the elements of the block. The sum is reduced to a standard number of digits and transmitted with the block. When the block of data gets to its destination, the same mathematical calculation is performed on the data by the receiving device and the result is compared with the received checksum. If the two checksums match, the integrity of the data has been maintained. If the two checksums do not match then an error has been made in transmitting the data and the receiving device requests the sending device to re-transmit the data. Even if one binary digit has changed in the data, the recalculated checksum does not match the received checksum and the data are rejected.

You may recognise a checksum as being similar in function to a parity bit for a byte or a check digit for a code number (such as the ISBN check digit in Chapter 2). More complex implementations of a checksum involve more complex arithmetic to try to detect a wider range of errors. Cryptography can be used to try to prevent someone from maliciously substituting different data with the same checksum.

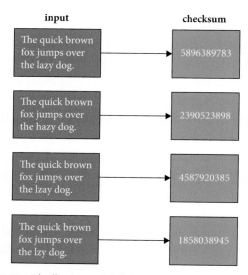

**Figure 4.13** Ideally, three slightly incorrect versions of a message each generate very different checksums from that of the original message.

3   Senine wants to print a photo from her PC to a high-resolution colour printer that is connected wirelessly and is on another floor. The printer has a large data buffer. Because of the distance involved, the photo is not transferred correctly. The printer detects that the checksum for the data is wrong. What is likely to happen next? What does Senine need to do?

6   Try to write down, in order, the steps that are needed for the operating system to save a file on a disk drive, when using a mouse.

## Summary

- An operating system is needed:
  - to manage the users, hardware, software and peripherals;
  - to provide a uniform environment for the processor;
  - to provide a user interface through which a user can run application programs and perform housekeeping tasks.
- Types of operating system include batch, multi-tasking, multi-access, real-time transaction processing, real-time process control and network.
- Types of user interface controlled by the operating system include command line and graphical user interfaces.
- A graphical user interface (GUI) often features windows, icons, menus and pointing devices.
- Operating systems with GUIs support folders and sub-folders to represent directory contents. The hierarchical structure of folders can often be viewed in a navigational file manager.
- User commands for file management include listing directory contents by opening a folder, moving and copying files and folders, and printing files.
- Methods of communication between the operating system and peripheral devices include the use of buffers, polling, interrupts with priorities, handshaking and a checksum.

## Examination practice for Paper 1

### Exam Questions

1.  Give **three** features of a typical operating system.                                        [3]

*Part of Question 3, Cambridge IGCSE Computer Studies 0420/01 Paper 1 May/June 2009*

2.  Many software applications use drop-down lists.
    (a) What is meant by the term 'drop-down lists'?                                               [2]
    (b) A user is filling out an order form on a website.                                          [2]
        (i) Give **one** example where a drop-down list could help the user.
        (ii) Give **one** example where a drop-down list should not be used to help the user.

*Question 9, Adapted from Cambridge IGCSE Computer Studies 0420/01 Paper 11 May/June 2010*

→

3. **(a)** What is an interrupt? [1]

   **(b)** How can an interrupt be generated? [1]

   **(c)** A computer function consists of an exchange of signals between two devices to allow communication to take place. What is the name of the computer function? [1]

   *Question 4, Adapted from Cambridge IGCSE Computer Studies 0420/01 Paper 1 May/June 2009*

## Exam-Style Questions

1. What is a buffer and what is its purpose? [2]

2. What is an interrupt and what is its purpose? [2]

3. What is a checksum and what is its purpose? [2]

4. State the key feature of a real-time operating system that makes it essential for the 'fly-by-wire' flight control system of an aircraft. [1]

5. Explain, with an example of each, **four** common features of a graphical user interface. [4]

6. Explain, with an example of each, **three** common commands for file management. [3]

# 5 Types of computer system

## When you have finished this chapter, you will be able to:

- distinguish between types of computer system
- describe what is needed to support various types of computer system
- explain the most suitable type of computer system for a given application and discuss the implications for the user
- describe problems in the management of the various types of computer system.

All computer systems involve input, processing and output. However, as we have seen in Chapter 4, different types of operating system can support different types of computer system. In this chapter, we extend these ideas and explore differences in timing, communication, interactivity and media.

When you read about the range and scope of computer applications in Chapter 7, try to work out which type of system would be used.

### 5.3.1 Batch processing systems

The key concepts in a **batch processing system** are the lack of any direct interaction between the user and the running program and its data, known as the 'job', or any immediate 'time dependency'.

If you are at the checkout in the supermarket, you expect the operator to find the price of an item immediately: the system works in 'real-time'. However, if you turn on your kitchen light and use the cooker, you do not expect a bill to be produced immediately for the use of the light and then another one for the use of the cooker. Your consumption of electricity is allowed to accumulate for a few months until it is large enough to make it worthwhile sending you a bill. If the bill arrives a day earlier or later than expected, you are not too concerned. Instead of your meter reading being processed individually, it is processed in a large batch with the readings of other customers, which is more efficient.

Batch processing has the following characteristics:

- a large amount of data is processed in one **batch**, or **job**, without operator intervention, usually at an off-peak time (e.g. overnight or at the weekend);
- the same processing is applied to all the sets of data in the batch;
- no other processing interferes with the batch job;
- the output from the process does not have to be produced quickly;
- the operating system holds jobs in a queue until the system is ready to process them.

Electricity billing is a good example of a batch process. The system carries out the following processing for all data sets:

1. Reads a meter reading and the customer details.
2. Calculates the bill.
3. Prints out the bill (see Figure 5.1).

No user interaction is required, except for staff to look after the printers and envelope-stuffing machines. The electricity supplier does not need to produce a bill to a tight schedule. The amount of data is enormous: for each supplier, tens of thousands of customer meters are read every day. The supplier's computer system is probably not doing anything at night when the offices are shut, so it can be used to produce all the bills.

A batch processing system requires:

- a batch operating system;
- a large batch of data all requiring similar processing;
- a suitable program to perform the required processing.

**Country Power**

page 1 of 4

Date: 07/06/2011

**Contact us:**
Tel: 123-456-789

We are open Monday to Friday 8 am to 6 pm, Saturday 9 am to 1 pm

Website: www.countrypower.com

Email: customer.service@countrypower.com

Mr Abiola Okeke
25 Main Street
Anytown

Dear Mr Okeke

*Your electricity statement*

*Account number: 1111 2222 345*
For the period 28/02/2011 to 31/05/2011

| | |
|---|---|
| Balance on your account brought forward: | –$ 206.40 |
| Your electricity charges: | $ 146.23 |
| Discounts: | –$ 11.43 |
| Tax | $ 15.19 |
| **You are in credit by:** | $ 56.41 |

*Full breakdown of the charges overleaf. Your monthly charge is* $ 58.00

Thank you for being a Country Power customer.

**Figure 5.1** Part of a typical electricity bill. Note the square, 2-D barcode near the top.

**Questions**

1  A payroll system is another application of batch processing. Explain why a payroll system is particularly suited to batch processing. What is the printed output in this case?

**SAQs**

1  Give two examples, other than utility billing and payroll, of where batch processing would be used.

### 5.3.2 Interactive systems

An **interactive system** allows the user to interact directly with a running program to influence the future course of processing.

The commonest form of interactive system is the PC that you may use at school or at home. The computer is under the user's control. The interface allows the user to give direct commands that the computer deals with immediately. Word processing software would be much less useful if you had to enter all your text before you could view it and make changes. Interactivity allows you to correct mistakes as you type and make changes as you develop a new document or edit an existing one.

An interactive system requires an interactive operating system and a user interface that supports the user's interaction with the system, such as a display screen, keyboard and mouse.

A PC is a **single-user system** because only one person can use it at a time. If more than one person can use the computer, there is a need for passwords to control access to the software and to the files. A **multi-user system** involves a single computer to which many users have apparently simultaneous access. Typically, each user accesses the system's **server** computer across a network, using a PC as a **client computer**. When a user wants some information from the system, the client computer sends a message to the server, which is interrupted and services the request.

Multi-user systems are used for online information systems where the server provides a single data source. Little processing power is required at the user end; all the processing for information retrieval is handled by the server.

A good example is an information system in a train station. There may be a kiosk-type terminal on each platform that passengers can use to ask about train times. The server, which is maintained centrally, has all the information and responds to queries. If an administrator updates a train time, it is immediately available to all the users. The system may even be web-based, so that users can access the system over the Internet from their PCs. A web server serves the multi-user system.

Multi-user systems in which the users modify a common pool of data are more complex, as it is necessary to prevent more than one user updating the same information at the same time. For example, an online booking system for concert seats must not allow two people to book the same seat. The booking system usually achieves this by temporarily 'locking' the data records for the requested seats until the user purchases them, abandons the booking, or the reservation period expires (Figure 5.2).

You have **20 minutes** to complete your purchase. Seats not purchased within this time period will be released to general availability.

My Basket

Below is the list of items in your shopping basket. Please check all details are correct before checking out.

Continue Shopping                                  Check Out

PROM 73
Wednesday 8 September 2010, 10:15PM                Remove

| Qty | Description | Total |
|-----|-------------|-------|
| 2 | 2T 30 Price Each: £15.00 Section: 2nd Tier Seats No(s): 1, 2 | £30.00 |

**Figure 5.2** An online booking for concert seats expires after a few minutes if you do not complete the purchase.

## Questions

2   Draw a diagram of a multi-user system in a supermarket that provides information to and collects data from the checkout tills. Add a terminal to your diagram that can be used by the management of the supermarket to control the system and update prices. What extra safeguards are necessary if the extra terminal is added?

5.3.3

## Network systems

In a **network system**, processing occurs independently in two or more computers that share controlled access to facilities such as file storage, servers and printers.

It is unusual nowadays to encounter a computer that is not part of a network. As I write this sentence, an Ethernet cable connects my computer to a broadband **router** and modem that provides a connection to the Internet. A laptop and a network-enabled, multifunction printer connect to the computer via the broadband router's wireless access point. Netbook and laptop users often use a mobile network modem, commonly known as a 'broadband dongle', to connect to the Internet via a mobile phone network.

A network can be as simple as two computers connected in a home network. The Internet is a very complex and extensive network. When I connect to the Internet, for example, I may access the following types of information:

- text and images on a public website, such as http://www.bbc.co.uk;
- data on a private file server in Cambridge;
- encrypted documents on a secure private website in Germany.

In each case, a number of computers linked by the Internet enable me to access shared resources.

### Access control

On your own computer, you have full control to read, change, create or delete files. Access to a network and its resources is usually controlled by usernames and passwords. If confidential or private information is stored, network communication may be encrypted.

On a school network, a file server's hard disk drive may have a folder that is set aside for your exclusive use. This 'user area' appears as a network drive in the file manager and the network's administrator is likely to give you full control to read, change, create or delete files in that area. Your access to other network drives or folders may be restricted so that you can only read software or data files.

There may be a number of shared resources on the network. For instance, it would be a good idea to separate student data from school administration data. Administration data have to be very secure, so this may be held on a separate file server with access closely controlled and monitored. Student data does not need to be as secure – a less tightly controlled file server would suffice. Data may thus be distributed around the network as appropriate.

A network system requires:

- networked devices, such as workstation or server computers, and network-enabled peripheral devices such as printers;
- metal cable, fibre-optic cable, wireless or satellite connections;
- sufficient copies of an appropriate network operating system.

### Network topologies

A network can be connected in different patterns or **topologies**. Three basic topologies are bus, ring and star.

In a bus network (Figure 5.3), the networked devices are all connected to a common cable known as the bus because, like the vehicle of the same name, it is shared by all. A bus network needs special devices at the ends of the bus cable called **terminators**. These absorb signals so that they do not get reflected back into the network and cause data corruption.

A bus network has a relatively short length of cabling but it may involve quite expensive types of cable and connector. If a break occurs in the cabling, the operation of the whole network is likely to be disrupted. Similarly, the network can be difficult to modify; some part of the network will need to be temporarily disconnected.

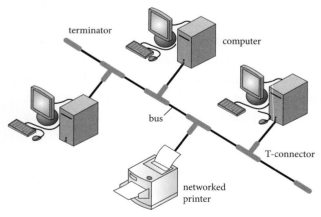

**Figure 5.3** A bus network.

All the data are sent along the shared cable so that all devices receive the data, although the data are usually addressed to only one of them and only that one acts on the data. The networked devices compete to use the bus, since no device should transmit data while another one is already doing so. When traffic is heavy, there is an increase in the frequency of nearly simultaneous data transmissions by different devices. These cause 'data collisions', when the two sets of signals interfere with each other and corrupt the transmitted data. This slows down the network, as both transmissions must be repeated.

In a **ring network** (Figure 5.4), separate segments of cable join the networked devices in a ring and data are transmitted from one to the next in a consistent direction. When a device receives data that are addressed to it, it uses the data; if the data are not addressed to that device, it forwards them to the next device. Data collisions are usually avoided by attaching data to one or more special signals, known as 'tokens'. Some ring networks employ two rings rotating in opposite directions to increase performance and enable automatic reconfiguration in the event of a fault. A ring network is often more difficult to install than a bus network. It also costs more because of the extra cabling.

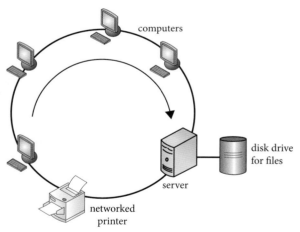

**Figure 5.4** Ring network.

Both bus and ring networks have a major disadvantage: if the main cable is damaged communication around the network is not possible. An alternative is that every device is separately connected to a central node that receives data and re-transmits them to some or all of the other devices. This type of network is called a **star network** (Figure 5.5). This is easier to set up and modify and is now cheaper to install than the other two types of network. If a cable is damaged, the network continues to operate for all the other devices. A wireless network is effectively a star network, with the wireless access point acting as the central node.

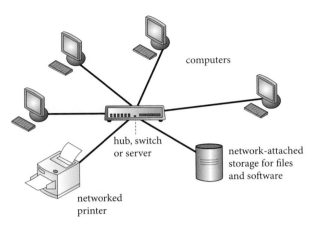

Figure 5.5 Star network.

## Types of network

A **local area network** (**LAN**) consists of a number of networked devices connected on a single site, perhaps in a single building or office. It enables computers to share peripheral devices. Because the size and scope of the network is limited, a subscription to an external communication medium, such as a telephone line, is not needed. They also normally allow higher rates of data transfer. Similarly, a LAN does not usually suffer from problems with control of the communication medium or interference by outside agents, such as hackers (although a wireless LAN, known as a 'Wi-Fi network', can have such problems).

Networked devices in a LAN are, typically, connected by network cables or wireless links and data are transmitted as electrical signals. If communication over greater distances is required, a **wide area network** (**WAN**) is set up. A WAN uses links such as telephone lines, fibre-optic cables or satellite links to connect computers over more than one site – possibly between continents. A WAN can connect LANs (see Figure 5.6). The best-known WAN is the Internet; it connects networks and host sites on the World Wide Web. A LAN that has users who need to connect to a WAN requires a **gateway** to connect it up to wider communication. A gateway allows communication between different types of network.

An organisation may provide its workers with access to its information systems by means of a private web server on its LAN. We call such web-based services on a LAN an **intranet** to distinguish them from public web services on the Internet.

It may also be necessary for workers to access the LAN remotely. For example, a sales representative may need access to a customer's records stored on the organisation's intranet while visiting the customer. The sales representative can access the intranet over an Internet connection. It would be unwise to allow public access to

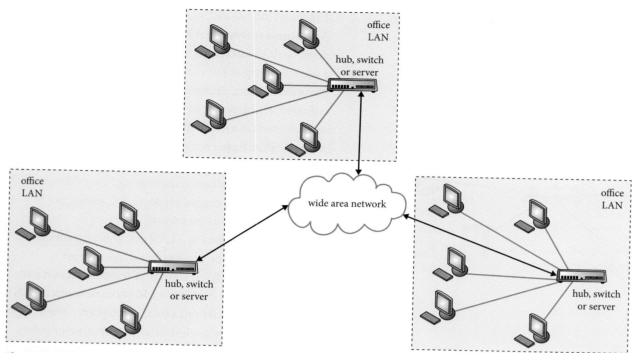

**Figure 5.6** A WAN connecting several LANs.

the intranet, so access must be controlled using usernames and passwords. A firewall would also be employed to restrict access to company employees only. Such an *ex*ternally accessible in*tranet* is known as an **extranet**.

**Questions**

4 Some schools have intranets. They allow students to access the school network from home but control the access so that other people cannot get onto the school system. Find out if your school has such a system. If it has, what is it used for? How can the use be expanded? If it does not have such a system, how could one be established?

## 5.3.4 Control systems

A **control system** consists of one or more computers used to regulate the operation of other devices. It may:

- allow monitoring and recording of physical quantities, such as temperatures or flow rates;
- provide analysis of performance, such as peak or average values;
- allow considerable user interaction.

Control systems are found in application areas such as oil refineries, chemical plants and integrated traffic-control systems (Figure 5.7).

**Figure 5.7** The computerised control console of a power station.

In most control systems, measurements of the results of the control process are used as **feedback** to optimise control under varying conditions (Figure 5.8). For example, if a control system switches on a heater to maintain the temperature of a chemical-reaction vessel as close as possible to a predetermined 'set-point', the system needs to sense the temperature change in the vessel caused by the heater. If the weather is unusually cold, the control system detects that more heat needs to be supplied to approach the set-point.

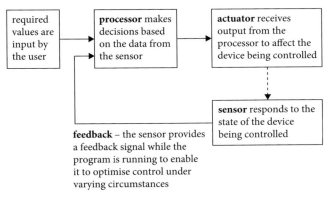

**Figure 5.8** Feedback in a control process.

Delays in sampling and processing the feedback signal tend to result in unwanted oscillations. The feedback signal needs to be sampled at, and processed within, sufficiently short intervals for the control process to be capable of maintaining adequate control over the system. For this reason, control systems are often referred to as 'real-time'. What constitutes real-time is likely to vary between control systems designed to control the temperature of a greenhouse and the core temperature of a nuclear reactor.

A control system requires:
- one or more sufficiently powerful computers;
- one or more control programs;
- suitable sensors for measurement and feedback;
- suitable relays and actuators;
- maybe a keyboard, mouse and display screen.

## Questions

5   Compare Figure 5.8 with Figure 4.2 (page 95). Where are the differences? What do the similarities tell us about a control system?

6   Redraw the diagram in Figure 5.8 to depict a computer used to control the temperature in a room using an air conditioner or a heater. Complete the boxes specifically for the temperature control system.

## 5·3·5 Automated systems

An **automated system** is similar to a control system. However, it is dedicated to a particular task and has limited scope for user interaction to re-configure it. Except in the case of an automatic weather station or data logger, an automated system usually has limited ability to record and analyse data.

As mentioned in Chapter 3, automated systems in appliances such as washing machines and cameras often contain embedded computers (Figure 5.9).

Using a computer to control an automated system has the advantage that if its ROM uses flash technology, improvements in a product's performance can even be made during its lifetime simply by upgrading its firmware. A digital TV receiver, for example, upgrades its firmware automatically, whenever a new version becomes available. Using a microcontroller has the added advantage that it may contain one or more timers, ADCs, DACs, or LAN or USB interfaces so the system may require hardly any additional electronic components.

**Figure 5.9** Camera electronics.

The microcontroller in a washing machine controls the wash cycle. Its automated system could not be used to control the temperature of the water in a fish tank or monitor the conditions in a nuclear reactor. A digital camera also has an automated system for adjusting lens focusing and measuring light in order to set the shutter speed and aperture of the lens. Details of such systems are discussed further in Chapter 7.

An electric oven is a further example of an automated system. The control program accepts a start time, duration and temperature; the oven's microcontroller does the rest – monitoring the temperature and increasing or shutting off the power to the oven's heating elements.

An automated system requires:

- a sufficiently powerful computer – often just a microcontroller;
- a single control program performing a single task with a fixed set of hardware;
- a few buttons or a keypad for input;
- suitable sensors for measurement or feedback;
- suitable relays and actuators.

An automated system may also have a small LCD screen for output. It would probably not have an operating system because it has only a single control program and relatively simple input and output. An operating system would increase development and manufacturing costs.

 ## 5.3.6 Multimedia systems and applications

In this context, a medium is a means of conveying information. There are many different types of media that human beings can recognise and that can be used as part of a human–computer interface. Computer applications use the following main ways to communicate information:

- text;
- audio;
- still images;
- animation;
- video;
- interactivity (such as hyperlinks, hotspots, image maps, buttons and mouseovers).

As we saw in Chapter 3, virtual reality also uses odours and vibration to provide haptic (tactile) feedback.

If a computer uses more than one of these media at a time, it is a **multimedia system**. Strictly speaking, that includes producing a page of text with a picture. However, we normally expect something a little more spectacular of a multimedia system. If your computer allows you to create or play an animation while playing some music, then it is a multimedia computer. A system that produces text with a picture involves only one of our senses, sight. A system that produces animation and music involves both sight and hearing.

If there is a delay of a couple of seconds in displaying an image with some text, it does not matter. A similar delay during an animation or the playing of a tune

distorts the output and may make it unusable. The various forms of output need to be synchronised otherwise the sounds may not match the pictures. To ensure this synchronisation, the computer needs a fast processor. A few years ago, this meant that only very powerful and expensive computers could cope with being multimedia machines. Today, any PC that you buy is powerful enough and all modern PCs can be classed as multimedia systems.

Multimedia authoring programs, such as Adobe Flash, can produce 'movie files' for web pages. Movie files are used for animated advertisements and games, as well as rich Internet applications (RIAs) and computer-aided learning (CAL) files. 'Browser plug-ins' enable a web browser to play the movie files in a web page.

Multimedia presentation programs, such as Microsoft PowerPoint, can produce and display slideshows with multimedia content, animated objects and transition effects between slides. Multimedia applications include presentation slideshows, web browsers, locally installed RIAs for online gaming and applications that involve video capture and virtual reality.

## Questions

 **7** Find the minimum processor clock rate, RAM, graphics memory and screen resolution for:
   **a** a multimedia authoring program;
   **b** a browser plug-in that plays multimedia.

 **8** What hardware might you need, additional to the hardware in a school computer, while testing or playing products of a multimedia authoring program?

 **9** List typical features and uses of presentation slideshows, web browsers, locally installed RIAs for online gaming and applications that involve video capture and virtual reality.

Specialist multimedia systems may require more powerful hardware:

- video-editing systems require a powerful processor with several gibibytes of memory, a dedicated graphics processor and a very large amount of backing storage;

- music production systems require a quiet, powerful processor with several gibibytes of memory, a dedicated sound card, a MIDI keyboard, a large monitor and a large amount of backing storage;
- a games computer requires a powerful processor with several gibibytes of memory, a 1600×1200 monitor, a very powerful dedicated graphics processor (to drive the high-resolution monitor at 35 frames per second) and a sound system.

 **SAQs**

2 Why do some multimedia computer systems need dedicated sound or graphics cards?

3 Why do video-editing systems need a large amount of backing storage? What size might be required for:
   a an individual;
   b a school?

## Summary

- A batch system processes a large amount of data as one job without operator intervention, usually at an off-peak time (e.g. overnight or at the weekend), to produce output that is not time-dependent.
- An interactive system allows users to interact directly with the running programs to influence the course of processing.
- An interactive system may have a single user or multiple simultaneous users.
- A network system uses network operating systems to allow two or more computers to share controlled access to facilities such as file storage, servers and printers.
- Three basic network topologies are bus, ring and star.
- A network may cover a local area (LAN) or a wide area (WAN).
- A control system runs one or more control programs that receive measurement and feedback from suitable sensors and activate actuators and user interface devices to regulate the operation of other devices.
- A control system monitors and records physical quantities, analyses performance and may enable user interaction.
- A control system is a 'real-time' system – it must be able to respond within a specified time to changes in conditions.
- Control systems are used in oil refineries, chemical plants and for integrated traffic control.
- An automated system is a microcontroller embedded in a specific device, running a single control program for a fixed set of hardware.
- An automated system includes sensors, actuators and a user interface with limited scope for interaction.
- Automated systems are used in washing machines, cameras and electric ovens.
- Multimedia include text, audio, still images, animation, video and interactivity.
- Multimedia software includes authoring programs for 'movie files', Rich Internet Applications (RIAs), multimedia player plug-ins and presentation programs.
- Multimedia applications include presentation slideshows, web browsers, locally installed RIAs for online gaming and applications that involve video capture and VR.

# Examination practice for Paper 1

## Exam Questions

1. Explain, with an example, the computer term 'batch processing'. [2]

   *Part of Question 1, Cambridge IGCSE Computer Studies 0420/01 Paper 11 May/June 2010*

2. Networks can have ring, bus or star topologies.

   (a) Draw and name diagrams to show **two** of these networks. [2]

   (b) Give **one** advantage of each chosen network. [2]

   *Question 13, Cambridge IGCSE Computer Studies 0420/01 Paper 11 May/June 2010*

3. Some microprocessor-controlled devices do not need an operating system.

   (i) Give **one** example of such a device. [1]

   (ii) Give **one** reason why it does not need an operating system. [1]

   *Part of Question 3, Cambridge IGCSE Computer Studies 0420/01 Paper 1 May/June 2009*

## Exam-Style Questions

1. Many computer systems are interactive.

   (a) Name **one** example of application software that is interactive. [1]

   (b) Explain, with an example, **one** advantage to the user of interactive application software. [2]

2. Explain what is meant by a 'local area network' (LAN). [2]

3. Control systems are more sophisticated than simpler automated systems.

   (a) State **two** features of a control system that would not be found in an automated system. [2]

   (b) Explain why control systems are often described as 'real-time'. [2]

# The system life cycle

Note that the whole of Section 2 of the syllabus is tested lightly in Paper 1 and in much more detail in Papers 2 (Coursework Project) and 3 (Alternative to Coursework). Each section in this chapter has a Coursework feature that tells you what you need to do for Paper 2. For Paper 3, you should practise producing similar work for the pre-released outline scenario. This outline scenario will only be very general, such as a 'database about ordering and stock control', but you can also use the scenario in the specimen Paper 3 question on page 284 or ask your teacher if you can use the scenario from a past paper.

## 2.1 Overview

An organisation may realise that one of its manual or computerised systems has problems. The organisation becomes the 'client' of a **systems analyst**. The analyst studies the system to determine where the problems are and how the system can be improved. The analyst then plans the development of the solution. Where a software solution is appropriate, the analyst hands the plans to a software development team. The team designs, builds and tests the solution. The analyst also plans how the new system will be implemented and maintained. This whole process is known as the **system life cycle**. It is referred to as a 'cycle', because it is often necessary to return to the beginning and repeat the process in the future. There are many different approaches to the cycle.

The current *IGCSE Computer Studies* syllabus summarises the stages of the cycle as:

- fact finding;
- feasibility study;

- analysis;
- design;
- building and testing;
- documentation;
- implementation (changeover);
- evaluation;
- maintenance.

The process of working sequentially through the stages is often called the **waterfall model** (Figure 6.1). This model shows progress as flowing steadily in one direction: downwards. Figure 6.1 does not include all the stages listed as part of the cycle. It is sensible to complete the fact finding and the feasibility study before starting on the stages of the waterfall model – once they are complete, their results may need to be revisited but they will not change during the rest of the life cycle. Documentation is not written in a specific stage – it is ongoing throughout the whole process. The important thing is not just to be able to copy the diagram in an examination, but to understand what the stages are and why they are in a certain order.

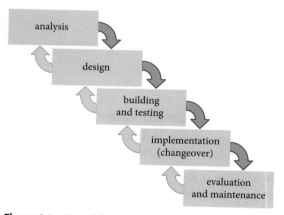

**Figure 6.1**  Waterfall model of the system life cycle.

It would not be sensible to work rigidly through the sequence of stages in Figure 6.1. People working on a project often reach the design stage and realise that they have to go back and find out something that was omitted in the analysis stage. Or they may find that something does not work as expected during software development, so they have to go back and modify the design. Sometimes the client changes the requirements, requiring changes to the

design and any subsequent work. In order to allow for going back to a previous stage to improve the outcome, 'water' in this 'waterfall' sometimes has to flow uphill!

## Defining the problem

A vital pre-requisite stage to solving any problem does not appear in the list of stages or in Figure 6.1: defining the problem properly. If a maths teacher asks you to produce an electronic mark book, the problem seems to be fairly simple to understand. So why not get on with going through the stages of the system life cycle?

Unless you make a lot of assumptions, you will soon have to ask: 'What is wrong with the current system?' Unless you obtain a detailed answer to this question, you are very likely to present the teacher (your client) with a solution that does not do what they expected. If you were a systems analyst in the real world, your professional reputation and payment would depend on satisfying, or even exceeding, your client's expectations.

The systems analyst and the client should each use their knowledge to ensure that the initial problem is properly understood. Only then can work start on finding a satisfactory solution. In this example, it may be that the teacher finds it difficult to make neat corrections in a paper mark book, that it is time-consuming and error-prone to calculate percentages or average marks and that it is difficult to include comments on students' work.

It should not be so challenging that you are doomed to failure. Your teacher can offer you guidance in the light of understanding your strengths and weaknesses.

A strong hobby or business interest may provide a suitable challenge. If not, do not invent an imaginary user; they will not set you a challenging problem! Talk to someone older than you, with experience of good ways of dealing with everyday business, domestic or social record-keeping or accounting transactions, who can provide you with a realistic problem. For example, talk to a parent, teacher or friend about their needs in the workplace or in managing a club activity or a hobby collection. The problem may involve a paper-based system that would benefit from computerisation or a computerised system that needs improvement or extension.

The *Guidance on the coursework* document on the Student CD-ROM contains further guidance on all the stages of the project. The 'Selecting the problem' section provides guidance on this step and on planning your work. The 'Write-up' section provides guidance on how to organise your written work.

## 2.1 Fact finding

An analyst must collect information about the system that has problems. The information will provide the basis for both a feasibility study and an in-depth analysis of the system in order to produce a solution. The analyst seeks answers to questions such as:

- what data are collected?
- what quantity of data is collected?
- how are the data collected and entered?
- how are the data stored and processed after entry?

For example, the teacher mentioned in the previous section may have made quite clear what they expect in their mark book, but the analyst will still have questions: How many students are there in each class? How many classes are there? Should the files be protected? Should copies be made in case the files are lost?

Information can be collected in a number of ways (Figure 6.2):

- **Observation of current procedures**: The systems analyst can learn a lot from simply watching what happens in the existing system. The advantages are numerous. It is possible to see exactly what is done, so that the analyst obtains reliable information. Little planning is necessary because it does not involve working directly with other people. It may be relatively quick and cheap to carry out. The disadvantages are that people tend not to work in the normal way if they know they are being watched – in particular, workers are unlikely to perform their usual 'workarounds' that do not conform to standard procedures. Also, if the observation is too brief it may give a false impression of what people spend most of their time doing.

- **Interview**: If the systems analyst wants to ask in-depth questions about what works well and, particularly, what works less well in the system, the obvious thing to do is to ask the people who use it. This should include the people who operate the system, as well as managers who receive information from it. An obvious advantage is that questions do not have to be completely fixed in advance. The analyst is able to alter the questions depending on the interviewee's precise role and their answers to previous questions. A simple example would be a question asking about the data that need to be stored. If the person being interviewed says that it is necessary to store data about their customers, the next question may be about security and privacy of this information: 'Does that mean that we need to protect the information by placing a password on the file?' On the other hand, if the reply is that the data stored are details of stock, the follow-up question might be: 'How often do the stock details change?' Other advantages are that the analyst may be able to encourage interviewees to give full and frank answers to questions. The disadvantages are that interviewing takes a lot of time and is, therefore, expensive and that interviewees cannot remain completely anonymous.

- **Questionnaire**: The analyst can give a questionnaire to all workers and even to some clients of the organisation. Advantages include the following.

Recipients feel that their views are valued. Questions can be answered quickly while allowing the recipient the opportunity to think about their answers. Recipients can remain anonymous. It is quick to analyse the answers obtained. Overall, a questionnaire is a relatively cheap way of obtaining information from a large number of people. Disadvantages are as follows. It is difficult to design an effective questionnaire. The questions cannot be changed halfway through the process. There is no direct method of asking for clarification of an answer. Some recipients may not take it seriously or even answer the questionnaire at all.

- **Inspection of documents**: The analyst can examine existing system documentation, written procedures or instruction manuals, data collection forms, log sheets and printed output from the system. An advantage is that the analyst can often gain information not obtained by any other method. A disadvantage is that documents are often difficult to understand for someone from outside the organisation, so it may be necessary to ask someone to explain them in an interview. Other disadvantages are that documents may say one thing, while people do something else and it can be a very time-consuming exercise.

**Figure 6.2** Fact-finding methods. **a** Observation. **b** Interview. **c** Questionnaires. **d** Documents.

1 In the scenarios below, each of the owners wants to install a new stock control system. Discuss how the analyst would collect information in each case, justifying your choice of method of collection.

a A small general store wants to install a computerised stock control system. All stock control has been done manually until now. The owner is the only person who works in the shop.

b A dress shop has used a computerised system for some time for selling items and giving receipts to customers. However, the stock is controlled manually. The owner looks after all the ordering of stock and record keeping but does not work in the shop. The owner has decided that she wants some help in dealing with suppliers and stock control in the shop. There are six shop workers.

c A large supermarket uses a fully computerised stock system together with POS terminals. The owner has decided that the present system needs updating, mainly because a rival supermarket has installed a more modern system. The supermarket stocks in excess of 30,000 items. More than 100 people work in the supermarket, some as shop assistants, some as supervisors, some in the accounts department and others in site management.

## Coursework

### Fact-finding methods

You should be able to justify the choice of suitable fact-finding methods. You can start by listing the advantages and disadvantages of each method for your problem and then decide which methods are appropriate for your purpose.

$\longrightarrow$

*Coursework continued …*

You need to decide when, where and how to use your chosen methods. You could start by making lists of observations to make, questions to ask and documents to examine. Then you can plan suitable arrangements for your fact-finding operation and carry it out, making careful notes. If you forget something, you may have to go back.

For **Paper 3**, you should practise writing a list of appropriate methods, why they are appropriate and how they could be used for the pre-release scenario.

## 2.1 Feasibility study

A feasibility study is a preliminary investigation of a problem. An organisation uses a feasibility study to decide whether a solution is feasible (possible) and what effects it might have. The terms of reference of a feasibility study define the objectives, boundaries and constraints of budget or time for the study. A feasibility study report includes:

- a description of the existing system, its problems and estimated costs;
- success criteria, such as the essential requirements and desirable features of the new system;
- an outline of possible solutions;
- a proposed solution;
- a development plan;
- a cost/benefit analysis.

The section of the report that considers the possible solutions will answer some or all of the following questions:

- Is the technology available to solve the problem? If it is not possible to solve the problem because a robot capable of carrying out the required actions does not exist then the problem needs to be redefined to take this into account or the solution should be abandoned.
- Is the solution economically possible? If the feasibility study finds that the solution requires more initial expenditure than the organisation can afford or that the running costs will make the organisation's products uncompetitive, then it is not sensible to continue.
- What are the likely social effects of the solution? If the solution is to computerise a production line then

a large number of people may be put out of work. Government authorities and employee organisations may object.

- Does the organisation have enough people with the correct skills to run the new system? If not, then at the very least the added cost of training will have to be considered
- What is the effect on the client? If the client sees no improvement, then is there any point in delivering the solution in the first place?

When a feasibility study has been produced, it should have enough information to allow the analyst and the client to make a sensible decision to carry on with the project or to abandon it. If the client approves the project, the analyst carries out a more comprehensive fact-finding exercise for a full analysis of the system.

## 2.1 Analysis stage

The first step in the **systems analysis** stage is to use the fact-finding methods to collect any further information needed to form a thorough understanding of the current system. There will be a large amount of information and it is helpful to divide it into three groups: data input, processing requirements and information output. Diagrams are often a useful way of summarising this information.

### Dataflow diagrams

It is often useful to draw a diagram to show where the various data come from, where they are stored, how they are processed and where they go. A diagram that shows all this information is a **dataflow diagram** (**DFD**). It is not necessary for you to be able to draw complex DFDs but you should be able to follow the logic and draw a simple diagram to illustrate the dataflow in your project work. There are many different versions of the symbols used in DFDs, but the symbols shown in Table 6.1 are widely used.

**Table 6.1** Dataflow diagram symbols.

| Symbol | Meaning | Example | Description |
|---|---|---|---|
| (oval) | An entity (a person or external organisation) that provides data or receives information | Teacher | The teacher provides the raw marks and uses the output information. |
| (process box) | A processing step: sequence number and process description | 2 / Sort marks in descending order | Process 2 sorts the marks in order. |
| (store box) | Storage of data: device type (e.g. D for disk drive, CB for manual cashbook), serial number of the device and file name | D2 StudentMarks | Data are stored on disk drive 2 in the StudentMarks file. |

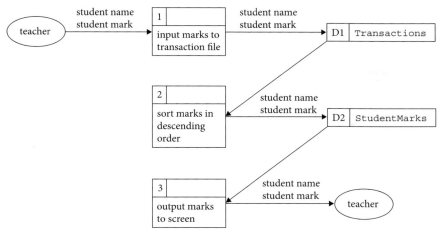

**Figure 6.3** Partial dataflow diagram for an electronic mark book.

The partial DFD in Figure 6.3 illustrates the flows of data for an electronic mark book. Each arrow representing a dataflow is labelled with a list of the data items being transferred. To avoid arrows looping back from output to input, the *same* entity, in this case 'Teacher', can be represented by more than one symbol.

## System flowcharts

A **system flowchart** is a diagram that places more emphasis on the different sorts of hardware used for input, storage and output. It also uses separate symbols for each sort of processing performed by the user or software, but still only describes processing in a general way and does not go down to a fine level of detail. As well as dataflow, the arrows can represent the 'flow of control' to and from terminator symbols.

Generic application software may have drawing tools for system flowchart symbols. Sometimes it also has 'connectors', which are lines and arrows that you can attach to the symbols. These lines move automatically when you adjust the positions of the symbols. Table 6.2 shows the most common symbols.

**Table 6.2** System flowchart symbols.

| Symbol | Name | Description or example |
|---|---|---|
| | Terminator | Start and end of the flowchart |
| | Manual operation | Data collection |
| | Input/output operation | Input or output of data |
| | Manual input | Keyboard entry of data |
| | Data processing operation | Manipulation or calculation of data to produce useful information |
| | Sort | Put data into alphabetical, chronological or numeric order |

**Table 6.2** *Continued*

| Symbol | Name | Description or example |
|---|---|---|
| | Merge | Join two files together |
| | Collate | Combine data into ordered sets |
| | Visual display unit | Monitor screen |
| | Document output | Printed hard copy |
| | Online storage | A device that is connected and available but the type of hardware is not specified |
| | File on hard disk | A named file |
| | File on magnetic tape | A named file |
| | Communication line | Telephone line |
| | Connectors | Link to or from another part of the diagram on the same page |
| | Connectors | Link to or from another part of the diagram on another page |

System flowcharts are easier to read if the data entry operations are situated at the left or top, data processing operations in the middle and storage and output operations on the right or bottom. A system flowchart for the electronic mark book is shown in Figure 6.4.

## Requirements specification

The next step is for the analyst to collate all the system requirements that have been identified during negotiations with the client. This list of system requirements must be translated into precise details of what the new system must do.

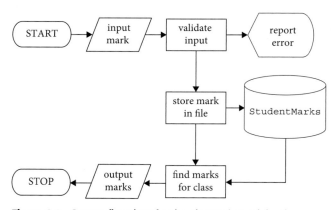

**Figure 6.4** System flowchart for the electronic mark book.

In consultation with the client, the analyst specifies:

- the services and functions that the new system will provide;
- the data items that need to be stored, with appropriate validation checks;
- the performance required in terms of data capacity, accuracy, security, reliability, response time, throughput and accessibility;
- any constraints on the design, such as how the organisation performs calculations, whether data should be stored in any particular format, and whether particular types of hardware or software should be used.

This **requirements specification** lists everything that the organisation has decided it needs and that the analyst has agreed can be delivered on time and on budget. The agreed requirements specification can be passed to a system designer, together with any sample data that the analyst has collected from the current system. The requirements specification must state, clearly and completely, what the system designer needs to achieve. Ideally, the system designer should not need to carry out further analysis activities.

## SAQs

1  What two documents need to be agreed by the end of the analysis stage? What do you think would happen if the client does not agree them?

## Questions

3  Look again at the three scenarios in Question 1:
   a  a small general store
   b  a dress shop
   c  a large supermarket.
   For each, consider ways in which the information collected can be represented. Also think about the information that is likely to be included in the requirements specification for each example.

## Coursework

### Analysis

You do not need to include a DFD or a system flowchart, although it may help. Your project report should:

- describe the background to the business or organisation (name?, type?, size?, what?, where?);
- describe the nature of the problem to be solved (what goes wrong?, when who does what?);
- describe the current system in detail, including data input (data capture methods and data dictionary, if applicable), data storage, processing and output;
- evaluate the current system, including its strengths, weaknesses and any suggested improvements;
- describe your proposed solution and at least *one* other possible solution.
- state an overview of your proposed system;
- list testable **objectives** for your proposed system, including areas such as navigation, menus, command buttons, input and associated validation and verification, storage, processing and output; objectives should use:
  - computer-related terms to state what you will provide;
  - general business terms to state what benefit you aim to achieve, for example:
    'I will provide a ____ to search a customer ____ to save ____ searching for a customer's ____ when answering a ____ enquiry';

The 'Analysis' section in the *Guidance on the coursework* document on the Student CD-ROM provides further guidance on this stage.

For **Paper 3**, you could practise drawing a DFD and a system flowchart and listing items for a requirements specification.

### 2.1  Design stage

The client should be consulted during the design stage to ensure that all the work really meets the requirements.

### 6.2  Planning

As soon as the system life cycle commences, it is necessary to plan and monitor the project in terms of expenditure of time and money and the use of human and physical resources. This requires project management skills.

Project management software is a useful tool that provides various sorts of diagram to visualise a project plan. A Project Evaluation and Review Technique (PERT) chart is a network of arrows representing stages of the project between circular nodes representing events marking the completion of stages. A Gantt chart (Figure 6.5), named after its inventor, is based on a calendar. It shows the durations of tasks and dependencies between tasks. It is relatively easy to understand and use. Even if you do not have time to learn to use project management software, you can produce something similar in a spreadsheet (or a word-processed table) with a series of dates as column headings and shaded cells. A Gantt chart created in project management software allows you to record the information listed in Table 6.3.

Some project management software has a feature to publish project updates to an intranet or to automatically email updates to relevant personnel.

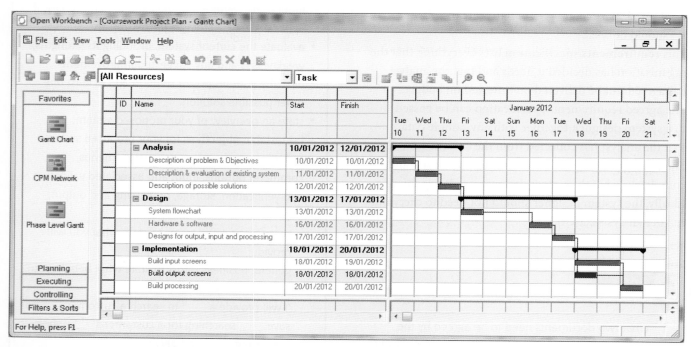

**Figure 6.5**   An incomplete project plan in a Gantt chart.

**Table 6.3**   Information in a Gantt chart.

| Information | Representation | Description |
|---|---|---|
| Phase | A horizontal bracket | A stage in a project (e.g. Analysis, Design) |
| Task | A coloured bar | The basic unit of work |
| Activity | A horizontal bracket | An optional group of tasks that form a 'sub-phase' |
| Time allocated | A coloured bar | Measured in days across dated columns |
| Milestone | A diamond marker | A significant event or date, against which progress is measured |
| Dependency | 'Waterfall' arrows between tasks | Waterfall arrows between bars show where one or more tasks cannot be started until another task has finished |
| Critical path | Colour-coding, usually red | The sequence of dependent tasks that determines the overall duration of the project |
| Progress on tasks | A percentage or a line on the task | The amount of the task completed, relative to the planned time |

### Introduction to the design process

Many people think that when you design something you should use a pencil, ruler, eraser and paper. There is nothing wrong with doing this, but when you consider the number of different design tools that are available on the computer, it often makes sense to draw the design straight onto the screen. It is certainly quicker to copy-and-paste similar elements of your design than to copy them by hand and, depending on your degree of skill with the software, making major amendments is also likely to be quicker.

### Selection of software

The sort of software to be used for the proposed solution is usually selected early in the design stage, as it has consequences for the rest of the design. The initial choice is between customising a generic application program or writing a bespoke program in a programming language. Further choices involve styles of user interface and file structures for data.

### Output screen forms and printed reports

All computer systems involve input, storage, processing and output. The designer starts by deciding what the output will look like. It may seem odd to start from what appears to be the end of the process but the purpose of the designer's role is to design a system that produces the set of outcomes (Figure 6.6) identified by the analyst and agreed with the client. Once the output has been designed, it is clear what inputs are needed to provide the data to produce the outputs.

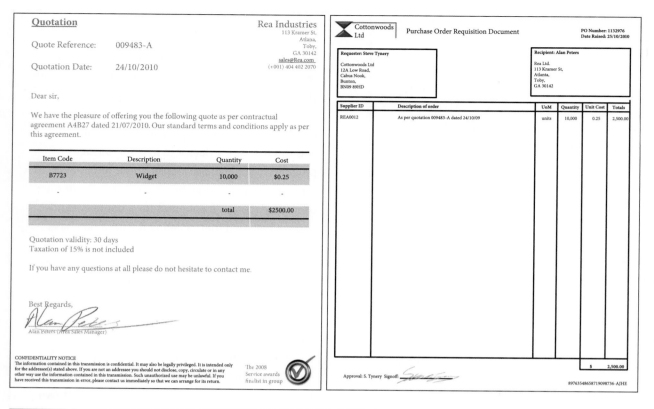

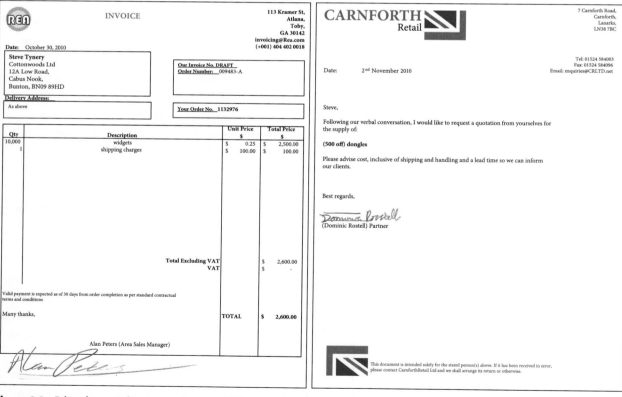

**Figure 6.6** Printed output forms are often part of the user's requirements.

Once the inputs have been decided, it is then possible to design the input screens that will capture the required data. After this, the processing that turns the input data into outputs is designed.

Imagine that an analyst has been asked to plan the development of a system that will allow call centre workers for a mail order company to take orders over the phone. The company's managers are only concerned with whether the workers can search to see if stock is available and then place an order. They are not really interested in how the system does it. The designer will design the output screens and then produce what is known as a **prototype**. It will not work yet because no processing has been designed and there is no data! The prototype is good enough for the management and workers to be able to tell whether it will be suitable for the tasks that they want it to do.

The following issues should be considered when designing on-screen forms for a system:

- a layout should use the entire area of the screen;
- too much detail should not be placed on a single screen;
- to draw attention to text, it can be made to flash or can be in a different colour;
- account should be taken of the contrast between the text colour and the background colour otherwise it will not be easy to read;
- the content of the output must be understood by the people who are going to use it.

At all stages, the management and the workers who will use the system must be able to comment on the acceptability of the screen designs.

The client may decide that the company logo must appear on every screen and that the corporate colour scheme should be used for the backgrounds. One of the workers may be colour-blind and some colour schemes should not be used. This sort of detail should have been found out in the analysis stage but it is sometimes missed. These things would force the designer to go back to the systems analyst and request a change in the requirements specification and, hence, the design.

## Coursework

### Output designs

Your output designs form part of your 'method of solution'. To gain full marks, they need to be described clearly and in detail. In your project report, you should draw, with a pencil or a computer, your designs for:

- output spreadsheets, charts or screen forms;
- any printed reports;
- any other form of output.

Your drawings should be clearly annotated using keys, footnotes and callouts (text boxes with arrows).

You should *not* include screenshots of outputs that you have started to prototype; a design is meant to be drawn or listed *before* any building takes place.

The 'Description of method of solution' section in the *Guidance on the coursework* document on the Student CD-ROM provides further guidance on this step.

For **Paper 3**, you could practise hand-drawing and annotating output screens and printed reports.

### Input screens

Once output has been designed, it is clearer what the data inputs should be. Once decisions have been made about the data that are required, the designer has to decide how the data will be collected and what method of data input should be used:

- Can automatic data capture be used? For example, will a sensor tell the system when someone enters a building or what the temperature of a process is?
- Will questionnaires be used as data collection forms? If so, should they be designed so that the answers can be automatically captured by a special OMR or OCR machine?
- Is the data going to be entered by someone using a keyboard and a screen?

It is then possible to design the data entry screen forms (Figure 6.7). These input screens go through the same prototyping process as the output screen forms.

When data are put into the system they need to be checked for validity and correctness because any computer system can only be as good as the data that

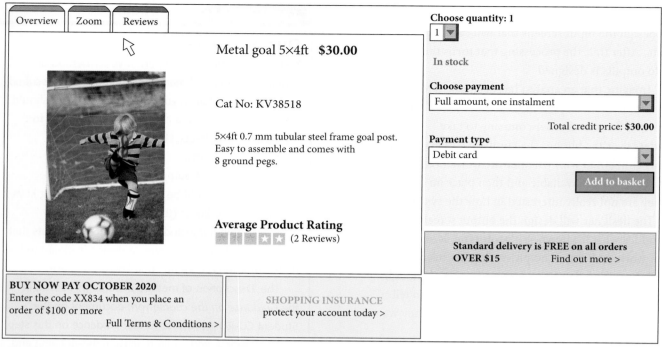

**Figure 6.7** An input form.

are used in it. As we saw in Chapter 2, validation checks are set up to apply programmed rules to check that the data being entered are sensible and reasonable. Verification checks are sometimes also set up to check the correctness of data. Error messages for these checks should be user-friendly, informing the user what the problem is and how to correct it.

## Coursework

### Input designs

Your input designs form part of your 'method of solution'. To gain full marks, they need to be described clearly and in detail. In your project report, you should draw, with a pencil or a computer, your designs for:
- input spreadsheets or screen forms;
- any other form of input.

Your drawings should be clearly annotated using keys, footnotes and callouts (text boxes with arrows).

You should *not* include screenshots of inputs that you have started to prototype: a design is meant to be drawn or listed *before* any building takes place.

→

*Coursework continued …*

You should also list:
- validation rules and informative error messages;
- verification methods and informative error messages.

The 'Description of method of solution' section in the *Guidance on the coursework* document on the Student CD-ROM provides further guidance on this step.

For **Paper 3**, you could practise hand-drawing and annotating input screens and listing appropriate validation and verification methods.

### Data storage

Now that the designer knows what the input and output are going to be, it is possible to design the data storage. Drawing also on the information about data and security in the requirements specification, the storage design should include:
- file types to be used by generic application software;
- file structures (see page 137) for any files that program code will have to manipulate;
- the structure of any database tables and their relationships;
- methods of controlling access to the data;
- the hardware needed for data storage and backup.

## Data storage designs

Your data storage designs form part of your 'method of solution'. To gain full marks, they need to be described clearly and in detail. In your project report, you should describe:

- the file types to be used by generic application software;
- the structures for any files that program code will manipulate;
- the structure of any database tables and their relationships;
- methods of controlling access to the data;
- the hardware needed for data storage and backup.

You should also draw, with a pencil or computer, your design for any relationships between database tables. Your drawings should be clearly annotated using keys, footnotes and callouts (text boxes with arrows).

You should *not* include any screenshots of any storage structures that you may have started to prototype, since a design is meant to be drawn or listed *before* any building takes place.

The 'Description of method of solution' section in the *Guidance on the coursework* document on the Student CD-ROM provides further guidance on this step.

For **Paper 3**, you could practise describing possible storage structures.

**4** Look again at the three scenarios in Question 1:

**a** a small general store;

**b** a dress shop;

**c** a large supermarket.

For each, decide on the important points about the output from and input to the system. What validation of the data input will be necessary? What form will the output take? What data needs to be stored? What are the important features of the data and how will these affect the hardware and the structure of the data files? How will the data be accessed?

**3.1.2** ## Top-down processing design

Finally, the designer can design how the input data should be processed to produce the outputs required. At this point there should be a good understanding of the system design and of how the different parts work together to achieve the required results.

If the solution to a problem is relatively simple, it can be thought of as single solution. If the problem is complex then the solution may be too complicated to think of all at once. It makes sense to split the solution into a number of steps that can then form a solution to the whole problem.

Consider the example of the electronic mark book. It is necessary to sort the marks into order and then print them out. The solution could be split into a number of steps: input the marks; sort them into numerical order; output the results. The input of the marks could be further split up into validating the marks that are input and then storing them on a file ready for use. Each time we split a solution into smaller steps, each step becomes easier to build in software.

A **structure diagram** (Figure 6.8), can document this **top-down design**. We start with the whole problem at the top of the diagram and divide it into simpler and simpler steps as we move down the diagram. We read the sequence of steps at any level from left to right. We study structure diagrams as a tool for top-down design again in Chapter 9.

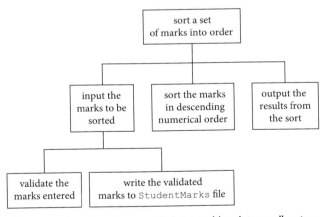

**Figure 6.8** Structure diagram splitting a problem into smaller steps.

Other advantages of designing the solution to a problem like this are:

- instead of one large solution, there are a number of smaller solutions, so each smaller solution can be given to a different member of a team of programmers;

- the smaller solutions are much shorter so there should be fewer errors and when they have been built they are easier to test and debug;
- many problems require the same smaller solutions.

It makes sense to save individual sections of program code, known as routines or **modules**, and re-use them when they are needed in another program. A module can conveniently be made available for re-use by adding it to a collection of modules, saved as a software **library file**.

## Questions

5 Look again at the three scenarios in Question 1:
   a a small general store;
   b a dress shop;
   c a large supermarket.
   For each, decide how the processing can be divided into modules if you were to follow a top-down design process.

## Coursework

### Processing design

Your processing design forms part of your 'method of solution'. To gain full marks, it needs to be described clearly and in detail. In your project report, you should draw, with a pencil or computer:
- a structure diagram for your top-down design;
- spreadsheet formulae or database queries on grids;
- algorithms in the form of flowcharts for program code that you will write.

You should also list:
- steps for macros that you will record;
- algorithms written in pseudocode for program code that you will write.

Your drawings should be clearly annotated using keys, footnotes and callouts (text boxes with arrows). At least one module of **pseudocode** or query code should be annotated to explain it, preferably using comments within the code.

You should *not* include any screenshots of any structures that you may have started to prototype, since a design is meant to be drawn or listed *before* any building takes place.

$\longrightarrow$

*Coursework continued ...*

The 'Description of method of solution' section in the *Guidance on the coursework* document on the Student CD-ROM provides further guidance on this step.

For **Paper 3**, you could practise drawing and listing processing design.

### Command buttons and menus

Menu design should include, as a minimum, appropriate command buttons on screen forms for navigation and processing. It may be possible to customise the menu system of generic application software or bespoke software forms. It may also be appropriate to design a 'main menu' (Figure 6.9) or 'start-up user interface'. This opens when the application runs and the user can return to it, to help them navigate the available options. It makes the application user-friendly.

**Figure 6.9** A main menu.

## Coursework

### Command button and menu designs

Your command button and menu designs form part of your 'method of solution'. To gain full marks, they need to be described clearly and in detail. In your project report, you should draw, with a pencil or computer, your designs for:
- command buttons on screen forms for navigation and processing;
- a 'main menu' or 'start-up user interface'.

$\longrightarrow$

*Coursework continued …*

Your drawings should be clearly annotated using keys, footnotes and callouts (text boxes with arrows).

You should *not* include any screenshots of anything that you may have started to prototype, since a design is meant to be drawn or listed *before* any building takes place.

You should also list any menu options for customising the menu system of generic application software or of bespoke software forms.

The 'Description of method of solution' section in the *Guidance on the coursework* document on the Student CD-ROM provides further guidance on this step.

For **Paper 3**, you could practise producing similar designs.

## Selection of hardware

It is possible that the old hardware for input, storage, processing and output will be good enough for the new solution. This is unlikely. The new hardware should be specified and ordered from suppliers.

### Coursework

## Selection of hardware and system flowchart

You need to select suitable hardware for input, storage including backup, processing and output for your proposed solution. This may include selecting one or more of the standard keyboard, computer and hard disk drive, display screen and loudspeakers or headphones available at school, with a USB flash drive for backup storage. You simply have to be able to justify their use for positive reasons.

In your project report, you should:
• list all the hardware you will use;
• justify each choice, by explaining why the device is needed for your proposed solution.

A table, with columns for the device and the reason, is a neat way of presenting this information.

$\longrightarrow$

*Coursework continued …*

The 'Hardware' and 'System flowchart' sections in the *Guidance on the coursework* document on the Student CD-ROM provides further guidance on this step.

Now that you have completed your design choices, you also need to produce a complete system flowchart for your proposed system, using the correct symbols (see Table 6.2, pages 123–4).

For **Paper 3**, you should practise justifying similar choices and hand-drawing a system flowchart.

## Selection of a test strategy and creation of a test plan

The purpose of testing a solution is to ensure that it meets the requirements specification. If the requirements specification and designs are clear enough, it should be possible to design the required tests before any software has been built. This is better than designing the tests after the software has been produced, as there might then be a tendency to make the tests fit the software, rather than the other way around.

A **test strategy** is a statement of the sorts of test necessary. One approach is to test the navigation, menus and command buttons, input and associated validation and verification, storage, processing and output. If bespoke software is to be written in modules, the strategy will probably include 'unit testing' of each module, followed by 'integration testing' of the complete system.

Unfortunately, you cannot test whether a piece of software will always work. Imagine a simple program that adds two numbers together. A sensible test to see if it works would be to input the numbers 3 and 4. If the software gives the answer 7, it passes the test. What about 5 and 9? What about 7 and 3.5? An infinite number of tests need to be carried out to show that the software always works, but that would be impossible to perform. A better approach to testing is to try to think of tests that will expose weaknesses in the software. When these tests are carried out and the software does not fail then you can be fairly confident that the software works. It may be motivational to arrange for test engineers to compete against programmers to try to 'break' the programmers' software.

**Test data** are data items that are specially chosen to test that a particular aspect of the system is working. For example, consider a system that allows examination marks out of 100 to be entered. A validation check is set up to ensure that marks greater than 100 are rejected. A test to show that the validation check is working might be to input a mark of 105 and see what happens. There are three sorts of test data:

- **normal data** – valid data that should be accepted by validation checks (for example, 87);
- **extreme data** – valid data at the limits of acceptability (for example, 100);
- **abnormal (erroneous) data** – invalid data that should be rejected by one or more validation checks and produce error messages (for example, 105).

Three types of test data can also be used with conditional processing; for example, calculating a fine only if the number of days overdue is greater than zero. It is probably also necessary to test whether a slight excess over the expected volume of data causes a problem. In the example of the electronic mark book, the system has been designed to work for 30 students in a class. What if another student joins the class: will the added volume of data make the system fail? To obtain sufficient data for this test, it is probably easier to use some **real data** supplied by the client during the analysis stage than to generate the required amount of test data.

Navigation in an area of a system with a GUI still needs testing. It is unlikely to require text or numerical data since a mouse will be used to click on a command button or menu option.

Following the strategy, it is possible to write a tabular **test plan** as shown in Table 6.4. The client has to be convinced that the new system works as agreed, so the test plan must be rigorous. If the testing follows the test plan and the results are satisfactory, the client will be satisfied with the product.

## Questions

6  In a new computer-based, customer database system, the customer's street name was defined as a text field of length 20 characters, including spaces. Give one example of each type of test data that should be used in the test plan. Can you foresee a problem with this choice of length?

7  Look again at the three scenarios in Question 1:
   a  a small general store;
   b  a dress shop;
   c  a large supermarket.

For each, consider the important parts of the test strategy. What areas of the proposed solution need to be tested? What validation testing is needed? What test data would it be sensible to include in the test plan? Is it any more important to test the third application than the first application?

**Table 6.4**  Part of a test plan: in this example, three tests are related to one objective of the test strategy.

| Test No. | Objective No. | Item tested | Method | Type of test data | Test data | Expected result |
|---|---|---|---|---|---|---|
| 4 | 3 | Customer first name length check: between 1 and 15 characters | Keyboard entry | Normal | Sunesh (6 characters) | Accepted |
| 5 | 3 | Customer first name length check: between 1 and 15 characters | Keyboard entry | Extreme | Adelaida-Sophia (15 characters) | Accepted |
| 6 | 3 | Customer first name length check: between 1 and 15 characters | Keyboard entry | Abnormal | Suneshhhhhhhhhhh (16 characters) | Rejected with error message |

## 2.2 Building and testing stage

One or more programmers use the designs to build and test the software, ideally without any further design activities. Figure 6.10 shows a fragment of program code.

 **SAQs**

2   What are two advantages of developing solutions in modules?

Once the software is built, the appropriate hardware and software should be installed and tested according to the test plan. A convenient way of displaying the test results is to repeat the relevant row from the test plan, followed by 'before' and 'after' screenshot evidence and a comment (Figure 6.11). When you test the system creating printed output, the actual output should be included as the 'after' evidence.

If testing shows that part of the solution does not work properly, the programmer, designer or analyst needs to go back to find the area of building, design or analysis that caused the problem and have another look at it, taking into account the test results. Changes may be needed to the design, the requirements specification, or both.

```
Sub DuplicateCurrentRow()

' Keyboard shortcut: Ctrl+Shift+D

    Selection.EntireRow.Insert                          ' Insert a new row at current selection
    ActiveCell.Offset(1, 0).Rows ("1:1").EntireRow.Select   ' Select the row below
    Selection.Copy                                      ' Copy the selected row
    ActiveCell.Offset(-1, 0).Range ("A1").Select        ' Select the new row above
    ActiveSheet.Paste                                   ' Paste the copied row
    Application. CutCopyMode = False                     ' Exit copy mode
    Cells(Selection.Row, 4).Select                      ' Select column D in the current row

End Sub
```

```
Sub CopyTopicToNextEmptyCell ()

' Keyboard Shortcut:Ctrl+Shift+T

    Cells(Selection. Row, 5).Select             ' Select current row, column E
    Selection.Copy                              ' Copy the selected cell
    Selection.End(x1Down).Select                ' Select the last occupied cell below - ASSUMPTION!
    ActiveCell.Offset (1, 0).Range ("A1").Select  ' Select the cell below
    ActiveSheet.Paste                           ' Paste the copied cell

End Sub
```

**Figure 6.10**   Two pieces of program code. Notice that the code is thoroughly commented.

| Test No. | Objective No. | Item tested | Method | Type of test data | Test data | Expected result |
|---|---|---|---|---|---|---|
| 6 | 3 | Customer first name length check: between 1 and 15 characters | Keyboard entry | Abnormal | Suneshhhhhhhhhh (16 characters) | Rejected with error message |

| Actual Result | | |
|---|---|---|
| **Before** | **After** | **Comment** |
| | | Length check succeeds in rejecting data of abnormal length.<br><br>Error message is not user-friendly because it does not tell the user what the problem is or how to correct it. |

**Figure 6.11** The result of test 6 from the plan in Table 6.4.

## Coursework

### Test results

For each test in your test plan, your project report should:

- clearly refer to the test performed – this is much easier for someone else to read if you copy-and-paste the relevant row from your test plan;
- show 'before' and 'after' screenshot evidence of the test:
  - be careful to include the *whole* of the application or form so that the context is clear; resize the window and scroll its content *before* taking the screenshot if this helps to cut out blank areas and keep the screenshot legible;
  - in the case of printed output, include the print as the 'after' evidence in an appendix to your report;
- comment on agreement (success) or disagreement (failure) between the expected and actual results.

To achieve full marks, you need to use all three types of test data and cover all aspects of your solution's functionality.

The 'Test results' section in the *Guidance on the coursework* document on the Student CD-ROM provides further guidance on this step.

## 2.2 Documentation

A small, simple problem can sometimes be solved by a single person who then uses the system they have produced. In this situation, it would not be necessary to write detailed notes about the solution. However, most problems are not like this. For anything bigger, full notes have to be kept about how the solution was produced (**technical documentation**) and how to use the new system (**user documentation**).

Documentation is not just tacked on to the end of a solution. It should be produced while the system is being developed. This is especially important for the technical documentation because there will almost certainly be more than one person producing the solution and each person involved needs to know what everyone else is doing. Unlike at the design stage, it is entirely appropriate to use screenshots to illustrate the documentation.

### Technical documentation

At some time after the solution has been implemented, the client is likely to need to ask a technician to carry out hardware or file maintenance on the system or a designer–programmer to update it to meet changed requirements. The technical documentation should provide these technical personnel with a detailed explanation of how the system works (Figure 6.12). It should also include information to

**Figure 6.12** A complete system requires documentation.

assist them in routine maintenance tasks and any future problem-solving or developments to meet new needs.

Technical documentation typically includes the following sections:

- **Purpose of the system:** This section defines the problem that the system solves, agreed with the client, including the scope of the solution.
- **Limitations of the system:** Some constraints may have been put on the system in the initial discussions between the client and the analyst. For example, an examination board might have wanted an electronic method to distribute examination results. Once the analyst had done some preliminary enquiries, it may have been decided that it would add too much cost or that it would mean that the project would not be ready on time. This constraint produces an expected limitation of the system.
- **Hardware and software requirements:** The hardware requirements of the system should include estimated file sizes so that storage choices can be justified. There may be diagrams to show how the servers, peripherals, storage devices, network and user terminals are interconnected. Software requirements should include details of software that has been bought in, software that has been configured to match the solution and software that has been written specifically for this solution. Minimum system requirements for running the software are also included.

- **System flowchart:** This can be useful to explain what has actually been built. The various processes are shown only in outline because the full details of the programs are covered in detailed program flowcharts.
- **Structure diagram:** This can be used to depict the top-down design of what has actually been built.
- **Program coding:** This section should clearly state the programming language used. It should also include detailed designs for the programs, possibly in the form of pseudocode algorithms or program flowcharts. Each of the program statements or blocks of statements in the program code should contain comments. Comments are notes within the program that explains what the code does and should enable another programmer to produce very similar code. Spreadsheet formulae can be shown in the 'formulae view' of the spreadsheet. A 'design view' of a query can be taken from a database application.
- **List of variables used:** Variables (see Chapter 9) that have been declared in the program need to be listed. This list includes the name of the variable, the reason it is being used and its data type. This list is not just to make sure that another programmer can follow the program if some maintenance needs to be done; it also helps to ensure that the same variable name is not used for more than one purpose.
- **File structures:** Information is needed about the types of data in each file so that the file structures can be altered if necessary. For example, if a file holds the data 'John Ahmed, 11DY, Computing', the structure should be described as: 'The StudentSubject file contains the following fields: StudentName (Text/String), Class (Text/String), Subject (Text/String)'. For complex systems, field names, data types and other relevant information are written in a table called the **data dictionary**. If data are stored in more than one database table, the relationships between the tables should be stated or shown in a clear diagram or screenshot.
- **Validation and verification checks:** Details of the validation and verification checks that are used to validate and verify the input data should be given, including the rules applied and error messages.

Further sections of the technical documentation may include annotated screenshots of the 'design views' of input forms, output forms and reports; sample runs with the test data and results; and known 'bugs' in the system.

**8** Produce a system flowchart for an application that inputs changes to be made to a membership system in a library. Include procedures that check on the validity of the inputs, use various files and produce outputs, which include lists of members and regular users.

**9** An entry in a list of variable names looks like this:

| | |
|---|---|
| Variable name | X |
| Description | This stores the total of all the items bought so far |
| Data type | Number |

Criticise this entry in the list and say how it could be improved.

**10** Claire inputs a telephone number to a program you have written and a message is output 'Wrong format'. How could you improve the error message, so that Claire would know what the correct format is?

**Coursework**

## Technical documentation

Your teacher can only give you marks for your solution if you provide documentary evidence of it. The obvious place to provide that evidence is in your technical documentation. There are also separate marks available for the quality and completeness of your technical documentation.

As with test results, apart from printed reports, screenshots are the only convincing evidence of what you have built. As before, be careful to include the *whole* of the application or form so that the context is clear, but resize the window and scroll its content *before* taking the screenshot if this helps to cut out blank areas and keep the screenshot legible.

→

*Coursework continued …*

You must clearly explain what you are presenting using suitable sub-headings, captions and annotation, which may be in word-processed callouts or handwritten.

In your project report, you should document your solution under at least the following headings:
- purpose of the system;
- limitations of the system;
- hardware and software requirements;
- build
  - programming:
    - structure diagram;
    - algorithms as pseudocode or program flowcharts;
    - programming language used;
    - commented program code;
    - list of variables used;
    - file structures, tables and relationships;
    - 'design views' of input forms and output forms and reports;
  - customisation of generic application program:
    - spreadsheet:
    - program used:
      - input and output sheets;
      - printed reports with header and footer;
      - formulae (in 'formulae view');
    - database:
      - 'design views' of input forms, output forms and reports;
      - queries (in 'design view');
      - file types, tables and relationships;
- validation and verification checks;
  - commented macro code.

The 'Technical documentation' section in the *Guidance on the coursework* document on the Student CD-ROM provides further guidance on this step.

For **Paper 3**, you should practise listing the items required in technical documentation for the scenario.

### User documentation

The other part of the documentation is provided for users of the system and is often called the 'user guide' or 'user manual'. Someone sitting at a computer and answering customer queries using a database does not need to know how the database is structured, what data type is used to store the price of the goods or how the database looks up items. They do not need to know the size of the database or the relationships between tables. They just need to know how to look up the price. The user documentation tells them what the system does and how to use it, but not *how* the system does it.

User documentation typically includes the following sections:

- **Purpose of the system:** This section states what the user can do with the system.
- **Limitations of the system:** This section should state what the system cannot do.
- **Hardware and software requirements:** This section should state what hardware and software the user needs to use the system.
- **How to use the system:** Annotated screenshots should show details of:
  - how to install a simple system;
  - how to launch the software and log in, if necessary for security;
  - the sort of data that needs to be entered, how to enter data and in what format;
  - how to delete or edit data;
  - how to perform sorting, searching and other processing;
  - how to print reports;
  - how to save files;
  - how to perform backup and recovery of files.
- **Sample runs:** This section includes outputs from some successful runs of the software with the test data used, so that the user knows what to expect from the system. These may be screenshots of input and output screens or printed reports, for example.
- **Error messages:** Things go wrong in any system and when they do it is important that the user is told in simple language what needs to be done to correct the error (Figure 6.13). This section should illustrate and explain the error messages that can arise. These vary from simple messages that inform the user that there is no paper left in the printer and what to do about it, to error messages informing the user that something serious has happened and that the system is attempting to recover data. This should include the set of messages that tells the user when there has been a validation

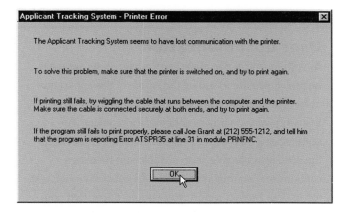

**Figure 6.13** A helpful error message.

or verification error, which data item was invalid or incorrect and what sort of input was expected.

- **Troubleshooting guide:** This section tells the user how to identify that something has gone wrong and what can be done about it. Otherwise, every time things go wrong, it will be necessary to call out a technician to solve the problem.
- **Frequently asked questions:** This should consist of a collection of questions that users may have posed, with corresponding answers.

 **SAQs**

3  As a result of testing the system, it is found that a module of code does not pass data to the next module as intended. It is rewritten and causes the user interface to change. Where would these changes be recorded and why?

 **Questions**

11  Look again at the three scenarios in Question 1:
    a  a small general store;
    b  a dress shop;
    c  a large supermarket.
    For each, decide who the audience is and what content is necessary in each of the user and technical guides.

## User documentation

As with technical documentation, screenshots are really helpful. If you are including the *whole* of the application or form so that the context is clear, be careful to resize the window and scroll its content *before* taking the screenshot if this helps to cut out blank areas and keep the screenshot legible. With suitable sub-headings, captions and annotation, you should not need much text.

In your project report, you should document your solution, in the form of a user guide or user manual, under at least the following headings:
- purpose of the system;
- limitations of the system;
- hardware and software requirements;
- how to use the system:
  - how to install the system;
  - how to launch the software;
  - how to enter data (including screenshots of data entry forms) and in what format (for example, whether it is necessary to enter two digits after the decimal point of a price);
  - how to delete or edit data;
  - how to sort, search and perform other processing on data (including screenshots of output forms);
  - how to print reports (including previews or scans of reports);
  - how to save files;
- error messages;
- how to perform backup and recovery;
- troubleshooting guide;
- frequently asked questions.

The 'User guide' section in the *Guidance on the coursework* document on the Student CD-ROM provides further guidance on this step.

For **Paper 3**, you should practise listing the items required in a user guide for the scenario.

## 2.2 Implementation (changeover) stage

When a system has been built and thoroughly tested, it has to be installed and commissioned in the organisation for which it was designed, according to the plan produced by the systems analyst. If the system is completely new, this may simply be a matter of installing the appropriate hardware and software and starting to use the system. However, in most cases, the system is designed to take over from an older system, which may not even be computerised.

A **changeover** plan is necessary to manage the change from an older system, involving installation of hardware, software and data, and training of users.

### Installation

The first thing to be done is to install any new hardware that is required for the new system. If this involves extensive work, it is possible that the business will need to shut down while it is carried out. However, it may be possible to install new hardware while the organisation is normally closed for business (overnight or over a holiday period). Then the system will be ready for operation when the organisation opens as normal. If no new hardware is required or entirely new hardware is required and there is space for both new and old equipment, workers may be able to continue to work on the old system. However, if old hardware items will be re-used with new ones, work on the old system may no longer be possible.

All new system and application software should be installed on the hardware for the new system.

The required data files have to be imported into the new system. The format of existing data files may need to be converted to the format required by the new system. Paper records may need to be scanned or have their data entered by manual keying or by optical character recognition (OCR). It may be necessary to employ specialist staff members temporarily in order to ensure that the data are entered efficiently, with adequate checks for accuracy.

### Training

It is necessary to train staff members in how to use the new system. If they are familiar with computer systems already, the training may not need to be very extensive. However, if they are not used to a computerised system, the training has to be very carefully planned and may need to start well in advance. An important question to be answered is 'What form will the training take?' The two main options are 'classroom training' and 'computer-based training' (CBT).

In classroom training (Figure 6.14), the staff members are students and a tutor is brought in to train them in various aspects of the use of the system. This type of training has big advantages: there is someone who can answer the specific questions that staff members may raise and the management can be sure that everyone has received the training. A disadvantage is that the staff members need time away from their work while the training sessions are held.

In computer-based training, the lessons are put onto a DVD and each member of staff is given a copy so that they can do the training when it suits them. Advantages of this are that the firm can run normally while staff members are learning. Also individuals can learn at their own speed – they can miss sections out that they already know about or they can redo sections that they find difficult. A disadvantage for staff members is that they have to use their own time to do the training.

Even with training, some of the staff may not be able to learn how to use the new system. This can cause a major social problem because these staff members may be moved to less-skilled jobs or made redundant.

**Figure 6.14** Adult users being trained in an IT classroom.

## Methods of changeover

As an example of a system to be changed over, we consider an examination board. It has a system that it uses:

- to input and store candidate results;
- to collate the results for each candidate from all the subjects that they have taken;
- to output the results for each candidate;
- to send the results to centres around the world.

The old system is very slow and unreliable because there has been a large increase in the number of candidates taking the examinations recently. They have designed a new system and are ready to implement it. There are four methods of changeover to be considered.

### Direct changeover

In a direct changeover, the old system is shut down, typically at the close of business at the end of a day or before a holiday period. The organisation starts using the new system at the beginning of the next working day.

Although this sounds a simple method of changeover, it requires careful planning. The new system must have been fully tested. All the files must be imported and ready to use, and all the workers must be properly trained when the new system is started. If something goes wrong, it is not possible to go back to the old system because it is no longer available.

Advantages of a direct changeover are that it is simple to understand; it keeps staff and running costs to a minimum because only one system is in use at a time; the benefits of the new system are obtained as soon as possible; and there is less likelihood of failure since the whole of the new system must have been tested.

## Questions

12 Make lists of the advantages and disadvantages of classroom and computer-based training from the point of view of:
   a  the staff;
   b  the management of the firm.
   What other forms of training could be used?

13 Look again at the three scenarios in Question 1:
   a  a small general store;
   b  a dress shop;
   c  a large supermarket.
   For each, consider the data files that will be needed. Decide how they will be produced and what measures should be taken to try to ensure the accuracy of the data. Also consider the need for training of staff members and how it will be carried out.

A major disadvantage is that if the new system does fail, the organisation faces an unscheduled shutdown.

For the examination board, if the calculation of results does not work properly, the results will not be produced in time. This is an example of a time-sensitive process that is very important to the organisation and hence a direct changeover is not appropriate.

### Phased changeover

In a phased changeover, one part of the system is changed at a time, while the rest of the system continues to use the old methods.

Advantages are that each part of the new system can be thoroughly evaluated before replacing the next part of the old system. If the latest part of the new system fails, it is possible to 'roll back' the changeover to the previous phase to ensure continued operation of the organisation's business.

Disadvantages are that a lot of planning and testing is required beforehand; staff members need to use both the old and new systems to process any set of data; business problems may be created by having parts of two different systems working at the same time; and the full benefits of the new system are delayed by evaluation of the successive phases. However, in important applications, it is often worth the extra work.

The examination board may choose to input marks using the new computer system while the processing and the production of the results are still done with the old system. Notice that all the results for all candidates in all subjects are treated in the same way. The system has been split up according to the processing rather than the data. After successful introduction of the first phase, another part of the system is changed over in the next phase, and so on until the whole system has changed over.

### Pilot changeover

In a pilot changeover, the system is split according to the data (or possibly the site), rather than according to the process.

Advantages of this method are that the scale of the problem is reduced if the new system is faulty, because only one set of data or site is affected. The pilot site's staff can be trained more rapidly than the whole organisation's staff. Staff and running costs remain at a minimum because only one system is in use at a time. The pilot site's data can provide a 'live' system on which to train further staff members.

Disadvantages are that some staff members need to use each system until the changeover is completed. If the pilot involves a direct changeover and the new system fails, the pilot site faces an unscheduled shutdown or needs to 'borrow' processing time from other sites.

The examination board may decide to produce the results for the IGCSE qualification from the new system, while the rest of the results are still produced on the old system. The IGCSE qualification is referred to as the 'pilot'. Instead of choosing a type of qualification, the examination board could have chosen an exam subject, such as Maths, as the pilot. In this situation, the whole of the new system processes some results, while the old system processes the rest. Once the pilot is seen to be operating correctly and there are no outstanding problems, the rest of the system can be changed over.

A large organisation may introduce a new system at a number of sites, such as the retail branches or warehouses of a supermarket chain. In this case, one of these sites may be the best choice for the pilot, so that workers on only one site need to be involved.

### Parallel running

The fourth method of changeover involves 'parallel running' of both systems at the same time. This means entering, storing and processing the data in both systems and producing two sets of output, until the managers of the organisation are convinced that there are no faults with the new system.

Advantages are that the method is simple to understand and it is very safe. If the new system fails or staff training takes longer than expected, the old system is still available. Parallel running provides an excellent way of testing the system using real data, because it is possible to compare the results produced by the two systems and any differences will reveal faults. The benefits of the new system are also obtained as soon as possible.

A disadvantage is that it is much more expensive than the other methods, since running both systems increases staff and running costs until a satisfactory evaluation of the whole of the new system is complete. Again, it may be worth it, if the system's results are very valuable to the organisation.

## SAQs

4   In industry, there are several terms that also mean 'changeover'. Can you name three?

5   Which of the four types of changeover do you think is also known as 'big bang'?

6   Which is the most risky type of changeover?

## Questions

14   Copy the following table and rate the costs of the four methods of changeover as Low, Medium or High.

| Changeover method | Financial cost | Work by users | Work by technical team | Impact in the event of failure |
|---|---|---|---|---|
| Direct | | | | |
| Phased | | | | |
| Pilot | | | | |
| Parallel | | | | |

15   Look again at the three scenarios in Question 1:
    a   a small general store;
    b   a dress shop;
    c   a large supermarket.
    For each, explain why some of the changeover methods are not sensible. Justify your choice of the one that should be used in each scenario.

## Coursework

### Changeover method

For **Paper 2**, you may document a suitable changeover method in your analysis or design sections, although you are not specifically required to do so.

For **Paper 3**, you should use the advantages and disadvantages of the four changeover methods to justify your choice of changeover method for your scenario.

---

2.2  ## Evaluation stage

### Evaluation against the requirements specification

Before the solution was produced, the systems analyst and the client agreed the requirements specification. This lists the things that the finished solution should do to be successful. A test plan was written to provide the evidence that the requirements were met and that the system does everything that was required of it.

In consultation with the client, the analyst now needs to write a formal evaluation of the new system. This includes:

- comparing the final solution with the requirements specification:
  - comparing test results from the new system with the expected results and with results from any previous system; by
  - comparing the performance of the new system with the requirements specification;
- evaluating the users' responses to using the new system.

If the system does not satisfy the requirements specification, the problem has not been solved. The analyst will suffer damage to his or her professional reputation and may not be paid. If the requirements are met, the solution to the problem is considered a success.

### Limitations and necessary improvements

The evaluation should identify any expected, or unexpected, limitations in the facilities or performance of the system. Sooner or later, other things that could have been done are likely to be found, or better ways of doing the things that have been done. The evaluation should describe and prioritise any necessary improvements that have already been identified.

The production of the finished solution is not the end of a linear process; continual improvements can be made by returning to earlier stages in the system life cycle. This is the reason for all that technical documentation, so that someone can come along later and change things when it becomes necessary.

### Live testing

The solution will have been tested by the people who produced it. However, these people tend to know about computers and know what the software is meant to do.

When the system has been introduced and formally evaluated and is being used by the ordinary workers in the organisation, they will find problems with it that the computer-literate testers simply did not think of. As such problems arise, further evaluation can take place in consultation between the client and a systems analyst.

### 2.2 Maintenance

The system will need to be maintained throughout its lifetime in the organisation. There are three types of maintenance that are likely to be necessary and which the technical documentation should support:

- **Corrective maintenance**: All complex software is liable to go wrong occasionally because it may contain errors that testing failed to identify. We call such errors in the program code 'bugs'. This term became common after an incident in the early days of computers in which a moth was found to have jammed an electromechanical relay! A programmer has to be able to find these software errors and fix them.

- **Adaptive maintenance**: Things are likely to change inside or outside the organisation. For example, the rate of Value Added Tax (VAT) or other data may change and require different calculations. This form of maintenance differs from corrective maintenance, because nothing has gone wrong with the system, but the requirements have altered. Adaptive maintenance is also required when the demands on a system grow as the volume of the organisation's business increases. Suppose that the examination board wants to offer its exams in a new country and the educational authorities in that country want the results to be presented in order of the marks awarded, as well as according to the centres where the candidates sat their exams. This will require added functionality for the software. Adaptive maintenance may involve hardware as well as software.

- **Perfective maintenance**: Organisations are always looking to improve their performance, by speeding up processes, making processes more efficient or by improving the quality of their products or services. The systems analyst has to consider how to solve such problems. The hardware may need improvements, for example faster or more reliable input or output devices or higher performance servers (Figure 6.15). The software may need improvements, for example changes to the structure of the data files from flat files to a relational database, or the use of a faster sorting algorithm.

Any changes will require careful planning, testing and introduction, to avoid disruption to the organisation's business.

**Figure 6.15** A computer engineer carrying out maintenance on a server.

7 A system has been operating satisfactorily for three months since its introduction. A user tries to do something differently that causes an error to be reported by the software. The user submits a bug report to the system support staff members who investigate the error. They conclude that the user is trying to do something for which the system was not designed.

a How will the support staff members have reached this conclusion?

b What can they do about the error?

**Questions**

16 Look again at the three scenarios in Question 1:

a a small general store;

b a dress shop;

c a large supermarket.

For each, decide what sort of evidence the analyst should provide to the management of the organisation so that the performance of the solution can be evaluated. Give examples of the types of event that would mean that the three different types of maintenance would be needed.

**Coursework**

## Development

You are asked to suggest some improvements or extensions to your solution. You do not have to build them, you only have to make some sensible suggestions. The suggestions must be realistic rather than complete flights of fantasy, so they need to use existing technology.

In your project report, you should write a number of realistic and substantial suggestions for improvement or extension, such as:

• a better method of data input, possibly involving a different input device;

• a better method of information output, possibly involving a different output device;

• an extra facility for the system.

The 'Future development' section in the *Guidance on the coursework* document on the Student CD-ROM provides further guidance on this step.

For **Paper 3**, you should practise writing the advantages and limitations of a new computer-based system, possible future developments and drawing detailed designs for websites, intranets and CBT.

## Summary

• A systems analyst can help a client to define their problem precisely.

• The stages of the system life cycle are fact finding, feasibility study, analysis, design, building and testing, documentation, implementation (changeover), evaluation and maintenance.

• Fact-finding methods used to collect information about the current system are observation, interviews, questionnaires and inspection of documents.

• A feasibility study includes a description of the existing system, its problems and estimated costs; success criteria for a new system; possible solutions; a development plan; and a cost–benefit analysis.

• Analysis involves using fact-finding methods to collect further information about the current system; summarising this information using a dataflow diagram and system flowchart; and writing a requirements specification.

• A requirements specification should include the required services, functions, data storage and performance, and any constraints on the design.

$\longrightarrow$

*Summary continued …*

- Design involves the selection of software; drafting of output forms and reports, data entry forms, validation and verification checks; selection of data storage, backup and hardware; description of processing; drafting of command buttons and menus; writing a test strategy and plan.
- Top-down design consists of dividing a desired solution into a number of smaller solutions that are simpler to produce.
- A structure diagram is a way of visualising a top-down design.
- A test strategy may include a range of test data; instructions for testing navigation, menus and command buttons, input, storage, processing and output; details of unit testing for each module followed by integration testing of the complete system.
- Testing should use real data and test data chosen to include normal, extreme and abnormal values.
- Technical documentation should include the purpose and limitations of the system; system flowcharts; program coding; a list of variables used; file structures; validation and verification checks; hardware and software requirements.
- User documentation, known as the user guide, should include the purpose and limitations of the system; hardware and software requirements; details of how to use the system; sample runs; error messages; a troubleshooting guide; and frequently asked questions.
- Implementation of a new system to replace an old one involves the choice of direct, phased, pilot or parallel running method of changeover, each of which has advantages and disadvantages.
- Evaluation should document a comparison of the final solution, including test results and performance, with the requirements specification and identification of any limitations or necessary improvements.
- Maintenance takes three forms: corrective, adaptive and perfective.

## Examination practice for Paper 1

### Exam Questions

1. A screen has been developed to allow the input of data into the following fields: *name, sex, address, date of birth* and *examination results*. A first attempt at designing the screen is shown below:

```
                           Student Records

Student name:................................. Sex:..........................
Student address: ..................................................................
...............................................................................
Date of birth:.......... / .......... / ..........
Exam results: Subjects and Grades
_____

Type in NEXT to go to next student or BACK to go to previous
student:.........................................
```

This is not a very good input screen. Give **four** ways in which it could be improved.　　　　　　　　　[4]

*Part of Question 7, Cambridge IGCSE Computer Studies 0420/01 Paper 12 May/June 2010*

2. Before the system is implemented, it needs to be fully tested. One of the tests will be to check that the company does not pay a worker more than $800 per week. Use examples of a worker's pay to explain what is meant by *normal* test data, *abnormal* test data and *extreme* test data. [3]

   *Part of Question 15, Cambridge IGCSE Computer Studies 0420/01 Paper 1 May/June 2008*

3. There are several methods used to implement new computer systems. Name **two** of these methods and for *each* named method give:

   (a) a brief description

   (b) **one** advantage compared with other methods

   (c) **one** disadvantage compared with other methods. [6]

   *Question 5, Cambridge IGCSE Computer Studies 0420/01 Paper 11 May/June 2010*

## Exam-Style Questions

1. Describe **four** stages of the system life cycle. [4]

2. Describe **three** fact-finding methods used by systems analysts. [3]

3. State **three** tasks performed in the *analysis* stage of systems analysis. [3]

4. State **three** tasks performed in the *design* stage of systems analysis. [3]

5. Explain what is meant by top-down design. [2]

6. State **three** items that should be included in technical documentation. [3]

## Examination practice for Paper 3

To answer the following questions you will need to read the garage scenario provided in Appendix A (page 284).

1. Describe what tools exist to help the analyst draw up an action plan and ensure that the project is completed on time and to budget. [4]

   *Question (a), Cambridge IGCSE Computer Studies 0420/01 Paper 3 Specimen for 2011*

   **Comments**

   Notice that this is a generic question. You simply have to list 4 of the available planning tools; you don't have to apply it to the scenario.

   $\longrightarrow$

2. Name **three** ways the analyst could gather information about the existing manual system. Explain how each method would be used to gather information. [6]

*Question (b), Cambridge IGCSE Computer Studies 0420/01 Paper 3 Specimen for 2011*

> **Comments**
>
> Notice that there are 6 marks awarded for naming **three** methods. This is because you also need to *Explain* how each method would be used. You would score 1 mark each for naming any three of the fact-finding methods. The other 3 marks would come from applying those methods to the specific scenario. So, think how each of the methods you list could be put into action in the garage.

3. Describe a test strategy for the new computer-based system. [4]

*Question (f)(i), Cambridge IGCSE Computer Studies 0420/01 Paper 3 Specimen for 2011*

> **Comments**
>
> For this question you need to include the different types of test data, as well as the strategy you would use to test each type.

4. Describe what items should be included in the User Manual supplied with this new system. [6]

*Question (g), Cambridge IGCSE Computer Studies 0420/01 Paper 3 Specimen for 2011*

> **Comments**
>
> Your answer can include any sensible points. It might help to first state what the user guide is and then list what items should be included in it.

5. Describe how the effectiveness of the new system could be evaluated. [4]

*Question (i), Cambridge IGCSE Computer Studies 0420/01 Paper 3 Specimen for 2011*

> **Comments**
>
> The answer will include the standard methods of evaluation. But these must be in the context of the scenario, in this case the parts department of the garage. You need to think what improvements could have been planned.

# Part II:
# Uses and implications

# 7 Range and scope of computer applications

When you have finished this chapter, you will be able to:

- describe the characteristics of an application of computer technology, ranging from the need that it was designed to fulfil, through its technical details to its effects on individuals and organisations

- demonstrate an understanding of a variety of computer applications from the following areas:

  - communication and information systems

  - commercial and general data processing

  - industrial, technical and scientific uses

  - monitoring and control systems

  - automation and robotics

  - expert systems

  - education, training and entertainment

  - use of the Internet.

## 1.1.1 Introduction

There are so many uses of computers that it would be impossible to study all of them in a book like this. We look at a number of typical computer application areas and study an example application from each area in further detail.

When an application is produced, it is designed to fulfil the need of an individual, an organisation or a market segment. Careful consideration is given to how the application works. When studying an application, we need to think about the following aspects:

- the purpose – what need is it intended to fulfil?
- the overall system design (including the computerised and non-computerised parts):
  - what hardware and software components are used and how are they organised?
  - what data are required, who collects and prepares them and how are they collected?
  - how are data captured, for example, is it manual entry on a keyboard or keypad, sensor with ADC or OCR?

- how are data structured for storage, for example, as files or databases?
- how are data processed?
- the required outcome – what output is produced and in what format?
- the user interface – are menus provided? If a GUI is used, what special screens are provided for input and output?
- system recovery – what means of recovery is there after loss of data and software?
- effectiveness – does it work well in practice?
- effects on individuals and organisations – are there good or bad effects of the application?

## 1.1.2 Communication systems

### Email

One of the most powerful features of a computer system becomes apparent when the computers are connected. For communication with a specific person there are several applications that can be used to send messages from one machine to another. The most important for use at work is electronic mail, known as email. The communicating computers must both have an email client application program, but it does not have to be the same program. An email system can be internal to an organisation. For example, in your school, it may be possible to send messages to other people on your computer system that they can read when they log in. If a LAN is connected to the Internet, it is possible to send messages all over the world.

The sender of an email composes a message, attaching one or more data files if required, and sends it to one or more recipients. A mail server can belong to the sender's organisation, their Internet Service Provider (ISP) or a webmail provider. An email address is similar to 'aperson@myorganisation.com'. The mail server uses the domain name, 'myorganisation.com', of the recipient's address to decide which Internet server to forward the message to. After several forwarding operations between servers, the message arrives at the recipient's mail server and is stored in their storage area, known as their 'mailbox'. To receive the message, the recipient logs in to the mail server and opens it. If they have a client email program, rather than webmail, this may download a copy of the message for local storage. The recipient can read the message, open or save the attached files and easily reply to the message.

Messages are stored until the recipient chooses to read them. This makes email suitable for international communication, where differences in time can make a real-time conversation, such as a phone call or video conference, inconvenient. It is even possible to have a rough translation of a message provided by a web translation service. Email does not require any special peripheral hardware.

Although emails can be sent and replied to in real-time, a real-time conversation between two or more people who are online is more fluent using instant messaging (IM). With some instant messaging systems, it is even possible to see your partner's keystrokes as they type a message. A business may provide an IM web application on its website to provide 'customer service chat'. One agent provides customer service to different people in separate conversations, nearly simultaneously. IM requires extra hardware if the application uses telephony or video.

## Video-conferencing

If it is important to see and hear each other in a computer-enabled dialogue, video-conferencing software is required, possibly based on VOIP telephony or IM. Although a video conference may involve only two people, it can involve a number of participants at a number of locations.

Video communication requires a high data transmission rate provided by a broadband private WAN or the Internet. For a conference between two people, it may be sufficient to attach a webcam, microphone and headphones to the computer. When there are more participants, a multimedia projector, loudspeakers and multiple microphones may be required.

Participants speak into one or more microphones, facing a webcam while viewing distant participants on screen and listening to them via headphones or loudspeakers. The software includes a network operating system and a *compressor/decompressor* (or '**codec**') to compress the stream of transmitted data and decompress the stream of received data. It also needs 'echo cancellation', especially if loudspeakers are used. This prevents sound received and picked up by microphones at one location being fed back to the location from which it came after a delay, sounding like an echo.

Video-conferencing is being used increasingly for a number of reasons:

- improved data transmission rates have improved the quality of images and sound;
- it is safer than travelling;
- it saves the time, monetary and environmental costs of travelling to meetings and accommodating people in hotels;
- participants can hold a meeting at short notice; there is no need to wait for people to travel to a venue;
- an electronic record can be kept of the meeting;
- it enables more flexible working arrangements for people with disabilities or caring responsibilities.

Disadvantages are that there may be time or language differences between participants; 'chairing' a multi-way conversation may be difficult, especially if there are significant transmission delays; it may be harder for participants to read others' body language as well as if they were meeting face-to-face; communications may be interrupted by loss of connection.

## Questions

 1 Explain how an email, asking about the syllabus, is sent from a teacher at your school to Cambridge.

 2 State the hardware and software needed to carry out a video conference among a number of participants in different parts of the world.

 3 Explain the difference between email and instant messaging.

 4 State three advantages and one disadvantage of video-conferencing for an organisation.

### Digital telephones

Many people interpret 'digital phones' as meaning 'mobile phones'. While mobile phones indeed have embedded digital computers, so do modern landline phones, even though they usually send and receive analogue signals to and from the local telephone exchange.

Modern telephone systems have a number of facilities that help to manage telephone calls:

- they can store names and phone numbers so that they can act like an address book – it is no longer necessary to remember numbers or to key them into the phone when making a call;
- they can display the caller's name when receiving a call;
- they can record 'voicemail' messages;
- they can provide automated messages and menu systems for callers phoning a call handling system.

### Mobile phones

Many digital telephones are no longer anchored to a landline but can be carried around by their users. This enables a user to avoid missing incoming phone calls and to make calls while they are away from their home or workplace. A mobile phone has extra facilities, such as the ability to take and transmit photographs.

A mobile phone works by maintaining radio communication with an antenna mast. The power of the transmitter in the phone is limited and it usually needs to be within about 8 km of a mast to work (Figure 7.1). Under ideal conditions, the range may be considerably greater. Usually, three antenna masts provide coverage of a hexagonal area using different radio frequencies or 'channels'. The hexagonal area is known as a 'cell', which is why mobile phones are often called 'cell phones'.

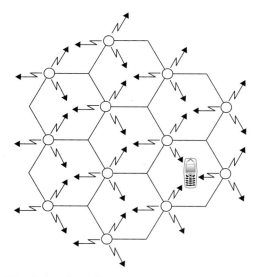

**Figure 7.1** A plan view of antenna masts serving hexagonal cells in a mobile phone network.

To make a call, a phone uses the antenna mast with the strongest signal (Figure 7.2). The signal from the calling phone is received by the mast and is then sent over an ordinary telephone network, known as a Public Switched Telephone Network (PSTN).

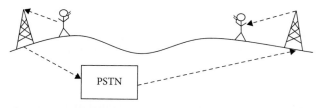

**Figure 7.2** Making and receiving a call using a mobile (cell) phone network.

In order to be able to deliver a call to a mobile phone, the computer system of the mobile phone network must keep track of the whereabouts of all phones connected to the network. It does this by broadcasting 'paging' messages to all phones at intervals from each antenna mast. The strength of the radio signals received when phones respond to the masts are recorded. The mobile phone network's computer system uses these records to route an incoming call to a phone via the mast currently receiving the strongest signal from the phone.

Emergency services and criminal investigators can obtain the approximate position of a mobile phone in the following way. The mobile phone network's computer system uses the differences in signal strength received by at least three masts to estimate the distance of the phone from each mast. These differences are used to 'trilaterate' the position of the phone.

Mobile phones can be very useful in business: people who are away from the office can be contacted almost anywhere. They do not need to keep their office informed of where they are. Usually, a company that requires its workforce to be mobile will issue mobile phones to them and pay all the bills. Similarly, parents may pay for their children to have mobile phones to keep in touch with them and assist with their transport arrangements when they are out of their homes.

In many parts of the world, people are far more likely to use a mobile phone than a computer to access the Internet. However, there are also many people who own only a landline phone or a mobile phone without Web access. Technologies are emerging for cheaply and rapidly creating application programs that enable phone access to information and services currently only available on websites. For example, an organisation could create an application program for booking train tickets or receiving information about the market prices for agricultural crops. A user can send an SMS text message to a published number to get the desired information sent to their mobile phone or can dial to connect to an interactive voice response (IVR) service to receive voice-based information.

Smartphones make up an increasing proportion of mobile phones being sold. They can run applications ('apps') designed to make use of their power and advanced networking capability. They can do more than just making calls and text messaging. For example, the user may be able to download an app that performs trilateration, using the strength of signal received from several cellular network masts to be 'location aware'. So the user can receive location-dependent information from the Web, such as local mapping, and information about local services, such as banks, hotels, restaurants, entertainment venues or transport services. Some 'high-end' phones also have GPS to locate the phone much more precisely and detect the direction of travel.

### Internet telephony

Internet telephony requires Voice over Internet Protocol (VoIP) software, a broadband Internet connection to a VoIP server, a microphone, loudspeakers or headphones and, optionally, a webcam for video. Some software may also provide instant messaging and file transfer.

VoIP services are used particularly by organisations who wish to employ people to work from home as part of a 'virtual call-centre'. The calls come from an organisation's customers to a central VoIP server that then forwards them via the Internet to workers at home. The organisation does not need to pay for office space or furniture to accommodate the workers, PCs, heating, air-conditioning, lighting and cleaning (the so-called 'overheads' – literally so, in the case of the roof and lighting!). The expenses related to providing some of these at home might be reflected in the workers' pay. The organisation does not even pay for the phone calls because the client who rings in will usually pay for the cost-bearing landline or mobile call. The segment of the call from the VoIP server to the worker is free of charges, although the VoIP server is a major investment and also requires maintenance.

## Internet connections

### Cable technology

The earliest method of accessing the Internet was through a **dial-up connection** over an ordinary telephone landline. The stream of *digital* data or signal produced by the computer cannot be sent directly down an *analogue* phone line. So a device called a 'dial-up **modem**' is needed to change the digital data into an analogue signal, consisting of a tone '*mo*dulated' in complex ways. The modem uses 'tone-dialling' to dial a connection over the PSTN to an Internet server operated by the ISP. Another modem is needed at the other end to '*dem*odulate' the analogue signal back into a digital signal that the receiving computer can process. The data transfer rate is limited to a maximum of 56 kilobits per second (kbps).

Fibre-optic networks, mobile phone networks, TV cable networks and many telephone landlines can all provide **broadband** connection to the Internet, with an appropriate modem. The data transfer rate from the Internet is measured in megabits per second (Mbps). Although this has not changed the physical speed of electrical signals in wires, optical fibres or radio waves, people refer to this as a much 'faster' connection.

A broadband modem is often combined with a number of hardware sockets or 'ports' for LAN cables to computers or network-enabled peripherals. Hence computers can share access to the Internet via the modem. A router is used to prevent local traffic from being sent to the Internet. A broadband router/modem combination is often the means by which a LAN is first created in a home or small business.

The advantages of broadband over dial-up include:

- the increased data transfer rate enables high-quality audio and video streams to be sent and received;
- the connection is always available, without the need to dial the connection to the ISP;

- the ISP charges a relatively low monthly fee, rather than the user paying per minute;
- a broadband connection can be accessed over a suitable landline while leaving the line free for making and receiving phone calls.

 **SAQs**

1  If a broadband connection has a transfer rate of 5.6 megabits per second (Mbps), how many times the maximum rate of a dial-up connection is this?

People who live in rural areas may have no access to any sort of cabled communication. On a dial-up connection, it can be very slow to browse media-rich web pages. For example, it may take several minutes to transfer and display just one high quality photo. The display of pages may be speeded up by turning off the display of pictures in the browser. However, this may make it difficult to use features of pages that rely on graphics, such as some menus. Even if there is a landline and the telephone exchange is equipped for broadband, the length of the line from the telephone exchange may severely limit the data transfer rate.

### Extension

Find out about some of the different communication services in your area. Look out for comments such as 'up to 10 Mbps broadband'. What speeds are really attainable? Why is it wrong to talk about the speed of communication? What type of communication link does your school have to the Internet?

### Wireless technology

A LAN that uses radio waves rather than cables to transmit data between computers or peripherals is called a **wireless local area network** (**WLAN**). WLAN products conforming with certain widely used international standards may be trademarked **Wi-Fi**, so a WLAN is often referred to as a 'Wi-Fi network'. The range of communication may extend to tens of metres indoors and hundreds of metres outdoors.

The absence of any LAN cables connecting devices in a WLAN means that a wireless broadband router/

modem provides a central 'access point'. It is a simpler and much more flexible way of connecting computers and peripherals, such as printers, while simultaneously providing Internet access. The data transfer rate within the LAN may be many tens of megabits per second (Mbps), but this may be lower than with LAN cables. Of course, the rate for Internet access is still limited by the level of service that the ISP supplies.

A user of a computer fitted with an internal or external wireless adapter can access the network from any convenient point that is within range of their access point, rather than having to work where a network cable is available (Figure 7.3).

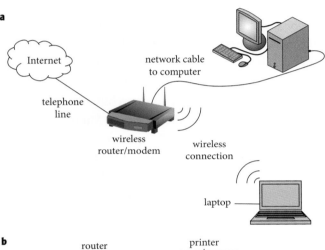

**Figure 7.3** **a** A wireless broadband router/modem enables computers to connect to the Internet via a network cable or its Wi-Fi access point. **b** A WLAN with several devices.

Organisations may provide public access to WLAN access points in areas known as Wi-Fi 'hotspots'. They may provide this service for a fee or free of charge to attract customers. Some communities provide community networks and when this is spread across a whole urban (or metropolitan) area it may be referred to as a 'Muni-Fi' network, run by 'wireless Internet service providers' (WISPs).

Smartphones and MP3/MP4 media players are often also equipped with Wi-Fi adapters. Some of these devices can even trilaterate from the strength of signals received from previously mapped Wi-Fi access points. This makes the devices 'location aware' and they can offer the user local mapping and advertisements for local services.

Sometimes, people have to use their ingenuity to make affordable antennas (Figure 7.4). This gives access to a mobile phone network outside its normal range or to the Internet via a community Wi-Fi network.

**Figure 7.4** A low-cost antenna made of wire wrapped around a plastic bottle for access to a community wireless network in a village in Mali, West Africa.

Apart from lower data transfer rates, WLAN technology has other disadvantages, which include:
- wireless range may be limited by metallic construction materials;
- other electronic devices, including other WLANs, may create radio interference;
- the owner of a WLAN needs to set up wireless security.

To avoid interference from neighbouring WLANs, it may be necessary to select a radio channel that is different from the ones they use. An unsecured WLAN allows unauthorised access to its LAN and Internet connection by other users within range of the access point. Organisations are generally well aware of this, but owners of home and small business networks may be less technically competent or motivated to realise this.

### Wireless Personal Area Networks

A **Wireless Personal Area Network (WPAN)** uses short-range wireless technology to connect devices within reach of the person using them, with a data transfer rate of just a few megabits per second (Mbps). For example, Bluetooth technology provides a WPAN for connecting a keyboard, mouse, printer, mobile phone, camera or headset to a computer without cables. It can also connect devices without the involvement of a laptop or PC, for example, a mobile phone to a headset or a camera to a photo printer.

There has been a 'convergence' of technologies for WPANs. To increase its data transfer rate, later versions of the Bluetooth technology have included Wi-Fi technology. It is also possible to use a computer's Wi-Fi adapter independently of a network access point, so that the adapter behaves as the access point for a WPAN, known as a Wi-Fi PAN.

## Multimedia systems

Presentations use multimedia to convey information effectively and maintain the interest of the viewer. A normal screen image containing text and graphics may be supplemented with animations, video and sound that are synchronised to the state of the screen.

Changes from one screen to another can use complex transitions to make an effect. Transitions may involve one screen fading into another or gradually being replaced. It can be distracting if this is used too much: the viewer may begin to look for the clever transitions rather than following the content closely. Hyperlinks can be included to give the user the choice of path through the information presented.

Typical examples of applications of multimedia are in presentations, advertisements on websites or computer-assisted learning (CAL) presentations. Multimedia in CAL presentations (Figure 7.5) give students a range of media through which to learn. A student may use a favourite medium to spark interest in a subject and a less favoured medium for extension work.

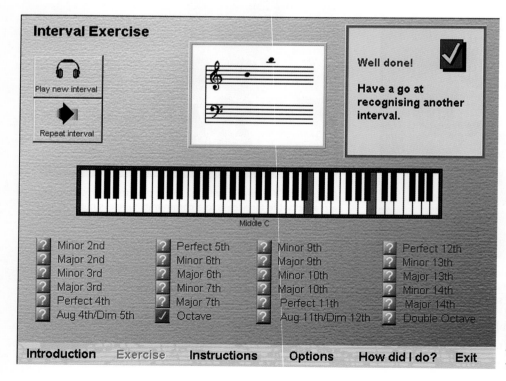

**Figure 7.5** A multimedia CAL presentation for learning aspects of music. The screen is interactive, providing both visual and auditory feedback as the student proceeds at their own pace.

A particular use in organisations is to aid the introduction of new computer systems by producing multimedia training courses. They are placed on DVD so that the employees can then learn the new system in their own time.

A multimedia presentation can also be in the form of a slideshow to be shown to an audience using a projector. The presentation is very similar to that produced for a single user. Usually such a presentation is run from beginning to end but experienced presenters will include hyperlinks to move between slides in response to audience feedback.

Many retailers use multimedia presentations within their stores, running in a loop. They typically use a lot of colour, fast cuts from one image to another and intricate transitions in order to keep the viewer's attention.

## Questions

8  Find some presentations that use multimedia software:
   * this could be software that you use in school for one of your subjects or by other departments in the school with other students;
   * see if advertising presentations are being used in a local store;
   * look at some websites to determine whether they use multimedia presentations.

   For each example that you find, identify the different features that have been used. If certain media or techniques have not been used, are these simply omissions or can you give a likely explanation of why they have not been used?

## Virtual reality systems

A **virtual reality** (**VR**) system creates computer-generated stereoscopic 3-D visual imagery and stereo sound of a simulated, 'virtual' environment. It gives the user the illusion of being able to move their gaze or even their whole body within that environment and possibly interact with it by handling virtual objects.

Looking at a screen while playing a game or using a computer for some other reason is impressive to the user, but is still just the output from a screen or projector within another environment. As soon as the user looks away from the screen, they see the room in which the screen is located. If the output from the computer controls *everything* that the user sees and hears, then the 'immersive' virtual environment that the computer produces is much more convincing because there is less to distract the user and break the illusion of this virtual reality.

This can be achieved by providing the user with a pair of goggles or a headset or 'helmet' that displays the computer's visual output, ideally in 3-D. If the headset includes headphones, they can deliver the computer's stereo audio output. If the equipment also contains sensors to detect the direction in which the user's head is pointing so that the software changes the computer's audio-visual output appropriately when the user turns around, the illusion is complete. The user can use a hand-held controller to control what they are seeing. Special gloves can send input to the computer and provide tactile sensory feedback to the wearer. It is possible to go further than this and use a complete suit that provides input to the computer and computer-generated feedback to the wearer. This hardware is described in Chapter 3. Other resources that may be needed are a relatively powerful computer with a large amount of RAM, compression software and broadband Internet access.

Virtual reality has many applications. For example, an estate agency can allow customers to 'tour' houses that are for sale without moving from the estate agent's office. A number of houses can be visited very quickly and there is no disruption to the lives of the people who are selling their houses. Tours may also be offered on a website or on CD or DVD. Similarly, CAD software can provide an animated walk-through or 'fly-through' view of a design for a real-world environment. This is useful when designing buildings, the layout of furniture in rooms such as kitchens, interior decor and gardens. Even vehicles and natural-looking people can be created to populate an architect's design. To get an idea of this, search http://www.youtube.com for 'walk-through' CAD.

VR can be used for training in fields ranging from dentistry and other forms of surgery, the operation of chemical or nuclear plants, infantry and armoured vehicle combat, road vehicle driving, flying an aircraft, and piloting submarines and space vehicles. In some cases, such as combat training, it may even be desirable to use an actuator to release an odour, such as the smell of cordite.

VR gives rise to endless possibilities for games. A game's VR environment can be similar to the real world or a fantasy world. VR techniques have also been applied in computer-generated imagery (CGI) and special effects in films, television and games software.

Cave Automatic Virtual Environment (CAVE) is a system for producing visual VR without the need for goggle or headsets by projecting images on the walls, the ceiling and even the floor of a room (Figure 7.6). In some simulations, this creates a 'wrap-around' visual environment for a seated participant that reacts realistically to their handling of the input devices. In this case, projectors can be sited inside the room. Other systems are designed for a participant to walk around, in which case the projectors need to be outside the room projecting onto translucent walls and floor. As participants walk around, sensors detect the position of their heads and the software adjusts the projected images to create the illusion that objects inside the room and outside the room, seen through virtual windows, are three-dimensional.

**Figure 7.6** A CAVE with stereoscopic 3-D images projected on the walls.

Depending on whether the VR simulates a fantasy world, a design, or real life, input data must be obtained from CAD or similar software or by sampling images and sound from the real world. For example, when creating a 'virtual tour' of a hotel for a website, photos are taken with a digital camera aimed in a number of directions from a single point, not too far from the centre of each room.

These photos can then be manipulated to create the tour. Image-stitching software can be used to 'stitch' these photos together into a seamless panorama. The image can be resized and the image quality adjusted for rapid display on a web page. Hotspots on the page need to be created to enable the viewer to rotate their virtual direction of view, by scrolling through the panoramic image. A plan of the hotel can have an image map created so that it will interactively 'move' the viewer to another room.

VR is a good way to experience environments that humans cannot enter. It is cheaper to build a VR environment than a prototype during early testing. It is also a way for people to experience emergencies that would be too dangerous to create deliberately. Training in how to respond to such emergencies is much more realistic with VR than simply thinking or talking through a series of events. It is safer to make 'virtual' mistakes than real ones during training.

## 1.1.2 Information systems

This is a very large range of applications that includes retrieving information from a database and updating the information in some way. An information system is a prime example of a system whose data needs to be protected from accidental loss through human error, failure of a storage device, natural disaster, fire or theft. A **backup** copy of data can be made continuously, perhaps by 'mirroring' to storage on another site, or at frequent intervals, so that there is always a recent copy of data available. Recovery after data loss consists of restoring the data to the system from the backup copy. In the case of loss of hardware or software, recovery will first require the replacement of the hardware and reinstallation of any missing software.

Seat booking systems involve accessing a database of seats for entertainment or travel, searching to find available seats and purchasing tickets, either with or without seat reservations. We look at three variations on the same basic type of information retrieval system.

## Seat booking systems

Theatre booking systems allow booking agencies in different locations to be in communication with a central computer database system that stores details of the available seats for shows.

A customer telephones or goes into the agency and states their requirements, which include the name of the show or concert and the date, number and type of seats required. The agent then connects to the computer system and searches for suitable seats. As soon as specific seats have been selected, the seats' database records need to be electronically 'locked' to prevent any other customer from booking the same seats while payment is arranged.

When the seats are agreed:
- the customer pays by debit card, credit card or cash;
- the seats that have been bought are changed to show 'occupied' or 'sold' on the computer system;
- the tickets are printed out or a receipt (an 'e-ticket') is printed out for exchange for the tickets at the theatre.

This system allows for the sale of all the tickets because there is never a risk of the same ticket being sold twice. This is an example of a real-time transaction processing application.

This system can be extended to allow the same sort of booking on a website. The advantage is that the customer can order tickets without having to telephone or visit an agency, although a booking fee is still usually payable. The customer simply sees the same screen that the agency worker sees when they book a seat for them (see Figure 4.5, page 97). Payment over the Internet requires adequate security to prevent interception of card details or cardholder authentication passwords. The customer usually receives an email confirming the booking (Figure 7.7) and including an e-ticket 'booking reference' or 'confirmation code'.

Cinema booking systems work in much the same way. A customer may book and pay on a website or an automated phone system that uses speech recognition or the keypad on a phone. The customer receives a booking reference number. For unreserved seats, the system only has to ensure that the total number of tickets sold for a screening does not exceed the seating capacity of the auditorium. At the cinema, the customer keys their booking reference number into a ticket machine (Figure 7.8) and inserts their debit or credit card to authenticate the reference number. The machine prints out the tickets.

```
From: info@ticketweb.co.uk
Sent: 07 September
Subject: Order Confirmation

Event: Amiina
Venue: XOYO
32-37 Cowper Street, London

Seating: GENERAL ADMISSION
Time: Tuesday, September 28 at 8:00 PM
Quantity: 1
Delivery: Box Office Collection
CONFIRMATION CODE: YXAY3Y78

-------------------------------------------
Tuesday, September 7 at 9:49 AM

You have purchased the following:
-------------------------------------------
Ticket face value:        10.00
Service fee:               1.20
Total charges:            11.20
-------------------------------------------
```

**Figure 7.7**  An email e-ticket.

**Figure 7.8**  Collecting pre-booked tickets from a machine in a cinema.

This allows the owners of the cinema to reduce their costs by employing fewer people than would otherwise be needed. If a cinema complex has a number of auditoriums of various seating capacities, the booking system can allocate the largest auditorium to any screening for which the ticket sales exceed the seating capacity of the second largest auditorium and so on. Assuming that there is no last-minute surge in demand for a previously less popular screening, this optimises the amount of seating available for each screening. There are a number of applications used here that have to work together seamlessly.

## Travel applications

The travel industry allows bookings to be made by individual customers using websites or by travel agents. It is just as easy for customers to do their own bookings as it is to use a travel agent, but many customers continue to use travel agents to book holidays. The reasons are:

- Some customers do not have Internet access.
- Travel agents may have insurance against the travel company going out of business. If the customer books the holiday themselves they may find it difficult to get their money refunded or may have difficulty if they are on holiday when it happens.
- The process is more complex than booking a cinema ticket and it may prove too daunting for some people to contemplate.
- Travel agents have access to some holiday packages that are not available on websites.

The basic principle of booking a holiday, or a seat on a plane or on a train or any other travel-related service, is the same as booking a seat in a theatre. Holiday and travel operators maintain central databases storing records of scheduled accommodation and travel services, so that double bookings cannot be made. The number of people involved in providing the service is reduced, which means that the wage bill is reduced and the cost of the service can be reduced.

Airlines commonly encourage passengers to book flights through their websites. Some low-cost airlines only allow customers to book or check in on their websites. The passenger is issued with a booking reference number, which is emailed to them after a successful booking has been made. Passengers are usually encouraged to 'check in' online or at self-service kiosks (Figure 7.9) shortly before travelling. They must supply their reference number, confirm their intention to travel, enter the number of items of 'hold baggage' they intend to take, confirm or change their allocated seating and print their boarding pass. The only contact required with airport staff is at a 'bag drop' desk, where the passenger shows their boarding pass and has their hold baggage tagged by an agent and sent to the aircraft. This saves the labour-intensive process of collecting and entering check-in data from passengers and also reduces the time spent in the airport by passengers before departure.

**Figure 7.9** Using a self-service check-in kiosk saves labour costs for an airline and time for passengers.

 **SAQs**

2 If you pay for tickets on a website, how can you be sure that the transaction is secure?

## Medicine information systems

When a doctor has diagnosed a patient's problem, he or she may prescribe medicine. There are thousands of medicines available each of which has possible side effects and which can have undesirable interactions with other drugs or foods. All this information can be found in large reference books that doctors use. However, things change so often that the books are always out of date.

What the doctor needs is all this information stored on a computerised information system (Figure 7.10). The doctor can search the system for possible medicines to prescribe and can see the information that is available on each one.

## Hospital information systems
### Patient records

What is different about patient records in a hospital from, for example, student records in a school? Apart from the need to keep 'sensitive' information even more secure, a major difference is how long they are stored. Your school records may be kept for some years after you leave school in case you ask for a reference in the future, but they will be destroyed eventually. Your medical records need to be stored for life because a doctor could need to see your medical history at any time. It is possible that something that happened to you as a baby may affect you at a later point in your life.

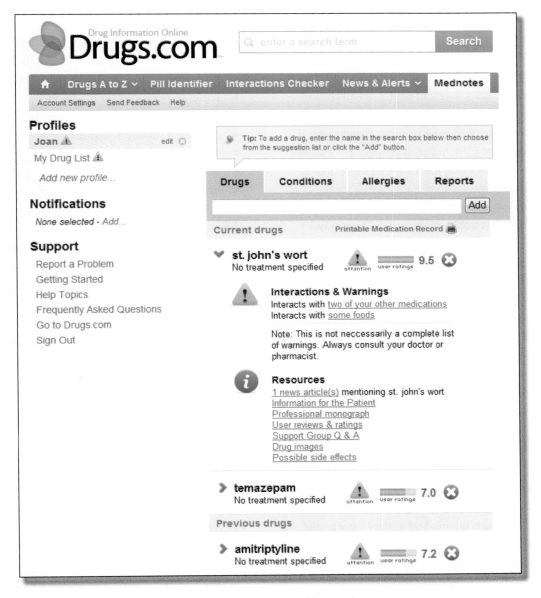

**Figure 7.10** Some medicine information systems are available to patients.

Each patient must be uniquely identified by a hospital number, a record key field in the database. Records need to include:

- the patient's medical history;
- monitoring data, such as temperature, pulse rate, blood pressure or electro-cardiogram (ECG);
- laboratory test results;
- high-quality images of X-rays and ultrasound or MRI scans;
- diagnoses;
- prescriptions.

These records have traditionally been maintained physically on paper and photographic film. Records stored electronically are potentially available via a private WAN or the Internet almost immediately at any location in the world.

The creation of an electronic patient record (EPR) system poses problems of managing the collection, input and storage of very diverse sets of data. Careful control of access to these data is needed to maintain patient confidentiality. These challenges become even greater if a regional or national EPR system is created. For reasons of both safety and efficiency, it is vital that these data are updated promptly. For example, time may be wasted if a patient cannot be contacted because a change of address or phone number has not been recorded. Time may be wasted and the health of a patient put at risk if the results of an earlier test have not been entered into the patient records system by the time the patient attends a consultation with a doctor.

Medical personnel can use PDAs or tablet PCs with barcode or RFID readers; they can identify patients by their hospital number on a barcoded or RFID-tagged wristband. They can also identify medication and blood products from their barcodes and enter these and other data directly into the hospital's EPR system via a WLAN.

## Extension

Investigate the use of computers and robots for carrying out surgical operations. What are the advantages and disadvantages for the patient and for the hospital? Investigate the use of the Internet, and particularly video-conferencing, when conducting complex surgical operations.

### Hospital administration

Records for the management of a hospital need to include data about:

- hospital personnel, their duty schedules and their clinical performance;
- patients' appointments for outpatient consultations and diagnostic and therapeutic procedures;
- patients' bookings for inpatient stays;
- ward management and scheduling;
- operating theatre scheduling;
- stock control for consumable supplies;
- equipment purchases and service histories;
- financial records including expenditure against budgets and payroll.

Advantages of electronic databases include easier tracking of the spending and performance of each department and improved efficiency in centralised, bulk buying of supplies.

Each of these applications is large and complex and discussion is beyond the scope of the syllabus. Many of them rely on working together and with other systems to achieve efficiency. For example, your family doctor or general practitioner (GP), may consult your medical records on the practice's patient administration system (PAS). The doctor may then book you an appointment online with a hospital doctor, email some notes to the hospital and update your records. A few days later, you get a letter confirming the date and time of your appointment with the hospital doctor. The hospital doctor may subsequently book you in for an operation that requires you to recover in a ward. Think of all the computer systems that have been used here. You will realise that healthcare, as well as most other sectors, is highly dependent on reliable applications of computer systems.

## Library systems

Computerised database systems are used in libraries to keep records of books and other resources that are available for loan; borrowers; and loans of resources to members. Possible names of various database tables are included below to explain how this works in detail, but in an exam it is sufficient to simplify this and refer to 'the loan record in the library's database'.

Each borrower usually has a library card with a barcode of the borrower's unique ID number. Each copy of a book can also have a unique number printed as a barcode (Figure 7.11). Input of these data requires barcode readers.

**Figure 7.11** A barcode, separate from the ISBN, can uniquely identify a specific copy of a library book.

### Questions

**10** Why does a library book's barcode need to replace the book's ISBN? Discuss differences between the school library system and a larger, public library system before reading any further. Note that there are no 'right answers' here because libraries tend to use similar but slightly different systems.

### Extension

What is the Dewey system of classification? What part does it play in a computerised library system?

Note the need for an ID number to identify the borrower in a public library rather than the name and class that may be used in a school library. The reason for this is that there are far more members of a public library than there are of a school library and it is very important to distinguish between two people with the same names. In a relational database, a borrower's unique ID appears in the record key field of their record, in the *Borrower* table and also as a reference to that record in each of their loan records, in the *Loan* table. Similarly, the *Resource* table has a unique ID number as its record key field and the value for the relevant resource also appears as a reference to that resource in loan records.

When a borrower borrows resources, their unique borrower's ID number is read from their card and the system prompts the librarian (or the borrower, if it is a self-service library) if resources are overdue. If the borrower has not exhausted their borrowing rights, the borrower's ID and the resource ID for each resource are entered into a new loan record. When a resource is returned, a query can use the resource's ID to find the relevant loan record and automatically update it by entering the current date into a *Date Returned* field.

Resources that are significantly overdue can be identified. The *Loan* table is searched each day for books that are overdue by at least a certain number of days. A suitable query can simultaneously look up the borrower's name and address from the *Borrower* table and the resource's title and author from the *Resource* table and, probably, a separate *Author* table. A suitable report groups these composite records by borrower, to avoid sending out multiple messages to the same borrower. These details can then be used to produce a letter (Figure 7.12) or email that is sent to the member reminding them that the resource is overdue and asking for it to be returned.

# AnyTown Library

Mr. T. Johnson
15 OurStreet
Anytown

9 May 2011

Dear Mr. Johnson

You borrowed:

The book *Promoting Harmony* by Sarah Idurise on 4 April 2011
The CD *Playing the Tenor Banjo* by Oliver Buxton on 4 April 2011

These resources are currently 28 resource-days overdue. The current fine payable is $28 \times 2c = 56c$.
Plase return the resources as soon as possible.

Yours sincerely,

L. Chrichton

Head Librarian

AnyTown Library

Address: Any House, 23 Any Road, Anytown, ANY 12345      Phone: 01234 567890      Fax: 01234 567890
Email: libname@anytownlib.hotmail.com   Website: http://www.anytownlib.com

**Figure 7.12**   A letter from a library reminding a borrower that a resource is overdue.

## Questions

11   Consider the letter in Figure 7.12.

a   Which parts of the letter are standard contents that will appear on every letter about an outstanding loan?

b   Which parts of the letter have come from the library's database and from which table does each of the pieces of information come?

c   Which parts of the letter are calculated by the system?

d   How can the tables be slightly altered so that a similar letter is not sent again tomorrow?

e   How can the system provide information about members who still do not return books despite having been sent a letter?

A library's cataloguing system can often be accessed by visitors to the library or even via a website. This may provide facilities for searching by title, author or subject. A relational database (Figure 7.13) to hold all this cataloguing and loan data efficiently is quite complex and way above the standard expected for this qualification.

## Office automation

The move from typewriters to word processing, from paper spreadsheets and accounting ledgers to electronic ones, and from paper-based records to electronic databases has greatly boosted the productivity of office workers. However, it has required them to learn many new skills, such as navigating a computer's operating system, file manager and the often complex and sometimes radically changing menu structures of these office 'productivity tools'. Organisations are adopting office automation, with the result that office workers have to understand and use new styles of working.

As computers became more common in the workplace, it became easier for different departments and individual workers to generate separate data files. Organisations realised that this was sometimes inefficient and could lead to up-to-date data not always being available. Many organisations use shared databases as a common pool of data with appropriate levels of access for workers according to their needs. Individuals

still have the flexibility of developing their own database objects or spreadsheets for generating their own information from the data. DTP and word processing software can use a database query or spreadsheet as a data source for a mail merge, to produce catalogues and personalised business letters.

An organisation may use a 'document imaging system' to capture and store scanned images of documents received by the organisation. A 'document management system', 'enterprise content management system' or 'digital asset management system' is used to track and store those images and computer-generated documents that the organisation receives or generates. Workers can often access information from wherever they are located, even using mobile devices.

A 'workflow management system' allows a manager to define a 'workflow' for a project, which is a sequence of tasks to achieve an outcome. As soon as one task is completed, the system automatically performs any file conversion required and notifies the relevant individual or team of workers that the data are available for the next task. The system follows up any uncompleted task and notifies the workflow's manager if there is a significant hold-up.

In a simple example, a document may be submitted into a workflow for approval, editing or commenting by other project members. They, in turn, can see each

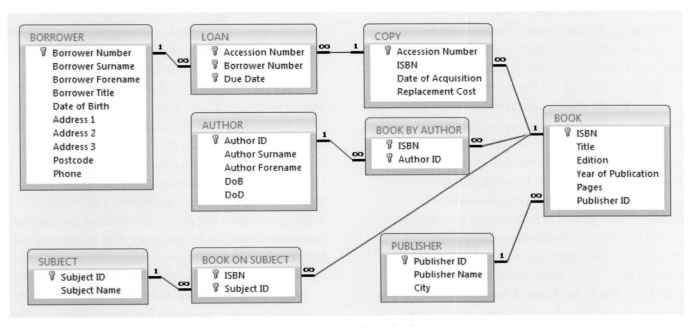

**Figure 7.13** The tables and relationships for a library book catalogue and loan database.

other's changes or comments and add their own. This enables the project's members to collaborate more effectively on the creation of the document. Previously, the originator would have emailed the document to all the project members, they would have returned their separate edited or commented versions and the originator would have had to combine all the changes and comments into a single document. This would then be sent out again for final approval – an unwieldy and time-consuming process.

Another area of development has been the creation of centralised application software that manages the content of a file in a database, while tens of workers or students with different levels of access collaborate by simultaneously editing or viewing the contents of the file in real-time.

Some companies host 'cloud computing' applications on remote servers. *Google Docs* is a free web application for creating, sharing, collaborating and publishing files. A 'wiki' (Hawaiian for 'quickly') is a web application for collaboratively creating and refining web pages; the foremost example is *Wikipedia*.

## 1.1.3 Commercial and general data processing

### Automatic stock control and order processing

An **automatic stock control system** records sales and deliveries and automatically reorders fresh stock when the stock level falls to a minimum level. Let us take the example of an automatic stock control system in a supermarket. Possible names of various database tables have been included to explain how this works in detail, but in an exam it is sufficient to simplify this and refer to 'the product record in the supermarket's database'.

Occasionally, supermarkets use four-digit 'price look-up' (PLU) codes to identify large items that cannot be passed over the point of sale (POS) terminal's barcode scanner or to identify self-service items, such as apples, which must be weighed. Otherwise, internationally unique product codes such as UPC or EAN-13 are printed in both human-readable and barcode formats on the labelling of all pre-packaged items. The full description of each product stocked is stored in a *Product* table, with the unique product code as the record key value. A *Product In Store* table in the supermarket's database contains a record for each

combination of product and store, in which the stock level can be stored. Each record uses a *Product Code* key value to refer to a product and a *Store Code* key value to refer to a store.

A customer takes their basket or trolley to the POS terminal, which may be a self-service kiosk. Each item's barcode is scanned by a barcode reader and a 'beep' or visual prompt confirms that a valid code has been read. A POS operator can manually key in the product code using a key pad, if the barcode cannot be read.

Depending on whether or not the supermarket varies the price according to the store, the terminal supplies the *Product Code* key value to a query to retrieve the product's description and price from the relevant record in either the *Product In Store* or the *Product* table. Another query uses the same *Product Code* key value and the *Store Code* key value to find the relevant record in the *Product In Store* table and subtract one from the value of the *Stock Level* field. If the value of *Stock Level* is less than or equal to that of the *Reorder Level* field in the same record, the system automatically reorders the *Reorder Quantity* from the supermarket's distribution depot.

This adjustment of the stock level and automatic reordering is done in real-time because the distribution depot needs as much notice as possible of the order, especially if the whole supply chain operates on a 'just-in-time' (JIT) basis. Although the *Reorder Quantity* is the default quantity to reorder, the order can also be automatically adjusted using past sales statistics, anticipated long-term trends, the weather, and scheduled local or televised sporting events. In such a system, the store manager may have little control over ordering.

This POS checkout procedure is repeated until all the items have been scanned, when the customer is told the total. The database also records the customer's payment for the goods, updates the points total of the customer's loyalty card account (which enables the supermarket to link sales to a particular customer) and prints an itemised receipt (Figure 7.14) showing a list of the items' descriptions and prices. The database can also use payment information to update the POS operator's cash takings in real-time. The store's takings can be updated in real-time or by totalling the sales at the end of the day.

When goods are delivered to the store, each package of products is likely to carry a barcode or RFID tag that

```
                ALDI
          LORDSCROFT LANE
             HAVERHILL

1969 PINK LADY APPLES           1.79  A
              SUBTOTAL          1.79
42919 YOGURT & CRUNCH 150G      0.35  A
42919 YOGURT & CRUNCH 150G      0.35  A
42919 YOGURT & CRUNCH 150G      0.35  A
42919 YOGURT & CRUNCH 150G      0.35  A
2907 FRESH SEMI-SKIMMED MILK    1.09  A
              SUBTOTAL          4.28
T O T A L                       4.28
6 ITEMS
C a s h           £             4.28

NET TOTAL        VAT  A         4.28
VAT              00.0%          0.00
*2565 776/010/001/122 14.08.11 13:30 A-00
             Permanently
           Lowering Prices
              Every Day
            www.aldi.co.uk
```

**Figure 7.14** An itemised supermarket receipt from the UK.

uniquely identifies that package. The ID code read from the barcode or tag is used to retrieve the relevant record from the database, containing the quantity and product code of the package's contents. The database automatically updates the relevant *Stock Level* by adding the quantity received in that package and will probably indicate a temporary storage location for the package.

At the distribution depot, the dispatch of an order for a product to a store is similarly used to reduce the *Stock Level* in the relevant record in the *Product In Depot* table for that depot. If the value of *Stock Level* is less than or equal to that of the *Reorder Level* field in the same record, the system automatically reorders the *Reorder Quantity* from the supermarket's supplier. The system uses the *Supplier Code* key value in the same record to look up the supplier's name and address in the relevant record in the *Supplier* table.

It is possible to run a query to calculate the gross profit generated by sales of each product over a period of time, ranging from a day to a year, for the store, a region or the whole supermarket, by subtracting the total cost of products purchased by the supermarket from the total income from sales of those products.

### Personnel records

The workers in an organisation are often referred to as its 'personnel' or 'human resources'. When you start to work for an organisation, they have to record a lot of information about you. Any personal information such as this has to be very secure so that only the personnel staff members in the organisation can access it. The information is used so that the organisation can:

- identify you – your employee number, name, date of birth, next-of-kin;
- send you information by post and email – your address, email address, telephone number;
- pay you – your salary or rate of pay, grade, date of joining the organisation, taxation reference code, tax payments, bank account details;
- record your attendance – periods of sick leave, annual leave entitlement used;
- record any disabilities – notes of adjustments needed to equipment and working conditions to enable you to work;
- gauge your progress – past salary increases, bonuses, grades, skills, training courses attended, projects completed, manager's appraisals;
- look after your future progress – target future training required, position in organisation;
- record good and bad experiences – quality awards, warnings.

All this information used to be stored in cardboard folders; it is now stored in personnel database systems, which have to be very flexible. Some of the items stored might, for instance, be scanned images of written material, such as appraisals. In well-designed, integrated systems, other systems access the personnel database to extract specific pieces of information. It is important to keep these records accurate and up-to-date. The organisation may periodically send you a copy of some of this information, so that you can verify it and make amendments, including any changes of address or telephone number. We see next how the payroll system uses personnel information.

## Payroll

Let us consider payroll calculations for workers in a factory who are paid weekly. Their pay depends on their rate of pay (taken from the personnel database) and the amount of work that they have done during the week. Suppose that batch processing of files is used to calculate the pay for the workers. The times that they work for the week and any relevant production statistics are collected in a serial 'transaction' file. Before processing, this needs to be sorted into the same order as the record key in the sequential 'main' personnel payment file, which may have been exported from the personnel database. The records from the main file are read in sequence and processed using all the relevant records from the sorted transaction file. Gross pay, tax payable and net pay are calculated. This system prints a 'payslip' providing each worker with notification of their pay (Figure 7.15). It can also produce a separate payments file, listing the electronic payments to be made to the workers' bank accounts.

---

Cottonwoods Ltd

Record of pay for week ending 04/05/11

| R. Thornton | Manufacturing Department |
| | Grade C employee |
| | Employee number 123456B |
| Bank Details | LancsBanks |
| Sort Code | 07-13-29 |
| Account No. | 6543 543 2345 |
| Tax No. | AD379684-25 |
| Number of hours at standard rate | 33 |
| Standard rate: | $7 |
| Number of hours at overtime rate | 6 |
| Overtime rate | $12 |
| | |
| Gross pay | $303.00 |
| Tax paid at source (Rate of 30%) | $ 90.90 |
| | |
| **Net pay** | **$212.10** |

Payment will be made to your bank account on the first working day following the date shown above.

**Figure 7.15** Simplified payslip output from the payroll application.

---

## Questions

12  The payslip shown in Figure 7.15 is a simplified version of a real payslip.

a  Which parts are standard contents that appear on every payslip?

b  Which parts are common to all workers in that factory?

c  Which parts are specific to the particular worker whose payslip it is?

d  Which parts are results calculated from data by the system?

e  If you were to receive a similar payslip, is there anything that you would like changed to make it easier to read or anything added to make it clearer?

## Banking systems

Banking application software is used to maintain a bank account as follows:

- It stores the cumulative result of all transactions, known as the account's 'balance'. When the account holder has funds in the account, it is said to be 'in credit'. If the account holder has been allowed to overdraw, the account is said to be 'in debit' because the holder owes a debt to the bank.

- Deposits into the account (or 'credits') are recorded and added to the balance. These may be cash deposits, cheques paid in from other accounts, or electronic payments such as 'direct credit' payments from an employer or a refund from a retailer.

- Withdrawals from the account (or 'debits') are recorded and subtracted from the balance. These may be cash withdrawals from the bank or an ATM, cheque payments, debit card payments at a POS or electronic payments (such as a 'direct debit' agreed by the account holder with a supplier of goods or services or Internet or telephone banking transfers).

- Any interest payable to or by the account holder is calculated and added or subtracted, respectively.

- Any charges (for example, for overdrafts or dishonoured cheques) are calculated and subtracted.

- A regular statement of the account's transactions is produced and may be sent to the account holder as well as being available for viewing using Internet banking.

### Cheque processing

Cheques are a paper-based technology for making payments from one bank account to another. Cheques are now rarely used but are still very convenient if the payer has no access to Internet banking facilities or the payee has no facilities for accepting debit card payments. Many banking systems are due to phase out cheques, although as yet there is no clear alternative such as the transfer of 'electronic cash' between e-cash cards.

A cheque is a pre-printed form, with ID codes for the bank, account and cheque. The codes are printed in MICR – simplified numeric and control characters in magnetic ink, which is hard to forge. The account holder completes the date, payee and amount to be paid. Figure 7.16 shows a completed cheque with the MICR characters highlighted in a red box. When the payee pays the cheque into their account, the bank has to claim payment from the drawer's bank. In the inter-bank, computerised, cheque-clearing system, a magnetic scanner and MICR software read the magnetic characters from the cheque, with an error rate of 1 per 20,000 cheques. Only the payment amount needs to be keyed in by an operator. The ID codes for the payee's bank and account are available in MICR characters on the accompanying paying-in slip.

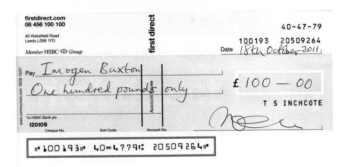

**Figure 7.16** A cheque with MICR characters that identify the bank, account and cheque number.

### Automated teller machines

Another piece of technology makes it less likely that a customer has to visit a bank branch personally. An automated teller machine (ATM) is a machine found

outside banks or shops (Figure 7.17), and sometimes in indoor locations. It gives a customer access to a limited range of banking transactions.

**Figure 7.17** ATM in use in a street.

The cardholder inserts their card into the machine, which contains a smart card reader. The cardholder enters a secret PIN to authenticate his or her identity. If the card and PIN combination is valid, the cardholder can then select a number of services from a menu, usually using buttons, as a touchscreen is less reliable when exposed to rain and snow. Services usually include viewing a balance and withdrawing cash, with or without a paper receipt showing the partial account number, date, time, location and amount. Before dispensing cash, the machine checks that the amount requested does not exceed the funds available and does not cause the total withdrawn during a certain period to exceed a maximum limit. This limit is intended to prevent a thief with knowledge of the PIN from emptying the account. A message travels from the ATM's operator to the card issuer requesting a transfer of funds from the cardholder's account to the operator's account (see the next section for more information about electronic funds transfer).

To be acceptable to customers, transactions must be processed in real-time. The machine always returns the card first, as it is more valuable than any cash dispensed and a customer could easily forget to remove this small object while handling the cash. Only when the card has been removed is the cash dispensed.

ATMs are a relatively cheap way of providing 24-hour access to cash, so they can be quite widely distributed. Their disadvantage is that they are in public locations where someone could observe cardholders entering their PINs and cardholders sometimes have to read ATM screens in unfavourable light conditions.

### Questions

**13** One service that a customer can select at an ATM is to request a statement for their account. Is this process a real-time process or a batch process?

1.1.2 ## Ecommerce

### Electronic funds transfer

An **electronic funds transfer** (EFT) is a computerised movement of financial credit from one account to another. A payroll system could produce a payments file listing the electronic payments to be made. This can be used to automate 'direct credit' payments from the employing organisation's bank account to the workers' bank accounts, without cheques or cash. For each payment, a secure electronic message is sent to the organisation's bank requesting that funds be taken out of its account and transferred to the worker's account, often at another bank. Within an inter-bank EFT system, the organisation's bank sends a similar secure electronic message to each worker's bank stating the amount to be credited to the worker's account. A simplified dataflow diagram is shown in Figure 7.18.

### Questions

**14** Is this process popular with the workers? Do they appreciate having their money paid into a bank account rather than being given cash in hand?

Card payments are accepted for many goods and services. Such card payments also use EFT. The cardholder inserts their card into the smart card reader at the POS terminal and enters their secret PIN to authenticate their identity (Figure 7.19). The card reader compares an encrypted version of the PIN with a similarly encrypted version stored in the card. If they match, a secure message is sent from the supplier of goods or services through a card payments system over a WAN to the card issuer. The message uses the ID number read from the card to request EFT from the cardholder's account to the supplier's account. If the card issuer authorises the transaction, the purchase is completed.

**Figure 7.19** Smart card reader used for payment for goods or services.

When an EFT system is integrated with a POS terminal, it is known as an **electronic funds transfer at the point of sale** (EFTPOS) terminal. Customers are

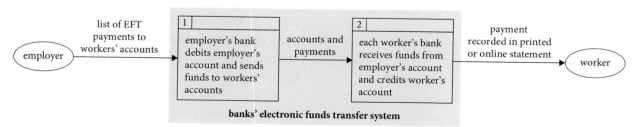

**Figure 7.18** Using EFT to pay workers.

often encouraged to pay by card because this reduces the amount of cash being handled at the tills and transported between the store and its bank.

Bank customers can also often use EFT through Internet banking. The customer logs in to a secure website using a username and password. They can view balances for their accounts, view statements or set up single or regular payments by EFT to a specified bank account of a specified amount on a specified date.

Bank customers may also be able to arrange to carry out telephone banking transactions. Here, the customer talks to a bank employee in a call centre (Figure 7.20), who carries out the required tasks on a computer at the request of the customer. Although some customers are concerned about security, these methods make banking highly accessible; only very rarely does a customer have to visit a bricks-and-mortar bank branch.

**Figure 7.20** Bank employees in a telephone banking call centre talking to customers.

### Internet shopping

Similarly, a cardholder can purchase goods and services from a website using EFT. The 'online shop' has to maintain a web-accessible database with an illustrated catalogue that customers can browse and search. A customer can add a specified quantity of a chosen item to a list of ordered items known as their 'basket' or 'cart'. They can also amend and delete items from their order. On completion of an order, the customer supplies their contact details, if they have not already registered them. They supply information about their payment card for EFT, including the card's ID number printed in embossed lettering on the front. Instead of using their secret PIN to authenticate their identity, the cardholder supplies extra security digits displayed on the other side of the card and, if the card issuer requires, a password.

An online shop's running costs are greatly reduced by this automated ordering. It does not necessarily needing any retail shop space and this can result in cheaper prices for customers. In other cases, retail outlets that offer specialist goods and services have been able to advertise and sell their products to a worldwide market by opening an online shop. This strategy is sometimes known as 'clicks-and-mortar'.

 **SAQs**

3   What do the following abbreviations stand for: EFT, POS, ATM, PIN?

### Debit and credit cards

Debit and credit cards are used for EFT as described earlier. The difference between a debit card and a credit card is the source of funds. With a **debit card**, a cardholder can only make a cash withdrawal or payment for goods or services with funds already in their bank account or with an overdraft (or credit) arrangement previously agreed with their bank. A 'debit' is recorded on the cardholder's account soon after they complete the transaction and shows up on a statement, which lists the date, location and amount of each transaction.

A **credit card** is so called because the card issuer provides the cardholder with borrowed funds with which to 'buy now and pay later'. As with a debit card, the EFT message arising from a card payment travels to the card issuer requesting EFT from the cardholder's account. This account has no funds in it, only debt owed to the card issuer, for which a high rate of interest is liable to be charged.

When the card issuer receives the EFT request arising from a card payment, it records the transaction. It adds the purchase price of goods or services to the cardholder's debt and sends funds to the account of the originator of the request, less a small fee for the use of the facility. This is why suppliers are sometimes unwilling to accept credit card payments, especially for small amounts.

ATM withdrawals are handled differently. The card issuer pays an EFT request from an ATM operator in full, but adds a small fee as well as the amount withdrawn to the cardholder's debt. The cardholder is liable to pay an even higher rate of interest on the 'cash' portion of their debt than on the 'purchases' portion.

The card issuer sends a monthly statement to the cardholder, listing transactions much like a bank statement. Depending on the contractual agreement between the card issuer and the cardholder, the cardholder is usually liable for interest on the cash portion of the debt from the date of its withdrawal. However, they may have an interest-free period within which to pay off the purchases portion.

The computer systems for managing both debit cards and credit cards have to process massive numbers of transactions. Many of these transactions involve the inter-bank EFT system, with real-time processing at least for the authorisation of payments and batch processing for the production of statements. Interest calculations are particularly complicated for different portions of credit card debt. The software must be highly accurate and reliable, with a high level of security.

In Kenya, in East Africa, banking and card payment services are not widely available or affordable. One mobile phone network made it possible for someone to purchase a number of call credits. These can be transferred to friends and relatives subscribing to the same network by means of a free SMS text message. People soon realised that they could use phone credit as a currency for informal EFT. The phone network has since developed a more formal phone-based EFT service (Figure 7.21) with millions of customers storing savings as phone credits and sending and receiving tens of millions of dollars every day.

Compared with paying by cash, cards for EFT are more secure and easier to carry. They can often be used in other countries. The disadvantages of payment cards are that the customer needs a bank account, cannot make very small payments, cannot see how much money

**Figure 7.21** *Sambaza* (Swahili for 'sharing') is a service that allows users to perform EFT through the transfer of phone credit by text message.

they have at all times and, in the case of a credit card, may be tempted to borrow money that they will not be able to repay.

 **SAQs**

4 Why do supermarkets not like being paid in cash?

5 What is the benefit to banks of the increasing use of EFT?

**Questions**

15 Two shops use traditional methods of serving customers. A member of staff fetches the goods for customers, adds up the amount owed and packs the shopping into the customer's bags. One shop decides

$\longrightarrow$

Question 15 continued …

to introduce a computerised system. Try to justify your answers to the following questions.

  a  How would you expect the state of the stock to differ between the two shops?

  b  Why does the store with the computerised system have fewer items that are specially discounted because they are nearing their 'sell-by' date?

  c  Why does the store with the computerised system have more special offers available?

16  The store with the computerised system decides to offer a service whereby customers can use a simple form of Internet shopping. A customer can email an order to the store over the Internet. The store will then arrange to have the order delivered.

  a  How can the store ensure that the goods are paid for?

  b  What are the disadvantages to the store and to the customer of using this form of shopping?

  c  What are the advantages to the store and to the customer of using this form of shopping?

  d  Is this very different from the old system that allowed customers to telephone in their orders?

  e  Is the system coming round full circle?

## Industrial, technical and scientific uses

### Modelling

Computer modelling is a tool for developing scientific understanding of physical, biological and social processes. A computer model does not involve a physical model. It uses program code based on a mathematical model, a set of formulae, to represent a real-world process (Figure 7.22). Data for the model can be obtained from previous measurements of the process. To be accurate, the model needs to be tested very thoroughly against the known behaviour of the target process. Departure of the model from known behaviour can be used to try to refine the model. Sometimes a spreadsheet is sufficient; sometimes complex specialised programming, a very large set of data and a supercomputer are needed.

### Simulation

A computer simulation is the use of a computer model to try to predict the future course of a process under specified external conditions. In some cases, it is performed simply to attempt to predict or forecast some behaviour or event, such as the occurrence and strength of hurricanes or earthquakes.

In other cases, computer simulation is used to attempt to engineer a solution to a problem. For example, structural engineers may simulate how different forms of building construction behave when subjected to hurricanes or earthquakes. They can then try to improve building construction standards to enable buildings to withstand these natural phenomena better.

For engineering tests, computer simulation is used when a physical scaled-down model cannot give reliable results and full-scale physical tests are:

- too expensive and time-consuming, such as crash-testing of a car or testing a prototype only to discover that it is not feasible or needs major modifications;
- not technically feasible, such as artificially hurricane-testing or earthquake-testing a building;
- too dangerous, such as testing the response of a nuclear power station to an incident.

Output is likely to be graphical as well as numerical and may be presented in real-time (that is, keeping pace with the real-world process) or faster or slower than real-time. Although a useful alternative to real-world testing, simulation is only as accurate as the underlying computer model in its predictions.

Some other applications of computer simulations are:

- forecasting the performance of a country's economy based on different scenarios;
- forecasting population growth based on different scenarios;
- forecasting how vehicles queue on congested roads or how customers queue at supermarket checkouts;
- testing proposed new road layouts or traffic lights;
- testing designs of chemical plants, nuclear plants or deep sea or outer space vehicles.

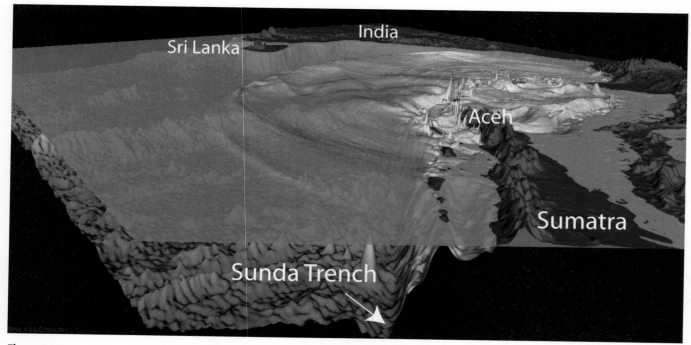

**Figure 7.22** A representation, generated by a computer model, of the wave heights one hour after the earthquake off the coast of Sumatra that triggered the Indian Ocean tsunami on 26th December 2004.

Software simulations have the following advantages:

- they may make it easier to try out alternative scenarios and configurations of equipment in order to arrive at the best solution;
- they may consume less time for both engineers and customers compared with performing real-life trials;
- they may be safer than real-life trials (for example, an inappropriate set of traffic light timings could contribute to an accident in real-life);
- they may be less expensive than setting up and performing real-life trials or simulations with actors.

### Simple simulations

Spreadsheets are often appropriate for simulating simple processes. With some software it is possible to switch a spreadsheet between different sets of data, known as 'scenarios', to answer 'what if' questions. A spreadsheet's graphical outputs can even be animated using programming techniques (Figure 7.23).

A small business could store its accounts on a spreadsheet and project its performance forward, by making certain assumptions about the continuation of trends in past data or about different future trends. Data could also represent assumptions made about future borrowing, inward investment, branch opening, recruitment of new staff, price changes or the price-sensitivity of sales. Formulae could calculate projected revenue, costs and profit. It is even possible to model a whole, new, proposed business using a spreadsheet.

### Weather-forecasting simulations

Let us consider a much more complex example: simulating the behaviour of solar radiation and the Earth's rotation, land surfaces, oceans and atmosphere for weather forecasting. Existing meteorological data have been collected and used to create, test and refine three-dimensional mathematical models for radiation, rotation, land, oceans and atmosphere.

The computer model of the atmosphere may consist of imaginary cubic segments of space. Each segment has gases and water vapour that flow in and out under the influence of pressure differences, convection currents and the Earth's rotation. Each segment also absorbs, re-radiates and transmits radiation and water droplets or ice particles form inside it. Mathematical equations enable the computer model to estimate how pressure changes within a segment and how gases, heat and water

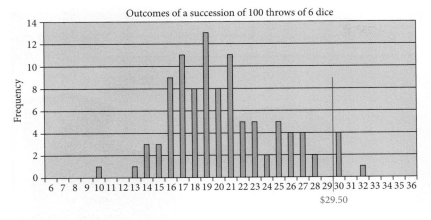

Outcomes of a succession of 100 throws of 6 dice

**Figure 7.23** A bar chart designed to illustrate possible distributions of the 'dice price' that theatre-goers could choose to pay to see a performance of *The Dice House*, instead of the standard price (marked in red). A player could see that they could end up paying a few dollars extra, but were far more likely to pay somewhere near the average throw of $21.

vapour flow between the segments in a given time, such as a few seconds.

Even if the cubic segments of the atmosphere are as large as one kilometre, there could be up to 50 billion segments for which complex calculations have to be performed for each element of time. Reducing the size of the cubic segments to 0.1 kilometres would have the potential to improve the accuracy of the model but there would then be up to 50 trillion elements for computation for the atmosphere alone. The forecast might be more accurate if each element of time was also smaller. However, the risk is that, even with a supercomputer, it may not be possible to obtain output from the simulation faster than real-time, so we may never be able to produce a forecast! There is no point in taking two days to forecast tomorrow's weather, however accurate the 'forecast' is.

Current data are captured at regular intervals from sensors (where necessary, with ADCs) measuring barometric pressure, temperature, humidity, wind speed and direction mounted on weather stations and meteorological balloons. Infrared and visible light images from remote sensors on meteorological satellites can provide information about cloud cover at various altitudes. These data are fed into the computer models. They are used to calculate predictions of pressure, temperature, humidity, wind speed and direction, cloud formation or evaporation, and precipitation over the Earth's surface at future times, ranging from a few hours to days ahead. From these results, it is possible to draw up weather forecasts for a locality or region and to draw maps representing forecast conditions over a region (Figure 7.24). Successive graphical representations of forecasts of cloud cover and precipitation can be animated to represent the unfolding distribution of

**Durban five-day forecast**

| Date | Local time | Weather | Max/Min temp | Wind Dir | Wind Speed | Pressure | Relative humidity | Visibility |
|------|-----------|---------|--------------|-----|-------|----------|-------------------|------------|
| Wed 20 Oct | Day | | 26 °C | NNE | 6 mph | 1014 hPa | 62% | Good |
| | Night | | 20 °C | | | | | |
| Thu 21 Oct | Day | | 25 °C | NNW | 9 mph | 1004 hPa | 21% | Moderate |
| | Night | | 18 °C | | | | | |
| Fri 22 Oct | Day | | 25 °C | SE | 6 mph | 1010 hPa | 83% | Good |
| | Night | | 19 °C | | | | | |
| Sat 23 Oct | Day | | 24 °C | SE | 4 mph | 1011 hPa | 89% | Good |
| | Night | | 19 °C | | | | | |
| Sun 24 Oct | Day | | 24 °C | SW | 7 mph | 1008 hPa | 87% | Good |
| | Night | | 17 °C | | | | | |

**Figure 7.24** A UK Meteorological Office weather forecast.

weather. Sometimes, the likelihood of rainfall during a day may be calculated as a percentage probability.

As computer processing power increases, the sizes of spatial and time segments can be decreased, improving the quality of forecasts produced by the computer models. Comparing each forecast with the actual weather provides further testing of the computer model. This may reveal systematic errors resulting from inaccuracy that requires further refinement of the models.

### Computer-aided engineering (CAE) simulations

When a designer pushes existing technology to its limits or uses an unfamiliar or innovative technology, there is no simple set of rules for judging the safety or reliability of the design. In such situations, it is possible to use **computer-aided engineering (CAE)** simulation software (Figure 7.25) to check the design before construction or manufacture. Strength of materials,

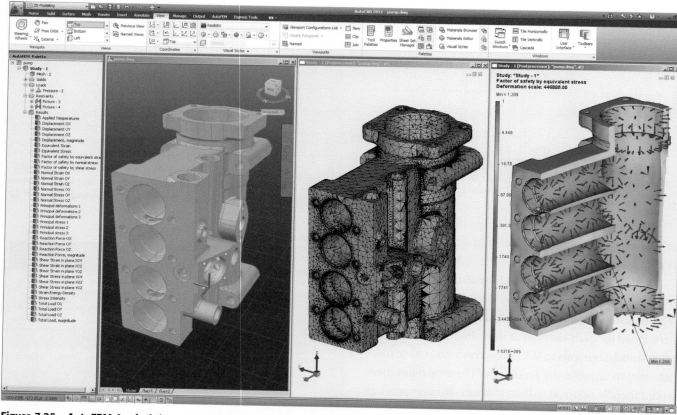

**Figure 7.25**   *AutoFEM Analysis* is an extension to the *AutoCAD* package that enables it to convert a CAD model into a mesh of small elements and use 'finite element analysis' (FEA) to show the distribution of stress applied to the 'virtual product' under certain conditions.

deflection under load, susceptibility to vibration, maximum load, and acoustic and thermal behaviour can all be modelled.

The architect of the interpretation centre (Figure 7.26) at Mapungubwe National Park, South Africa, used adaptations of the sort of thin-skinned

**Figure 7.26**   The designs for these vaulted roofs at Mapungubwe National Park, South Africa, were checked by structural engineers using CAE simulation software similar to that shown in Figure 7.25.

vault design shown in Figure 1.15, a technology from Catalonia in Spain. The vault designs were checked by an international team of structural engineers using CAE simulation software prior to construction.

### Architectural simulations

Architects often use simulations to test other aspects of their designs. For example, an architect who has designed a new shopping mall must assess the proposed procedures for evacuating many hundreds or even thousands of people from the mall if a fire were to break out. In many countries, building designs must not simply be constructed in appropriate ways but also conform to performance standards. Even if the mall were built so that its performance could be tested, it would still not be possible to set fire to it and certainly not with people inside! The alternative of hiring a crowd of people to perform simulated evacuations in response to fire alarms is also expensive and time-consuming.

Fortunately, computer models exist for estimating the time taken for a number of people to leave a building via exit routes of various lengths, widths and types. The architect could use software with these models to provide an evacuation simulation. Data for a simulation could include:

- CAD data for the building's design;
- the locations of the visual and audible alarms;
- the locations of the evacuation signs and the direction in which people are directed to leave the building;
- the locations of exits;
- the number of people and how they will be distributed around the building;
- the number of children and people with mobility or sensory impairments, who may take longer to become of aware of the need to evacuate or to move to an exit;
- the location of a fire.

The results could be as simple as the time calculated for everyone to leave the building. The output could also include graphical representations of the building and its occupants at various stages during the simulated evacuation (Figure 7.27). These graphics could also be animated into a video of the simulation. The architect may run the simulation using different scenarios, such as changing the location of the fire or blocking one of the exits because of maintenance work. The architect can adjust some aspects of the building's design, perhaps increasing the width of a long walkway, including an extra audible alarm or moving a cinema auditorium to a lower floor. This continues until simulations achieve the required evacuation performance for all scenarios. The results of these simulations would be used as evidence that the design achieves the required evacuation performance standards when applying for permission to construct the building.

Software also exists that can simulate the spread of a fire through a building, which can be used to produce even more informative simulations of an evacuation.

### Virtual reality

Virtual reality is a more 'immersive' method of interacting with a computer simulation than simply looking at a screen. One application of VR is to allow an operator to interact with a simulation of the control room of a planned industrial plant, an aircraft cockpit or an assistive device for someone with a disability. This provides a relatively cheap way of testing ergonomics and allows a design to be modified before building an expensive mock-up or prototype.

Another application could be to allow an engineer to fly through normally inaccessible spaces, such as hazardous environments or tiny channels, or even to 'see inside' solid parts of a proposed chemical or nuclear plant. Colour-coded, graphical information about normally invisible properties such as temperature, mechanical stress or radiation strength could accompany the view of the structure itself. For a fly through of a design, this extra information would be simulated to provide engineers with an additional method of checking designs. For a working plant, the extra information could be processed from data obtained from sensors or cameras within the plant and could help operators to monitor the plant's safety and troubleshoot faults.

The sounds of engine and wind noise and animated graphics on a normal computer screen are sufficient to create a moderately strong illusion for users of driving or flight simulation software. VR techniques can make the illusion even more convincing for trainees undergoing initial or 'refresher' training. The trainee can be provided with a realistic steering wheel, flight yoke or joystick and other controls that provide input data to the computer. They receive feedback from instrument hardware, screens providing side (and, in the case of a vehicle, rear) views as well as a forward view, and hydraulic actuators that move or rotate the vehicle seat or aircraft cockpit

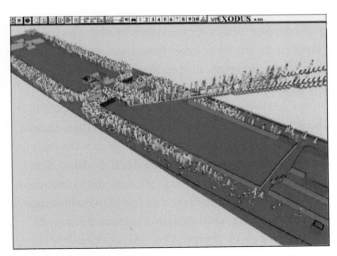

**Figure 7.27** Evacuation simulation for an underground railway station.

(Figure 7.28) to simulate the movements and vibrations experienced on the road or in flight. VR hardware and software such as this is known as a **simulator**.

**Figure 7.28** An engineer working on an airline flight simulator.

A simulator can be used to expose trainee drivers to simulated road traffic, traffic signals and pedestrians. Similarly, it can expose trainee pilots to taxiways populated with other aircraft and ground vehicles, runways, airspace and radio traffic, including conversations with air traffic control centres. Trainees can experience daylight or night-time in varying weather conditions.

Trainees can be repeatably exposed to realistic normal or emergency scenarios to enable them to practise correct procedures for dealing with situations they may face in a vehicle or aircraft. Scenarios can include extreme atmospheric conditions that cannot be created and mechanical failures or 'near misses' that cannot be created safely. Mishandling the simulated vehicle or aircraft causes no harm to the simulator. Trainees can make errors that could prove fatal in reality without exposing themselves or any passengers to any danger. Even a highly sophisticated VR simulator is cheaper than a large aircraft.

A disadvantage of using a simulator for training is that, however realistic the simulation, the trainee retains an awareness that it is only a simulation and may take a risk that they would not take in a real vehicle or aircraft.

 **SAQs**

6   What are the advantages of simulations?

## Computer-aided design

Designers use computer-aided design (CAD) software to design products ranging in scale from jewellery to airliners. Some simpler CAD software is cheap enough to be affordable for home users and small businesses. CAD is now used for designing even the simplest of products because it is quick to create a design, modify it and accurately re-use proven parts of the design in new products. More complex CAD software is needed to design complex products. In some cases, the software can verify the performance of the design by running tests on a simulated 'virtual product'. It can produce estimates of materials required and costs of production.

Application areas include: aircraft and space vehicles, or 'aerospace', design; architecture; vehicle, or 'automotive', design; civil engineering, including roads, railways, bridges, tunnels and dams; design of domestic appliances, such as fridges and washing machines; office and industrial workstation design, or 'ergonomics'; clothing design; garden and landscape design; heating, ventilation and air conditioning design; interior design; lighting design for buildings and entertainment; mechanical, electrical, electronic, chemical and nuclear engineering; naval architecture.

In very large-scale integrated circuits, such as processor or memory chips, so many millions or even billions of component units are repeated that electronic engineers have even invented 'electronic design automation' software. Programs can be written in a special programming language whose statements specify the facilities required in the chip. The software can then 'compile' this program 'to silicon'. This means that a detailed design for the layout of all the required components and their interconnections in the silicon chip can be automatically produced and verified without any further intervention from the user.

A CAD system often requires a relatively powerful PC and non-standard input and output devices. These include a light pen, a trackball, or a graphics tablet; a 3-D mouse for zooming, panning and rotating graphical models; a high-specification graphics card; multiple, large, high-resolution screens; and a plotter to draw scale and full-size drawings.

CAD has many advantages over manual drawing of designs using pen and paper. One CAD operator is about five times as productive as someone drawing a design by hand because of the use of library components and the ease of modifying the design. Automated validation and verification of a design save money, as do automated estimation of the raw material and component requirements and the cost of production. CAD's vector graphics are more accurately and clearly scalable than a drawing; designs that formerly occupied large sheets of paper are now rarely printed. Electronic copies or PDF versions can be easily and cheaply distributed via a file or web server or as email attachments. CAD files can be exported directly to a computer-aided manufacturing (CAM) system, which increases the efficiency of prototyping and production for the manufacturer. The accurate re-use of some or all of a proven design can improve product reliability.

Disadvantages of CAD are that people who used to produce design drawings manually with great skill may feel that they are being 'de-skilled'; the cost of training someone to use CAD software is relatively high; there are potentially fewer job opportunities in CAD within an organisation; and, finally, since the work is highly portable, it can easily be 'outsourced' to an organisation with lower labour costs.

## Monitoring and control systems

As we saw in Chapter 5, a control system consists of one or more computers used to regulate the operation of other devices. The system acquires data at frequent intervals from suitable combinations of sensors and, where necessary, analogue-to-digital converters (ADCs). Software processes the input data and usually provides the user with information for monitoring physical or chemical quantities (such as temperature, flow rate or oxygen concentration) and warning signals if limits are exceeded. The data may also be recorded, as in data-logging, for future analysis of performance, such as peak or average values. Input data may also be used as feedback from a system being controlled so that software can make decisions about the output required to actuators, such as heaters or motorised valves. The output to an actuator may need to be converted to analogue form by a digital-to-analogue converter (DAC). The system may allow the user to interact with the information displayed and, possibly, to override automatic control.

### Monitoring hospital patients

Hospitals are major users of computer-controlled patient monitoring equipment. This equipment monitors the bodily functions of a patient under assessment or known to be critically ill. The equipment allows constant monitoring of patients; if this were done by a human being; they would likely get tired and could misread the data. The equipment would also take more precise readings in general. Sensors include a temperature sensor for body temperature, infrared and visible light sensors for pulse rate and blood oxygenation, a pressure sensor for blood pressure, a stretch sensor in a chest band for respiratory (breathing) rate and self-adhesive chest electrodes for electro-cardiogram (ECG). A diagnostic station (Figure 7.29) is a stand-alone, dedicated, processor-based device for monitoring and possibly for recording the monitored functions. It displays information about the functions monitored on one or more digital displays or an LCD screen. It could include an ECG trace in real-time of a recorded abnormality. It can also provide warning beeps or light signals to alert medical workers if a reading becomes too high or low, or changes suddenly. Some monitoring may be performed by connecting sensors to a PC, with a range of software to provide further analysis and interpretation of the data.

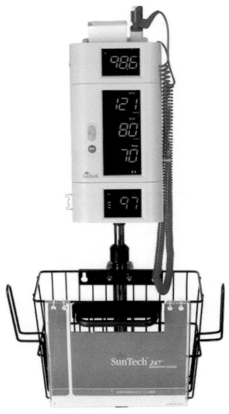

**Figure 7.29**  A portable diagnostic station for monitoring temperature, pulse and blood pressure, and blood oxygenation.

## Burglar alarms

A computerised security system monitors premises for the presence of intruders and generates alarm signals if an intruder is detected. Sensors can include microswitches or reed switches to detect when a door or window is open, pressure-sensitive mats to detect foot-fall and PIR movement sensors. Some systems may include emergency (or 'panic') buttons to summon assistance, even when the intruder alarm is disarmed.

Depending on the design of the system, a sensor can request the processor's attention either when the processor polls it or by sending an interrupt signal (see Chapter 4). The software could react in different ways to an intrusion signal from a sensor. For instance, it could pan, tilt and zoom a closed-circuit television (CCTV) camera onto the area protected by the sensor and start recording the camera's video stream. To alert local security personnel and deter the intruder, the system can switch on siren or flashing-light actuators to provide warning signals. The system can also automatically page, send an SMS text message, or email remote security personnel or police.

For maximum security, the control panel for a burglar alarm (Figure 7.30) must be sited inside the area that it is protecting. The alarm system's software must allow for a short exit delay after arming the alarm, to allow the user to leave the premises without triggering the alarm. A short entry delay allows the user to enter the premises

and disarm the system by entering a code on the control panel's keypad. Some systems allow different zones of the premises to be armed and disarmed independently. Such a system would indicate the zone in which an intrusion had occurred on the control panel's LCD.

 **SAQs**

7  How do movement sensors ignore small animals?

## Weather monitoring

A school's geography department, a farmer or an amateur meteorologist may wish to monitor barometric pressure, temperature, humidity, wind speed and direction, rainfall and sunshine with their own weather station (Figure 7.31). They may do this to try to refine the available forecasts for their locality or to log data over a period of decades in order to observe trends in climate. It is unlikely that any alarm would be triggered by weather monitoring, other than perhaps to warn someone drying laundry that it had started to rain!

**Figure 7.31**  A weather station.

 **SAQs**

8  What kind of sensors are needed to make computerised meteorological measurements? Where would you mount these sensors?

9  You want a light to come on at dusk when it is freezing. Which two sensors do you need?

**Figure 7.30**  The control panel of a burglar alarm.

17  Make a list of events in your life – in school, at home, in the area that you live in – that require measurements to be made. For each one consider:
- what is being measured;
- how accurate the measurement needs to be;
- how often the measurements need to be made;
- for how long the measurements need to be made;
- how easy it would be for a human to be able to make the measurements.

18  Make a list of the various experiments that you have done in science lessons.
- Which ones used any form of computerised measurement?
- In which did you make the necessary measurements?
- In these experiments, was it essential that you took the measurements or would it have been better to have used sensors linked to a computer?

**Extension**

Sometimes computerised monitoring is on a truly global scale: military satellites perform monitoring to gather intelligence; a satellite has been put into orbit to map the Earth's gravitational field accurately; another space mission is mapping the sea bed. Try to find out about these and other measurements that are taken from space. How can measurements about the Earth be taken from space? What types of measuring instruments are used?

## Environmental monitoring

Environmental monitoring may involve long-term data-logging and computerised monitoring of the current values of environmental quality indicators in order to detect a sudden deterioration in atmospheric or aquatic

conditions. Sensors may be required for pollutant gases, such as carbon monoxide and nitrogen dioxide in the atmosphere or for oxygen or pH in river water.

If relatively infrequent sampling is planned for long-term data-logging, it is important to avoid misleading results due to sampling at the wrong time of day. For example, if data are only to be sampled once per day in a study to monitor the atmospheric carbon monoxide concentration in a city street, capturing data at 4 am is likely to give a very different picture from capturing data at 4 pm (Figure 7.32).

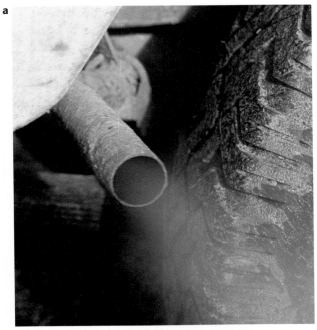

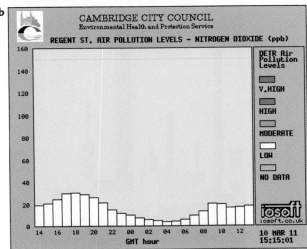

**Figure 7.32**  **a** Motor vehicle exhaust fumes produce carbon monoxide pollution. **b** Some cities monitor pollution levels in their streets.

The system may be programmed to signal an alarm if environmental conditions deteriorate below a certain level. Data for short-term events or long-term trends could be presented as information in the form of a table, or as a graph or chart that may be easier to understand. Future conditions could be simulated by extending the historic trend into the future. Data collected from a number of locations could also be displayed on a map.

## SAQs

10 In environmental monitoring, what are the important timings that need to be decided?

## Questions

19 Consider a river. It is necessary to ensure that the river's water quality is maintained to make sure that the water can sustain the fish and other creatures that live in it. A factory built on the bank of the river takes water from the river for use in its production process. It then discharges the water that it has used back into the river further downstream.

Question 19 continued ...

The important environmental question is: has this affected the quality of water in the river? Decide what sensors are necessary to answer the question. Decide where these sensors should be placed. Explain how and at what time intervals data are captured from the sensors. Describe how the data are used when they have been captured.

## Monitoring and control of industrial plants

Industrial plants (including chemical plants, breweries, steelworks, vehicle factories and nuclear power stations) benefit from computerised monitoring and control systems (Figure 7.33). A computerised system makes reliable, precise and accurate measurements to enable operators to monitor a plant's functioning and respond rapidly to control the production process. For example, they may shut off a valve when a fluid reaches a certain level in a reaction vessel, maintaining the temperature of beer during brewing to within 1°C or opening a pressure-relief valve when the pressure in a chamber reaches a certain level.

Monitoring and control software needs to happen in real-time and requires a real-time operating system in order to guarantee a response within a specified maximum time. The software uses a wide range of sensors to continuously capture data representing physical and chemical quantities. Temperature and pressure sensors play a particularly important role in chemical plants. Precisely controlled temperatures and pressures are vital for achieving the optimum yield and quality of a product. They must not be allowed to rise so high that reaction vessels or pipework could explode. In chemical plants, gas sensors may provide data for monitoring pollutants in the air around the plant. In nuclear power stations, radiation sensors provide data for monitoring radiation levels in and around the station.

Software processes the captured data to provide the plant's operators with information on display screens about the status of the plant, such as temperature, pressure, gas concentration or radiation levels, at various points. Alarm signals using sound or light actuators warn that critical levels have been reached.

**Figure 7.33** A generator unit's control panel in the control room of a coal-fired power station.

The software also processes the data to provide appropriate feedback to make decisions about the actuator output needed to control the plant's production (Figure 7.34). For example, in response to changes in the demand for electricity, an electrical power station's monitoring and control system must act. It automatically increases the current through a generator's field electromagnet and opens a valve to increase the supply of steam from the boiler to the turbine driving the generator, without changing the frequency or phase of rotation of the generator. If the temperature or pressure of the steam supplied by the boiler falls, the system must, within safety limits, automatically increase the supply

of fuel to the furnace heating the boiler (in a gas-, oil-, wood- or coal-fired power station) or raise the control rods (in the core of a nuclear power station's reactor). It may also be possible for an operator to override the control system, if the system fails.

In 'safety-critical' applications, where failure could cause death or injury, or damage to equipment or the environment, control software can place safe limits on a system's response to requests from the operator. There is no need for an operator to override the control system if it is made fault-tolerant through redundancy, as we saw in Chapter 4.

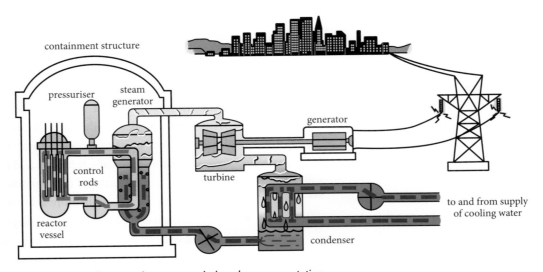

**Figure 7.34** A diagram of a water-cooled nuclear power station.

## Monitoring and control of traffic

Consider the control of traffic lights at a road junction (Figure 7.35). The purpose of the system is to optimise the flow of traffic. Electromagnetic sensor loops buried in the surface of the roads or laser distance sensors mounted next to traffic lights can detect the passage of vehicles approaching the junction. These signals may need to pass through an analogue-to-digital converter and can be used as data for a system that monitors the flow of traffic. This is usually by counting the number of vehicles in successive intervals of time.

**Figure 7.35**  Traffic lights at a road junction.

Real monitoring data, together with simulated data representing accidents, breakdowns or exceptionally heavy traffic, can be supplied to a simulation program. This applies various scenarios of the number of vehicles allowed through or of time for which traffic is allowed to flow in each direction. The results of these simulations can be used by engineers when they choose the best number of vehicles or timings for traffic lights. The advantages of a simulation are that it is faster and cheaper to perform simulations than to adjust real traffic lights to perform trials; it is safer because it is likely to prevent traffic jams and accidents that might occur through inappropriate settings of the real lights; it is also possible to try out more scenarios to find the very best settings.

A control system can generate the standard sequences of output signals. These have the correct timings for the stages from 'stop' to 'go' and from 'go' to 'stop' to control each set of lights together with the other sets of lights at that junction. When the number of vehicles that have passed in one direction or the time for which a 'stop' signal has been displayed reaches a stored value, a vehicle's arrival at the junction may be used by the control system to change its output signals. Some traffic will be halted and other vehicles allowed to proceed.

If the time for which a 'stop' signal has been displayed reaches a larger stored value, the control system may change the signals to halt other traffic and allow vehicles to proceed in any case. This is necessary because a bicycle may not trigger an electromagnetic sensor loop, especially if the bicycle is made of carbon fibre rather than steel. The timings may be adjusted to reflect greater flows of traffic in certain directions at different times of day.

The advantages of computerised systems over human systems for monitoring and control are:

- *Reliability*: Measurement data are usually captured more reliably, round the clock and on time. Measurements and control decisions do not depend on people turning up for work and are not subject to disruption by fatigue, stress or changes of shift.
- *Frequency*: Measurements and control decisions can occur more frequently, many times a second if necessary. This makes more data available and improves the speed of response to changes in conditions.
- *Precision*: Electronic measurements can be more precise than a human's, especially if the human is reading an analogue scale.
- *Accuracy*: Measurements can usually be made with less disturbance of the system whose properties are being measured. For example, a human being might need to put a thermometer into the reaction vessel to measure the temperature or a heater may need to be turned off to allow the human to get close enough to take the measurement. A tiny sensor can remain permanently in place with minimal disturbance. Automatic data capture avoids human transcription errors, so data are usually recorded and timed more accurately. Calculations and comparisons for control decisions can also be made more accurately.
- *Analysis*: Data can be automatically displayed and analysed to discover trends or anomalies.

Together, these advantages can lead to improved production efficiency for a plant and improved quality of monitoring and control of safety-critical processes.

# Automation and robotics

## Automated systems

An **automated system** is very similar to a computerised control system. Usually it is restricted to a single task, provides only limited interactivity for the user and lacks facilities for monitoring and analysing data. Unless it is designed for data-logging or audio, photographic or video recording, it is also less likely to include facilities for saving data. Examples of automated systems are found in household appliances such as washing machines and electronic equipment, such as digital still or video cameras. The automated system's embedded microprocessor is usually in the form of a microcontroller. The microcontroller stores a control program with read-only lookup table data in its non-volatile memory. The capacity of the non-volatile memory may be measured in kilobytes and a skilful programmer is needed to optimise the program code to fit into this tiny space.

## Household appliances

### Washing machine

In Chapter 3, we used a washing machine as a case study in the use of sensors and actuators and looked at some of the inputs, outputs and decisions for its control program. The automated system in a washing machine receives inputs from its control panel switches (Figure 7.36), door closure microswitch and temperature and pressure sensors. It also sends outputs to one or more inlet water valve actuators and water heater, drum motor and drain pump or valve actuators to control the operation of the machine.

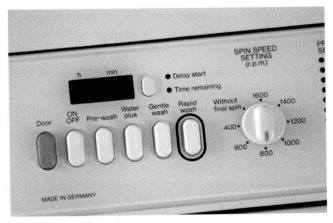

**Figure 7.36** A washing machine control panel.

The user can select a pre-programmed 'cycle' (or 'programme') of washing, rinsing and spin drying using a specific water temperature and spin speed, together with optional variations. A delay timer may allow the user to take advantage of cheaper off-peak electricity.

The control program ensures that water enters the machine carrying washing powder into the drum and that the required water level and temperature are achieved. It ensures that the drum rotates in alternating directions for the required time and that the waste water is released or pumped out. This process is briefly repeated for the appropriate number of times with cold rinsing water. The control program also makes sure that the drum spins the load dry at the appropriate speed for the required time. The machine's progress through the programme may be indicated by LEDs or an LCD.

A fully automated machine is easier to use than a manually controlled one. Compared with a motorised switch controller, a microcontroller-based automated system may cost more. However, it may reduce the labour cost during assembly of the machine. It is usually more reliable, can offer more wash programmes and may be able to use temperature sensor data to control water temperature more accurately, thereby reducing running costs. It can automatically initiate sensor calibration and a test cycle in the factory, reducing manufacturing costs. It can store a fault code if a fault occurs during use, reducing repair costs. It is relatively easy to change the microcontroller's firmware to improve performance or provide extra facilities for new, or even existing, models.

It may be possible for a repair technician to use a portable computer, such as a PDA, to capture the fault code directly from the microcontroller. This speeds up fault diagnosis and repair and provides prompt and accurate feedback to the manufacturer on failure rates, which reduces the cost to the manufacturer of evaluating and improving its products.

## Questions

20  How may the automated system tell if a washing machine is lightly loaded or overloaded with laundry?

21  How does the system sense how much water there is in the machine so that it knows when to turn off the inlet valve water actuator?

### Automated cooker

At its simplest, an automated cooker or oven has two inputs from the user via the control panel (Figure 7.37): the desired temperature and the length of cooking time. A more sophisticated automated system may include a delay timer to allow the user to delay the start of cooking so that it will be completed at a time of their choice. It may also allow the setting of different temperatures during different phases of the process, or a choice of pressures for a pressure cooker.

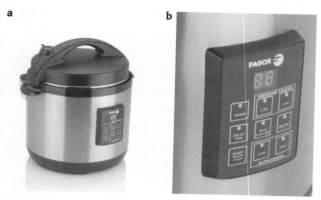

**Figure 7.37  a** An automated electric cooker. **b** The cooker's control panel.

A microcontroller repeatedly captures data from a temperature or pressure sensor within the cooker. It compares them with the desired temperature to decide when to activate a relay as an output actuator to switch on a heating element to raise the temperature or pressure and maintain it at the required level. When a timing process ends it switches off the heating element and alerts the user using a light or sound signal.

Some microwave ovens can use the barcode printed on food product packaging to automatically set the cooking time and power setting. These are known as 'smart' or 'intelligent' ovens, as they provide additional automation. They may be able to 'learn' in the sense of accepting fresh cooking instructions for new food products, but they are *not* 'intelligent' in the sense of automatically learning from past events.

One manufacturer has equipped a microwave oven with a barcode reader for reading a food product's ID barcode. The microcontroller's control program uses the ID number to search a database of several thousand products stored in its non-volatile memory. It automatically reads and uses the stored time and power setting, with instructions to the user such as 'stir' or 'uncover' shown on a display. This oven can also use an Internet connection to download records for new food products to its database.

Another manufacturer has provided a 2-D barcode reader for reading an extra 2-D barcode (like the one in Figure 5.1) on the food product packaging. This provides the cooking instructions, timings and power settings directly, as a 2-D barcode can encode far more information than a normal barcode. It does not depend on storing a database of cooking instructions and settings, but relies on food manufacturers printing the appropriate 2-D barcode on each of their products.

Such automated systems have the potential to improve food safety by avoiding under-cooking and to reduce wastage of food by avoiding over-cooking.

### Lighting control

A torch with more than one light source (Figure 7.38) may have a microprocessor-controlled switch. It may use as few as twelve components, including a tiny microcontroller chip, which can cost as little as 50 cents when a torch manufacturer buys 10,000 pieces. For such a torch, successive presses of a single push-switch could cause the switch to cycle through incandescent, LED, both and neither ('off'). Students of electronics might be able to design an equivalent circuit whose components are cheaper. However, if this involves more components, the increased labour cost of assembling the switch could easily make the overall cost higher. A microcontroller-based switch can easily be reprogrammed to suit different numbers of light sources for different models of torch. It could be 'intelligent', learning to start the cycle with the most frequently chosen option.

In some cases, a lamp such as a street light is turned on at dusk and off at dawn by a light-sensitive switch. If such a system is microcontroller-based, it uses data from a light sensor facing the sky above the lamp to decide whether or not to activate a relay as an output actuator to control the lamp. Again, it is relatively easy to change the microcontroller's firmware to alter the switch's behaviour.

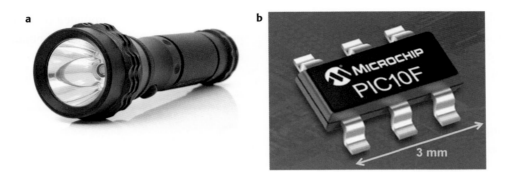

a    b

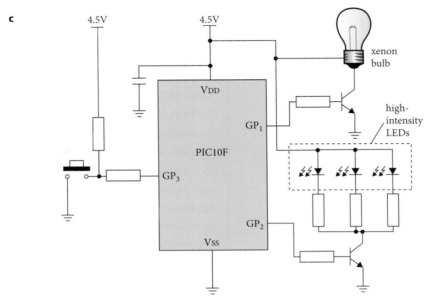

c

**Figure 7.38**   **a** A torch with more than one light source. **b** A suitable tiny microcontroller.
**c** A circuit diagram for a microcontroller-based switch.

**Questions**

22   What can stop a street lamp being turned on
if a bird sits on the light sensor during the day
or if there is an eclipse of the sun?

Imagine a more sophisticated lighting control system
in a house. It is intended to deter burglars when the
house is unoccupied by switching one or more lights on
and off through the night. This creates the impression
that someone is at home. In this case, input data come
from a light sensor facing the sky outside the house
and a random sequence of switching decisions are
made for lights. There are rules about the minimum or
maximum time for which a light would plausibly remain
switched on.

A specialist automated lighting system may be
much more sophisticated and include fading as well
as switching of lights. For example, as daylight fades
in an office, it could raise the level of artificial light
to maintain a minimum level. An automated stage-
lighting system (Figure 7.39) allows the user to control

**Figure 7.39**   An automated stage-lighting console.

lights manually and to program complex lighting transitions, dry ice and pyrotechnic effects. This enables one lighting engineer to control lights and effects in a way that might previously have required a team of engineers.

### Heating, ventilating or air conditioning control

An automated system for controlling the temperature and humidity within a building is likely to need to switch off the system or reduce (or 'set back') the required level (or 'set point') at certain times of day, such as the night. Such a system is likely to include a software clock and timer. The user can enter not only the room temperature or humidity required but also the programmed times at which the system switches on and off or sets back the set point on each day of the week.

The automated system receives inputs from its control panel switches (Figure 7.40) and one or more temperature sensors or thermostat switches, one of which may be external to the building. The control program compares the clock time with the programmed times and sensor data with the appropriate set point. It uses these to decide the appropriate output signals to send to one or more relays that are actuators controlling the heating or cooling equipment. The system may show information about the programmed times and temperature or humidity on an LCD. The system could also report to the user on the LCD the failure of the temperature to change significantly after a reasonable period of time. The user would then have to check whether a window was open or the heating or cooling

equipment had failed. Automated control has the potential to improve the comfort of building occupants and reduce energy consumption.

### Questions

**23** What might happen if a microprocessor only senses the room temperature every 30 minutes?

### Extension

Consider other examples of computer control and, for each, work through the desired outcomes, inputs, processing, alarms and control outputs to explain how it works. You could start by looking at simple systems to control household items, such as toasters, irons and alarm clocks. This can be extended to more complex applications, such as control of the environment in an aquarium or a garden pond. What about the automated feeding of a herd of cows when they come in for milking?

### Embedded web technology

Embedded web technology (EWT) enables a user to use a web browser to monitor and interact in real-time with a remotely located embedded microprocessor control system. The embedded processor runs real-time web server software to enable it to act as a website. The user can use a web browser on a computer or mobile phone to log in to the target system using 'user credentials', such as a username and password, to prevent unauthorised access.

First developed for remote management of scientific experiments in outer space, EWT can also be used with a suitably equipped domestic appliance. For example, a manufacturer of EWT automated ovens (Figure 7.41) has provided a website through which the user can log in to their oven and control it using the same GUI as the oven displays on its own touchscreen. This enables the user to place a meal in the oven and start a cooking cycle from a remote location. The manufacturer has also provided an interactive voice response (IVR) service

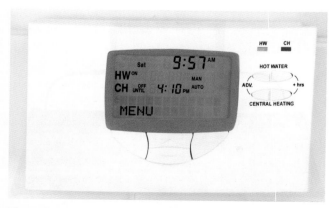

**Figure 7.40** A central heating programmer.

to make this web application voice-accessible using a phone. Some models include refrigeration for keeping food cool in the oven until cooking starts.

**Figure 7.41** The user can control this automated oven remotely using embedded web technology.

## Electronic equipment

Many smaller items of household and office equipment used for communications, entertainment and printing are automated systems containing a microcontroller or other embedded computer.

### Cameras

A camera is likely to have an automated system, whether it uses digital imaging or photographic film. The automated system receives inputs from the camera's control panel and displays a GUI on an LCD. For a digital-imaging camera this is the same screen that is used as a view finder and for displaying stored photographs. A camera may be equipped with GPS (see later in this chapter), so that a photo can be automatically 'geotagged'. This means that the location where the photo was taken is included in the form of geographical co-ordinates.

In the case of a digital-imaging camera, an array of light sensors provides the input data for the photograph. As mentioned in Chapter 3, the more pixels there are, the more detailed or 'higher resolution' the image

is. Even when stored in a compressed format, such as JPG, a high-resolution photo may easily occupy several mebibytes of storage. This means that a camera may require one or more gibibytes of storage to store hundreds of photos.

The automated system's control program uses the user's settings and data from one or more light sensors to control:

- **Shutter speed**: The length of time that the film is exposed to the scene being photographed or over which the array of sensors averages the light each pixel receives. A long exposure shows 'motion blur' if the subject moves relative to the camera, which may be a nuisance or required for artistic effect.
- **Focus**: The distance of the camera's lens from the film or array of sensors is adjusted to get the clearest possible (or sometimes a deliberately blurred) image. This can be automatically adjusted for one or more target areas of the image.
- **Zoom**: A more complex, motorised camera lens can offer optical magnification of the image. 'Digital zoom' enlarges the available data from the centre of a sensor array and discards the rest without improving the level of detail visible, although it saves the user from having to crop the photo later.
- **Aperture**: In most cameras, this literally controls the size of an approximately circular opening behind the lens. The larger this is, the more light from the scene is available, so the exposure time can be reduced. The 'depth of field', or range of distance from the camera at which subjects are clearly focussed, is also decreased, which may be useful for emphasising a single subject by blurring the background. However, the smaller the aperture is, the larger the depth of field.
- **Flash**: It may be possible to switch flash illumination between 'off', 'auto', 'red-eye reduction' and 'on'.

The camera may be able to store the user's preferred settings between uses (Figure 7.42). The automated system can display a warning when it cannot focus the image. A digital-imaging camera has further advantages. It is possible to view images without making prints, so it may be possible to re-take a shot while the subject is still available. It is possible to delete unwanted photographs to release storage. There is no cost of developing film. The user may be able to perform limited editing on the camera, such as cropping or adjusting colour, brightness or contrast. The user can transfer photos from the camera to a photo printer or computer through a USB port, Bluetooth or Wi-Fi.

**Figure 7.42** The display on a digital camera.

A disadvantage of a camera with automatic geotagging of digital photos is that the user may be unaware that the photos that they publish on websites contain geotags. The user may therefore unintentionally reveal the location of their home. When advertising a valuable item for sale, the user may reveal where the item is, together with an indication of when they will be at home to receive phone calls and, thus, when their home is likely to be empty and vulnerable to burglary.

### Television sets

A television set's automated system uses data entered by the user through its control panel or remote control and stored in non-volatile memory to:

- display a GUI on the screen;
- tune to or select a television broadcast channel;
- select alternative sources such as a 'set-top box' or a DVD and CD player;
- adjust picture and sound settings;
- reset to factory settings stored in ROM.

An automated system gives more reliable operation than manual tuning, push-button channel selection and adjustment of picture and sound settings.

For some countries' terrestrial services and for almost all satellite services, the signals carried by television broadcasts are digital. A digital television receiver (or 'tuner') may be built in to the television set or purchased as a separate set-top box, which helps to keep older television sets in use and is required to gain access to subscription-only channels. A digital television tuner contains embedded computer technology for decoding the digital signals, correcting any errors, selecting the required programme (or 'channel') from the combined (or 'multiplexed') stream and extracting the video, audio and data streams from the selected programme stream. Digital television tuners are immune to interference and provide very clear video and audio.

### Satellite navigation devices

Earlier in this chapter, we met the idea of a mobile phone trilaterating its position on the locally two-dimensional surface of the Earth. It uses the distances from at least three cellular network masts or Wi-Fi access points, estimated from their signal strengths. This is not very accurate, but enables the phone to be 'location-aware'.

A global satellite navigation system (GNSS) is a system of at least 24 satellites in various orbits at an altitude of approximately 20,000 kilometres. The satellites broadcast frequent messages that enable a small satellite navigation (satnav) device containing a radio receiver and an embedded computer to calculate its geographical location to within a few metres. To calculate its location on the locally two-dimensional surface of the Earth, the device needs to receive sufficiently strong radio signals from at least three satellites. For greater accuracy and to calculate its location in three dimensions, including elevation, the device needs to receive sufficiently strong signals from at least four satellites.

The device decodes each message received from a 'visible' satellite to obtain data about the precise orbit of that satellite. It also receives the precise time at which the message was sent according to a highly accurate atomic clock on the satellite. The device synchronises its own less accurate clock with the satellites' atomic clocks. Then it is able to calculate the time that each message took to travel from a known point in each satellite's orbit to the device. Using the known speed of radio waves in space, the device is able to calculate its distance from at least three points in space and hence its location at or near the surface of the Earth (Figure 7.43).

The Global Positioning System (GPS) is a US military GNSS. It is said to be capable of navigating a cruise missile through a targeted office window, but it is used

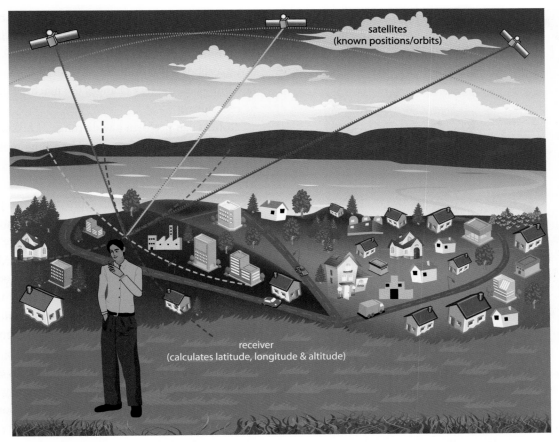

**Figure 7.43** A satellite navigation device finds its location by calculating its distance from each satellite – only three satellites are shown here for simplicity.

at less than full precision by any other user. It has more than the minimum of 24 satellites in orbit, so that at least eight of its satellites are 'visible' from any unobstructed point near the Earth's surface at all times. At the time of writing, it is the only fully operational satellite navigation system available to all, although European and Chinese systems are due to become operational within the next few years.

Some satnav devices simply display their position as longitude, latitude and, sometimes, altitude for surveying purposes or to assist navigation with a paper map. GPS-enabled smartphones and devices for vehicles combine this position-finding capability with navigation functions such as:

- storing mapping data, which may be displayed on a screen as a map together with an icon representing the user's position (Figure 7.44);
- calculating the shortest or fastest route and providing navigational instructions via text, speech synthesis or a pictogram of the next manoeuvre, such as 'turn right', to the driver of a vehicle or pilot of an aircraft or boat;
- providing drivers with information on points of interest (POI), such as fuel stations, speed cameras or restaurants; warnings when a speed limit is exceeded; suggested alternative routes using historical or real-time data on traffic conditions or real-time data on road closures.

A satnav device may also log its position at predetermined intervals of time. Such a log can later be used to track and analyse a journey. The location of a vehicle or an emergency beacon can also be monitored or 'tracked' in real-time if the device can connect to a cellular or satellite phone network to transmit location data to a remote computer.

Advantages of satnav devices include not having to maintain a collection of paper maps; driving more safely without having to read a map or list of directions and

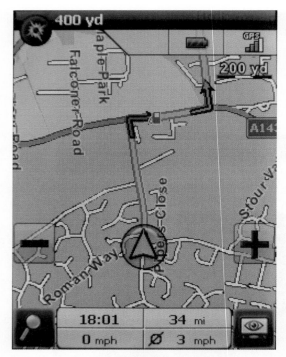

**Figure 7.44** Satellite navigation software running on a PDA with a GPS receiver – the user's position is represented by the yellow arrowhead and the map automatically orientates so that 'up' on the map represents 'ahead' on the ground.

reducing errors such driving the wrong way down a one-way street. They provide much more information about points of interest. They make it easy to find the shortest or fastest route and ease re-routing mid-journey if traffic is heavy or a road is closed. Mapping data are updated electronically.

Disadvantages of satnav devices include: receiving incorrect directions if the stored maps are out of date; no location information or directions if reception from at least three satellites is not available (for example, in a tunnel); inaccurate positioning can result from poor reception of satellite signals or errors in the mapping data; over-reliance on the directions or incorrect choice of destination or settings for the route can result in the driver following an inappropriate route.

### Industrial robots

A robot is a machine that can repeatedly carry out a task under the control of a computer and whose task can be changed by reprogramming its computer. The name 'robot' is the root of the Slav word for 'work'.

A robot's computer may be embedded in the robot or it may be a separate computer system to which the robot is connected by cable or wireless link. A machine is not a robot if it repeatedly carries out the same task but when the task changes the machine has to be redesigned.

Robots can perform a wide range of tasks, including welding, painting and handling materials. In 'pick-and-place' applications, a robot picks products from a conveyor belt and places them in a carton or picks electronic components from a belt and places them on an electronic circuit board. A common type of pick-and-place robot, known as a Selective Compliance Articulated Robot Arm (SCARA) can not only position but orient an item in the horizontal plane. It is compliant (or yielding) to forces in the horizontal plane, so that the robot can accommodate small inaccuracies in tightly fitting parts when performing 'peg-in-hole' tasks.

Robots are of two types: fixed and mobile. Some robots are fixed to a single point in the factory (Figure 7.45) and the work that needs to be done is brought to them. This type of robot is usually called a robot arm. Like a human arm, it is fixed at one end and yet has a large degree of movement available.

**Figure 7.45** A robot arm in a car factory.

A robot arm consists of rigid sections of different lengths connected by joints that allow the attached sections to move. The length of each of the sections depends on the distances that the robot arm is expected to reach. The number of joints dictates the flexibility of the arm and the complexity of the control program that the processor needs to run in order to operate the arm effectively. A fixed robot may have to rely on other equipment (maybe another robot) correctly positioning the workpiece.

Some robots are mobile and can move from place to place. Robots like these can be used on a production line to move workpieces from one place to another. A car's body shell on a robotic platform (Figure 7.46) may first move to the station where robot arms fit the wheels. It then moves to another station where more robotic arms fit the seats and so on until the car is built. The robotic platform may be programmed to take it to particular stations where different things are added according to the model of car being produced. One shell may need cloth seats; another may be for a GLX model that goes to another station to have leather seats fitted by a different robotic arm.

**Figure 7.46** Car shells being carried on robotic platforms to a succession of different robot arms.

A robot can obtain data about its work environment from other robots or from its own 'vision system' cameras or other sensors. These data may include whether a workpiece has arrived in position, whether there is an obstruction in its path, or whether the supply of components or paint has run out. The robot receives feedback data about the position of its own machinery from sensors within it. It also has electrical or hydraulic actuators to move its machinery.

A robot's task program can be written directly for it, or it may 'learn' the correct sequence of movements from a human operator who models the task. For example, a skilled paint spraying operator may manually move the robot's arm to spray a car body with paint. The robot's computer records data from the arm's position sensors and spray control valve many times per second. It is then able to use its actuators to reproduce this motion precisely and repeatably.

Robots have a number of advantages over human workers in factory production lines:
- they produce more consistently precise results than human workers, improving overall product quality and reliability and reducing wastage and environmental impact;
- they can work continuously without a break;
- they are usually more productive because they can often perform a certain task in a shorter time;
- they do not require heating or lighting;
- although they cost a lot to buy, they have lower running costs than the pay and 'on costs' of human workers;
- they can work in areas or with materials that would be dangerous for human workers;
- they can relieve humans of the need to do arduous or very repetitive and boring work, leaving them free to do quality control or other more skilled work.

Disadvantages of robots include that:
- unless they have been programmed to cater for exceptions, such as a missing component, they are unable to deal with them in the way that a human can;
- they tend to put humans out of work, increasing unemployment, at least locally and temporarily;
- manual skills are lost from the workforce, known as 'de-skilling';

- once production can be supervised by semi-skilled or unskilled workers, it can be 'outsourced' to locations offering cheaper labour, which also increases local unemployment.

## Questions

**24** A bar of metal is presented to a robot. The robot needs to drill a hole in the middle of the bar and turn it through 90 degrees.

**a** Instructions given to robots must be very precise otherwise they can be misinterpreted. What is wrong with the instructions here? Are they unambiguous?

**b** Try to write a set of instructions that tells a robot how to carry out the task. You do not need to use a programming language but try to be precise.

**25** If money were not a problem, consider how a robot could be used to boil an egg. Could this idea be taken further to produce meals in the school canteen? Could robots be used to serve the meals to students? How could robots be used to collect the plates from the tables and then clean the tables?

## Extension

Rewrite the set of instructions in Question 24 to drill a series of holes in a line, with each hole 2 cm from the previous one.

## Closed-circuit television

Closed-circuit television (CCTV) means using video cameras to produce video signals that are not broadcast. A CCTV system consists of one or more video cameras (Figure 7.47) and a monitor screen to display the images. It can also include a recording device to record the video stream from the camera for later use if necessary.

The camera may be an ordinary video camera or an infrared one that allows pictures to be recorded without visible light. CCTV is usually used for some form of surveillance for safety or security purposes. The camera may be remotely controlled by an operator or by a

**Figure 7.47** A CCTV surveillance camera.

computer that receives data from sensors signalling an event of interest in a particular area. As we saw when considering burglar alarms earlier in this chapter, the computer's software could react by panning, tilting and zooming the CCTV camera onto the area protected by the sensor and starting to record the camera's video stream.

The outputs to control the camera may consist of digital pulses to drive a 'stepper motor'. Alternatively, the digital output may go to a digital-to-analogue converter (DAC) to provide an analogue signal to control an electric motor known as a servo (or 'slave') motor. In each case, the computer needs a feedback signal from a rotation sensor, which may be built into the motor. This confirms that the motor has actually moved the camera to the required position.

Some software can analyse the video stream from a camera without the need for other sensors, to provide automatic sound or light alarm signals to the user and highlight an area of interest on a monitor screen. Such analysis may include motion detection to provide warning of an intruder on unoccupied premises; crowd formation or other scene change detection software to provide warning of possible public disorder; unattended object detection to provide warning of a suspicious object; or missing object detection to provide warning of the removal of an item on display.

## Expert systems

An **expert system** (or 'knowledge-based' system) is a computer program that aims to achieve the problem-solving competence of a human expert in a specific task area. It uses the knowledge and rules of inference gathered from one or more human experts. Types of problem-solving include diagnosis, interpretation of data, prediction, planning, scheduling, design, configuration, debugging and prescription. Task areas include medical diagnosis; identification of animal, plant or fossil specimens; choice of most likely sites for oil or mineral prospecting; games of strategy such as chess; ship design; fault diagnosis; route planning for deliveries; financial planning; and choosing a make and model of car to suit the user's requirements.

An expert system can often solve problems using incomplete data, where the user answers 'don't know' to a question or is not completely sure about their response (Figure 7.48). An expert system may be called a 'decision support system' and deliver 'advice' rather than 'solutions'. This avoids deterring users who may already be relatively experienced and therefore reluctant to have a computer tell them how to do their job.

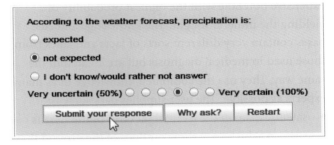

**Figure 7.48** An expert system asking a question to which a 'don't know' or uncertain answer is acceptable.

The essential components of an expert system shown in Figure 7.49 are a **knowledge base** that stores facts; a rule base that stores rules for decision-making, usually in the form of if…then… statements; an **inference engine** that processes the user's problem using the contents of the knowledge and rule bases; and a **user interface** that enables the user to communicate with the inference engine. Many expert systems also have a 'knowledge

base editor' for updating the knowledge base. They may have an 'explanation system' to explain to the user why questions have been asked and the reasoning used by the system for one or more suggested solutions.

Information is collected from one or more experts. Factual information is placed in the knowledge base and decision-making rules are placed in the rule base. The developer then creates an inference engine that processes the facts, rules and data obtained from the user and a user interface. The interface needs to ask the user questions about their problem, as input, and deliver solutions, as output. It may also be able to explain why questions are asked and solutions are suggested. The system must be tested with a variety of inputs for which certain outputs are expected. The developer will also produce a user manual and train users, as with any system.

In operation, the user interface presents the user with a series of questions for which the user is constrained to yes/no answers, multiple choice answers or selecting items from lists. The user may be able to request the explanation system to explain why questions have been asked. The inference engine uses the user's responses with the facts in the knowledge base and rules in the rule base to present one or more possible solutions via the user interface. Again, the user is likely to ask the explanation system to explain the expert system's reasoning. This is potentially very helpful in extending the user's own expertise.

When used to diagnose faults or illnesses, an expert system outputs one or more possible diagnoses and corresponding suggestions as to how to correct the fault or treat the illness. Often the probability of the diagnosis is stated as a percentage, to assist the user in deciding what action to take.

Expert systems have the following advantages over other sources of knowledge and guidance: they follow all the necessary logical steps without bypassing any; they provide consistent solutions to problems; they take less time to solve a problem; they can produce good outcomes with less skilled workers, thereby potentially saving money.

Disadvantages of expert systems include: any errors in the knowledge or rule bases could lead to many users making incorrect decisions; operators need careful training to ensure that they use the systems correctly; they are very expensive to create; the knowledge and rule

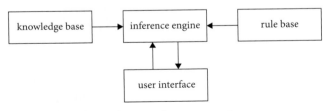

**Figure 7.49** A block diagram of an expert system.

bases need updating whenever new expertise becomes available; they are totally dependent on their knowledge and rule bases and programming and are unable to deal with unusual situations in the 'common sense' way that humans can.

## Medical diagnosis

A patient goes to see a doctor and presents symptoms. The patient goes to see a doctor because of the doctor's expertise and experience, but no doctor can be expected to be expert in every area of medicine. There is so much information about diseases and symptoms that doctors need help to make sure they have not missed anything, especially a rare condition that they have learned about but rarely, if ever, see. Doctors used to get this extra information from books but nowadays this has been superseded by information held in medical diagnosis expert systems. These can hold more information, be updated relatively easily and searched much more rapidly for relevant information. An expert system is a powerful tool, whose correct use can help even junior doctors to make world-class diagnoses and to learn in the process.

Typically, the system asks the doctor the age and sex of the patient and to enter symptoms from a list. For example, the doctor might enter 'child (1–12 years)', 'male' with symptoms 'rash', 'conjunctivitis', 'shock', 'diarrhoea' and 'pyrexia' (high body temperature). The system might respond with a list of 15 possible diagnoses. These would probably be listed in order of probability to enable the doctor to concentrate on the most likely diagnoses first. If the doctor were familiar with this combination of symptoms in male children, the doctor would probably have remembered all the 'top' diagnoses without the expert system. However, if the most likely diagnoses are ruled out by tests, the rarer diagnoses are present in the list to remind the doctor that they are also possible explanations for the symptoms. The system is also useful for combinations of symptoms that the doctor rarely sees.

Medical diagnosis expert systems cannot reliably be used to make a diagnosis by a non-expert, as a non-expert lacks sufficient background knowledge and experience and does not know what tests to conduct to confirm a diagnosis. However, simplified systems are sometimes used to check symptoms as part of a 'triage' process for screening patients to discover whether they

need to see a doctor and, if so, how urgently. Such a system enables people with relatively little training to follow a set of steps and rules known as a 'protocol' to carry out triage. When provided on a website, it even allows a patient to check their own symptoms (Figure 7.50).

### SAQs

11 What advantages may a doctor who uses a medical expert system have over a doctor who does not use one?

## Mineral prospecting

Mineral prospecting differs from medical diagnosis because the problem involves the interpretation of survey data and choice of the location for drilling an expensive borehole with the highest probability of yielding the mineral sought. The knowledge and rule bases contain very different sorts of facts and rules from those used in medical diagnosis but are created in the same way. They use the combined knowledge of as many experts as possible. The user supplies data such as:

- satellite data, in the form of pictures of the Earth's surface, which may show outlines of the ground that are not otherwise visible;
- sensor data, that captures tiny shifts or vibrations, which may show that there is seismic activity in the area;
- geological survey data.

An explosion on the surface may be set off some kilometres away from sensors that are placed on the surface. From the length of time that it takes the shock wave to bounce off layers of rock deep below the surface and reach the sensors and the strength of those shock waves, it is possible to create 3-D maps of what lies beneath the surface.

Using all these data, the expert system can then make predictions as to the likelihood of finding particular minerals in that area. Note that what is produced is a prediction – certainty of outcome is not possible. This type of expert system gives a probability of the presence of a particular mineral as a percentage. 'Iron ore 20%' would mean that it was not very likely that iron would be found there, whereas 'Iron ore 80%' would mean that it was highly likely that iron would be found.

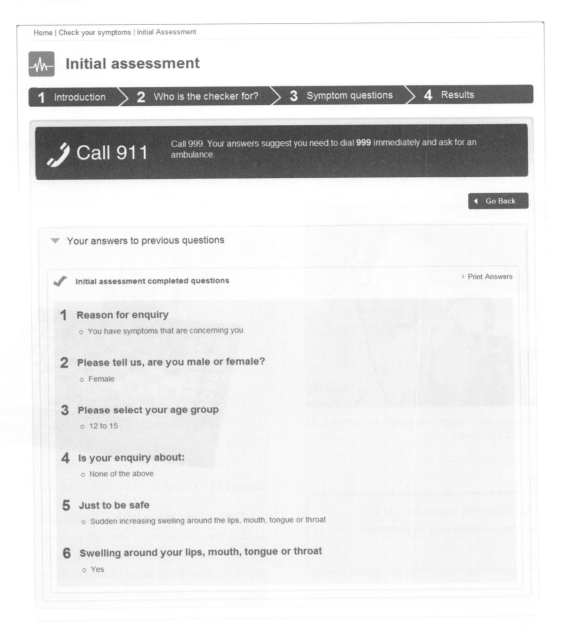

**Figure 7.50** A simplified expert system for non-expert users, showing the advice given and the history of answers to questions.

**SAQs**

12 In what other ways can iron ore be detected? How could this be used as data in an expert system?

## Vehicle engine fault diagnosis

Information about things that can go wrong with vehicle engines is collected from experienced mechanics and stored in the knowledge base of the system. When a vehicle is brought into the garage, a mechanic can input details of the faults by answering a series of questions through the user interface. The system interrogates the knowledge base and uses the rules in the rule base to produce a result for the mechanic on the screen. This is the standard way to use an expert system, but this application can be set up to be rather more automatic.

Many vehicles have an onboard microcontroller-based computer that continuously monitors the working of the engine. It can warn the driver of unusual performance and suggests that they take the vehicle to a garage. In this case, the mechanic would connect the car's onboard computer to the expert system (Figure 7.51) and the details of the unusual performance are downloaded automatically. The expert system may also be able to capture data automatically from an electronic exhaust gas analyser.

**Figure 7.51** A mechanic uses a diagnostic system to capture data from a vehicle's onboard computer.

**Extension**

Try to find out what types of sensor are used to provide evidence for a vehicle engine diagnosis expert system.

Similar diagnostic systems can also be used for diagnosing problems with electronic devices.

## Chess computers

Chess-playing computers are expert systems. Originally they were given lots of good moves for particular circumstances that might be met in a game. These moves were the result of asking many expert players. The problem with this is that chess is a very complex game with a massive number of possible situations; it is therefore very difficult to predict all the moves that may happen in a game.

Better chess computers are programmed with strategies. They are able to quantify how good their position and the opponent's position are. At each turn, they work through possible moves trying to analyse what the outcome will be and hence find the strongest move. Many chess computers display a virtual chessboard on a display screen. Others have real chessboards from which input data are captured by a peg on a chess piece which activates switches in holes in the squares from and to which it is moved. A chess computer has even been sold with a pick-and-place robot arm for moving its own pieces (Figure 7.52).

**Figure 7.52** A chess computer with a pick-and-place robot arm.

The best machines have a degree of intelligence in that they can learn when they do something wrong. When these computers are beaten, they analyse the moves so that if the same situation arises in a future game they do not make the same mistake again. Expert systems that 'learn' in the way that the best chess-playing systems do have gone one stage beyond a normal expert system and are said to have '**artificial intelligence**'.

## 1.1.8 Education, training and entertainment

### Computer-based learning

**Computer-based learning** typically consists of the multimedia presentation of interactive learning activities. This type of application is also known as **computer-assisted learning** (**CAL**) or **computer-based training** (**CBT**), although the letter term tends to be reserved for training in work skills rather than academic learning.

Computer-based learning can engage many students because it is more than simply reading and viewing images. It can be highly effective when it includes computer-based assessment to provide feedback on progress. It allows students to study independently of a teacher or trainer and to ask for their assistance when required. CAL presentations can give students the chance to manage their own learning. Students can work at their own pace, repeat sections that they found difficult and omit sections they already know.

Computer-based learning is often web-based, so students can access it from anywhere there is a PC with a web browser. All kinds of multimedia can be used to illustrate the topic being taught and enrich the experience to maintain interest. Hyperlinks can point students to relevant websites or stored files. Different routes can be taken through the application according to the student's choice. Sometimes the software chooses a route that reinforces or repeats a topic in a different way. Software can feed scores directly back to the student so that the student can repeat the question or can feed final assessment scores to a tutor.

Computer-based learning is advantageous because:

- students can learn at times that are more suitable to them;
- students have more control over the pace of their learning;
- it is less embarrassing if they fail to answer a question or if they ask a tutor for help as, even if other students are in the room, they are likely to be engaged in their own learning;
- it is easier to omit parts students already know;
- it is easier to repeat parts students have not understood;
- students can often get more immediate assessment of their performance;
- it is easier for authors to illustrate work with multimedia content;
- it is easier for authors to amend computer-based learning and keep it up to date;
- learning providers may have reduced costs, because they need fewer teachers and classrooms.

The disadvantage is that there may be less (or no) face-to-face help available from a tutor or support from other learners. However, some virtual learning environments (VLEs) make tutor and student support available through email, IM or forums.

## Virtual reality in training

We have previously met VR simulation, a form of interactive, multimedia experience that can give the user the illusion of being able to interact with their environment and virtual artefacts within it. This can be extremely useful in training, as it can provide a trainee with visual and haptic (tactile) instruction from a virtual tutor. In complete safety, they can practise techniques that would otherwise be hazardous to the trainee or others.

It is very difficult to prepare for working in dangerous environments. VR simulations can be used to give workers the experience of working under hazardous conditions without the associated risks. They are used for safety training and certification in several industries, such as mining, construction and power generation, particularly nuclear power plants. VR simulations are also used by some armed forces to prepare their troops for combat. They are a spin-off from the computer games industry. The advantages of using VR in training are that workers have higher levels of skills and competence before entering the real work environment, which reduces injuries and increases productivity.

Traditionally, dentists have been trained on real patients (under constant supervision) or on physical models. VR using a head-mounted display (HMD) can be used to create simulations of a patient's head and mouth cavity. The trainee uses a virtual drill (or 'handpiece') with haptic feedback to practice drilling and filling teeth with realistic contact and resistance (Figure 7.53). VR with haptic feedback is sometimes known as augmented reality (AR). A real patient's head can even be scanned and the data from the scan used to simulate the patient's head and mouth in VR or AR. This means that an operation on a specific patient can be rehearsed beforehand.

The advantages of an AR system are that it does not consume materials, such as model teeth, and it can record the performance of students for assessment. It can also help to evaluate the effectiveness of different types and durations of training programmes.

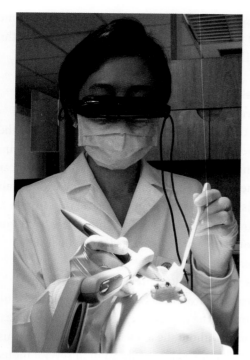

**Figure 7.53** A trainee dentist wears an HMD with camera that captures the position of an AR marker on her dummy mirror. The HMD shows her an AR mirror-view of the virtual teeth inside a physical model's mouth, on which she can work with a haptic device instead of the 'handpiece' usually used for drilling.

## Applications in music

### Composition

It is possible to use software to compose music by writing notes with the software's notation tools. The notes are positioned by a mouse or other pointing device on a stave displayed on the monitor screen to produce a musical score. It may also be possible to input notes using mouse-clicks on the keys of an on-screen keyboard or the frets of an on-screen guitar fretboard (Figure 7.54).

In Chapter 3, we met a MIDI keyboard as an input device. Some composition software can use input from a MIDI keyboard, MIDI guitar or computer keyboard to record the notes played in all or part of a performance. For example, when one of the MIDI keyboard's keys is struck, it sends signals representing the start of a note of a particular pitch and volume, any changes in finger pressure while the key is down and the end of the note. The MIDI keyboard can also accept multiple simultaneous key presses.

Software is also available for capturing notes from an optical scan of an existing handwritten or printed score (the musical equivalent of OCR). It can also capture notes from an audio stream, such as music sung or played into a microphone and input to a computer through the sound card's ADC.

Software can edit a composition, including transposing it to another musical key, and save it as a file. It can also play the composition, generating sound output using a software synthesiser or sounds sampled from real instruments and the sound card's DAC. This is useful as the composer adds successive instrumental parts to, or 'orchestrates', the composition, as well as for playing the finished piece. The software may also be able to produce visual output on an on-screen keyboard, fretboard or other representation of an instrument (Figure 7.54). This is useful for learning how to play the relevant instrument. The composition can be printed as a complete score for a conductor and as separate parts for different instruments.

There are major benefits to composing in this way. The composer can hear immediate feedback of a new part of the composition and can also isolate particular instruments in the orchestration or even groups of instruments. The composer can edit the composition immediately and send it anywhere in the world electronically. Composers can collaborate on the same piece of music with people all over the world. Also, intermediate results can be sent to other places for inspection before carrying on with different parts of the composition. An example is a composer living in Britain who is writing the music for a film that is being made in the USA. As different sections of the music are produced, the results are sent to the director for approval.

### Performance

Pitch correction software is widely used to adjust the pitch of a vocal or instrumental performance either on an audio stream in live performance, often using an embedded computer, or on a digital recording. The software detects repeating features of the audio waveform and measures the time interval (or 'period') between similar points in the waveform. If this differs from the period of the nearest note on a standard tuning, the pitch of the note is liable to be perceived as 'out of tune'. The software automatically recreates the same waveform with the correct period and perceived pitch.

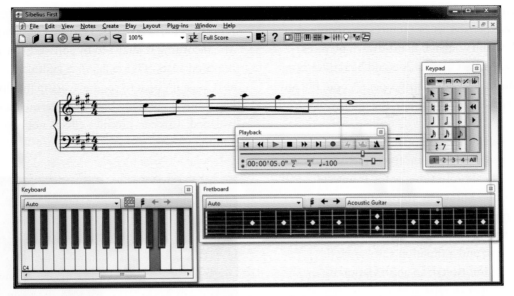

**Figure 7.54** Musical composition software showing a melody written on a stave, with accompanying chords, being played with visual output on both on-screen keyboard and guitar fretboard.

Pitch correction software may also be able to create chorus or harmony effects. It does so by deliberately shifting one or more copies of the audio stream or recording to other slightly different notes for a chorus effect or to completely different but appropriate notes for a harmony effect. Other computerised effects include reverberation, vibrato and various forms of distortion.

A synthesiser can combine simple waveforms in complex ways to mimic other instruments or produce novel sounds. It may also produce automated percussion and chord accompaniment.

A sampler can sample a note from an instrument, shift it to several pitches and map each pitch to a different key on a keyboard. In performance, a musician can record a sequence of sampled percussion sounds and one or more successive layers of accompaniment that automatically loop. This allows them to create their own 'live' backing for their instrumental or vocal performance.

### Recording

In a recording studio, a computer can be used as a digital audio workstation (DAW) to apply effects to separate recordings (known as 'tracks', from the era of multiple analogue recording tracks on magnetic tape) and mix them into a finished piece of music (Figure 7.55).

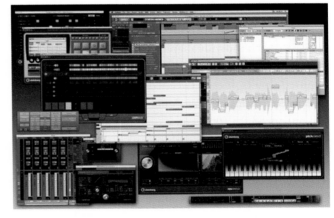

**Figure 7.55** Music software.

### Animation

Animation consists of displaying a rapid succession of 2-D or 3-D graphics or model arrangements to create the illusion of movement. Animation is used for web presentations and advertisements and for film and television. Computer animation is the process of using computer hardware and software to create moving images.

Before the use of computers, animations were created by producing thousands of drawings, each of which differed very slightly from the previous one. Each one was photographed as one frame of a motion picture film and when the images were projected, the effect was to create a moving picture. This process was highly skilled and very expensive as 24 pictures are required for one second of film – 86,400 hand-drawn pictures for a one-hour animated film. This could be reduced by cutting down the number of pictures per second, but any reduction also caused a reduction in the quality of the finished film.

To produce realistic motion of animals and humans, an animator would often trace line drawings from optical projections of the frames of a movie film, a process known as 'rotoscoping'. Animators can now use software to automate rotoscoping. Graphics software is used to digitally illustrate the figures, and animation software is used to interpolate (or 'tween', an abbreviation of 'in between') frames between relatively few 'key frames'. Software can also assist with the complex process of synchronising the animation of facial movements with a character's speech.

Automated rotoscoping, digital illustration and tweening all raise the productivity of the animator. However, each individual graphical object must be placed in a separate layer for tweening to produce the required results. If each tweened frame is separately illustrated in considerable detail, the animator may still only produce 100 frames, or about four seconds of animation, per week. So a film may take 75 person-years to produce.

A simple animated GIF file consisting of a succession of photographic images or 2-D drawings is often used as an avatar to represent a contributor to a web forum or message board. Animated 3-D avatars are used to represent characters in computer games.

In 3-D animation, graphics software similar to CAD software is used to produce a 3-D 'stick model' for each animated object. An 'animation variable' (or 'avar') stores a number representing the position of one of a character's stick-model elements and facial features. For example, one character in the animated film *Toy Story* used over 700 avars, of which over 200 were for the face alone.

There are several ways of generating successive sets of avars to represent the object's or character's position in each frame of the animation. An actor's performance while wearing a 'motion-capture suit' carrying lights or reflective markers can be recorded by a video camera. The recording is analysed by software to calculate the required avars (Figure 7.56). A skilful animator can also use a joystick to set the avars manually for each key frame, between which the intermediate frames are tweened. This can produce effects not easily modelled by a human actor.

**Figure 7.56** A researcher (left) performing facial motion capture for an animated character (right). The coloured spots of theatrical make-up on the researcher's face represent markers whose position is recorded by the helmet-mounted video camera in front of his face.

Once the stick model is satisfactorily animated, the avars can be used to calculate the elements of a wire-frame model. The final process of rendering, which can take hours of processing time for each frame, adds coloured, textured and shaded surfaces over the wire-frame model. Even though 3-D animation consumes a lot of processing time, it still enables producers to make considerable savings in the overall cost and duration of a production. It may soon be possible for animators to create a human figure which moves and interacts with a realistic environment so convincingly that viewers cannot tell whether the scene is computer-generated or a film of real actors.

Rotoscoped animation can be used to add special effects to conventional films, such as the 'lightsabres' in *Star Wars* films. The 'bluescreen' technique (also known as 'colour-separation overlay') can be used to separate the video of one or more actors from their blue background. In this way, the actors can be superimposed over an animated cartoon or computer-generated imagery (CGI) of a fantasy world. A CGI landscape can be created by an algorithm that uses random numbers and fractal mathematics to mimic the appearance of a natural landscape. CGI can include characters populating a scene, so that there is now less employment for film 'extras' for crowd or battle scenes.

## Use of the Internet
### Websites

A website is a collection of web pages containing text, graphics, video and sound. A website is hosted on a web server on the Internet. The information in the website can be viewed by other Internet users using a web browser. Websites are used to raise the profile of a person or an organisation and to communicate with others.

Storage space for text is rarely limited so, when designing a website, attention should be paid to maximising the information that users of the site may require in order to minimise the need for additional communication by email or other means. Menus and hyperlinks can easily provide access to separate pages to make additional information available without overwhelming users with information that they do not need immediately or allowing any one page to become excessively long. Hyperlinked text or command buttons to other websites should preferably open a fresh browser window or tab, so that the user does not lose touch with the website.

An interactive web form can be used to allow the user to register for a service, send a message, or make a purchase or other transaction. A web form needs careful design to provide sufficient space in boxes for entering data in text boxes, adequate validation and restriction of data using controls such as drop-down lists, check boxes and option buttons.

A website is published on a web server. The usual way to do this is to hire space from a web hosting company or ISP. The website is built on a local computer and uploaded to the web server via a secure connection.

A school website (Figure 7.57) is used to raise the profile of the school in the community, which can help students when they apply for jobs. It is used to communicate with parents and other interested people to ensure that they feel fully involved with the school. The website is also used to advertise the school to people that currently have no connection with the school, particularly potential new parents. It is also used to advertise events at the school.

The Internet is a new technology that had no direct predecessor, so it has created new markets and new jobs. There are companies that host thousands of websites; there are companies that will even build your school website for you. The World Wide Web is now widely used for advertising. Consequently, some old-style advertising has decreased and the advertising industry has had to adapt to this new medium.

### Online shopping

An online shopping website is likely to need at least the following facilities:

- a cookie to enable the web server to recognise the user as soon as their browser requests a web page from the website;
- a search facility to enable a user to search for an item by category, possibly using drop-down boxes to select a category or by keyword, such as the item's name, brand, or genre;
- advertising facilities, giving messages such as 'of customers who viewed this item, X% bought this item and Y% bought item Z' or ' when customers bought this item, X% also bought item Y'; or special offers available, such as 'bundle' deals;
- detailed descriptions of products, the ability to listen to a sample of music or to view a sample of video;
- currency conversion for international customers;
- a shopping basket, trolley or cart to store the items and quantities selected for purchase;
- saved customer details for delivery and possibly payment;
- customised pages, such as a Buy Later List or Wish List;

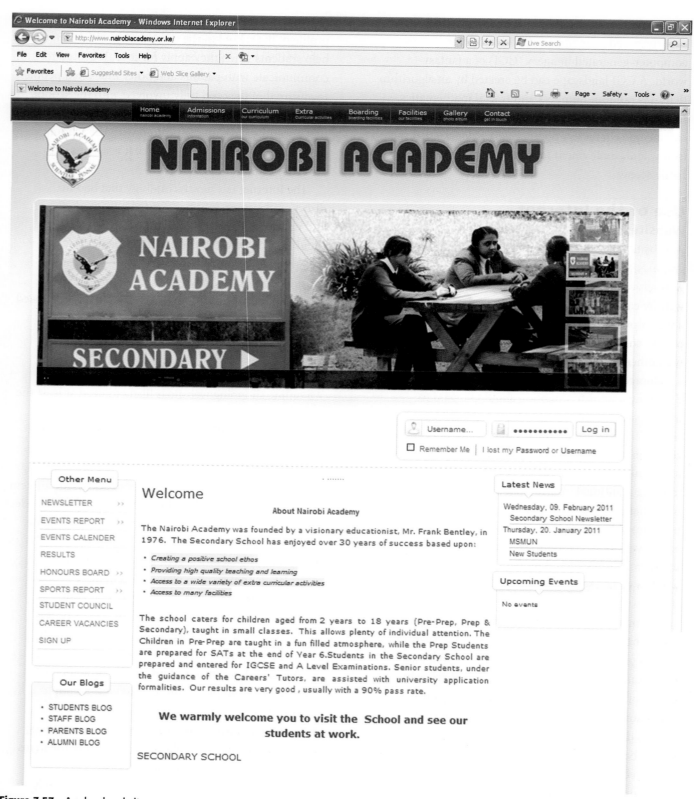

**Figure 7.57** A school website.

- a secure connection when paying by debit or credit cards;
- order or payment confirmation by automatic email;
- tracking the status of orders;
- help, such as a page of answers to Frequently Asked Questions (FAQs);
- contact details for the company.

The possibility of sound output from the site means that it is useful for the user's computer to have loudspeakers or headphones as well as a monitor screen. A shopping website with such facilities has considerable interactivity. The user can enter text to register with the site and provide details for debit or credit card payment, choose from a list or enter a search term to find information, and click command buttons to select items to purchase. When the user clicks a 'Proceed to checkout' button, the web server is likely to present the user with a succession of pages, requiring the user to:

- log in to their account via a secure connection, using HTTPS instead of the usual HTTP protocol;
- confirm the delivery address or add or select an alternative;
- select a carriage (or 'shipping') option;
- view a list of the items selected for purchase, with their unit prices and 'extended prices' calculated by multiplying the default value for quantity by the unit price and the total value of the order;
- select or add a method of payment;
- confirm or amend the order.

### Online banking

Online banking websites offer facilities for anyone to view information about banking services available. Customers can log in to their account, using the secure HTTPS protocol, with a username, password and possibly additional security questions. Facilities for customers are interactive in similar ways to those for online shopping. However, they focus on: viewing the account balance and recent transactions; viewing statements for past months; adding, amending or cancelling a payee; making a payment; adding, amending or cancelling a standing order; and changing security details such as a password or additional security questions (Figure 7.58).

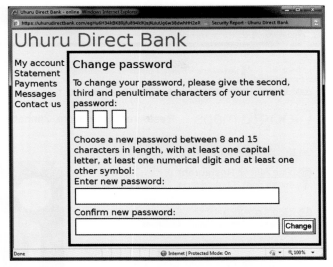

**Figure 7.58**  Changing the password for an online bank account. Notice the requirement to re-enter parts of the existing password and verification of the new one by double entry.

## Questions

26  Websites are used widely in ecommerce applications and in online banking.

a  What are the features that a shopper would expect to see when using an online shopping site?

b  What are the problems associated with online banking applications and which may worry some potential customers? What measures can be taken?

### Other sorts of website

Many web applications use interaction and dynamic screens to display content. For example, some mapping websites provide satellite photographs of the Earth's surface on relatively cloudless days, stitched together to provide an aerial view of anywhere on Earth. The user can zoom in and out by clicking buttons or rotating a mouse wheel. This can be useful for exploring the terrain in various parts of the world or for planning a cross-country trek.

For planning a road journey or finding your way around a city, a map can be superimposed over the satellite images so that you can view street and place names (Figure 7.59). The user can use their web browser

**Figure 7.59** This website supplies maps that can be superimposed on satellite imagery with map pins marking the addresses of local services.

to locate a landmark on the aerial view and then look at place names or vice versa. The user can take a virtual stroll along a street in any city in the world. In some cities, photographs of streets have been taken at ground level and made available with the aerial view so that the user can get an even better idea of what the area or even a specific building looks like. Such map websites often carry adverts for local services. They may provide a facility for the user to input two addresses or postal codes and receive the shortest or quickest route calculated between those points, highlighted on the screen map.

### Search engines

The Internet is the largest network of computers in the world. Its web and older File Transfer Protocol (FTP) servers store many billions of resources such as web pages, documents and images. Many users visit familiar websites for information, but the Internet is also a useful resource for finding new sources of information. Though users need to be aware that it is much easier to publish incorrect information on a website than in a book,

which is usually subject to some process of verification by its publisher.

To find new sources of information efficiently, a user needs the help of a web application known as a **search engine**, which searches its database for Internet resources that match the user's search criteria. A search engine's web-crawler program is an automated browser that systematically explores the content of web and FTP sites, updating its database (or 'index') of the content of, and possibly number of links to, each resource.

The user's search criteria are supplied to the search engine via a web form and used to search the database for relevant resources (Figure 7.60). The search engine's web server supplies the user with search results (colloquially known as 'hits') in the form of a list of hyperlinks. Different search engines produce different results for the same search criteria because they vary in how they construct their databases, query them and order the results. For this reason, each user should try out different search engines in order to select one that suits their needs.

When words contained in a resource are used as search criteria, there are a number of techniques for

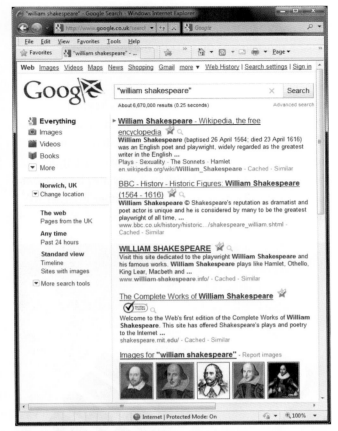

**Figure 7.60** Results from a search engine with a search criterion consisting of a phrase enclosed in double quotation marks.

improving the efficiency of the search. A single common word typically yields billions of potential results, so that the usefulness of the first screen-full of results is highly dependent on the way the search engine has ordered the results. A relatively long piece of text, especially if searched for as a phrase (meaning that all the words must appear in a precise order), may yield relatively few results. This is very helpful if the user is looking for the source of a quotation or the Internet location from which they have previously copied all or part of a resource, but it can also lead to a very limited, or even empty, set of results.

There are several ways of grouping words used as search criteria. The user may simply enter a number of words as search criteria, for example:

### vacation hawaii golf

In this case, most search engines automatically only return results that include *all* of the search criteria regardless of order, as if the user had entered:

### vacation +hawaii +golf

which is shorthand for:

### vacation AND hawaii AND golf

To search for resources that include an exact phrase (a group of words in a particular order), the user simply puts double quotation marks around the search criteria:

### "the long and winding road"

In most search engines, to search for either *smoke* or *fire*, the user can enter *smoke OR fire. AND* and *OR* are called Boolean operators and can operate on criteria consisting of single words or phrases. Your search term may have more than one meaning. For example, *bass* could refer to fishing or music. The user can focus their search by putting a minus sign (-) in front of words related to the meaning they want to avoid. To search for resources about bass in lakes but *not* bass in music, the user can enter:

### bass –music

Many search engines have a link to an *Advanced Search* page that provides alternative ways of using words as search criteria without having to type quotation marks or operators. It will apply other search criteria, such as reading level; language; file type; domain; how recent the resource is; country; price range; as well as size, type and colour of image.

 **SAQs**

**13** You want to find information about one of the characters in a particular Shakespeare play. What search criteria would you use?

### Internet security
During the process of logging in to a webmail account there is a risk that the user's password may be intercepted. The interception of a few emails may not be a major problem, but the interception of the password would enable someone to read all the account holder's email at their leisure, or even worse, to hijack the user's

account to generate spam or spread viruses. To combat this risk, you may have noticed that the log in page of a webmail account uses the secure HTTPS protocol that we mentioned for online shopping and banking. To prevent the interception of shopping account, card payment or bank account information, the whole of a shopping checkout or banking session is likely to use the secure protocol.

The HTTPS protocol relies on **encryption**, or secret encoding, of data during transmission. Similarly, for business email, encryption can be used to:

- create a 'digital signature' to be sent with an email to authenticate the identity of the sender and that the message has not been tampered with during transmission;
- encrypt the text of the email to prevent anyone who intercepts it from reading it.

### Extension

Investigate SSL (or TLS) certificates.

Just like a server responsible for security in a LAN, webmail, online shop and bank servers usually store users' passwords in encrypted form in case someone gains unauthorised access to them and to prevent abuse of passwords by those who administer these servers. To avoid having to expose the whole password to interception as it is sent over the Internet, an online banking server often asks for a random subset of the password's characters, as in Figure 7.58.

A smart card reader is frequently built into a computer keyboard to provide a swift and secure method for a user to log in to a business network or to read the identity cards of colleagues or customers. Ideally, each user of online shopping and banking would use a similar smart card reader to allow the server software to require the debit or credit card to be authenticated by entry of the user's PIN. Unfortunately, not all computers are yet equipped with smart card readers.

Some banks have developed an alternative system in which a user can opt to use a small hand-held smart card reader to add an additional layer of security

when logging in to online banking (Figure 7.61). Someone attempting to initiate an online banking session must supply the correct username and password, and they must also insert a smart card associated with the account into the smart card reader and input the user's PIN on the reader's keypad. The reader generates and displays a numerical one-time password (OTP), which must be immediately entered into the web form. Since an account may have more than one card associated with it, it may also be necessary to enter some digits from the card number in order to identify the card used.

**Figure 7.61** A hand-held smart card reader used to increase the security of online banking.

The disadvantage for the user is that they have to carry around a relatively bulky reader as well as their card. To address this problem, one inventor devised a smart card with an embedded microcontroller, in-card display and battery that can generate and display an OTP simply by pressing a button on the card. However, without a complete embedded keypad with which to enter the PIN, such a card is unable to make the generation of the OTP dependent on the user supplying their PIN.

Since an online shopping card payment typically requires only a card number, expiry date, card security code and cardholder name, all of which are visible on the card, some card issuers also require password authentication of a card payment for online shopping.

People are sometimes worried about the risks when using the Internet for shopping. These include encountering offensive websites while searching for goods or services; downloading viruses during a transaction; being deceived by a bogus website and paying for counterfeit or non-existent goods; interception of shopping account, card payment or banking account information making them vulnerable to unauthorised access to their accounts ('hacking') or fraudulent transactions; receiving unsolicited email after they have been required to supply a valid email address in order to register for an account. People also worry that browser 'cookie' files that identify their computer to a web server can enable a trader to 'retarget' them. That means that the trader will display personalised advertising based on products previously viewed on the trader's site when the user views other websites.

## Effects of the Internet on society

Computer technology enables people to do things differently to the way they were done in the past. It has many benefits, but it is important that we are aware of the drawbacks that also come with such technology. Increasing access to the Internet has had many social effects. Tables 7.1–7.3 consider the positive and negative impacts of various uses of the Internet. You can probably think of similar effects for many of the other applications of computers in this chapter.

However much the Internet helps to increase efficiency and reduce environmental impact, we should not forget that its use has some widespread negative effects. The installation and maintenance of the satellite, cable, wireless and server infrastructure to support the Internet itself has a significant environmental impact. The connection to the Internet of our own computers and those of businesses and governments who hold information about us increases the risk of unauthorised access to data ('hacking'). Since people can access so many services and so much entertainment by staying at home and using a computer, they have less incentive to interact with other people and tend to get less physical exercise, contributing to an increasingly obese and unhealthy population.

**Table 7.1**  Purchase of goods and services online

| Positive social effects | Negative social effects |
| --- | --- |
| • Shopping and banking are available 24 hours a day, 7 days a week (known as '24/7'), which is helpful to people who work during the normal working day. | • Bricks-and-mortar shops and banks are closing in both urban and rural areas, leading to loss of jobs. |
| • It may save the shopper's time. | • There is increased exposure to risk of fraud by offer for sale of counterfeit or non-existent goods, or misuse of debit or credit card details. |
| • People with disabilities that make it difficult for them to travel or who live in remote locations have improved access to shopping and services. | • Increased postal delivery of goods increases the environmental impact resulting from increased packaging and possibly decreased efficiency of delivery. |
| • There is improved access to international shopping and banking. | • Service has become more impersonal. |
| • Less travel to shops and banks results in decreased transport-related environmental impact. | • There is less opportunity to view or test the goods and judge their quality before purchase. |
| • Decreased 'overhead' costs and increased competition between online shops results in greater efficiency and reduced prices for customers. | |
| • There is increased access to other shoppers' reviews of products and services. | |

While access to the Internet opens up new societies, cultures and social values to people all over the world, it can also have an adverse effect on local culture because young people see a very biased picture of what life is like in other cultures and there is a danger that they may reject their own culture. Inappropriate information is also available and protecting people from such information is now more difficult.

**Table 7.2**   Obtaining news and other information online

| Positive social effects | Negative social effects |
|---|---|
| • Breaking news is available 24/7, worldwide.<br><br>• People with disabilities that make it difficult for them to travel or who live in remote locations have improved access to news and information.<br><br>• There is increased access to information from other countries and in other languages with online translation.<br><br>• Less transport of newspapers and books results in less transport-related environmental impact.<br><br>• Decreased costs of distribution results in cheaper or even free access to news and information. | • Newspapers, book publishers and printing businesses may close, leading to loss of jobs.<br><br>• There is increased risk of exposure to unreliable information unless the user is careful to check it and try to obtain it from reputable sources.<br><br>• People may lose book-based skills, such as using an index. |

**Table 7.3**   Use of the Internet in education

| Positive social effects | Negative social effects |
|---|---|
| • A virtual learning environment (VLE) makes structured learning resources available 24/7, which is helpful to students who need to fit education around work or caring commitments.<br><br>• People with disabilities that make it difficult for them to travel or who live in remote locations have improved access to educational facilities.<br><br>• There is improved access to international educational resources.<br><br>• Less travel to access education results in decreased transport-related environmental impact.<br><br>• Decreased 'overhead' costs and increased competition between online education providers results in greater efficiency and reduced costs for taxpayers or fees for students. | • Bricks-and-mortar colleges may close, leading to loss of jobs.<br><br>• Help from teachers or tutors may be less immediately available than in a classroom. |

## Intranets

In Chapter 5, we met the idea of web-based information services accessible only within an organisation's private network. These are known as an intranets to distinguish them from the public web services on the Internet, which can be accessed from anywhere else on the Internet. Most of the websites hosted by the millions of web servers in the Web can be accessed by anyone. In contrast, an intranet usually improves security by requiring separate user log-ins, first to gain access to the organisation's network and then to gain access to one or more intranet servers.

Providing information through web applications over an intranet may reduce the need to install expensive application software on the organisation's computers. If the organisation provides Internet access for its workers, as the majority do, a single router–modem can share Internet access with all the computers connected to a LAN.

If the organisation does not provide Internet access for its workers, the organisation can use an intranet to ensure that workers have access to available reliable information about the organisation's products and business. They can use the intranet to search for required information more effectively. Workers are prevented from distracting themselves by accessing websites or from accidentally accessing offensive material. Since contributors to intranet forums are relatively small in number, the views that are posted are more likely to be relevant. Security is improved since email remains internal to the organisation, unauthorised network access by persons outside the organisation is much harder and viruses cannot enter the organisation's network via the Internet.

If students and teachers have access to an intranet resource such as a virtual learning environment (VLE) at school, it may also be accessible from elsewhere on the Internet, such as a home computer. As we also mentioned in Chapter 5, an intranet that is available to authorised persons from outside the organisation's network is called an extranet.

In another example, an employee of an organisation in Dubai may be temporarily working in London. The employee can use a laptop computer to access the Internet using Wi-Fi or mobile broadband and then connect to the organisation's extranet by pointing their browser to the correct web address and securely logging in with their username and password. The employee is able to use the extranet's resources in the same way as if they were accessing the intranet in their office in Dubai. Some organisations also make an extranet available to aid communication with their business partners, business customers and suppliers.

**Questions**

27 If your school has an intranet, why does it have one? If it does not, discuss whether or not your school would benefit from one. Describe what it could be used for by:

a teachers;

b students.

## Summary

- The characteristics of an application of computer technology are: the need it is designed to fulfil; its hardware and software components; the collection, preparation and capture of its data; its data storage structure; the outcome required and format of output; user interface; method of backup and system recovery; effectiveness; effects on individuals and organisations.
- Communications systems include email, video-conferencing, digital telephones, Internet telephony, broadband and dial-up connections, wireless technology, multimedia applications and virtual reality.
- Information systems involve databases and include seat-booking systems, medical information systems (medicines, patient records and hospital administration), library systems and office automation.
- Commercial and general data-processing applications include automatic stock control and order processing, personnel records, banking systems and ecommerce.
- Industrial, technical and scientific uses include modelling, simulation and computer-aided design.
- Monitoring systems make measurements for display or analysis, including patient monitoring, burglar alarms, weather monitoring and environmental monitoring.
- Control systems use measurements to provide feedback in order to control a process, including the control of chemical plants, nuclear power stations and road traffic.
- Automated systems involve microcontrollers embedded in household appliances, such as washing machines and cookers, and electronic equipment, such as digital cameras and televisions, satnavs and CCTV.
- Robots are computer-controlled machines for repetitive production tasks such as welding; painting and handling materials; 'pick-and-place' for assembling components; and packing finished products.

$\longrightarrow$

*Summary continued …*

- An expert system is designed to support problem-solving by using the knowledge and rules of inference gathered from one or more human experts in task areas ranging from medical diagnosis to ship design.
- Education and training applications include CAL and CBT and may include VR or AR.
- Entertainment applications include musical composition, performance and recording, and animation.
- Internet applications include websites providing information, online shopping and banking, and search engines.
- Internet security depends on encryption during transmission of passwords and debit or credit card details, and additional security questions or one-time passwords generated by a portable smart card reader.
- People's worries about Internet shopping range from encountering offensive websites while searching for goods or services to interception of shopping account, card payment or banking account information making them vulnerable to unauthorised access to their accounts ('hacking') or fraudulent transactions.
- Effects of the Internet on society depend on the application, but may include improved convenience, time-saving and accessibility to information and services; reduced cost of goods and services, transport-related environmental impact and availability of bricks-and-mortar shops, banks and colleges; increased risk of fraud or misleading information; loss of employment from physical shops, banks and colleges; reduced face-to-face social interaction and exercise; increased health problems and vulnerability of personal data; global culture may undermine local cultures.
- Intranets are web-based information services accessible only within an organisation's private network.
- Extranets are intranets made available to members of an organisation while off-site, or to people with whom the organisation does business.

# Examination practice for Paper 1

## Exam Questions

1. (a) State **two** items of hardware needed to enable a standard computer system to take part in video-conferencing. [2]
   (b) State **two** additional items of software that would be needed for the video conference to take place. [2]
   (c) Describe **two** potential problems when using video-conferencing. [2]

   *Question 12, Cambridge IGCSE Computer Studies 0420/01 Paper 12 May/June 2010*

2. Describe how a supermarket would use computer technology to carry out automatic stock control. [3]

   *Question 7, Cambridge IGCSE Computer Studies 0420/01 Paper 11 May/June 2010*

3. Weather forecasting using computer models has made predicting weather more accurate.
   (a) Describe how data is gathered for the computer model. [2]
   (b) How does the computer model make its prediction based on the new weather data input? [2]
   (c) Describe **two** ways the predicted weather for a week could be conveyed to the user. [2]

   *Question 2, Cambridge IGCSE Computer Studies 0420/01 Paper 1 Specimen for 2011 onwards*

$\longrightarrow$

4. Aeroplanes use onboard computer power to allow them to operate more efficiently and safely.

   **(a)** How are data during a flight collected and fed back to onboard computers?                                      [2]

   **(b)** Why are computer systems thought to be safer than human pilots?                                                 [2]

   **(c)** However, pilots are still used on all flights. Why is this?                                                     [2]

   **(d)** What recent developments have led to more use of computer control in newly designed aeroplanes?                 [1]

   **(e)** Describe how the computer would know when to make course corrections during a flight.                          [2]

   *Parts of Question 15, Cambridge IGCSE Computer Studies 0420/01 Paper 1 May/June 2009*

5. A safety system has been developed to stop vehicles getting too close to each other on the road.

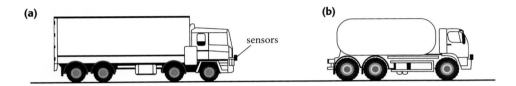

   If vehicle **A** gets too close to vehicle **B**, the brakes are automatically applied by a computer system in vehicle **A**.

   **(a)** What type of sensors could be used on the vehicles?                                                             [1]

   **(b)** Describe what the safety system does to constantly monitor how close the vehicle is to the vehicles in front and decide when to take action.                                                                                    [4]

   **(c)** Describe **two** potential problems with this safety system.                                                    [2]

   *Question 14, Cambridge IGCSE Computer Studies 0420/01 Paper 12 May/June 2010*

6. An expert system is being developed to help engineers diagnose faults in aero engines. Describe the steps taken to develop this new expert system.                                                                                  [4]

   *Part of Question 6, Cambridge IGCSE Computer Studies 0420/01 Paper 12 May/June 2010*

7. A large city has decided to computerise totally its traffic management system. Traffic lights and electronic road signs are now under automatic computer control.

   **(a)** Sensors are placed around the city to gather information about traffic. Describe what information would need to be gathered.                                                                                                   [2]

   **(b)** Describe **two** ways the information from the sensors could be sent to the central computer which is located several miles away.                                                                                             [2]

   **(c)** Give **two** advantages of having the traffic in the city controlled in this way.                              [2]

   *Question 10, Cambridge IGCSE Computer Studies 0420/01 Paper 1 Oct/Nov 2008*

8. A company has set up an Internet website to sell their electrical goods online.

    (a) Give **two** features you would expect to see on the website. [2]

    (b) Payments for goods can be made by credit/debit cards. Data from the cards is encrypted.

        (i) What is encryption? [1]

        (ii) Why is data encrypted? [1]

    (c) Apart from credit card fraud, people have other fears about buying from the Internet. Describe **one** of these fears. [1]

    *Question 16, Cambridge IGCSE Computer Studies 0420/01 Paper 11 May/June 2010*

## Exam-Style Questions

1. (a) Explain the term *virtual reality*, including the special hardware devices that may be used for input and output. [3]

    (b) Give **one** example of a system that uses virtual reality. [1]

    (c) Give **three** advantages of using virtual reality. [3]

2. (a) Give **one** advantage and **one** disadvantage of using Wi-Fi to connect a computer to the Internet. [2]

    (b) State **one** other device that can connect to the Internet using Wi-Fi. [1]

3. Some organisations provide their workers with access to an intranet, but not to the Internet.

    (a) Give **two** differences between an intranet and the Internet. [2]

    (b) Give **two** reasons why an organisation might choose to make such provision. [2]

4. Some websites provide aerial photographs of the whole of the Earth's surface.

    (a) How are the photographs of the Earth's surface obtained? [1]

    (b) Such a website often allows the user to see a road map placed on top of an aerial photograph. What advantage does this give to the user? [1]

    (c) State **one** additional facility often provided by such map websites. [1]

# Examination practice for Paper 3

To answer the following question you will need to read the garage scenario provided in Appendix A (page 284).

1. Now that the garage has all their spare parts stored on a computer system, they have decided to advertise on the Internet. A website has been created to enable customers to obtain information and also order items from the website using their credit cards.

   Use the space below to design a web page for this garage to allow customers to order spare parts. [6]

   *Question (k), Cambridge IGCSE Computer Studies 0420/01 Paper 3 Specimen for 2011*

## Comments

In this type of question, it is a general rule that you will score 1 mark for your design looking how it would appear on the screen from the website. So make sure your drawing is neat and clear. The other marks (in this case 5) would be awarded for including standard items expected on a website relevant to the scenario.

It is a good idea to include more items on the screen than the number of marks available. In this example it would be sensible to include 7 items on the list. The 7 items in addition to the final mark for overall design, would give you 8 chances of earning the 6 marks.

# 8

# Social and economic implications of the use of computers

**When you have finished this chapter, you will be able to:**

- demonstrate an understanding of some social and economic effects of computer use on people and organisations, including:
  - de-skilling
  - relocation of business operations
  - benefits of 'new technology' agreements in the workplace
  - economic reasons for using computers
  - changes to methods, services and the working environment
  - health and safety aspects
  - re-training to meet changes in employment
- describe measures needed to maintain privacy and integrity of data
- describe the features expected in data protection legislation
- describe an application's requirements for security and reliability
- demonstrate an understanding of threats to security and measures to combat them, including:
  - hacking and other computer crime
  - computer viruses
  - internet security
- describe some recent developments in the use of the Internet.

## Introduction

As we saw in Chapter 3, although people have been building calculating devices for centuries, electronic computers were only developed in the early 1940s. Your grandparents probably remember a time when computers were only read about in science fiction or adventure novels, where they were used by evil people who wanted to take over the world until James Bond or some other hero came along to stop them. Computers did exist in real life but most people rarely came across them and certainly did not study them in school.

However, in less than a century, they have directly or indirectly changed the lives of most people on the planet. Computers, in all their forms, are used by most of the world's students and much of the world's trade, industry, education and entertainment now depends on them.

The economic reasons for using computerised systems can be summarised as increased productivity compared with manual systems. This results from the ability of computer systems to communicate and process data repetitively, accurately and rapidly; to store data in relatively little space; to make backup copies of data rapidly and reliably; to search for information rapidly and reliably; and to produce output in a variety of formats. For example, an organisation may be able to improve its economic position by:

- using less space for storing bulky paper documents;
- reducing the risk of losing vital information;
- operating a 'just-in-time' (JIT) ordering strategy with automated reordering;
- making its sales system available to customers through a website;
- responding faster to customers' requests;
- making good-quality information available through the use of an intranet;
- using CBT to improve the quality and flexibility of staff training;
- maintaining or increasing production with fewer workers.

## Changing employment

Often, computerisation requires changes to the working environment, business methods or processes and to the services provided by an organisation. The success of a new computer-based system may be limited by factors such as:

- poor communication with users during the analysis and design stages;
- delays in development during which the organisation's requirements change;
- lack of compatibility with the organisation's existing hardware and software;
- incorrectly designed business procedures;
- insufficient testing of the solution or training of users.

Some of the effects of computers on individuals, organisations and society in general have already been discussed in Chapter 7. As we begin to look at other aspects in this chapter, let us look at a case study.

### Case study: Computerisation in a steel works

Ahmed worked in a steel works. His was a very **skilled job** that took years to learn. He had to stand next to great furnaces full of molten metal (Figure 8.1) and

decide when to add extra ingredients, such as carbon to make carbon steel. He would also decide when to pour the molten metal off. He knew when these things should be done because of subtle changes to the colour of the metal in the furnace.

**Figure 8.1**   A steel works.

He was forced to retire early when the foundry introduced computer systems to do his job. The company is very happy with the new system because the computers get the timing right every time. This means that the finished steel is as perfect as it can be. The costs are lower because the system is automated, which means that fewer people have to be employed. The sales are up because the quality of the steel is very high and it is cheaper.

However, there are no longer any people left who have the skills that Ahmed had. Soon, there will be nobody left who remembers that the job can be done by human beings simply by using their sight. What will happen if the machines can no longer do the job properly? This loss of skills is known as **de-skilling**.

Ahmed is happy in one way: his son was going to follow him as an apprentice in this very dangerous job. Ahmed is grateful that his son has instead got a job in the control room (Figure 8.2) that controls the robots that manipulate the containers of molten metal. This job is not as skilled as Ahmed's used to be but still requires training to be able to do it. Ahmed's son is said to be **semi-skilled**.

Ahmed's daughter worked in the administration department but applied to go on a course about robotics when plans were announced for introducing computer systems to her department and it was obvious that

**Figure 8.2** The control room of an automated steel works.

**Figure 8.3** Teleworking from home.

some of the workers would be made redundant. Having finished her course, she is now one of the technicians servicing the robots in the works. She changed her job by learning the skills necessary for another one and hence has **re-skilled**.

The workers who are still employed in the administration department have also had to re-skill to learn to use the new technologies. It may take longer to learn to use relatively complex computers and software than to learn how to use a typewriter and paper-based document, record-keeping and accounting systems. However, a worker can usually rapidly become much more productive. For example, whereas it would have taken a lot of practice before a typist could have rapidly typed a document without a significant chance of making an error, a word processor has a facility for checking spelling. Also an electronic documents can be edited, without having to re-type it all again as would have been the case with a typewritten document.

The sales team no longer need to make so many visits to customers as most of their business can be conducted over the Internet using various communication tools including email and video-conferencing (see Chapter 7). It is not only sales visits that are reduced. The sales team do not even need to visit their own company offices very often, so these workers can largely work from home using computers and telephones – they are known as teleworkers (Figure 8.3). Benefits to workers of teleworking include less time and money spent travelling to and from their workplace and possibly increased flexibility in when they do their work, allowing them to plan their working hours around family commitments.

## SAQs

1  What are the essential hardware requirements for working at home if you are working as a salesperson?

### Questions

1  Discuss the advantages and disadvantages of being able to work from home rather than going in to work every day:
a  for the worker;
b  for the company;
c  for society in general.

### Computerising existing jobs

The introduction of new technology has changed many types of employment. In the steel works that Ahmed worked in, three people in the payroll department worked with typewriters, calculators and tax tables. The management of the company considered outsourcing the payroll system, but decided to keep it in house and computerise it. This had a large effect on the payroll workers:

- A 'new technology' agreement was struck between the workers' trade union and the management because there was a mutual recognition that computerisation and changes in employment were necessary for the company to remain in business in a fiercely competitive industry. Such agreements can lead to greater productivity for the company and better working conditions for the workers.

- The new system was more efficient, contributing to the overall efficiency of the company. However, the company now only needed one full-time post and one part-time post in the payroll department, so that two full-time posts were made redundant and replaced by one part-time post. This was very stressful for the workers whose posts were affected.
- The two people who remained needed to go on training courses in order to be able to use the new system. At first, they were worried that they would find the new skills difficult to learn and were uncertain about their futures, although they both adapted well to the new system.
- The workers' higher level of training has made them more highly qualified and the company has slightly increased their rates of pay. Their extra training will also make them more employable if they need to change jobs.
- The jobs that they do have changed. Computers have relieved them of many tedious, repetitive tasks requiring a high level of concentration and accuracy. They also feel de-skilled now that their responsibilities have been reduced to entering and updating data, printing payslips and transmitting the electronic direct credit payments file to the company's bank. This has made it harder for them to feel proud of what they do and that their jobs give them a place in their society.

## Questions

**2** Two shops on the same street sell food, general produce and household goods. Customers who go into either shop are met by an assistant who greets them and asks what they need. The assistant gets their purchases from behind the counter and keeps a total of what they spend on a piece of paper. This system has worked perfectly well in the two shops for many years, but the owner of one of

→

---

*Question 2 continued …*

the shops decides to introduce a computerised system. The system uses POS terminals reading barcodes on products that shoppers select for themselves. Investigate the answers to the following questions.

**a** What are the things that the shopper will notice when they go to the shop with the new system?

**b** Will all the shoppers from both shops be drawn to the one with the new system or can you recognise some reasons why some will still want to shop in the other shop?

**c** What will be the effects on the workers in both shops? Do not forget to include all the people who work in the shops.

---

You may be able to identify other areas in which de-skilling of the workforce has occurred. CAD software has tended to de-skill drafting jobs. Expert systems are sometimes used to enable less highly trained people to do work previously done by professionals.

### Off-shore outsourcing

Computer technology has enabled some jobs to be relocated anywhere in the world, especially now that VOIP technology has made international telephony so cheap. For example, the steel-making company could move its customer service system, for responding to customers' phone calls, to another country. If the company does not want to manage its own real or virtual 'off-shore' call centre, it may 'outsource' this service to a company in that other country. At the time of writing, India and South Africa are major providers of off-shore call centre facilities to companies in the UK.

Advantages to companies of using an off-shore call centre may include:

- a highly educated workforce with reduced labour costs;
- possible financial incentives for foreign investment from the government;
- the flexibility to transfer some or all of the workload at relatively short notice;

- workers in different time zones can contribute to round-the-clock customer support during normal working hours in their own time zone.

Disadvantages of such an arrangement may include:

- negative effects on the company's existing local workforce, such as redeployment, redundancy and early retirement;
- language differences (even between variants of the same language!);
- cultural differences that hinder understanding;
- customers' lack of confidence in an overseas call centre;
- the cost and time taken in training call centre workers for their new role;
- time differences that require workers to work outside normal working hours to provide service during the required periods of the day.

## Health and safety

People who work with computers, in all their forms, often have relatively clean and comfortable working conditions. However, we need to be aware that spending long periods using a computer can make workers susceptible to a range of health risks that can be prevented (Table 8.1).

 **SAQs**

2   What simple thing can you do to avoid sore eyes? Racing drivers also have to remember to do this but only for a tiny fraction of a second!

**Table 8.1**   Preventing health risks.

| Health risk | Cause | Prevention |
|---|---|---|
| Reduced physical exercise<br><br>Poor circulation in the legs | Long periods sitting at a workstation | Regular changes of task<br><br>Regular rest breaks, during which the worker should stand up and walk around |
| Back, shoulder and neck problems | Long periods sitting at a desk with poor posture | A chair that supports the worker's back<br><br>A keyboard at the right height for the forearms to be horizontal<br><br>A screen level with or just below eye level<br><br>Regular changes of position |
| Sore eyes, caused by a lack of tear fluid to lubricate the eye and focusing muscles not being exercised over their full range | Long periods looking in one direction at a computer screen | Regular changes of gaze (look away from the screen)<br><br>A screen correctly adjusted to avoid too little or too much brightness or colour contrast<br><br>A screen at right angles to a wall containing a window<br><br>An anti-reflective screen filter<br><br>Regular eye tests by an optician |
| Repetitive strain injury (RSI), which feels a bit like arthritis | Long periods holding hands over the keyboard and pressing keys or clicking mouse buttons | A padded wrist support<br><br>Regularly stretching wrist and arm muscles in different ways |

## Training methods

A worker who works with a computer system needs to be trained properly when using a new system or an upgraded version of a familiar system. The worker may need training not only in how to use the new system's hardware and software but also in the business processes to be used with it.

Training used to involve a specialist trainer taking a class or a small group of people and leading them through the types of task that they were expected to do. The specialist would have to be paid and workers would have time off to be trained. If all the members of a department needed to be trained simultaneously, this meant that nobody was available in that department while the training was being carried out. In some cases it was even necessary to close down the organisation during the training. This was very expensive and when the training was over there was nobody to ask for help when problems arose with the system.

What often happens nowadays is that the training course is a specially written computer program, usually in the form of a multimedia presentation on CD-ROM or DVD-ROM. Using this, the worker can work at their own pace and can skip parts of the training that they are already comfortable with and they can repeat stages that they find difficult. Workers can also be expected to do the training in their own time. The training program is always available so that it can be used again if the worker finds difficulty with a particular aspect of the work. Further details of this type of training were discussed in the education and training section of Chapter 7.

### Questions

3  List advantages and disadvantages of training using computer-based software rather than having a human being to run the training.

## Privacy and integrity of data

One of the great benefits of using computers is that large quantities of stored data are easily accessible, both locally and over networks. As the use of computers has become more widespread, keeping stored data private has become increasingly important. Governments try to keep military, intelligence and diplomatic information secret. Smaller organisations need to keep private both personal data about their workers or clients and commercially sensitive information about their products, services, processes and future intentions.

For example, if the data consist of the prices that a supermarket is charging for its stock items, it does not matter much if anyone sees them. However, if the data contain the prices that the supermarket intends to charge in the future, the company would not want another supermarket to gain access to them, because the competitor could then set its prices accordingly.

Even records as seemingly trivial as those of customers' purchases from a shop are actually quite important to keep private. If an unauthorised person can gain access to a record of a customer's purchase of a valuable item, that customer is at risk of being burgled.

Maintaining the **privacy** (or 'confidentiality') **of data** involves trying to prevent:

- unauthorised access to data, also known as 'hacking' (see later in this chapter);
- accidental disclosure through inappropriate procedures, such as leaving a computer screen at a reception desk visible to visitors or placing unshredded documents in a waste bin;
- deliberate disclosure through a malicious act by a worker.

**Integrity** of data refers to their completeness and correctness during processing, storage, copying and transmission. Maintaining data integrity involves trying to prevent unwanted changes to data, known as **corruption** (Table 8.2), caused by:

- a computer hardware, software or network error;
- a virus (see later in this chapter);
- unauthorised access;
- the incorrect or malicious action of an authorised user.

Although we cannot completely prevent corruption, we can compensate for it by keeping backup copies of files from which we can restore fresh working copies. Such files may include the 'grandfather–father–son' file generations often used in a batch-processing system, in which two previous generations of master and transaction files are kept in case the latest master file is found to be corrupt and needs to be recreated.

**Table 8.2** Preventing data corruption.

| Cause | Prevention |
| --- | --- |
| Incorrect operation of the computer, such as incorrect use of software or incorrect power down of the system | Thoroughly written user manuals and thorough training for users |
| Power loss | An 'uninterruptible power supply' (UPS) |
| Hardware faults, especially hard disk crashes | Fault tolerance can be provided through the use of a Redundant Array of Independent Disks (RAID) system, or even two or more redundant (or 'parallel') whole computer systems (see Chapter 4) |
| Software faults | Fault tolerance can be provided through use of two or more redundant (or 'parallel') whole computer systems with different, thoroughly tested software |

An 'uninterruptible power supply' (UPS) contains a microcontroller that detects a power loss before the output of the computer's internal power supply collapses. It uses a rechargeable battery and an 'inverter' to supply the computer with power for a few minutes until the computer can be properly shut down.

Maintaining privacy and integrity of data is a challenge even with a stand-alone computer, which is not connected to any others. Someone who can gain physical access to the computer may attempt to gain unauthorised access to any data stored in the computer. The computer could be safeguarded by physical security such as: not leaving it unattended at any time; locking the room in which it is kept, perhaps with a keycard system; monitoring the room with CCTV as a deterrent; locking the computer to a security cable (Figure 8.4); equipping the computer with a key-operated power switch.

**Figure 8.4** Physical security for a PC.

Maintaining privacy and integrity of data is even more of a challenge when computers are linked together in a network. In a network, a number of users interact with a number of computers. Hacking into a LAN from an unattended workstation or via the Internet becomes a possibility. There is also a risk of corruption of data during its transmission between computers.

As discussed in Chapter 4, a checksum can be used to detect corruption caused by signalling errors during transmission of a data packet. A checksum is calculated from the data packet by the transmitting computer and transmitted at the end of the data packet. The receiving computer recalculates the checksum from the received data and compares this with the received checksum. If they differ, the data packet has been corrupted and transmission must be repeated until the checksums agree. If the checksums still do not agree after a certain number of repeats, the transmission has failed.

A LAN or single computer connected to the Internet is usually protected behind protective software (and possibly hardware). This hardware and software, known as a **firewall**, blocks unwanted network communication with your computer (Figure 8.5). For example, a firewall may only allow specified programs to receive data from the Internet. The firewall protects the LAN from external attack, such as unauthorised requests for data via other programs. However, it allows authorised persons who are off-site to log in to an extranet or to authenticate to a secure 'virtual private network' (VPN). Some operating systems include firewall software.

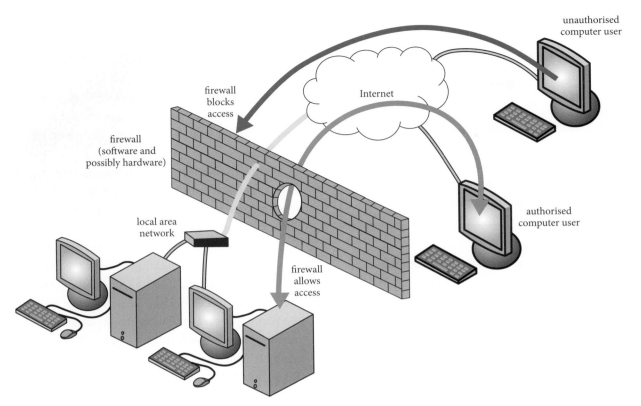

**Figure 8.5** Accessing a LAN through a firewall.

## Security and reliability of data

**1.2.5**

The **security of data** can be defined as maintaining the privacy and integrity of data, together with protecting data against loss when failure of a storage device occurs, a computer is stolen or destroyed by fire or natural disaster, or data are accidentally or maliciously deleted.

To help maintain privacy and to reduce the risk of data corruption or loss being caused by people, file systems allow different access rights or **permissions** to files, directories or drives to be given to different users and groups of users. Users may be given no access rights to files that they have no need to use. Other users may be given read-only access rights, which enable them to read files but prevent them from accidentally or deliberately modifying or deleting files. As with data corruption, although we cannot completely prevent loss of data, we can compensate for it by keeping backup copies of files.

Sometimes a failure that wipes out files is just annoying – imagine that your teacher told you at the start of a lesson that your project work had been lost and that you would have to start it again! Sometimes it can be far worse. Goods in a supermarket do not have the prices on them, just barcoded ID numbers. If a supermarket that depends on computers to look up each item's description and price were to lose its database of stock items, the checkout computer would still read each item's ID number, but would be unable to look up the item's price. The supermarket would not able to sell anything and would have to shut temporarily. Similarly, if a bank lost all its data, it would go out of business because it would not know who owed it money or to whom it owed money.

You may have noticed that networked computers usually do not have a *Recycle* or *Trash* bin. If you have accidentally deleted a file or it has become corrupted on your school's network, you may have had to ask if you could have your file restored from a backup copy. If your school creates backup copies once a day of files that you store on the network, you cannot lose more than a day's work. Losing customer records or even a single day's transactions would still be ruinous for a bank, so its files are usually backed up far more often. Any changes to the files are probably also backed up continuously, to minimise the risk of losing any data.

## Questions

4  What problems could arise with the integrity of data if a lot of backup copies are made? How can these problems be overcome?

Storing backup copies anywhere near the computer means that the backups are just as vulnerable as the computer to theft or destruction by fire or natural disaster. So backup copies need to be kept away from their computer system. Ideally, someone should take home a backup (on a USB memory stick, a portable hard drive or a magnetic tape cartridge) of the data for a school or a small business at the end of the day. If backup copies are left on the premises, they should be locked in a fire-proof safe. Another possibility is to use an 'online backup' service available on the Internet, to which files can be uploaded for backup and from which they can be downloaded to restore files when necessary.

Large companies have to take even greater precautions and often store backups in separate, secure buildings, well away from their offices. Fibre-optic network cable is frequently used as the volume of data can be so great. Some organisations even go so far as to build or lease a duplicate site that remains on standby in readiness to run their operations in case their offices are affected by a fire or natural disaster.

Backup copies of files are often compressed to reduce storage requirements, although compression slows down the process of creating the backup and of restoring the data if required. A backup utility program can be scheduled to perform this processor-intensive activity automatically at a convenient time, such as overnight. Even the data on a home computer should be backed up to a separate drive. Many students have lost important homework, coursework, or their photograph or

music collections through failure to do so. You have been warned!

The security of data affects their **reliability**, or how available they are, often expressed as a percentage. For example, an availability of 99.999% (known as 'five nines') means that, on average, the data are only unavailable for 0.001% of the time, or five minutes in each year.

Although discovering corruption or loss of payroll files would be a nuisance, it is likely to be acceptable if it takes some minutes to restore these files from backup copies. However, in a safety-critical application, such as fly-by-wire or air traffic control, there could be a catastrophic failure if backup copies of the data were not immediately available if a working copy were to become corrupted or lost.

Very high levels of data reliability can be achieved through redundancy of disk drives, or even of whole computers. For example, in one version of RAID, multiple exact copies of data files are written to multiple hard disk drives, known as a 'mirrored set'. If one disk fails, the disk controller can immediately read the data from another drive in the mirrored set. Backup copies of these data can be made by removing one of the disks from the mirroring process, making a backup copy of its data and then 're-building' its contents to reflect the current data of the mirrored set.

 ## Data protection legislation

We mentioned earlier in this chapter that an organisation needs to keep private personal data that it holds about its workers or clients. Of course, they are also valuable data that would take considerable amounts of both the organisation's and the workers' or clients' time and effort to replace.

So conserving the security and privacy of personal data are necessary both as a respectful way of dealing with people and to comply with data protection laws. The relevant laws include those in an organisation's own country and those in any country from which the organisation wishes to receive personal data for 'processing', which includes its use in a call centre, for example.

Data protection legislation is typically based on principles such as the following:

- personal data may only be obtained and processed fairly, lawfully and for specified purposes;
- data must be accurate, kept up-to-date, sufficient, relevant, not excessive, and deleted when no longer needed;
- individuals have a right of access to the data held about them and to have *factually* incorrect information corrected;
- data must be protected from corruption, loss and access by or disclosure to people who are not authorised to see them (note that this requires attention to all the aspects of data security described earlier);
- data must not be transferred to another country unless that country provides a similar level of legal protection for personal data.

## Questions

5   Find out the name and main requirements of any data protection law in your country.

Many organisations maintain privacy by applying a 'need to know' principle and giving different access rights to data to different people. For example, in a doctor's surgery, very sensitive data is stored about patients. Receptionists need access to patients' names, addresses and telephone numbers so that they can send out letters and phone patients when it is necessary to change the time of an appointment, but they should not be able to see patients' medical records. Doctors need to have access to patients' medical records. The practice manager and doctors who are partners in the practice need to be able to see all the doctors' records.

For convenience in managing access rights, user accounts are put into groups and the groups are given access rights to resources. For example, each of the receptionists' user accounts would be put into a group called *Receptionists*, which could be given read-only access to the patients' address and telephone number records and read–write access to appointment records.

## Questions

6   Explain the log-in process for a doctors' surgery system and how the system decides what access rights the user should have.

7   Data about students are stored on a school computer system. Many people have access to different parts of the data that are held. Make a list of the types of data held about students in your school. Divide the different types of data up into groups that you would expect to be accessible by different personnel in the school.

## ? SAQs

3   Explain the difference between data privacy and data security.

## 1.2.6 Computer crime

As the use of computers has grown, there has been a growth not only in the use of computers as tools to assist in the commission of other crimes but also of crimes directed towards computer systems themselves. Computer crime may be committed by an 'insider' (someone who works within an organisation) or by an 'outsider'.

### Hacking

**Hacking** is a commonly used term for gaining unauthorised access to a local computer or to a remote computer via a network (Figure 8.6). In many countries, this is itself a crime, even if no damage is caused or other crime committed. Hacking poses a risk of the loss of privacy and integrity of data, but also a risk of the total loss of data if a hacker accidentally or deliberately deletes them.

Hackers have a variety of motives. They may gain access just to prove that a system is vulnerable. They may want to alter or destroy data for some malicious reason. Alternatively, they may be intent on committing some other form of computer crime.

**Figure 8.6** Protect your computer from hackers.

Hacking can be combated by the physical security measures mentioned earlier in this chapter and the use of user credentials to authenticate the user's identity when they log in to a system. Each authorised user is given a **username** that is not secret. It represents a claimed identity and the user chooses a secret **password** to prove their claim. A legitimate user can supply both a valid username and the matching password, their **user credentials**, and gain access to the system. A hacker has to discover or guess a valid username and guess or otherwise gain access to the matching password.

To prevent someone from guessing a password, it needs to be 'strong', which means that it should be long and complex. Ideally, a password should have at least 14 characters, combining upper case and lower case letters, digits, punctuation and other symbols.

As mentioned in Chapter 7, a smart card reader built into a computer keyboard can provide an additional layer of physical security, because a smart card acts as a keycard that must also be physically present in order to supply the correct password when a PIN is entered via the keyboard.

When the computer is left unattended, the user should place the computer's operating system into *lock*, *sleep* or *hibernate* mode with a password required to return to normal operation. If the user does not do that, he or she should log out or shut down the computer.

To guard against hacking, all attempts to access a system should be automatically logged, whether or not they are successful. The resulting audit trail may provide evidence of, or at least clues to, the hacker's true identity.

Encryption (secret scrambling or encoding) of passwords stored in a computer system prevents a

hacker, who has gained access by guessing a set of user credentials, from simply reading any other users' passwords. Encryption can also be used to make individual files or emails unreadable without the relevant password, but this is not a reliable method of stopping a hacker gaining access to them. It simply provides an extra layer of security: a hacker has to 'crack' one password to gain access to the system and then another to decrypt and read the contents of a file or email.

## Questions

8   Investigate techniques of encryption.

    **a**   The ancient Romans used a simple method of encryption. It consisted of two concentric rings with the letters of the alphabet on both. The inner ring could be spun around. As long as you knew the setting, a message could be encrypted or decrypted very quickly and easily. Imagine the rings are set so that the letter on the inner ring is three ahead of the letter on the outer ring. Then A on the outer ring becomes D on the inner one, B becomes E, and so on, until W becomes Z, X becomes A, and Z becomes C. Then HELLO would become KHOOR. To decipher the message the letters would be found on the inner ring and the new letter would be on the outer one. Try to design your own encryption machine.

    **b**   What are the weaknesses in this form of encryption? Would it take long for an unauthorised person to break the encryption, particularly with the help of a computer?

    **c**   Find out about some other forms of encryption.

    **d**   Search for the name 'Sarah Flannery' on the Internet. She was just 16 years old when she won a prize for discovering a powerful form of encryption.

    **e**   Try to discover your own encryption technique.

User credentials are used for authentication when a user logs in to a computer system, but slightly different forms of authentication are used with embedded computers. When someone uses an ATM, the account number is read from the debit or credit card, which is equivalent to a username. In case the card has been stolen, confirmation is required that the user of the card is the legitimate cardholder. The personal identification number (PIN) is a short, numerical equivalent of a password.

Apart from using a firewall, another way of ensuring that data are kept secure is not to store them on the computer system while the system is networked. This would involve storing the data on a removable storage device and removing it from the system before using the network. This means that even if the defences of the computer are breached, the data are not there and cannot be stolen or corrupted by a remote hacker.

## Other sorts of computer crime

Forms of 'cybercrime' in which computers are used as tools to assist in the commission of other crimes include:
- data theft;
- theft of authentication credentials (commonly known as 'identity theft'), including phishing and pharming;
- fraudulent trading;
- banking fraud;
- espionage;
- infringement of the copyright of software or music;
- distributing or acquiring child pornography;
- harassment (also known as 'cyberstalking');
- child grooming.

Forms of cybercrime directed at computer systems or devices themselves include: distribution of malicious software, such as computer viruses, scareware, spyware and crimeware; and denial-of-service attacks.

## 1.2.7  Computer viruses

The term 'virus' is often used loosely to include all forms of **malware** (malicious software), which can potentially affect computer systems and devices with embedded computers, such as mobile phones and media players.

Strictly speaking, a **virus** is a piece of program code within a data or program file that copies (or 'replicates') itself and 'infects' other files in the same or another host computer, by analogy with a biological virus that replicates itself and infects other cells in the same or another host organism. Under certain conditions, such as opening the file, the virus can run and deliver its malicious effects (or 'payload'). This may simply involve replicating itself but often includes delivering an attention-seeking message or corrupting or deleting operating system or user files.

Such a virus spreads between computers when a user, usually unknowingly, copies an infected file to another computer using a network or a portable medium, such as a CD, DVD, USB drive or portable HDD. The virus' payload may include using an email client program to send copies of the infected file to addresses in the email client's address book.

A worm is another type of self-replicating malware. It differs from a virus in that it does not need to embed itself within another file and it may be able to send copies of itself through a computer network without any action by a user.

Other forms of malware are not self-replicating, so they have to be actively downloaded. A **Trojan horse** is a piece of malware that seems to be, or is bundled with, useful and desirable software in order to deceive a user into downloading it from the Internet and installing it. It is called a Trojan horse from the story of a platoon of Greek soldiers that hid in a wooden horse, which was pulled into the ancient city of Troy by its citizens. At night, the soldiers emerged and opened the city gates to allow their army to enter. A computer Trojan horse may deliver a worm to the user's LAN or may open a 'back door' that later allows an intruder to gain remote access to the user's computer system, rather like the opened gates of Troy.

As with hacking, the only complete defence against malware delivered from a network is to work on a stand-alone computer, but this is not very practical for most users. A properly configured firewall is a major defence against malware being delivered to a computer via the Internet. Even with a firewall, a user would be wise not to view an email or its attachments from an unknown sender.

Similarly, a user should be cautious about copying files from someone else on portable storage media. Bearing in mind the risk of a Trojan horse, it is wise to install software only from an original CD or DVD or website, rather than as part of a bundle produced by a third party.

The most reliable way of detecting and removing malware once it has arrived at a computer is **anti-virus software,** also known as a **virus scanner**. This software scans files as they are opened, copied and saved. If malware is detected, it prevents the malware from running. The software may be configured to automatically or manually remove (or 'heal') malware. This consists of removing the malicious code from a file infected with a virus or deleting the whole of any other sort of malware file.

Some anti-virus software can also monitor a computer for malware activity that could lead to identity cloning, block a website known to be the source of malware or check links provided by a search engine for threats. Although anti-virus software is not usually included in an operating system, every computer should be protected by it and free editions are available for personal use (Figure 8.7).

## Extension

3  Try to find out about some examples of different types of malware and what they are intended to do.
4  Note the different measures needed to remove different types of malware.
5  If you install anti-virus software on your computer, why is it necessary to download updates regularly?

## ? SAQs

4  You have just discovered that a part of your hard disk is inaccessible, possibly corrupt, and you suspect a virus. What can you do?

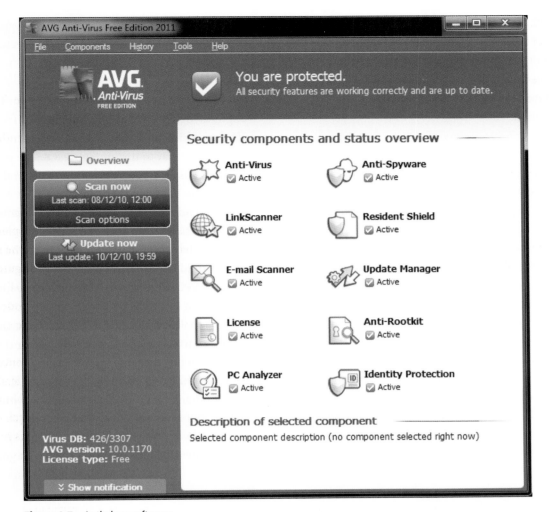

**Figure 8.7** Anti-virus software.

**10** When would it be sensible to have a computer system that is not connected to other systems? Are there any ways that a hacker or a virus could still gain access to the system?

**11** Most schools have two types of computer system: one that is used by students and teachers and one that is used for school administration. As a group, quiz your teacher about the system that holds student projects. Ask whether the school's administrator would be willing to talk to your class about the school administration system. Try to get answers to the following questions about each of the two systems.

  **a** What files are stored and how are they arranged?

  **b** What measures are used to stop people looking at things they should not see?

  **c** What sort of backups are done, how often and where are they kept?

  **d** What protection does the system have from malware?

  **e** Has the problem of hacking been considered and what measures are taken to protect the system from hackers? Discuss the differences between the two systems.

## Internet security

A number of threats to a computer's overall security are created or made more serious by connection to the Internet. These include hacking and malware, both of which have been extensively considered in the previous section.

### Spyware

One particular form of malware deserves further attention. **Spyware** is malware that secretly collects various types of personal information. One type of spyware is known as a 'keylogger' because it literally records all keyboard activity. Spyware can also collect data from the clipboard; the screen, which can include an on-screen keyboard; text entered into a form, including passwords, search engine queries and IM conversations; application programs; websites visited; sound from a user's microphone; and video from the user's webcam.

Spyware may be used for eavesdropping on communication, diverting a browser request to a competitor's web server or monitoring web-browsing activity to gather marketing statistics or display unwanted pop-up adverts. It may also be used for theft of ID data such as authentication credentials or debit or credit card details. Like other malware, spyware is frequently a Trojan horse download, bundled with a useful freeware program.

### Phishing

An Internet-based deception (or computer-based 'social engineering') known as **phishing** is used for theft of ID data. Phishing works by an attacker sending a user an email similar to that in Figure 8.8. The message in Figure 8.8 is an actual message in which only the name of the bank has been changed.

The sender's email address may look genuine, but banks *never* send such messages. Although some messages have even fewer typos than the one shown, the spelling and grammar are often below the standard one would expect from a bank. The message usually contains a hyperlink to a website. You may have noticed that in professionally produced documents, hyperlinks usually consist of words such as 'click here', rather than a web address. In this case, the message is likely to display a genuine address in an attempt to distract the recipient from noticing that the actual address to which it links is similar, but is actually that of a fake website.

The fake website may have an address such as www.welltrustedbank.randomsite.com (it goes to the

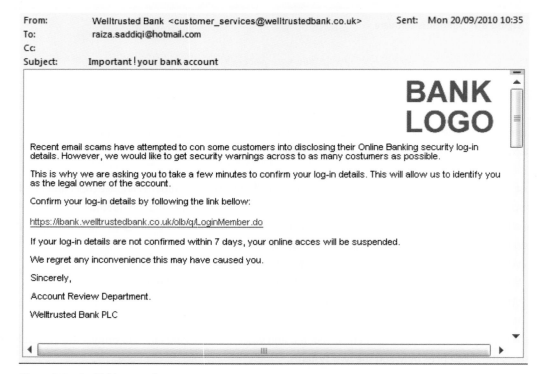

From: Welltrusted Bank <customer_services@welltrustedbank.co.uk>    Sent: Mon 20/09/2010 10:35
To: raiza.saddiqi@hotmail.com
Cc:
Subject: Important ! your bank account

BANK LOGO

Recent email scams have attempted to con some customers into disclosing their Online Banking security log-in details. However, we would like to get security warnings across to as many costumers as possible.

This is why we are asking you to take a few minutes to confirm your log-in details. This will allow us to identify you as the legal owner of the account.

Confirm your log-in details by following the link bellow:

https://ibank.welltrustedbank.co.uk/olb/q/LoginMember.do

If your log-in details are not confirmed within 7 days, your online acces will be suspended.

We regret any inconvenience this may have caused you.

Sincerely,

Account Review Department.

Welltrusted Bank PLC

**Figure 8.8**   A phishing email.

welltrustedbank section of the randomsite.com website) or even just www.randomsite.com instead of www. welltrustedbank.co.uk. The true address of the fake site should be visible in the lower left hand corner of most web browsers while the mouse is hovering over the link, even if the site itself appears with the genuine address in the address bar when the link has been followed.

Fortunately, most people receive quite a few of these messages from banks at which they are not customers before they ever receive one from their own bank. In some cases, an attacker uses spyware to harvest information about which online banks people use and then uses that information to target a phishing attack at customers of a particular bank. As well as bank customers, phishing attacks have been directed against customers of online payment services, taxpayers and users of social networking sites. Experiments have reported that around 70% of phishing attacks on social networks are successful. Do you always remember to resist being asked to log in a second time or to check the link address and address bar carefully?

## Pharming

**Pharming** is an attack by hacking. It intercepts browser requests sent from a computer to a website and redirects them to another, fake, website on which the attacker attempts to steal authentication credentials, or debit or credit card details, as in a phishing attack. A pharming attack can be carried out by altering a computer's local 'hosts' file. This file is used by an operating system's Internet Protocol (IP) code to map an Internet 'hostname', such as www.welltrustedbank.co.uk, to an IP address, such as 200.35.92.99.

Alternatively, an attack can be made on the configuration (or 'settings') or even the firmware of a computer user's Internet router, which may serve the whole of a LAN. An attacker could specify a Domain Name System (DNS) server (which a computer's operating system usually uses to resolve domain names to IP addresses) that is under the attacker's control instead of a legitimate one.

A wireless Internet router is very convenient for its users, but the router is often left with its default administrator name and a default or easily guessed password. This allows an attacker to alter settings or install malicious firmware wirelessly in a so-called 'drive-by' pharming attack.

## Advance fee fraud

In a more direct form of computer fraud, known as an advance fee fraud scam, the attacker sends an email such as the one in Figure 8.9, which is an actual message.

It appears that criminals have been known to send people letters similar to this message since the end of the eighteenth century, but the advent of email has turned it into a criminal 'growth industry'. A modern twist is to set up a fake online bank website complete with user credentials that the attacker shares with a potential victim

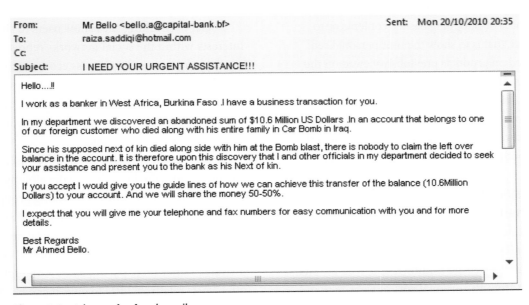

**Figure 8.9** Advance fee fraud email.

to try to convince them that there really is a large sum of money residing in a bank account waiting to be claimed.

If the recipient were to be lured into this criminal conspiracy, they would receive a request for a fee of a few hundred dollars to be paid in advance to cover various 'expenses' that the sender would claim needed to be incurred. After the recipient paid the fee, they would receive no further communication from the attacker. They would have conspired to commit fraud, which might deter them from reporting the scam to the police. In any case, the fact that this is often a cross-border crime makes it even less likely that a victim would ever see their money again.

### Other Internet security problems

Some other Internet security problems are generally more of a nuisance, unless they lead to some of the problems mentioned above. Spam consists of unwanted messages advertising goods or services. Email spam is sent using illegally gathered email addresses or by hacking into a mail server in order to broadcast a message to all holders of email accounts on that server. It can be blocked by suitable settings of the spam or junk mail filter in the user's webmail account or email client settings. Other forms of spam occur in social networking, instant messaging, web forums, blogs, wikis, and online classified ads.

As we have noted earlier, browser **cookie** files are useful for identifying a user's computer to a web server prior to log in. They can also be used by a trader to store a user's preferences or 'shopping basket' contents or to 'retarget' the user, that is to show the user personalised advertising based on products previously viewed on the trader's site when they view other websites. A web browser will allow you to block cookies from domains other than that shown in the address bar (third party cookies) or from specific sites. **Adware** displays unwanted pop-up adverts, which may be both distracting and time-consuming.

### 1.2.8 Recent developments in the use of the Internet

A modern website often allows account-holding users to contribute to the site's content via a form viewed in a web browser. Such a website is known as a **Web 2.0** site, to distinguish it from the original sort of website that only the owner of the site could modify. The best known

examples of Web 2.0 sites are social networking websites and web forums. They are usually funded by advertising, rather than by subscription.

### Social networking websites

Humans are very social animals and use computers extensively for social, as well as strictly business, communication. A relatively recent development is a **social networking website**, a Web 2.0 site that allows a user to:

- create a page (or 'profile') containing personal information (Figure 8.10);
- upload photos, videos and music to which no one else holds copyright;
- post blog entries;
- send email;
- participate in chat rooms;
- hold private IM conversations;
- search for users with similar interests;
- add users to a list of contacts (or 'friends');
- submit 'threaded' comments to their friends' profiles;
- invite friends or the public to 'events'.

These sites usually allow users to choose who can view their profile or contact them. This control over a user's privacy does not always prevent users from publicly revealing a lot of personal information that makes it relatively easy for an attacker to obtain ID data. It may also have an adverse effect on the way that a current or potential employer views them.

Social networking sites allow users to share ideas and interests within the social networks represented by their overlapping contact lists across economic, political and geographical boundaries. Participants report finding that social networking can become addictive, particularly if opportunities for face-to-face contact are limited by lack of transport or sheer distance.

Although sites provide facilities for users to build elaborate individual profiles, media albums and blogs, they also provide facilities for creating group profiles to cater for shared interests and to hold discussions in forums. Co-operation in these social networks can be seen as encouraging the 'gift economy' and 'paying forward', rather than 'paying back'. Although information often costs relatively little to give, it can be shared and valued by many.

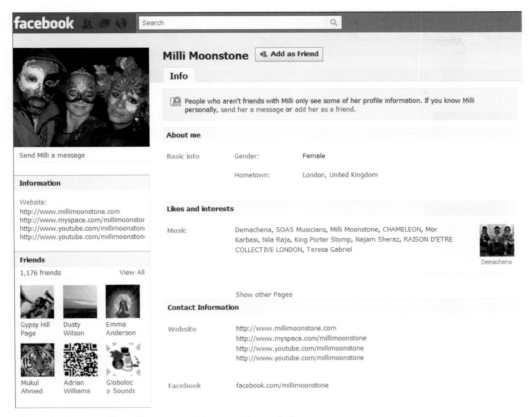

**Figure 8.10** A user's profile on a social networking website.

Since students and their parents are often very experienced in using social networking websites, teachers are beginning to create user-friendly VLEs by creating groups, chat rooms and forums to extend classroom discussion; setting work, tests and quizzes; helping students with homework; allowing parents to raise concerns and ask questions.

Social networking sites are also used:

- by scientists to share scientific information and know-how outside their immediate peer groups and subject disciplines and without regulation by journal publishers or professional associations;
- by political activists as a flexible and very low-cost means of organising campaigns and demonstrations;
- by businesses to create brand awareness, for public relations, for recruitment, to generate discussions between their customers on improving products or services through which they can learn about new technologies and competitors, and to attract potential customers to their own websites.

## Web forums

A web forum, or message board, is a Web 2.0 site where users can hold public conversations by posting messages (Figure 8.11). This differs from a chat room in that messages are not shown in real-time, since a message may be delayed by waiting for approval by a moderator and even then only becomes visible when the relevant page is refreshed in the user's browser. To post messages, users usually have to register with the forum and then log in to post a message.

A forum may have sub-forums, where a user can start a topic of conversation. The conversation may be linear, so that each reply follows the last, or threaded, so that a reply can branch off from an earlier post.

## Wikis

**Wiki** is a Hawaiian word for 'fast'. A Web 2.0 site can use wiki software to allow one or more contributors to create and edit a set of interlinked web pages. Content is created and edited via forms, stored in a database and used by

**Figure 8.11** A web forum.

the web server to serve pages. Wikis are often used for personal note-taking, to create collaborative websites within corporate intranets and to create collaborative community Internet websites. Currently, the best-known wiki is *Wikipedia*, a collaborative encyclopaedia.

### Digital media sharing websites

A **digital media sharing website** is a Web 2.0 site devoted to allowing account-holders to upload audio-visual media files, to which no one else holds copyright, for sharing with friends and other account-holders. Depending on the account-holder's privacy settings, friends and other account-holders can post comments on the media file. Each site is usually devoted to photos, videos or sound files.

### Tagging

**Tagging** is the process of adding keywords to a media file or blog post to make it easier to find later. For example, a user could tag an uploaded photo with words such as 'Anahita hiking mountain trail'. To find other photos of Anahita, a visitor to the site can just click the hyperlinked 'Anahita' tag. Some sites may allow a user to tag a friend's media files, if permitted by the friend's privacy settings. A list of tags used in a website forms an index to its contents.

## Blogs

Short for 'we*b log*', a **blog** is a Web 2.0 diary created by the account-holder for others to read. Some websites are devoted exclusively to blogging, but blogs may also form part of a social networking site or web forum. By default, blogs are publicly visible, although a blogger may restrict visibility to their friends.

A relatively recent development is microblogging, in which blog posts are limited to 140 text characters, to facilitate posts by SMS text. The best-known example is Twitter.

## Feed readers

A blogger or news service can offer their readers a subscription through an RSS feed. This is a standardised format used for automatic publication of the full or summarised text, together with 'metadata', such as publication date and time and authorship. A **feed reader** is part of a web browser or email client that checks for and retrieves, at user-determined intervals, new content from all the feeds to which the user has subscribed. This enables the user to read all the feeds in a single convenient personalised virtual newspaper, rather than having to visit multiple websites. An 'aggregator' is a web application that performs a similar function.

Subscribing to someone's blog or microblog is known as 'following' them and subscribers are known as 'followers'. Feeds are sometimes described as 'pull' technology, in which the subscriber chooses what to pull to their feed reader, as opposed to 'push' technology such as email or IM, in which the sender chooses what to push to the recipient.

An RSS narrator is an application program that uses speech synthesis to convert text feeds into audio files. This is useful for people with a visual impairment or to enable someone to listen to their feeds while driving a vehicle. A feed narrator may even allow a user to set up an alarm clock to wake them up every morning with their personalised news.

## Podcasts

A **podcast** is a series of audio or video files that are published on a website and usually made available as a feed. Most feed readers can automatically download files from the feed and, in some cases, can automatically load them onto portable MP3/MP4 media players when they are connected to the user's computer. Teachers can often supply useful educational material to their students in this way.

## Peer-to-peer file-sharing protocols

A **peer-to-peer (P2P) file-sharing protocol** is used for distributing large data files. P2P file-sharing protocols are among the most common protocols for distributing large files and represent a very substantial proportion of all Internet traffic in some parts of the world.

Rather than downloading a file from the original distributor's server, a user downloading with a P2P file-sharing protocol joins a 'swarm' of other downloaders' computers to download from, and upload to, each other simultaneously. Even lower-power computers (such as mobile phones) with lower bandwidth are able to contribute to the distribution of files.

Relative to using standard HTTP or FTP servers, this sort of protocol reduces the heavy load on the original distributor's file server and the bandwidth of its Internet connection, thereby reducing the distributor's costs. It also provides redundancy against technical problems and so reduces the dependency of a user performing a download on the immediate availability of the original file server. The disadvantage from the downloader's point of view is that downloads can take time to rise to full speed because it may take time for enough peer-to-peer connections to be established.

P2P file-sharing protocols have been widely used for the illegal downloading of copyrighted files because the original source for the file is generally only temporary and therefore harder to trace than a standard, enduring file server. However, their advantages have also encouraged publishers or licensed distributors to adopt them for the legal distribution of film, video, music, podcasts, TV programmes, games software, open source and free software, and government statistics. Some publishers even distribute their own specialised or simplified P2P client software with which users can download their files.

Some large-scale web services such as social networking and microblogging each require tens of thousands of servers and P2P protocols may be used to distribute software updates to these servers. For example, it may be possible to distribute a few hundred mebibytes of data to tens of thousands of servers in just one minute, a task that might otherwise have taken hours.

### Mashups

Many new web applications combine data, presentation or processing from two or more sources to create new services. Such a hybrid web application is known as a mashup. One type of publicly available mashup uses a mapping application to display (or 'visualise') the locations of contributions to a Web 2.0 site. At the time of writing, *WikipediaVision* (*WPV*) displays the locations (where known) of recent contributions to *Wikipedia* in English and some other languages. It reads data from a *Wikipedia* page listing recent changes, uses a web service to look up the likely geographical location of the contributor's IP address and uses a programming interface to display details of the contribution on a world map from a mapping website.

## Summary

- The economic advantage of computerisation is increased productivity resulting from computers' ability to communicate and process data repetitively, accurately and rapidly; to store data compactly; to make backup copies of data; to search for information; to produce output in a variety of formats.
- Computerisation has a tendency to result in the de-skilling of some jobs.
- Some jobs can be carried out by teleworkers and others are liable to be moved 'off-shore'.
- Computer use involves risks to circulation, spine, eyes, arm and hand muscles, all of which can be prevented by suitable action.
- CBT is often a good way to re-train to meet changes in employment.
- Maintaining privacy of data involves preventing unauthorised access and accidental or malicious disclosure.
- Maintaining integrity of data involves avoiding corruption by computer hardware, software or network error, viruses, an error or malicious act by someone with authorised or unauthorised access or an error during transmission.
- Keeping backup copies allows fresh working copies to be restored in the event of data corruption.
- It is important to maintain physical security measures around computer systems.
- Data security can be defined as maintaining the privacy and integrity of data, together with protecting data against complete loss.
- An application's requirements for security and reliability may include assigning different access rights to different users and groups of users, making backup copies that are kept in a remote location and providing high availability by the use of redundant storage devices or even whole computers.
- A data protection act is typically based on principles of obtaining sufficient, relevant and not excessive personal data lawfully and for specified purposes; keeping data accurate and up to date and deleting them when no longer needed; giving individuals right of access to data held about them and to correct information; protecting data from corruption, loss and access by people who are not authorised; not transferring data to another country unless that country provides a similar level of legal protection.
- Hacking (gaining unauthorised access to computer data) is combated by physical security, user credentials for authentication, the extra security layer of encryption, and the use of an Internet firewall.
- Computer crime includes data theft; ID data theft, including phishing and pharming; fraudulent trading; banking fraud; espionage; infringement of the copyright of software or music; distributing or acquiring child pornography; cyberstalking; child grooming; distribution of malware; denial-of-service attacks.
- Malware (viruses, worms, Trojan horses, scareware, spyware and crimeware) can be combated by anti-virus software.
- Security is particularly challenging when computers are connected to the Internet.
- Users are vulnerable to phishing, pharming and advance fee fraud attacks and to spam and potentially intrusive cookie files.
- Recent developments in the use of the Internet include: social networking websites; web forums; wikis; digital media sharing websites; tagging; blogs and microblogs; feed readers and narrators; podcasts; peer-to-peer file-sharing protocols; and mashups.

## Examination practice for Paper 1

### Exam Questions

1. You have been asked to produce a presentation on the social impact of computers on shop workers.
   What could you include in your presentation to show how the workers would be affected?                                                    [2]
   *Part of Question 3, Cambridge IGCSE Computer Studies 0420/01 Paper 11 May/June 2010*

2. A company is concerned about three aspects of the security of data stored in computer files:

   - data corruption

   - data loss

   - illegal access to data.

   For each of the above, give **one** reason why it could occur and state **one** method of prevention. Your reasons must be different in each case.                                                    [6]
   *Question 4, Cambridge IGCSE Computer Studies 0420/01 Paper 11 May/June 2010*

3. Give **four** features of a *Data Protection Act*.                                                    [4]
   *Question 4, Cambridge IGCSE Computer Studies 0420/01 Paper 12 May/June 2010*

4. A bank is worried about computer crime. One of their concerns is online access to customer accounts.

   **(a)** How can a customer's access details be discovered by criminals?                                                    [2]

   **(b)** Why would a customer using a credit card for online shopping be more of a security risk than a customer using the same card in a shop?                                                    [2]

   **(c)** Describe what measures the bank can take to safeguard customer accounts.                                                    [2]
   *Question 5, Cambridge IGCSE Computer Studies 0420/01 Paper 12 May/June 2010*

### Exam-Style Questions

1. A pharmaceutical company employs seven people who answer customers' technical queries over the phone. The company has decided to provide this customer service by instant messaging 'live chat' on its website rather than by phone.
   Describe **two** ways in which this change would affect the seven employees.                                                    [2]

2. Data corruption sometimes occurs in computer systems.
   Give **two** ways that corruption could occur and, for each, suggest how data may be protected.                                                    [4]

3. Authentication credentials such as a username and password are required for access to a computer system.
   If someone still manages to gain unauthorised access to the computer system:

   **(a)** What could be done to prevent data being used?                                                    [1]

   **(b)** What could be done to prevent loss of data?                                                    [1]

   **(c)** What could be done to enable restoration of data after their loss?                                                    [1]

4. Viruses are one form of malware that can affect computer systems.

   **(a)** What is a virus?                                                    [1]

   **(b)** Describe **two** effects of a virus.                                                    [2]

   **(c)** How can a computer's administrator protect it from viruses?                                                    [1]

   **(d)** Why does making backup copies of data not guard against the effects of viruses?                                                    [1]

## Examination practice for Paper 3

To answer the following question you will need to read the garage scenario provided in Appendix A (page 284).

1. Describe **three** advantages in adopting the new computer-based system when compared to the paper-based system. [3]

*Question (j), Cambridge IGCSE Computer Studies 0420/01 Paper 3 Specimen for 2011*

### Comments

Remember that the advantages must specifically refer to the scenario. It might help to first think of the generic advantages of a computer-based system and then think how these would benefit the garage in the scenario.

# Part III:
# Problem solving with programs and logic gates

# Algorithm planning and design

---

**When you have finished this chapter, you will be able to:**

- describe the stages in making an overall plan to solve a problem
- explain algorithms and their relationship to a larger system
- describe and use tools to design programs and algorithms
- design, interpret and test algorithms.

---

## Creating a plan

Whenever there is a problem to solve, whether or not we use a computer to assist with the solution, we need to establish a plan that we can apply. This plan consists of several stages and is closely linked with systems analysis (see Chapter 6). The four main stages are:

- understand the problem;
- create a solution;
- document the solution;
- test the solution.

## Understand the problem

To demonstrate the process of creating an algorithm, we are going to look at a particular problem: 'Read in a date and calculate the number of days since the start of the calendar year'.

At first, the problem appears to be quite simple, but when we consider it in more detail, it becomes more complicated. For example, at the input stage we need to consider the format of the input date. It could be any of the following:

- 1 July 2013;
- 1st July 2013;
- July 1st 2013;
- 1 July 13;
- 1/7/13;
- 7/1/13;
- 010713.

Other variations are also possible. So the first step is to specify a single date format or allow for different formats. What happens if the current year is a leap year? The solution will need to take that into account before it can calculate the number of days.

## Create a solution

### The scope of the solution

It is important to define the scope of the solution to a problem. The **scope** means the limits of the facilities that the solution will provide.

In our date example, the scope might be that we want to perform this calculation for dates from 1930. In scoping a problem, we are deliberately constraining ourselves to a limited solution.

In this case, there is a good reason for this constraint; it was not until 1926 that all countries adopted the Gregorian calendar that gives us our current rules for calculating leap years. For use in a particular country, you could re-scope the solution to go back as far as the year after that country adopted the Gregorian calendar. The scope of the overall solution has implications for the scope of any sub-solutions that we design.

### Top-down design

A good technique for creating a solution to any complex problem is to use top-down design, which we met briefly in Chapter 6. You may remember that this means breaking down the solution to a problem or task into a number of steps that can be considered as separate sub-solutions or sub-tasks. We can continue the process by breaking down the sub-solutions or sub-tasks into smaller solutions or tasks, until we reach sufficiently simple steps. Top-down design is also known as **stepwise refinement**.

Advantages of top-down design include reducing the solution to a large and complex problem to a set of smaller, simpler sub-solutions; making the design well-structured and easier to understand, modify and debug; speeding up development; allowing each sub-solution, or module, to be given to a different member of a team of programmers. A good strategy is to break down the solution according to the input–storage–processing–output model of computer systems.

For our example problem, we are not concerned with storage, so the solution can be broken down into three steps:

1. Input the date.
2. Calculate the number of days since 1 January of that year.
3. Output the result.

However, Steps 1 and 2 can be divided into smaller tasks. Step 1 must accept only correctly formatted dates and reject any incorrect date. The user could be prompted to input the date in a specific format or the user could input the date in any format and the solution would recognise the format. Obviously, the second option is much more difficult to achieve, since there are so many possible formats for a date.

Step 2 can be broken down into sub-solutions as follows:

2.1 Identify the year of the entered date.
2.2 Calculate the difference in days between 1st January of that year and the entered date.

If, as is highly likely, the programming language has a Date data type, sub-solution 2.2 simply involves subtracting 1st January from the entered date. Otherwise, calculating the number of days involves using rules that specify month length and leap years.

We can illustrate top-down design by working through a simple problem to read in ten numbers and display their total. Starting with the input–storage–processing–output model, we are not concerned with storage, so we might expect top-down design to give

us three sub-solutions concerned with input, process and output.

This problem involves calculating a cumulative, or 'running', total. Something that you would assume when calculating a running total, but which a computer's processor must be instructed to do, is to set the running total to zero and the count of how many numbers have been added to one. We can then use a structure diagram (Figure 9.1) to represent how this problem has been broken down into sub-solutions, which are read as a sequence from left to right.

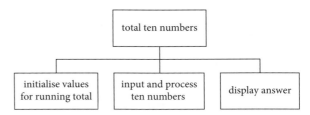

**Figure 9.1** Structure diagram for calculating the total of ten numbers.

The second step, processing the numbers could repeat, ten times, the process of entering a single number and adding it to the running total. Such a process of repeating a sequence of steps is called **iteration** (or **repetition**). We also refer to each repetition of the sequence as an iteration. In order to ensure that we repeat the process of entering a number and accumulating the result ten times, we need to count the number of iterations.

A programmer can define a uniquely named location in memory in which a single data item can be stored while the program is running. The programmer does this by declaring a **variable** in a piece of program code called a variable declaration. It helps to make a program self-explanatory or 'self-documenting' if we give the variables meaningful names. We can use the variable `Total` to store the cumulative total of the numbers and the variable `Count` to count the number of numbers. This iteration (or repetition) should only continue while the value of `Count` is less than or equal to ten.

We can now break our problem down into further, smaller sub-solutions (Figure 9.2). Notice that an asterisk (*) is used to indicate iteration (or repetition) of the sub-solutions below it. The left-pointing arrow (←) is the assignment operator. You can read it as 'is made equal to' or 'takes the value'; for example, `Count` takes the value 1.

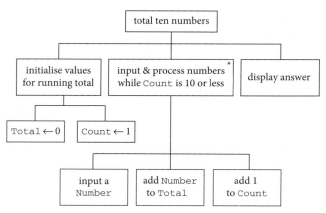

**Figure 9.2** Refined structure diagram for calculating the total of ten numbers.

## Questions

1 Write down the steps required to solve the following problems:

   **a** Read a list of numbers that represent the cost of buying five items. Display the total cost of the items.

   **b** Read a list of numbers that represent the cost of buying a number of items. The end of the list is indicated by a cost of 0. Display the total cost of the items and the number of items purchased.

   **c** Read a list of numbers that represent money being paid into your bank account (positive numbers) or money being taken out of the account (negative numbers). The end of the list is indicated by a value of your choice. Display the total money paid in and the total of the money taken out of your account.

   **d** Read a list of numbers that represent money being paid into your bank account (positive numbers) or money being taken out of the account (negative numbers). The end of the list is indicated by a value of your choice. Check that the data being input is not text; if it is text, then reject the item and print a suitable error message. Display the total money paid in and the total of the money taken out of your account.

## Algorithms

An **algorithm** is a sequence of steps to solve a given problem or execute a given task. It may describe the solution for a complete system or one part of the system, such as a sub-solution in a top-down design. In the case of an algorithm for a complete system, it may need to pass control to, or 'call', one or more algorithms for sub-solutions.

An algorithm can be initially drafted as a list of steps in plain English but becomes much more useful when represented as a program flowchart or pseudocode (see Chapter 10), which is a stepping-stone to program code.

## Modules of code

In Chapter 6, we mentioned that program code written to provide a sub-solution is often saved as a routine (or 'subroutine', 'module' or 'procedure') in a collection of routines known as a library file. When we later need code with which to program an algorithm for a sub-solution, it may be possible to re-use a suitable routine from such a library file. In this case, the program for the complete solution would call the routine from the library file by temporarily passing control to it.

## Menus

When a program does not simply run through a fixed sequence of data input, processing, storage and output, it often provides facilities for opening previously saved files and using a number of editing, searching and formatting commands. In order to exploit the freedom to interact with the program in these ways, the user needs an interface through which to issue the desired commands.

In a graphical user interface (GUI), this is most often done through one or more menus on a display screen. A menu provides a set of options, each of which may become highlighted when pointed to by a pointing device and may be selected by clicking the pointer's switch. The menu may be displayed as a set of buttons or hotspots, a drop-down menu of commands, a fixed list of data entry options, or a drop-down list of data entry options associated with a list or combo box. A menu may also consist of a toolbar of buttons, whose functions are often symbolised by icons rather than words.

The advantages of menus are that they prevent the user from issuing inappropriate commands and remind the user of the commands that are available.

## Document the solution

**3.1.2**

### Structure diagrams

We briefly introduced the use of a structure diagram to represent a top-down design in Chapter 6 and we used structure diagrams to show the refinement of a design earlier in this chapter.

Here we consider refining structure diagrams to document another simple problem: calculate the sum of the numbers 1 to 100. Starting from the input–storage–processing–output model, we realise that no input or storage is needed. The cumulative total requires an initialisation step for the values involved in an iterative (repetitive) processing step. Notice that the iteration (repetition) itself needs an exit condition; otherwise, it becomes an 'infinite loop'. Finally, we need an output step (Figure 9.3).

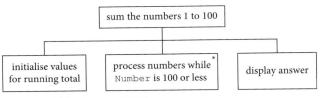

**Figure 9.3** Structure diagram for summing the numbers 1 to 100.

The first two steps can be further subdivided into smaller sub-solutions (Figure 9.4).

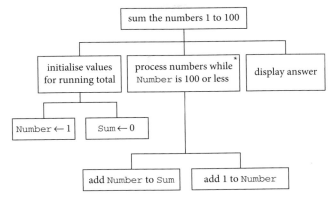

**Figure 9.4** Refined structure diagram for summing the numbers 1 to 100.

When we have broken the solution down into smaller, more manageable sub-solutions, we can devise an algorithm for each sub-solution.

### Questions

**2** Choose one of the following tasks and draw a structure diagram:

**a** renting a DVD from a local video shop

**b** borrowing a book from a school library.

**3** Consider the structure diagram for producing a sales report, shown in Figure 9.5. Notice that a circle is used to indicate each option in a process of selection. Which part of the design can be repeated to produce a sales report for a number of salespeople?

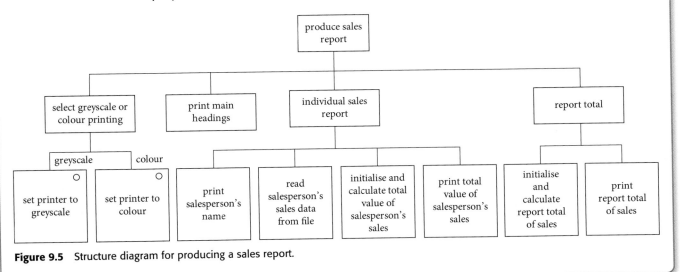

**Figure 9.5** Structure diagram for producing a sales report.

## Program flowcharts

In Chapter 6, the system flowchart was shown as a method of representing dataflows between hardware and processing steps. A similar graphical method is a **program flowchart** that represents the finer level of detail of processing required for an algorithm. A program flowchart uses only the symbols shown in Table 9.1. The arrows in a program flowchart show the order of operation within the algorithm, known as the 'flow of control', *not* the flow of data.

Consider the simple problem of converting a distance given in metres into centimetres. The solution is to input the distance in metres, multiply it by 100 and output the distance in centimetres. We could represent this in the form of a flowchart (Figure 9.6).

We again consider the problem of calculating the sum of the numbers 1 to 100. The cumulative total requires an initialisation step for the variables involved in an iterative processing step. The iteration (or repetition) requires a decision in order to iterate while the value of Number is less than or equal to 100, but stop iterating when Number exceeds 100. Finally, we need an output step (Figure 9.7).

Notice that iteration (or repetition) requires a loop in the flow of control, in which control is passed back to an earlier step. For this reason, a process of iteration

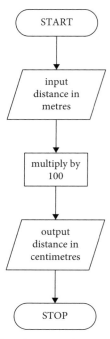

**Figure 9.6**  Flowchart for converting metres to centimetres.

(or repetition) is often called a **loop**. We need to be aware that the flowchart looks very similar when control is passed *forward* to a later step, bypassing steps, in which case there is no iteration (or repetition). We just need to pay attention to the direction of the arrow.

**Table 9.1**  Program flowchart symbols.

| Symbol | Name | Description |
|---|---|---|
|  | Terminator | Start and end of the flowchart |
|  | Input/output operation | Input or output of data |
|  | Data processing operation | Manipulation or calculation of data to produce useful information |
|  | Decision | Choices are presented to decide the direction of flow |

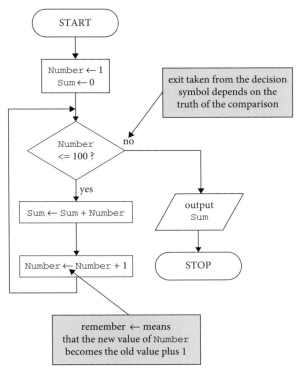

Figure 9.7   Flowchart for summing the numbers 1 to 100.

Question 5 continued ...

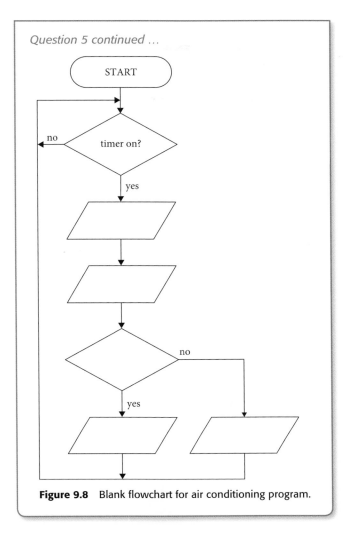

Figure 9.8   Blank flowchart for air conditioning program.

## Questions

4   Draw a flowchart to add together two numbers.

5   A microprocessor is used to control the air conditioning unit to cool a house.

   a   What air temperature will make the microprocessor start the air conditioning?

   b   What processing of the temperatures takes place?

   c   What action does the microprocessor take in response to the data processing?

   d   Copy the program flowchart shown in Figure 9.8 and complete it for the program that controls the air conditioning.

⟶

## System flowcharts

Program flowcharts are useful for clarifying programs, but they can become complicated and show far too much detail when dealing with a large, complex solution. There are often many interconnected links and the chart may extend over several pages, making it difficult to see the overall solution. An alternative way of describing how the system works, without the details of each processing step, is a system flowchart, which we saw in Chapter 6.

System flowcharts have the advantage that they show the hardware required to support processes. For example, output may be as simple as a result in a text box on a PC screen. Alternatively, data may be captured automatically every second over a month, requiring a large storage space, and then processed and output as a series of colour graphs on a colour laser printer.

To illustrate this, we create a system flowchart to represent a pupil database within a school. An enrolment form is printed with a barcode representing the unique identification code of each applicant. Administrative workers *collect* pupils' completed enrolment forms and, for each form, *scan* the barcode and *key in* the other data. The system *validates* the data and *displays* any errors. The system uses the accepted data to *update* the pupil database.

At intervals, administrative workers *generate* and *print* a barcoded report of personal details for each pupil on a greyscale printer. Teachers ask the pupils to check the accuracy of their personal details and to provide any amendments and updated information, for example, address or telephone numbers. Teachers *collect* these amended reports and administrative workers repeat the process of *scanning* and *keying in* the data. At any time, a member of staff can *search* the database to *display* information on an individual pupil and, if required, *print* it in colour. This system is summarised in Table 9.2.

This system can be represented in the system flowchart shown in Figure 9.9. Notice that specific types of input and output hardware are implied by, or mentioned in, the shaded symbols.

**Table 9.2**  Pupil database system.

| Input data | Processing | Output |
|---|---|---|
| Enrolment form data collected, scanned and keyed in | Validate. Update pupil database. | Display errors. |
| | Generate reports of personal details. | Print reports on a greyscale printer. |
| Amendments to personal details | Validate. Update pupil database. | Display errors. |
| Target ID or name | Search for pupil record. | Display record on screen. Print record on colour printer. |

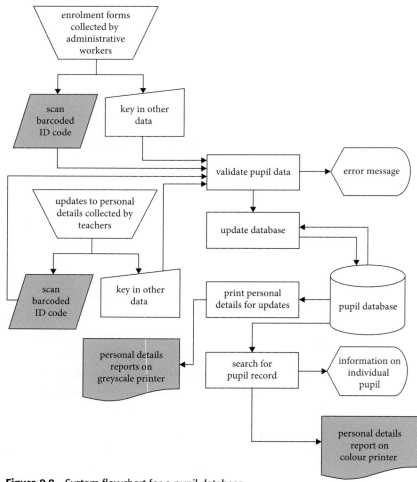

**Figure 9.9**  System flowchart for a pupil database.

## Questions

6 A company uses a computer system to process employee salaries. Data are collected about new employees and a data entry clerk enters them into the system. The system generates validation error messages; the clerk corrects any errors and re-enters the data into the system. Similarly, data about employees leaving the company are collected, entered and validated. Each month, the system calculates salaries, and generates and prints reports for payslips. It also generates a bank payments file and uploads it across a WAN to the employer's bank.

Draw a system flowchart to represent the payroll system. You may find this easier to do if you start with a blank table similar to Table 9.2 and use Figure 9.9 as a guide.

## SAQs

1 How can we make system flowcharts easier to read?

2 What are the four main stages in finding the solution to a problem?

3 Why do we scope a problem?

## Testing and interpreting algorithms
### Dry running

A designer or programmer often has to read an algorithm and work out its purpose or function. The algorithm may have been created by someone else and may not be clearly documented. The designer or programmer performs a **dry run**, a mental run through the algorithm, a step at a time, to see what it does.

Most algorithms follow the input–process–output model but they often contain an initialisation stage

followed by some kind of loop structure. First, you need to determine the purpose of the initialisation stage; it often sets the variables, including any iteration counter, to the required initial value and any running total to zero. The loop structure allows repeated input or calculation while, or until, a given condition is satisfied.

Unless the loop is for a pre-determined number of repetitions, the input must be tested for a certain value, known as a 'dummy' or 'sentinel', that the user can enter to end the loop. If the input is not the dummy value, the loop continues; if the input is the dummy value, the loop ends and control passes to the remainder of the algorithm.

What does the algorithm represented by the flowchart in Figure 9.10 do? See if you can work it out before going on to read about it.

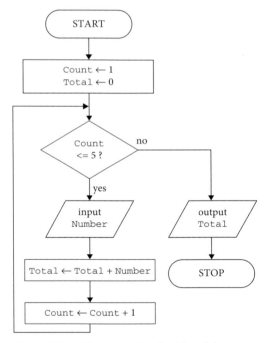

**Figure 9.10** What does this algorithm do?

The algorithm in Figure 9.10 initialises the `Count` variable, which holds the iteration number, to 1 and the `Total` variable to zero. While `Count` remains less than or equal to five (that is, for five iterations), the iteration, repetition or loop repeatedly inputs a value and holds it in `Number`, adds `Number` to `Total` and stores the result in `Total`, and increments `Count` by 1. When `Count` reaches 6, control passes from the iteration (or repetition) and the algorithm outputs the value of `Total`. In other words, the purpose of the algorithm is to add five numbers and display the total.

What does the algorithm represented by the flowchart in Figure 9.11 do? See if you can work it out before going on to read about it.

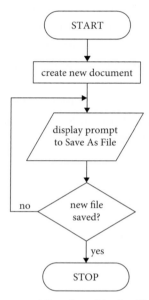

**Figure 9.11**  What does this algorithm do?

The algorithm in Figure 9.11 shows the decision at the end of a loop, rather than at the beginning. This ensures that there is always at least one iteration of the loop. The algorithm creates a new document and prompts the user to save it as a new file. If the user does so, the algorithm ends. If the user fails to save the document, the prompt to save is repeated until the user does save it. The purpose of the algorithm is to force the user to save a new document before doing any further work.

Notice that this is an 'indefinite' loop, because the designer or programmer cannot predict how many times the loop will be iterated. In this case, there is no need to count the number of iterations in order to control the loop. You could modify the algorithm to keep a count of the loop's iterations and give a modified prompt or even an escape route after a certain number of failures to save.

## Trace tables

While a simple dry run can be done entirely in one's head, programmers often perform a dry run involving a loop using a **trace table**. A trace table (Table 9.3) has a column for each variable, usually in the order in which their values are first assigned within the loop. Each row is then completed with the values of the variables whenever they change, moving to the next row when necessary. We leave unchanged values blank so that we can focus on changes. The benefits of this more organised approach to dry running are that the designer or programmer:

- is less likely to make a mistake;
- has evidence of the dry run;
- can check back to find any mistake in the dry run.

**Table 9.3**  Partially completed trace table for the algorithm in Figure 9.12.

| Number | Total | Count | output |
|--------|-------|-------|--------|
| 0 | 0 | 0 | |
| 5 | | | |
| 6 | | | |
| 0 | | | |
| −9 | | | |

Thorough dry running with a trace table aids our understanding of an existing algorithm, which may involve a complex loop with multiple decisions and exit points, by allowing us to track its complete behaviour. A trace table is also useful while designing an algorithm, for checking that it uses correct logic and for testing that it generates the required results for a given set of test data. It is also useful for identifying errors when troubleshooting an algorithm.

Dry run the algorithm in Figure 9.12 by copying Table 9.3 and completing it for the input data: 5, 6, 0 and −9. What does the algorithm do? Is its purpose clear? Could it be simplified or improved?

The algorithm initialises the variables and enters a loop. It adds together all non-negative numbers entered; when a negative number is entered, it displays the total. See Table 9.4 for the completed trace table. Notice that we leave unchanged values blank.

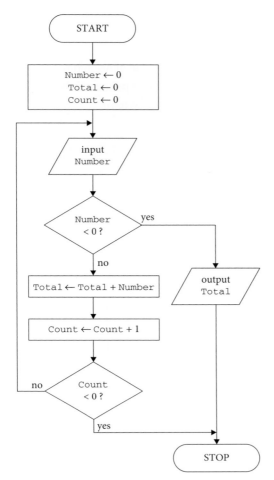

**Figure 9.12** What does this algorithm do?

**Table 9.4** Complete trace table for the algorithm in Figure 9.12.

| Number | Total | Count | output | Notes |
|--------|-------|-------|--------|-------|
| 0 | 0 | 0 | | Initialise relevant variables |
| 5 | 5 | 1 | | First iteration |
| 6 | 11 | 2 | | Second iteration |
| 0 | | 3 | | Third iteration |
| −9 | | | 11 | Exit the loop and output `Total` |

The purpose is slightly unclear because the loop contains two decisions. The second decision would stop processing if `Count` were to become negative. `Count` is initialised to 0, and increments by 1 on each iteration, so `Count` can never become negative. Did the designer once intend the user to enter a fixed number of numbers to be added?

The algorithm could be simplified by removing the second decision and the initialisation of `Number`, as this is assigned an input value on each iteration *before* its value is compared in the first decision. The initialisation and incrementation of `Count` could also be removed, unless the final value of `Count` were to be output as well as the `Total`, perhaps for calculating the mean value.

The algorithm could be improved by prompting the user to enter a positive number for addition or a negative number to terminate processing.

## Questions

**7** Look at Algorithm 9.1.
**Algorithm 9.1**

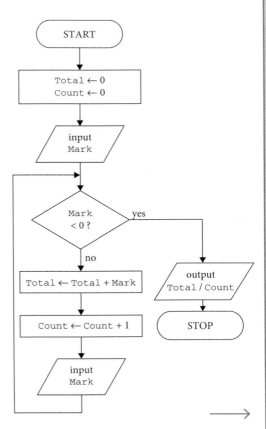

*Question 7 continued …*

*Questions continued …*

**a** Copy and complete the trace table, adding as many rows as needed, for Algorithm 9.1 with the input data 7, 8, 3 and −1.

| Total | Count | Mark | output |
|-------|-------|------|--------|
|       |       |      |        |

**b** What is the purpose of this algorithm?

**c** What happens if the first value is −1?

**8** Look at Algorithm 9.2.

**Algorithm 9.2**

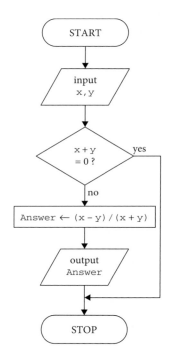

**a** Dry run this algorithm with the values 7 and 3.

**b** Dry run this algorithm with the values 7 and −7. What is the outcome avoiding in this case?

**c** Dry run this algorithm with the values 5 and 5.

**9** What is the purpose of Algorithm 9.3, which represents part of a program to be used in a shop's computer system?

**Algorithm 9.3**

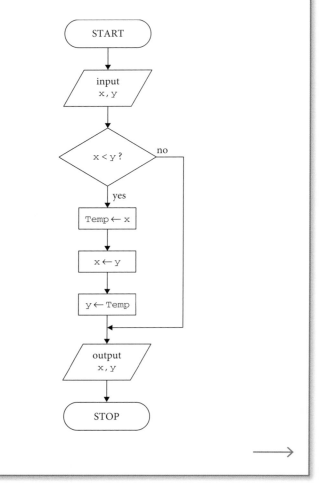

**10** Look at Algorithm 9.4.

**Algorithm 9.4**

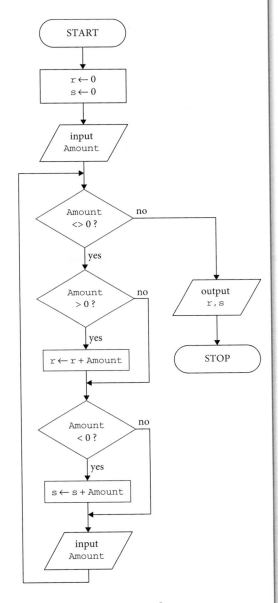

**a** What does `r` represent?

**b** What does `s` represent?

**c** What is the purpose of this algorithm?

→

**11** Look at Algorithm 9.5.

**Algorithm 9.5**

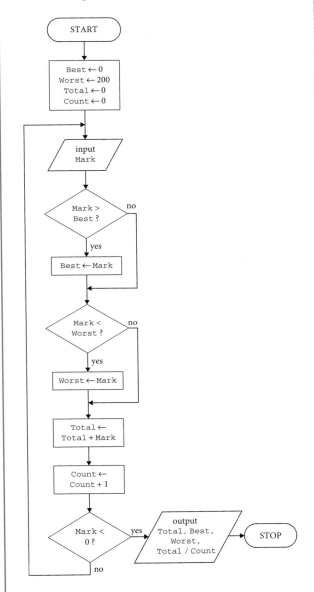

**a** What is the purpose of this algorithm?

**b** What are its weaknesses?

**c** What is the best integer number to choose as the dummy value to exit the loop?

**d** Dry run the algorithm with the values 25, 13, 45, 34, −23.

**e** How can this algorithm be improved?

## Summary

- The main stages of planning any solution are: understanding the problem; defining the scope of the solution; creating the solution; testing the solution; and documenting the solution.
- An algorithm is a sequence of steps required to solve a given problem or task.
- An algorithm may describe the solution for a complete system or just one sub-solution.
- An algorithm can call an algorithm for a sub-solution.
- We can create an algorithm by using top-down design and considering input, storage (if required), processing and output.
- Structure diagrams and program flowcharts are techniques for documenting an algorithm.
- System flowcharts are a technique for documenting the hardware required in a solution.
- A program may re-use previously saved routines by calling them from library files.
- Menus, toolbars and fixed and drop-down lists provide an interface through which the user can select from a limited choice of commands.
- Dry running is the process of thinking through the operation of an algorithm, to test it during design, for troubleshooting and to work out its purpose, if not stated.
- A trace table is a record of a dry run, consisting of columns for variables and rows for their successive values as the algorithm changes them.

## Examination practice for Paper 1

### Exam Questions

1. What is meant by top-down design when developing new software? [1]

   *Part of Question 10, Cambridge IGCSE Computer Studies 0420/01 Paper 11 May/June 2010*

2. Program code for an algorithm has been placed in a library of routines. Give **one** advantage of doing this. [1]

   *Part of Question 9, Cambridge IGCSE Computer Studies 0420/01 Paper 1 May/June 2008*

3. The following flowchart shows what happens when a customer uses a credit card to pay for goods at a supermarket. Ten of the boxes are blank.
Using the items from the list, insert the **ten** missing statements using the appropriate number only. Each statement may be used once only. [5]

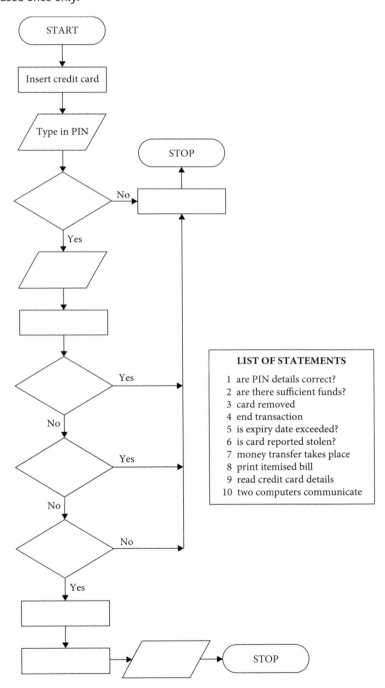

**LIST OF STATEMENTS**

1 are PIN details correct?
2 are there sufficient funds?
3 card removed
4 end transaction
5 is expiry date exceeded?
6 is card reported stolen?
7 money transfer takes place
8 print itemised bill
9 read credit card details
10 two computers communicate

*Question 16, Cambridge IGCSE Computer Studies 0420/01 Paper 1 May/June 2009*

*Examination practice for Paper 1 continued ...*

### Exam-Style Questions

1. Explain **three** benefits of using a top-down approach when designing a computer program. **[3]**

2. How can one or more algorithms be used when designing a solution to a problem? **[2]**

3. Explain what a library file is and how it can be used by a programmer. **[2]**

4. Give **two** advantages of using a menu when creating a software solution. **[2]**

5. Explain what is meant by a dry run and give **three** possible uses of it by a designer or programmer. **[4]**

## Examination practice for Paper 3

To answer the following question you will need to read the garage scenario provided in Appendix A (page 284).

1. Draw a systems flowchart to show how the new computer-based system will work. Include: what happens when a customer makes an enquiry, how a part is identified, how the database is updated when a part is sold, how new orders are produced and how a check is made on the daily money taken. **[8]**

*Question (d), Cambridge IGCSE Computer Studies 0420/01 Paper 3 Specimen for 2011*

### Comments

Remember that in a systems flowchart emphasis is on input, processing, storage and output. You will need to have the correct process AND the correct symbol for each stage of input, process, decision and output to score full marks. In most cases, you will score 1 mark for each correct stage.

**254**  Part III: Problem solving with programs and logic gates

# Programs and pseudocode algorithms

## The concept of a program

**3.2.1**

A computer **program** is a sequence of instructions or programming language statements that a programmer must write to make a computer perform certain tasks. To write a well-structured program, a programmer requires a programming language to support the following 'program constructs':

- **sequence** – execution of the program usually following the order in which the steps are written;
- **selection** – a decision between alternative routes through the program that involves at least one condition;
- **repetition** – a step or sequence of steps repeated within the program as an iteration or loop;
- **subroutine** – a sub-program such as a procedure or function that can be started or 'called' by a program instruction and can return control to the next instruction after the 'calling' instruction on completion of its processing.

A computer's processor can only run a computer program in the form of a file of **machine code**, which is a sequence of binary codes representing instructions for the processor. Each series, or 'family', of processors has

a specific **instruction set** that contains an instruction for each operation that the processor family has been designed to perform. An instruction set can be thought of as the 'language' in which machine code is written for that family of processor.

An instruction set includes data transfer instructions for:

- setting the value held in a register (a small, temporary memory location within the processor);
- moving data from an internal memory location to a register or *vice versa*;
- reading data from an input or storage device and writing data to an output or storage device.

An instruction set also includes arithmetic and logic operations for:

- adding, subtracting, multiplying or dividing the values of two registers;
- comparing the values in two registers;
- performing bit-wise logic operations.

An instruction set also includes instructions for controlling the flow of a program, including:

- jumping to an instruction at an *earlier* point in the same sequence of instructions, to produce an iteration, repetition or loop;

- conditionally jumping to an instruction at a *later* point in the same sequence of instructions, producing a **decision**;
- jumping to the beginning of a subroutine – before executing the jump, the processor saves the 'return' address of the next instruction as the point to which to return; the subroutine ends with a return instruction on which the processor jumps back to the return address.

When machine code runs, the processor fetches (meaning gets) an instruction from internal memory, decodes it and carries out ('executes') the required operation. It then repeats this cycle with the next instruction. Sometimes the processor has internal firmware, called 'microcode', to simplify its electronic circuitry for decoding and executing complex instructions.

## Programming languages

Computer programming languages can be divided into two types: low-level, closer to machine language, and high-level, closer to a human language such as Arabic, English or Hindi. Each type has its own advantages and drawbacks.

### 3.2.3 Low-level languages
#### Machine language

**Machine language** has the lowest level of language, because the long string of zeros and ones in machine code is so difficult for a programmer to read or write. Even when some of these bits represent a number, the binary number system is not one in which people think most fluently. Each complete machine language instruction consists of an operation code (known as an 'opcode'), which may be as short as a single byte, even for a 32- or 64-bit processor. For example, the following is one opcode from the instruction set of a PIC16F627 microcontroller:

```
110000
```

Some opcodes require one or more operands, which are numerical values or memory addresses upon which they operate. The operand follows the opcode in the program, for example:

```
110000    01011010
```

Machine code can be represented in a slightly more programmer-friendly format where each group of four bits (half a byte or a 'nibble') is coded as one hexadecimal (base-16) digit. Each 'hex' digit can have

one of sixteen values: 0, 1, ..., 8, 9, A, B, C, D, E and F. For example, the operand 01011010 can be split into two nibbles: 0101 and 1010. In hexadecimal, 0101 is 5 and 1010 is A, so the operand can be written as 5A. Although this is easier to read than binary, it is not at all clear to the reader what it means, as the following fragment of machine code shows:

```
:100000006E280000000000000090025088A01820710
:10001000603431343234333461343434353436344A
:1000200062343734383439346334 2A343034233446
:100030006434293084008316831 39B0183161C14B7
:100040001A088000840A9B0A83122D300402031DC3
```

It is fairly safe to say that no one *writes* whole programs in machine language today.

#### Assembly language

As an alternative to machine language, programmers developed an **assembly language** for each family of processor. Assembly language is considerably easier to read and write than machine language. A short word or abbreviation acts as a memory aid, or 'mnemonic' code, for each machine language instruction's opcode. For example, a valid instruction in the PIC16F627 microcontroller's assembly language is:

```
MOVLW    0x5A
```

The mnemonic MOVLW stands for **MOV**e the **L**iteral operand into the **W**orking register and represents the six-bit machine language opcode 110000. A *literal* operand simply means the value of the operand itself, so the operand is the hexadecimal (for which 0x is a marker) value 5A. So MOVLW 0x5A represents the machine language instruction that we met earlier:

```
110000    01011010
```

This instruction moves the hex value 5A (90 in everyday, denary numbers) into the microcontroller's working register. The assembly language instruction is more compact and easier to understand than the machine language instruction.

The following fragment of assembly code shows that you would still need considerable experience of the assembly language before you would begin to feel fluent in it. Almost the only whole words are in the comments, preceded by semicolons.

```
Label        Opcode        Operands and comments
             ORG           0x2100
             DE            "1234"      ; default code stored in EEPROM
vectors      ORG           0
             GOTO          main
             NOP
             RETFIE        ; ignore interrupt
ktable                     ; determine pressed key's code from kcode
             MOVF          kcode, W
             CLRF          PCLATH
             ADDWF         PCL, F
             DT            0x60 ; data lookup table directive
             DT            "123a"
             DT            "456b"
             DT            "789c"
             DT            "*0#d"
eep_read                   ; copy EEPROM contents to RAM from cod to cod_end-1
             MOVLW         cod
             MOVWF         FSR
             BSF           STATUS, RP0
             BCF           STATUS, IRP
             CLRF          EEADR
```

Assembly code must be translated into machine code before it can be run by a processor. This can be done manually, but it is time-consuming and error-prone to look up all the opcodes to substitute for the mnemonics. Fortunately, it is a relatively straightforward task to write a translation program called an **assembler** for an assembly language. The assembly code input to the assembler is known as the **source code**. The assembler rapidly and reliably looks up the mnemonic and converts it to machine code output, known as **object code**. The translation process produces one machine language instruction for each assembly language instruction.

Low-level languages are very machine-oriented, because they refer to hardware such as the processor's registers, input and output ports and specific locations in internal memory. An advantage of this characteristic of low-level languages is that a skilful programmer has complete freedom of choice of instructions and direct control over the processor's communication with its input, output and storage devices. The programmer can write very efficient programs that:

- fit into limited storage space;
- require limited RAM;
- run rapidly.

The disadvantages of low-level languages are that:

- their lack of relation to a human language makes them difficult for a programmer to read;
- their machine-oriented nature makes them hard for a programmer to learn;
- the processor-specific nature of the instruction set means that programs are not transferable or **portable** between families of processor.

### 3.2.2 High-level languages

**High-level languages** look far more similar to a human language or mathematical notation than low-level languages. This makes them easier to read and write, test, debug and maintain. They are intended to help programmers to solve problems rather than to micro-manage the computer's hardware. A high-level language is independent of the instruction set of any particular family of processor. Different languages are designed to solve different sorts of problem (Table 10.1).

**Table 10.1** High-level programming languages.

| Use | Language |
|---|---|
| Business applications | COBOL (Common Business Oriented Language) |
| Scientific applications | FORTRAN (FORmula TRANslation) |
| General-purpose use and education | BASIC (Beginners All-purpose Symbolic Instruction Code)<br>Visual BASIC<br>Pascal<br>Delphi<br>LISP<br>LOGO<br>C and C++<br>Java |

Depending on the type of high-level language, a program consists of procedural steps, called **statements**, or of facts and rules. Procedural languages provide the programmer with statements that include:

- reading input from a keyboard and assigning it to a variable;
- displaying or printing output expressions or graphics;
- performing calculations and comparisons on variables with different data types and data structures;
- selection of a route through the program;
- repetition of part of the program;
- calling function and procedure subroutines;
- creating, writing to and reading from files on storage media.

A high-level language program must be translated into machine code before it can be run by a processor. However, high-level language statements need translation software that is more complex than an assembler. One statement in a high-level language is translated into one or more machine language instructions. Consider the simple task of adding together two numbers represented by variables B and C and assigning the result to variable A. In a high-level language, the programmer might write:

```
A ← B + C
```

In a low-level language, the programmer might write:

| | |
|---|---|
| LDA B | Load the contents of the memory location whose address is represented by the variable B into the accumulator register. |
| ADD C | Add the contents of the memory location whose address is represented by the variable C to the contents of the accumulator, holding the result in the accumulator. |
| STA A | Copy the contents of the accumulator into the memory location whose address is represented by the variable A. |

Table 10.2 compares the features of high-level and low-level languages. Source code written in a high-level language is portable between families of processor and operating systems, provided that someone has written a translation program to create the appropriate object code for the target processor and operating system.

There are two types of translation program that differ depending on the high-level language (Table 10.3). A **compiler** program translates all the high-level source code into object code by a process known as 'compilation'. Compilation must be completed before the program can be run. An analogy is translating text from English into another language and then giving the complete translated text to someone to speak. If there are errors in the source code, the compiler produces an error report, the programmer corrects the errors and compiles the whole program again. The debugging of a large program before it can be run can be a slow, iterative process. Once there are no errors in the source code program, the compiler produces a machine code program that the processor can run rapidly.

**Table 10.2** Comparison of high-level and low-level languages.

| High-level language | Low-level language |
|---|---|
| Program statements are problem-oriented. | Program instructions are machine-oriented. |
| One statement translates to many machine code instructions. | One assembly language instruction translates to one machine code instruction. |
| Programs are portable between different types of computer. | Programs are not portable between different types of computer. |
| Programs must be translated to run on a processor. | Machine language needs no translation. |
| Translation to machine language is relatively complex. | Translation from assembly language to machine language is relatively simple. |
| Programs are relatively easy to read and write. | Programs are relatively hard to read and write. |
| Programs are relatively easy to test, debug and maintain. | Programs are relatively hard to test, debug and maintain. |

**Table 10.3** Comparison of translation programs.

| Assembler | Compiler | Interpreter |
|---|---|---|
| Translates processor-specific assembly code into machine code for a specific processor. | Translates high-level code into machine code for a specific processor and operating system. | Translates high-level language statements and executes them on a specific processor and operating system. |
| Translates an entire program but does not run it. | Translates an entire program but does not run it. | Translates and executes a program on the target processor, usually one statement at a time, but does not create machine code. |
| Translates one source code instruction to one machine code instruction. | Translates one source code statement to one or more machine code instructions. | Executes one source code statement as one or more instructions. |

An **interpreter** translates a high-level language program in a very different way. The interpreter runs directly on the target processor, usually analysing one source code statement at a time and running appropriate subroutines to give effect to, or 'execute', it. An analogy is translating text from English into another language and speaking the translation aloud sentence by sentence without writing down the translation – if you want to speak the translation again later, you have to repeat the translation. If the interpreter finds an error in the source code, it produces an error report and stops the execution. The process of translation slows the execution, but an interpreter can speed up the debugging of a large program, as the program does not need to be re-compiled after every edit.

 **SAQs**

1   What are the benefits of writing in a high-level language?

2   What is the connection between source code and object code?

3   Describe two differences between an assembler and a compiler.

4   In which sort of situation is it better to use a low-level language rather than a high-level language?

## Pseudocode

For this course, you do not need to be able to write programs in any particular language, but you do need to be able read, troubleshoot and write algorithms represented in pseudocode, as well as by the more graphical program flowchart that we met in Chapter 9. Pseudocode describes an algorithm's steps like program statements using English, mathematical notation and keywords commonly found in high-level languages. It is not bound by the strict rules of vocabulary and syntax of any particular programming language.

Pseudocode is used for learning programming concepts as we are doing here and to sketch out ideas and structures in algorithm design before coding begins. Figure 10.1 shows a typical pseudocode solution to the problem of sorting names into alphabetical order.

```
REPEAT
    enter name into an array of strings
UNTIL no more names
REPEAT
    set swapped to false
    look at the first pair of names
    REPEAT
        IF names out of order
            THEN
                swap names
                set swapped to true
        ENDIF
        look at the next pair of names
    UNTIL no more pairs of names
UNTIL swapped is false
OUTPUT list of names from array
```

**Figure 10.1** Pseudocode statements for an algorithm that sorts names into alphabetical order.

### Arithmetic operators

In pseudocode, we use the arithmetic operators shown in Table 10.4.

### Assignment

In Figure 10.1, the following statement indicates assignment:

```
set Swapped to False
```

**Table 10.4** Arithmetic operators.

| Operator | Meaning |
|---|---|
| + | Addition |
| − | Subtraction |
| * | Multiplication (× in mathematical notation) |
| / | Division (÷ in mathematical notation) |
| ^ | Raise preceding number to the power of the following exponent; for example, 2^3 is equivalent to $2^3$ in mathematical notation and evaluates to 8 |

Another way of indicating assignment is to write:

```
Swapped ← False
Count ← 1
```

The left-pointing arrow symbol means 'assign (or write) the value or expression on its right to the variable (or memory location) on its left'. Some programming languages and conventions for writing pseudocode use different symbols for assignment, such as := or =. You can read the statement Count ← 1 as 'Count is assigned the value 1', 'Count is made equal to 1' or 'Count becomes 1'.

If an algorithm needs to use the value of a variable *before* it assigns input data or a calculated value to the variable, the algorithm should assign an appropriate initial value to the variable. This is known as 'initialisation'. In the case of a cumulative total, the appropriate value is usually zero. In the case of a 'control variable' to count the number of iterations of a process, the appropriate value is often 1, to indicate the first iteration.

### Input

In pseudocode, we indicate input by words such as INPUT, READ or ENTER. Notice that ENTER Name means 'input a string of characters and assign its value to the variable Name'.

### Output

In pseudocode, we indicate output by words such as OUTPUT, WRITE or PRINT. Notice that we can specify any combination of text strings (in quotes) and variables:

```
WRITE "Name is ", Name
PRINT Count
```

## Totalling and counting

We can use a variable such as `Total` or `Sum` to hold a running total and an assignment statement to update it, such as:

```
Total ← Total + Number
```

This statement means 'the new value of `Total` becomes the old value of `Total` plus the value of `Number`'. We can also indicate adding to the running total with a statement that does not explicitly mention assignment, such as:

```
add Number to Sum
```

It is sometimes necessary to count how many times something happens. To count up or increment by 1, we can use statements such as:

```
Count ← Count + 1
increment Count by 1
```

To increment by a different number, we use a different numerical value. We can also count down (or decrement):

```
Length ← Length - 5
decrement Length by 5
```

## Conditions

A **condition**, or logical test, is often used to control an algorithm's route through a loop or selection structure. A condition is a **logical expression** that evaluates to either True or False. A logical expression often involves a comparison, such as `number > 1`, whose truth is tested to produce a value of True or False. It may help you to read the comparison as the question 'Is `Number` greater than 1?', to which the answer is either 'Yes, the comparison is True', or 'No, the comparison is False'. Comparisons can operate on text strings as well as numbers and use the operators in Table 10.5.

It may help to read the condition `Number = 0` as 'Is `Number` equal to 0?'

## Repetition

Many problems involve repeating one or more statements, so it is useful to have structured statements for controlling an iteration, **repetition** or loop. There are a number of types of **iteration statement** available:

**Table 10.5** Comparison operators.

| Comparison operator | Meaning |
| --- | --- |
| = | Equal to |
| <> | Not equal to ($\neq$ in mathematical notation) – literally 'less than or more than' |
| < | Less than |
| > | Greater than |
| <= | Less than or equal to ($\leq$ in mathematical notation) |
| >= | Greater than or equal to ($\geq$ in mathematical notation) |

- WHILE ... DO ... ENDWHILE
- REPEAT ... UNTIL
- FOR ... TO ... NEXT

Although these are similar to one another, they have distinct differences. In the following examples, the variable `Number` is used to hold the value of a number being input, `Count` is used as a counter to hold the number of times we have repeated the process and `Total` is used to hold the total of the input numbers.

### WHILE ... DO ... ENDWHILE loop

This statement can be used when we do not know how many times the process is to be repeated. The statements between `DO` and `ENDWHILE` are repeated *while* a certain condition is True. This condition is tested at the *beginning* of the loop. In Figure 10.2, the condition is `Number >= 0`.

Note that we use indentation to help to clarify which statements lie within the loop.

Notice that the statement `INPUT Number` occurs once *before* the loop, so that the `WHILE` condition can be tested on the first occasion, and once *within* the loop as part of the repeated process. If the user first inputs a positive number, the `WHILE` condition is True on first evaluation and the statements within the loop are executed. Control then passes back to the start of the loop and the condition is evaluated again. As soon as the user inputs a negative number, the `WHILE` condition `Number >= 0` is False and control passes to the `ENDWHILE` statement to continue the algorithm.

```
Total ← 0
INPUT Number
WHILE Number >= 0
    DO
        Total ← Total + Number
        INPUT Number
ENDWHILE
OUTPUT Total
```

These two statements are repeated in sequence as long as Number is greater than or equal to 0.

**Figure 10.2** Pseudocode using a WHILE ... DO ... ENDWHILE loop.

```
REPEAT
    OUTPUT "Please choose between options by entering A or B"
    INPUT Response
UNTIL Response is "A" or "a" or "B" or "b"
```

These statements are repeated until the value of Response is equal to A, a, B or b.

**Figure 10.3** Pseudocode using a REPEAT ... UNTIL loop.

If the first number input is negative, the WHILE condition is False the first time it is evaluated and the statements within the loop are not even executed once.

### REPEAT ... UNTIL loop

This statement can also be used when we do not know how many times the process is to be repeated. It differs from the WHILE ... DO ... ENDWHILE loop because it is repeated *until* a certain condition *becomes* True. This condition is tested at the *end* of the loop so, even if the condition is initially True, the statements within the loop are *always* executed at least once. In Figure 10.3, the UNTIL condition is expressed in English, as you are not expected to know any particular way of expressing it.

### FOR ... TO ... NEXT loop

This statement is used when we know how many times the process is to be repeated. It is possible to increment a variable to control the number of iterations in a WHILE ... DO ... ENDWHILE loop. Figure 10.4 is a version of Figure 10.2 that always adds together 10 input numbers.

The 'control' variable Count is initialised to 1 and incremented on each iteration, until it reaches 11 at the end of the tenth iteration. Most programmers would

prefer not to have to remember to initialise a control variable before the loop and increment it within the loop.

Fortunately, the FOR ... TO ... NEXT loop looks after the details of this for us. The loop is repeated *for* a specified number of iterations. We specify the initial (lower) and final (higher) values of a control variable in the opening statement of the loop. These values are not restricted to numerical values: they can be expressions involving variables. The control variable is automatically (by default) incremented by one each time the loop reaches the NEXT keyword at the end of the loop and is tested at the *beginning* of the loop. The loop is repeated while the control variable remains less than or equal to the specified final value. For example, Figure 10.5 is equivalent to Figure 10.4 but is two lines shorter:

If we want to end a loop *either* on a specific input *or* when a maximum number of iterations is reached, we can revert to using a WHILE ... DO ... ENDWHILE loop.

 **SAQs**

5　Write an iteration (or repetition) in pseudocode to print the numbers 1 to 10,000.

**1** You may know that the factorial of a positive integer *n*, written as *n*!, is the product of all the positive integers less than or equal to *n*. For example, 4! = 4 × 3 × 2 × 1 = 24. 0! is a special case that is defined to be 1. Write an algorithm in pseudocode that uses an iteration (or repetition) to calculate the factorial of any non-negative integer. Dry run your algorithm with a trace table with the test data 0, 4 and 7.

**Hints:** You first need to input the number and carefully initialise a variable for the result. You can use the number entered as the number of iterations. You can also think of 4! as 1 × 2 × 3 × 4.

**2** If you enjoy mathematics, you might like to write another algorithm in pseudocode that uses an iteration (or repetition) to produce a sufficiently good approximation to the square root of a positive number, *N*, input by the user. You may have met the idea that a better guess, *B*, of the square root of *N* is (*G* + *N*/*G*)/2, where *G* is a previous guess. If you iterate this calculation, recycling your previous value of *B* as your new value of *G*, *B* converges on the square root. Try to recall or work out why it works so well. The method is attributed to Isaac Newton. You can stop when the magnitude of *G* − *N*/*G* is less than a chosen fraction (for example, 0.01) of *G*, depending on the number of significant figures you desire in the final value of *B*. Dry run your algorithm with a trace table with the test data 0, 3, 4 and 207. Which sort of loop statement can you use to perform at least one iteration of the loop?

**Hints:** When a human uses this algorithm they can pick their own initial value for *G*. For a program algorithm, the programmer has to either invite the user to enter their own guess or initialise a variable for *G*. Assuming that you do the latter, pick *any* positive value! Obviously, it helps if you know what range of number for *N* your user will most often use.

```
Count ← 1                                    Count is initialised to 1.
Total ← 0
WHILE Count <= 10
      DO
          INPUT Number
          Total ← Total + Number
          Count ← Count + 1                  Count is incremented by
                                             1 on each iteration.
ENDWHILE
OUTPUT Total
```

**Figure 10.4** Pseudocode using a WHILE loop for a specific number of iterations.

```
Total ← 0
FOR Count ← 1 TO 10                Count is assigned the initial
     INPUT Number                  value, 1, on the first iteration.
     Total ← Total + Number        Before every iteration, the loop
NEXT                               tests whether Count is less than
OUTPUT Total                       or equal to the final value, 10.
```

**Figure 10.5** Pseudocode using a FOR ... TO ... NEXT loop to perform the same task as Figure 10.4.

## Selection or conditional statements

There are two types of structured **conditional statement** for controlling selection, which is a decision between alternative routes through the algorithm.

### IF...THEN...ELSE...ENDIF statement

An IF...THEN...ELSE...ENDIF statement uses a single condition to control a choice between two routes through an algorithm. The choice of routes may be as simple as including or bypassing one or more statements:

```
IF Number > 0
    THEN
        WRITE "this is a positive number"
ENDIF
```

Sometimes the choice of routes is between two sequences of one or more statements; we want to do one thing when the condition is True and another thing when it is False. In this case, we add an ELSE clause after the THEN clause, as shown here:

```
IF Number > 0
    THEN
        WRITE "this is a positive number"
    ELSE
        WRITE "this is zero or a negative
        number"
ENDIF
```

It possible to use multiple IF statements to control a choice between multiple routes through an algorithm. We often do this by 'nesting' one IF statement inside another, rather like Russian dolls (Figure 10.6).

**Figure 10.6** Russian 'nesting' dolls.

For example, two nested IF statements can control three routes through the algorithm. In Figure 10.7, if the value of Number is greater than 0, the first WRITE statement is executed and control passes to the outer ENDIF. If not, the ELSE route is followed and the number is tested again.

```
IF Number > 0
    THEN
        WRITE "this is a positive number"
    ELSE
        IF Number = 0
            THEN
                WRITE "this number is zero"
            ELSE
                WRITE "this is a negative
                number"
        ENDIF
ENDIF
```

**Figure 10.7** Pseudocode using two nested **IF** statements to control three routes through an algorithm.

### CASE...OF...OTHERWISE...ENDCASE statement

It is quite tedious to program an extra IF statement for each extra route required. When the multiple conditions all involve a similar expression (testing the variable Number in our example), it is quicker and clearer to use a CASE...OF...OTHERWISE...ENDCASE statement.

Consider Figure 10.8, in which the user inputs a number representing a day of the week (1 = Monday, 2 = Tuesday, etc.) and the pseudocode algorithm assigns the name of the day to the variable DayName.

Unless a comparison other than equality is used, the comparison conditions in the OF clause are assumed to be DayNumber = 1, DayNumber = 2, etc. In another algorithm, we could use a comparison other than equality for each condition in the operator OF clause, but the statements are executed for the *first* condition that is True. This means that the order of such conditions is important, just as it would be within nested IF statements.

Notice that the OTHERWISE clause is useful to handle unforeseen values of the variable DayNumber. Without it, the user might not realise that they had made an error and the value of DayName would not just be 'Unknown' but indeterminate. When a program runs, an uninitialised variable holds whatever was last

```
INPUT DayNumber
CASE DayNumber OF
    1: DayName ← "Monday"
    2: DayName ← "Tuesday"
    3: DayName ← "Wednesday"
    4: DayName ← "Thursday"
    5: DayName ← "Friday"
    6: DayName ← "Saturday"
    7: DayName ← "Sunday"
    OTHERWISE
        WRITE "You have not entered a number in the range 1 to 7"
        DayName ← "unknown"
ENDCASE
OUTPUT "Today is ", DayName
```

**Figure 10.8** Pseudocode using a `CASE...OF...OTHERWISE...ENDCASE` statement.

written into that location in internal memory before the program ran. As far as the programmer is concerned, that is random or 'garbage' data. However, a good programmer would anticipate user error and validate the input number by placing the `INPUT DayNumber` statement within a suitable `REPEAT...UNTIL` loop.

### SAQs

6  Write a conditional statement in pseudocode so that the output is 'Pass' if the value of the variable `Total` is greater than or equal to 40, otherwise the output is 'Fail'.

### Questions

3  Write a conditional statement in pseudocode so that the output is 'Distinction' if `Total` is greater than or equal to 80, 'Merit' if `Total` is greater than or equal to 60, 'Pass' if `Total` is greater than or equal to 40, and otherwise 'Fail'.

   **Hint:** If you tackle this with nested `IF` statements, be careful that the way in which you express your conditions and the order in which you nest your statements does not result in some grades never being awarded.

## Producing algorithms in pseudocode

In earlier chapters, we have thought of an algorithm only as a list of steps in plain English or as a flowchart. Now you have the option of writing an algorithm in pseudocode, which is no longer graphical, but is one step closer to writing program code in a high-level language.

Let us consider how to write a pseudocode algorithm. In a certain country, citizens who wish to use motor vehicles on public roads pay an annual tax that is based on the engine capacity, as shown in Table 10.6.

**Table 10.6** Tax rates based on engine capacity.

| Engine capacity at or above (cc) | Tax rate ($ per cc) |
| --- | --- |
| 3000 | 0.25 |
| 1000 | 0.15 |
| 0 | 0.10 |

We will write a pseudocode algorithm to allow the user to enter an engine capacity, calculate the tax and output the tax for an unknown number of vehicles. When the value zero is entered, the number of vehicles in each tax rate is output and the algorithm ends.

We need to initialise the values of counters for the three tax rates to zero. We then need a WHILE loop to enter and process data for an unknown number of vehicles. Within the loop, we need a CASE statement to select the correct route to calculate the tax and increment the appropriate counter. We can use a 'greater than' comparison, in which case the processing statements are executed for the *first* condition that is True (Figure 10.9).

Let us consider how to write a pseudocode algorithm that will enable a teacher to enter 25 test marks, validated to ensure that they are in the range 0 to 30, and output the maximum, minimum and mean marks scored.

We need to initialise the value of Max to the lowest possible mark, from which any higher mark can move it up, and Min to the highest possible mark, from which

any lower mark can move it down. We then need a FOR loop to enter and process 25 marks. This will contain a REPEAT loop to validate the input data and IF statements to adjust the values of Max and Min (Figure 10.10). The IF statements cannot be nested because, although a mark cannot usually both exceed the previous value of Max and fall below the previous value of Min, the very first mark entered is very likely to do so, because of the extreme initial values of Max and Min.

## Testing and interpreting pseudocode algorithms

In Chapter 9, we learned how to read an algorithm in the form of a program flowchart, and work out its purpose or function by performing a dry run. We now need to do the same for algorithms in the form of pseudocode. Consider the pseudocode in Figure 10.11.

```
NumberAt25Cents ← 0
NumberAt15Cents ← 0
NumberAt10Cents ← 0
INPUT Capacity
WHILE Capacity <> 0
    DO
        CASE Capacity OF
            >= 3000:
                Tax ← Capacity * 0.25
                NumberAt25Cents ← NumberAt25Cents + 1
            >= 1000:
                Tax ← Capacity * 0.15
                NumberAt15Cents ← NumberAt15Cents + 1
            > 0:
                Tax ← Capacity * 0.10
                NumberAt10Cents ← NumberAt10Cents + 1
        OTHERWISE
            Tax ← 0
            OUTPUT "You have entered a negative number"
        ENDCASE
        OUTPUT Tax
        INPUT Capacity
ENDWHILE
OUTPUT "Vehicles taxed at $0.25 per cc: " NumberAt25Cents
OUTPUT "Vehicles taxed at $0.15 per cc: " NumberAt15Cents
OUTPUT "Vehicles taxed at $0.10 per cc: " NumberAt10Cents
```

**Figure 10.9** Pseudocode algorithm to calculate road tax.

```
Max ← 0
Min ← 30
Total ← 0
FOR Count ← 1 TO 25
    REPEAT
        OUTPUT "Please enter a Mark between 0 and 30"
        INPUT Mark
    UNTIL Mark is between 0 and 30
    IF Mark > Max THEN Max ← Mark
    IF Mark < Min THEN Min ← Mark
    Total ← Total + Mark
NEXT
OUTPUT "Maximum Mark: ", Max
OUTPUT "Minimum Mark: ", Min
OUTPUT "Mean Mark: ", Total / Count
```

> ENDIF is not needed if the whole IF...THEN statement is written on a single line

**Figure 10.10**  Pseudocode algorithm to process marks.

```
Line 1  Exponent ← 0
Line 2  REPEAT
Line 3      Result ← 2 ^ Exponent
Line 4      PRINT "2^", Exponent, " = ",
            Result
Line 5      Exponent ← Exponent + 1
Line 6  UNTIL Result > 100
```

**Figure 10.11**  What does this pseudocode algorithm do?

**Table 10.7**  Trace table for pseudocode in Figure 10.11.

| Result | PRINT | Exponent | Notes |
|--------|-------|----------|-------|
|        |       | 0        | Initialise variable |
| 1      | 2^0 = 1 | 1      | 1st iteration |
| 2      | 2^1 = 2 | 2      | 2nd iteration |
| 4      | 2^2 = 4 | 3      | 3rd iteration |
| 8      | 2^3 = 8 | 4      | 4th iteration |
| 16     | 2^4 = 16 | 5     | 5th iteration |
| 32     | 2^5 = 32 | 6     | 6th iteration |
| 64     | 2^6 = 64 | 7     | 7th iteration |
| 128    | 2^7 = 128 | 8    | 8th iteration |

To dry run the algorithm, we construct a trace table (Table 10.7) and work through the algorithm a line at a time, writing the values in the trace table:

- line 1 initialises the value of the variable Exponent;
- line 2 is the beginning of the loop structure;
- line 3 calculates 2 raised to the power of the value of the variable Exponent and assigns it to the variable Result;
- line 4 prints the result in the format '2^0 = 1';
- line 5 increments the variable Exponent;

- line 6 is the end of the loop structure, which iterates until the value of Result exceeds 100.

The purpose of the algorithm is to print a list of the powers of 2 starting at $2^0$ until it reaches the first one over 100. Notice that the variable Exponent is initialised and incremented just like our usual control variable Count, but it is *not* being used to control the loop. The algorithm could have used it for that purpose, with exactly the same output, if line 6 had been:

UNTIL Exponent > 7.

Dry run the algorithm in Figure 10.12 by completing a trace table for the input data: 5, 7, 0 and −9 (after you have tried it yourself, look at Table 10.8). What is the purpose of the algorithm?

- line 1 initialises the value of the variable Sum to zero;
- line 2 initialises the value of the variable Count to zero;
- lines 3 to 6 use a REPEAT ... UNTIL loop to prompt the user for Number and validate the input so that it does not exceed 100;
- line 7 is the beginning of a WHILE ... DO ... ENDWHILE loop that ceases to iterate when Number has a negative value;
- line 9 adds the value of Number to the value of the running total Sum;

- line 10 increments the variable `Count` to hold the number of values processed;
- lines 11 to 14 are identical to lines 3 to 6. They prompt and validate the input of `Number` within the loop;
- line 15 is the end of the `WHILE` loop that starts on line 7;
- line 16 checks that the value of `Count` is not zero and outputs the mean of the numbers entered. If the first

value input were negative, `Count` would be zero and would cause an error when a real program calculates `Sum / Count`.

The purpose of the algorithm in Figure 10.12 is to prompt the user to enter and to validate numbers between 0 and 100. The algorithm keeps a running total of the numbers, until the user enters a negative number, when it displays the mean of the numbers.

**Table 10.8**   Trace table for pseudocode in Figure 10.12.

| Sum | Count | OUTPUT | Number | Notes |
|-----|-------|--------|--------|-------|
| 0 | 0 | \<prompt\> | 5 | Initialise variables and enter 1st number. |
| 5 | 1 | \<prompt\> | 7 | 1st iteration of WHILE . . . DO . . . ENDWHILE loop |
| 12 | 2 | \<prompt\> | 0 | 2nd iteration of WHILE . . . DO . . . ENDWHILE loop |
| | 3 | \<prompt\> | −9 | 3rd iteration of WHILE . . . DO . . . ENDWHILE loop |
| | | 4 | | Final output |

```
Line 1   Sum ← 0
Line 2   Count ← 0
Line 3   REPEAT
Line 4    OUTPUT "Enter a number between 0 and 100 for addition, or a negative number to finish"
Line 5     INPUT Number
Line 6   UNTIL Number <= 100
Line 7   WHILE Number >= 0
Line 8    DO
Line 9      Sum ← Sum + Number
Line 10     Count ← Count + 1
Line 11     REPEAT
Line 12       OUTPUT "Enter a number between 0 and 100 for addition, or a negative Number to finish"
Line 13        INPUT Number
Line 14     UNTIL Number <= 100
Line 15  ENDWHILE
Line 16  IF Count <> 0 THEN OUTPUT Sum / Count
```

**Figure 10.12**   What does this pseudocode algorithm do?

## Questions

**4** Consider the following pseudocode:

```
INPUT x
INPUT y
IF x + y <> 0
    THEN
        Result ← (x - y) / (x + y)
        OUTPUT Result
ELSE
        OUTPUT "Cannot calculate"
ENDIF
```

**a** Dry run this algorithm with the values 7 and 3.

**b** Dry run this algorithm with the values 7 and −7. Why has the algorithm been designed to do this?

**c** Dry run this algorithm with the values 5 and 5.

**5** What is the purpose of the following algorithm, which is part of a program to be used in a shop's computer system?

```
INPUT x
INPUT y
IF x < y
    THEN
        Temp ← x
        x ← y
        y ← Temp
ENDIF
OUTPUT x
OUTPUT y
```

**6** Consider the following pseudocode:

```
n ← 0
p ← 0
FOR Count ← 1 TO 6
    INPUT x
    IF x < 0 THEN n ← n + 1
    IF x > 0 THEN p ← p + 1
NEXT
OUTPUT n
OUTPUT p
```

*Questions 6 continued …*

**a** Copy the trace table below, adding as many rows as needed, and complete it for this algorithm with the input data 7, −8, 0, −3, 5 and −1.

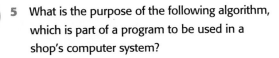

| n | p | Count | x |
|---|---|-------|---|
|   |   |       |   |

**b** What does n represent?

**c** What does p represent?

**d** What is the purpose of this algorithm?

**3.2.1** **Finding and correcting errors in pseudocode algorithms**

You also need to be able to identify errors and suggest corrections in a pseudocode algorithm. Common errors include:

- missing or faulty initialisation of variables;
- faulty initial and final values for the control variable or 'loop counter' in a FOR loop;
- incrementing the loop counter in a FOR loop, which interferes with the automatic counting;
- failing to increment a counter variable in the other sorts of loop;
- failing to complete a structured statement with the requisite ending keyword: ENDWHILE, UNTIL, NEXT, ENDIF or ENDCASE;
- misplacing a keyword, so that statements are inappropriately inside or outside a loop.

Cover up Table 10.9 on the next page and try to identify five errors in the pseudocode algorithm in Figure 10.13 (also on the next page) and possible corrections for these errors. Then check your answers with those in Table 10.9.

```
Line 1      Max ← 0
Line 2      Min ← 30
Line 3      FOR Count ← 25 TO 1
Line 4          REPEAT
Line 5              OUTPUT "Please enter a Mark between 0 and 50"
Line 6              INPUT Mark
Line 7          UNTIL Mark is between 0 and 50
Line 8          IF Mark > Max THEN Max ← Mark
Line 9          IF Mark < Min THEN Min ← Mark
Line 10         Count ← Count + 1
Line 11         Total ← Total + Mark
Line 12     OUTPUT "Maximum Mark: ", Max
Line 13     OUTPUT "Minimum Mark: ", Min
Line 14     OUTPUT "Mean Mark: ", Total / Count
```

**Figure 10.13**   Debug this pseudocode algorithm.

**Table 10.9**   Errors in pseudocode in Figure 10.13.

| Line number | Error | Correction |
|---|---|---|
| 11 | `Total` not initialised before use. | Insert `Total ← 0` before line 1. |
| 2 | `Min` initialised to too low a value. | Amend to `Min ← 50` |
| 3 | Reversed initial and final values for `Count`. | Amend to `FOR Count ← 1 TO 25` |
| 10 | `Count ← Count + 1` interferes with the automatic counting in the `FOR` loop. | Delete line 10. |
| 12 | `FOR` loop not complete before output starts. | Insert `NEXT` before line 12. |

## Summary

- A program is a sequence of instructions or programming language statements written to make a computer perform certain tasks.
- Machine code is a sequence of binary codes representing instructions for the processor.
- The instruction set for a family of processors consists of an instruction for each operation that the family has been designed to perform.
- Programming languages support sequence, selection, repetition, subroutine call and facilities for data transfer and manipulation.
- Machine language uses binary codes and assembly language uses mnemonic codes to represent individual processor instructions; they are low-level programming languages.
- Low-level programming languages are machine-oriented and programs can be very efficient, although they are relatively difficult to write and debug and are not portable between different families of processor.
- High-level programming languages (e.g. BASIC, COBOL, Pascal, JavaScript) use statements similar to English or mathematical notation.

→

*Summary continued ...*

- High-level programming languages are problem-oriented, are much easier to write and debug and are portable between different families of processor, provided a translation program is available.
- An assembler translates assembly language programs into machine code.
- A compiler translates high-level language programs into machine code.
- An interpreter executes a high-level language program.
- Pseudocode uses keywords commonly found in high-level languages, mathematical notation and English to describe an algorithm's steps; it includes assignment, input and output, and structured statements for repetition and selection.
- Iteration, repetition or loop, statements are used to solve problems involving repetition; they include:
  - a `WHILE ... DO ... ENDWHILE` loop, used when the exact number of repetitions is not known; the condition is checked before the loop statements are executed;
  - a `REPEAT ... UNTIL` loop, used when the exact number of repetitions is not known; the condition is checked after the loop statements are executed;
  - a `FOR ... TO ... NEXT` loop, used for a known number of repetitions.
- Selection, or conditional, statements are used to select alternative routes through a program they include:
  - an `IF ... THEN ... ELSE ... ENDIF` statement, used to decide between two routes;
  - a `CASE ... OF ... OTHERWISE ... ENDCASE` statement, used to decide among many routes.
- Producing an algorithm for a solution to a given problem in pseudocode typically includes initialising variables for totalling and counting, using `REPEAT ... UNTIL` for input validation, an appropriate loop structure for repetition of data entry or other processing and conditional statements to select appropriate processing alternatives.
- Dry running with a trace table and test data helps to understand the behaviour and work out the purpose of a pseudocode algorithm.
- Common errors in pseudocode algorithms include missing or faulty initialisation, faulty initial and final values for the loop counter in a `FOR` loop, missing or unnecessary incrementation of a loop counter, omitting the ending keyword from a structured statement and misplacing a keyword, so that statements are inappropriately inside or outside a loop.

# Examination practice for Paper 1

## Exam Questions

1.  (a) Compilers and interpreters translate high-level languages. Give **two** differences between compilers and interpreters.  [2]

    (b) Programs can be written using high-level or low-level languages. Give **one** advantage of using each method.  [2]

    *Part of Question 10, Cambridge IGCSE Computer Studies 0420/01 Paper 11 May/June 2010*

    $\longrightarrow$

2. A group of students were monitoring the temperature every day over a one-year period. Readings were taken ten times **every** day (you may assume a year contains 365 days).

   Write an algorithm, using pseudocode or flowchart, which:

   - inputs all the temperatures (ten per day)
   - outputs the **highest** temperature taken over the year
   - outputs the **lowest** temperature taken over the year
   - outputs the average temperature **per day**
   - outputs the average temperature **for the whole year**. [7]

   *Question 18, Cambridge IGCSE Computer Studies 0420/01 Paper 11 May/June 2010*

3. A golf course charges $10 for each game of two people. Each additional person incurs a further charge of $2 per game. If they book two or more games in advance, they get a 10% discount on the total charge.

   The following program has been written in pseudocode to calculate the charges for a game.

```
1 ExtraCost ← 0
2 INPUT NumberPeople, NumberGames
3 Charge ← 10 * NumberGames
4 ExtraPeople ← NumberPeople - 2
5 IF NumberPeople < 2 THEN ExtraCost ← 2 * ExtraPeople * NumberGames
6 Charge ← ExtraCost
7 IF NumberGames > 1 THEN Charge ← Charge * 0.1
8 PRINT Charge
```

   There are **three** errors in the program. Locate these errors and suggest a correct piece of coding. [6]

   *Question 12, Cambridge IGCSE Computer Studies 0420/01 Paper 11 May/June 2010*

## Exam-Style Questions

1. (a) Write a pseudocode algorithm to input 20 numbers and output their total. [4]

   (b) Write a pseudocode algorithm to validate a number by repeating its input until it is in the range 1 to 10. [3]

2. A website publishes monthly values for the price of rice over a five year period.

   Use a program flowchart or pseudocode to write an algorithm that inputs the price for each month over the five year period and then gives the following outputs:

   - The lowest price
   - The highest price
   - The number of times when the price was above $600 per tonne
   - The average (mean) price [5]

3. State **three** types of pseudocode error. [3]

## Examination practice for Paper 3

To answer the following question you will need to read the garage scenario provided in Appendix A (page 284).

1. As part of the scenario described in Appendix A, it is necessary to scan barcodes on spare parts. The computer system needs to validate that the part number input is within the range 100000 to 999999.

   (i) Write a pseudocode algorithm to prompt the user to scan the barcode or type the part number until the input is within the required range. [3]

   (ii) Suggest three test part numbers for dry running the validation algorithm. Copy and complete the following partial test plan for dry running your algorithm, indicating **three** types of test data, suitable values and whether you expect the input to be accepted or rejected. [6]

| Type of test data | Test data | Expected result |
|---|---|---|
| | | |
| | | |
| | | |

**Comment**

You will typically score 1 mark for each of: correct loops; initialisation of total and control variables; conditional statement; calculations; and output.

# 11 Logic gates and circuits

## When you have finished this chapter, you will be able to:

- define the functions of five types of logic gate and recognise their symbols
- write a truth table for a given gate and recognise a gate from its truth table
- produce a truth table for a given logic circuit
- design a simple logic circuit to provide a solution to a written logical statement of a problem.

## Logic gates

An electronic **logic gate** is a relatively simple digital electronic circuit, with as few as three components. It processes two-state signals according to a logical rule. Each gate has one or more inputs and a single output.

Electronics engineers can use these simple logic gates as building blocks for complex circuits of gates, or **logic circuits**, in which the output of a gate forms an input to one or more other gates for further processing. Apart from the obvious use for logic gates in processing logical expressions, the fact that they process *two-state* signals also makes them suitable for processing and temporarily holding the *binary* numbers that almost all digital computers use to represent numbers and text. The processor in a PC consists of many thousands of logic gates.

Logic circuits with feedback from output to input can have outputs whose values depend on the history as well as the current values of their inputs; they are called **sequential logic circuits**. A suitable circuit can form a memory element. Sets of these elements can form the registers that a processor uses to hold the current program instruction and the data on which it is operating. Thousands or millions of these memory elements can form a RAM chip.

Logic circuits without feedback from output to input have outputs whose values depend only on the current values of their inputs; these are called **combinatorial** or **combinational logic circuits**. Although they do not remember previous inputs, they can perform useful

processing operations. Figure 11.1 illustrates how 16 logic gates can form a 1-bit arithmetic and logic unit (ALU) used in a computer's processor.

This circuit only processes two 1-bit operands. To process two 64-bit operands, we would need the equivalent of 64 of these, or a 'gate count' of about 64 × 16 = 1024. You may be relieved to know that our studies are limited to studying this simpler, combinational sort of logic circuit, with a maximum of just six gates.

Different families of logic gate use different specifications for the voltage ranges that represent the two **logic levels**: high and low. These two logic levels can be associated with a number of meanings. The associations with logic levels in Table 11.1 are arbitrary: although they are commonly used, they are not universal. However, *IGCSE Computer Studies* has chosen to adopt them, so you can safely assume that they always apply in exam questions, unless otherwise stated. The values True and False refer to the truth or falsehood of logical statements that the signals in logic circuits can represent.

We only need to consider the five simplest types of logic gate: AND, OR, NOT, NAND and NOR. The gates can be represented by the symbols shown in Table 11.2. Diagrams in exams will use the preferred, distinctively shaped, symbols, although you may draw answers using the circular symbols. Although the distinctively shaped symbols do not need to be labelled, we include the labels to help you associate the shape with the gate's function.

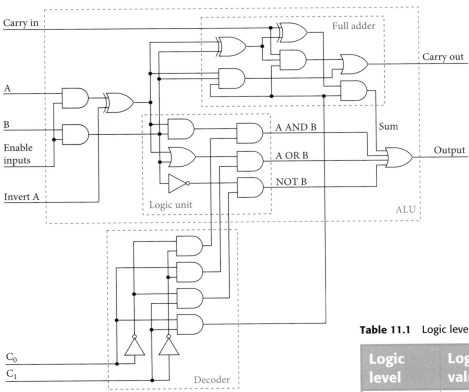

**Figure 11.1** Logic gates as building blocks for a 1-bit arithmetic and logic unit (ALU), as used in a computer's processor.

**Table 11.1** Logic level associations.

| Logic level | Logical value | Binary value | Switch value |
|---|---|---|---|
| High | True | 1 | On |
| Low | False | 0 | Off |

**Table 11.2** Logic gate symbols.

| Preferred symbol (label is optional) | Alternative symbol (must have a label) | Behaviour of gate |
|---|---|---|
| AND | AND | An AND gate has at least two inputs. The output has the value True only when its first input *and* its second input *and* other inputs have the value True; that is when *all* the inputs have the value True. |
| OR | OR | An OR gate has at least two inputs. The output has the value True when *either* its first input *or* its second input *or* any other input or combination of inputs has the value True; that is when *one or more* of its inputs has the value True. |
| NOT | NOT | A NOT gate has only one input. The output is the opposite of its input, so it is also called an 'inverter'. The output has the value True only when the input does *not* have the value True; that is when the input has the value False. |
| NAND | NAND | A NAND gate is an AND gate followed by a NOT gate. The output has the value False only when *all* its inputs have the value True. This is equivalent to saying that its output has the value True only when *not all* of its inputs have the value True. |
| NOR | NOR | A NOR gate is an OR gate followed by a NOT gate. The output has the value False only when *one or more* of its inputs has the value True. This is equivalent to saying that its output only has the value True when *none* of its inputs has the value True. |

## Truth tables

A **truth table** is used to show the output of a logic circuit for all possible combinations of input values. Although it is called a 'truth' table, we usually use the binary values 1 and 0 as shorthand for True and False. The truth tables that define the behaviour of each of the five types of logic gate are shown below. We only need to consider gates with a maximum of two inputs. You need to be able to remember the truth table for a given gate and identify a gate from a given truth table.

The output of an AND gate (Figure 11.2) is 1 (True) only when A AND B (both of its inputs) are 1 (True), as shown in Table 11.3.

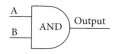

**Figure 11.2**   An AND logic gate.

**Table 11.3**   Truth table for an AND logic gate.

| Input A | Input B | Output A AND B |
|---------|---------|----------------|
| 0 | 0 | 0 |
| 0 | 1 | 0 |
| 1 | 0 | 0 |
| 1 | 1 | 1 |

The output of an OR gate (Figure 11.3) is 1 (True) only when A OR B (either or both of its inputs) are 1 (True), as shown in Table 11.4.

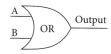

**Figure 11.3**   An OR logic gate.

**Table 11.4**   Truth table for an OR logic gate.

| Input A | Input B | Output A OR B |
|---------|---------|---------------|
| 0 | 0 | 0 |
| 0 | 1 | 1 |
| 1 | 0 | 1 |
| 1 | 1 | 1 |

The output of a NOT gate (Figure 11.4) is 0 (NOT True) only when A (its input) is 1 (True), as shown in Table 11.5.

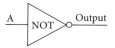

**Figure 11.4**   A NOT logic gate.

**Table 11.5**   Truth table for a NOT logic gate.

| Input A | Output NOT A |
|---------|--------------|
| 0 | 1 |
| 1 | 0 |

The output of a NAND gate (Figure 11.5) is 0 (NOT True) only when A AND B (both of its inputs) are 1 (True), as shown in Table 11.6.

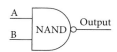

**Figure 11.5**   A NAND logic gate.

**Table 11.6**   Truth table for a NAND logic gate.

| Input A | Input B | Output A NAND B |
|---------|---------|-----------------|
| 0 | 0 | 1 |
| 0 | 1 | 1 |
| 1 | 0 | 1 |
| 1 | 1 | 0 |

The output of a NOR gate (Figure 11.6) is 0 (NOT True) only when A OR B (either or both of its inputs) are 1 (True), as shown in Table 11.7.

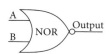

**Figure 11.6**   A NOR logic gate.

**Table 11.7**   Truth table for a NOR logic gate.

| Input A | Input B | Output A NOR B |
|---------|---------|----------------|
| 0 | 0 | 1 |
| 0 | 1 | 0 |
| 1 | 0 | 0 |
| 1 | 1 | 0 |

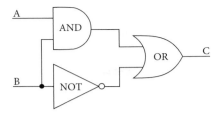

**Figure 11.7** A logic circuit with AND, NOT and OR gates.

1 If you only have AND, OR and NOT gates available for your project, how can you produce the functionality of NAND and NOR gates?

**Questions**

1 Which logic gate is represented by the following truth table?

| Input A | Input B | Output |
|---------|---------|--------|
| 0 | 0 | 1 |
| 0 | 1 | 0 |
| 1 | 0 | 0 |
| 1 | 1 | 0 |

2 Which logic gate is represented by the following truth table?

| Input A | Input B | Output |
|---------|---------|--------|
| 0 | 0 | 0 |
| 0 | 1 | 0 |
| 1 | 0 | 0 |
| 1 | 1 | 1 |

## 3.3.3 Combinational logic circuits with two inputs

Logic gates can be combined to produce one or more outputs from two or more inputs. We call such a combination a logic 'circuit', even though we are only referring to the flow of signals from the inputs to one or more outputs, not to the technical details of an electronic circuit.

In Figure 11.7, input B goes to both the AND gate and the NOT gate.

For any logic circuit with two binary-valued inputs, there are $2^2 = 4$ possible combinations of values, as shown in the truth tables for the two-input gates. You need to be able to produce a truth table for a circuit, to show the values of C for each of these four combinations of input values. We place these four combinations in a

consistent order in the rows of a truth table, which is equivalent to counting from zero (00) to three (11) in binary numbers, with input A as the twos column and input B as the units column.

Since it may be quite hard to think through the behaviour of all the relevant gates to work out the output of a logic circuit, it is usually helpful to include a column in the truth table for the values at each intermediate output between the inputs and one or more outputs, shown as D and E in Figure 11.8.

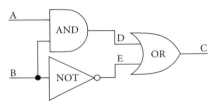

**Figure 11.8** The logic circuit from Figure 11.7 with named intermediate outputs.

In Table 11.8, we include a column for the values for D, the output from the AND gate with inputs A and B. We also include a column for the values for E, the output from the NOT gate with input B. D and E form the inputs to the OR gate, for which we need to work out the values for output C. If you are not given these extra columns in an exam, you can always add them to the side of the table. Using our knowledge of the behaviour of AND and NOT gates, we first complete the columns for D and E. Then we use our knowledge of the behaviour of OR gates to complete the column for C.

**Table 11.8** Truth table for the logic circuit in Figure 11.8.

| Input A | Input B | D = A AND B | E = NOT B | Output C = D OR E |
|---------|---------|-------------|-----------|-------------------|
| 0 | 0 | 0 | 1 | 1 |
| 0 | 1 | 0 | 0 | 0 |
| 1 | 0 | 0 | 1 | 1 |
| 1 | 1 | 1 | 0 | 1 |

Notice that we can write the words AND, OR, NOT, NAND and NOR as operators in logical equations (strictly speaking, identities) that express the behaviour of the outputs D, E and C. We can also substitute the expressions for D and E in the logical equation for C, using brackets to indicate that the logical operation within the brackets takes priority:

C = (A AND B) OR NOT B

Remembering that 1 is a numerical value representing True, we can read this as meaning:

C = 1 only if ((A = 1) AND (B = 1)) OR ((NOT B) = 1)

Since (NOT B) = 1 means B = 0, we can read this as:

C = 1 only if ((A = 1) AND (B = 1)) OR (B = 0)

or in plain English as:

C is 1 only if A *and* B are 1 *or* B is 0

You should find that this agrees with the truth table above.

## Questions

Copy and complete the following truth table for each of these questions.

| Input A | Input B | Output C |
|---------|---------|----------|
| 0 | 0 | |
| 0 | 1 | |
| 1 | 0 | |
| 1 | 1 | |

 **3** To which single gate is the following circuit equivalent?

A
B
AND — NOT ○— C

⟶

*Questions continued …*

**4** To which single gate is the following circuit equivalent?

A
B
NAND ○— NOT ▷○— C

**5** Note that both inputs A and B in the following circuit go to both the AND gate and the NOR gate.

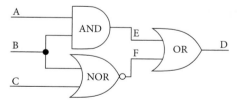

A
AND
D
NOR ○— C
E
B
NOR ○

# Combinational logic circuits with three inputs

Three inputs and six gates is the most complex circuit for which you need to be able to produce a truth table. For any logic circuit with three binary-valued inputs, there are $2^3 = 8$ possible combinations of values. To work out all eight combinations and place them in a consistent order in the rows of a truth table, we can count from zero (000) to seven (111) in binary numbers, with input A as the fours column, input B as the twos column and input C as the units column. Figure 11.9 shows an example of a logic circuit with three inputs.

A
AND
E
B
OR
D
F
C
NOR ○—

**Figure 11.9**   A logic circuit with three inputs.

Again, we fill in the truth table (Table 11.9) for the intermediate outputs E and F, to make it easier to see what the final output D should be.

**Table 11.9** Truth table for the logic circuit in Figure 11.9.

| Input A | Input B | Input C | Output E = A AND B | Output F = B NOR C | Output D = E OR F |
|---|---|---|---|---|---|
| 0 | 0 | 0 | 0 | 1 | 1 |
| 0 | 0 | 1 | 0 | 0 | 0 |
| 0 | 1 | 0 | 0 | 0 | 0 |
| 0 | 1 | 1 | 0 | 0 | 0 |
| 1 | 0 | 0 | 0 | 1 | 1 |
| 1 | 0 | 1 | 0 | 0 | 0 |
| 1 | 1 | 0 | 1 | 0 | 1 |
| 1 | 1 | 1 | 1 | 0 | 1 |

*Questions continued …*

**7** Notice that input B is connected to both the NAND gates. It can be seen as controlling or 'gating' the other inputs A and C. Complete the following statement:

When input B is 0, output D is always ____.
When input B is 1, output D is 1 when either A is ____ or C is ____, or ____.

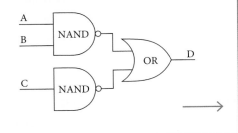

## Questions

Copy and complete the following truth table for each of the following questions.

| Input A | Input B | Input C | Output D |
|---|---|---|---|
| 0 | 0 | 0 | |
| 0 | 0 | 1 | |
| 0 | 1 | 0 | |
| 0 | 1 | 1 | |
| 1 | 0 | 0 | |
| 1 | 0 | 1 | |
| 1 | 1 | 0 | |
| 1 | 1 | 1 | |

**6** To which three-input single gate is the following circuit equivalent?

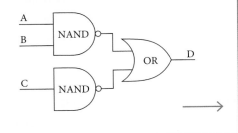

### (3.3.4) Designing simple logic circuits

Apart from their use in processors and other computer components, logic gates can be purchased in smaller, cheaper integrated circuits, each containing one or more gates of a particular type. For example, a 14-pin package (Figure 11.10), about 2 cm long, can contain four two-input gates. If an automated system for monitoring or control only requires a fixed pattern of output for all the possible combinations of inputs, it is sometimes cheaper to design and 'hard-wire' a solution, than to program a microcontroller or computer.

You need to be able to design simple combinational logic circuits from logical statements such as:

If A AND B are **on** AND C is **on**, then the light (L) is **on**.

We can rewrite this statement with brackets to clarify the value for each variable and the priority of logical operations as:

If ((A is **on**) AND (B is **on**)) AND (C is **on**), then the light (L) is **on**.

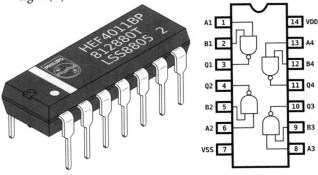

**Figure 11.10** A 14-pin integrated circuit.

We can rewrite this in terms of logical operators and binary number values as:

L = **1** if ((A = **1**) AND (B = **1**)) AND (C = **1**)

Recalling again that 1 represents True, we can rewrite this as a logical equation for L:

L = (A AND B) AND C

All this looks like over-kill in such a simple example, but it is the kind of process that we can reliably use for working out the logic circuit required. Writing something similar to either of the last two equations above may earn you marks for working in an exam. In this example, there are three inputs A, B and C. Starting with the brackets, A and B need to be connected to the inputs of an AND gate whose output is D. D and input C need to be connected to the inputs of another AND gate whose output is L (Figure 11.11). To check that the logic circuit is correct, we can draw up a truth table (Table 11.10).

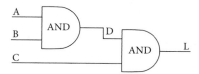

**Figure 11.11**  Constructing a logic circuit for a light.

**Table 11.10**  Truth table for the logic circuit in Figure 11.11.

| Input A | Input B | Input C | D = A AND B | Output L = C AND D |
|---------|---------|---------|-------------|---------------------|
| 0 | 0 | 0 | 0 | 0 |
| 0 | 0 | 1 | 0 | 0 |
| 0 | 1 | 0 | 0 | 0 |
| 0 | 1 | 1 | 0 | 0 |
| 1 | 0 | 0 | 0 | 0 |
| 1 | 0 | 1 | 0 | 0 |
| 1 | 1 | 0 | 1 | 0 |
| 1 | 1 | 1 | 1 | 1 |

You may already have realised that this circuit of two-input AND gates is equivalent to a single three-input AND gate.

As a further example, suppose that you have been asked to design a logic circuit from the logical statement:

If A AND B are **on**, OR B is **on** AND C is **off**, then the pump (P) is **on**.

We can rewrite this as equivalent statements with brackets, with logical operators and binary number values, substituting (NOT C) = 1 for C = 0, and finally as a logical equation:

If ((A is **on**) AND (B is **on**)) OR ((B is **on**) AND (C is **off**)), then the pump (P) is **on**.

P = **1** if ((A = **1**) AND (B = **1**)) OR ((B = **1**) AND (C = **0**))

P = **1** if ((A = **1**) AND (B = **1**)) OR ((B = **1**) AND ((NOT C) = **1**))

P = (A AND B) OR (B AND (NOT C))

To construct the circuit (Figure 11.12), we start with the innermost brackets where they are nested and work outwards. A and B need to be connected to the inputs of an AND gate whose output is D. Input C needs to be connected to a NOT gate whose output is E. B and E need to be connected to the inputs of another AND gate whose output is F. Outputs D and F need to be connected to the inputs of an OR gate, whose output is P.

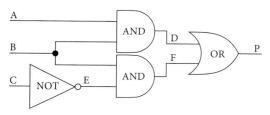

**Figure 11.12**  A logic circuit to control a pump.

## Questions

**8**  Design logic circuits for the following logical statements. Show your working before you draw the table and check your circuit by producing a truth table.

   **a**  If A or B is on, then the actuator Q is on.

   **b**  If A and B are on and if B or C is on, then the actuator Q is on.

   **c**  If A and B are on or B and C are on or C and A are on, then the actuator Q is on.

   **d**  If A and B are on and C is off, then the actuator Q is on.

## Testing logic circuits

We have seen how to produce truth tables and use them to check logic circuits designed to solve a given problem, rather as we use trace tables for dry running flowchart or pseudocode algorithms. However, it is helpful to have other means of experimenting with logic circuit design. The main choice of techniques for building and testing circuits is between using simulation software and using some sort of hardware.

## Simulation software

Simulation software uses a computer as a tool for modelling the sorts of components from which a logic circuit is made. A simulation program represents inputs, gates, output indicators and their connections graphically (Figure 11.13). It uses built-in truth tables to calculate the output of each gate. As the user changes the input values, simulated LEDs or other indicators change in response. Professional engineers use simulation software unless they are speed testing a new form of chip technology. Some simulation software is available as freeware.

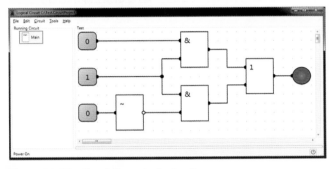

**Figure 11.13** Simulating a logic circuit.

## Electronic circuitry

Experimenting with logic gates using electronic circuitry is highly recommended if you have an interest in electronics. It is relatively cheap. For a start, you do not need an expensive computer. However, you must be aware of the safety implications of experimenting with electronic components.

### Safety warning

Working with electronic components gives you the freedom to connect them in ways that their designers did not intend. This exposes you to hazards from fire and explosions that, though small, could permanently damage your eyesight. You are therefore strongly advised to:

- experiment with electronic circuitry only under the supervision of a suitably experienced teacher or other competent person;

$\longrightarrow$

### Safety warning continued …

- ensure that you have adequate information about the components you use;
- wear protective laboratory goggles or safety spectacles whenever your circuitry is connected to an electrical supply.

Some school science or design and technology departments have logic gate modules with convenient plugs and sockets for connecting inputs and outputs. Hence you do not have to concern yourself with individual electronic components, but you still need to understand how to make and change connections in such a way that you neither damage a gate nor create a short circuit between the terminals of the power supply. Without a safety fuse, some rechargeable batteries can deliver tens of amps and set fire to plastic insulation on wires when short-circuited.

Building experimental circuits from components is best done on a 'solderless breadboard', a plastic base with holes into which you can insert the wire leads of components (Figure 11.14). Hidden underneath the holes are spring clips attached to conductive strips that make connections between components plugged into holes in the same column. Further details are beyond the scope of this book, but again your safety is important. For example, an LED used to act as an indicator can develop a gas bubble within its plastic encapsulation and explode if connected directly to the power supply.

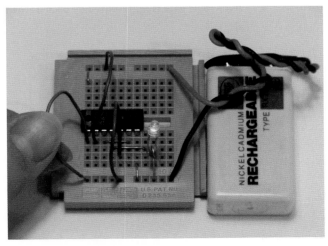

**Figure 11.14** A solderless breadboard.

## Summary

- A logic gate is an electronic circuit that processes two-state signals according to a logical rule.
- A logic circuit, consisting of two or more connected gates, can process logical expressions and binary numbers.
- Unless otherwise stated, we associate True with 1 and On, and False with 0 and Off.
- The five simplest types of logic gate are: AND, OR, NOT, NAND and NOR.
- A truth table is used to show the output of a logic gate or circuit for all possible combinations of inputs; we usually use the binary values 1 and 0 as shorthand for True and False.
- Truth tables need four rows for two-input gates or circuits (00 to 11 in binary) and eight rows for three-input gates or circuits (000 to 111 in binary).
- When producing a truth table for a circuit, it is helpful to include a column for intermediate outputs as well as for the final outputs.
- We can use the names of the gates as operators in a logical equation, such as L = (A AND B) OR NOT B, with brackets to indicate which logical operation takes priority.
- We can design a logic circuit to solve a written logical statement of a problem, by rewriting the statement with brackets to clarify the binary value for each variable and the priority of logical operations or as a logical equation.
- We can draw up a truth table or use simulation software to check that a logic circuit solves a stated problem.

## Examination practice for Paper 1

### Exam Questions

1. Draw a logic circuit and truth table for the following logic problem:

   "A sprinkler (S) is **on** if
      EITHER temperature alarm (T) is **on** AND cooler alarm (C) is **on**
      OR vent alarm (V) is **off** AND cooler alarm (C) is **on**"
   Show your working before you draw your logic circuit.

   [9]

   *Question 12, Cambridge IGCSE Computer Studies 0420/01 Paper 1 Specimen for 2011*

### Exam-Style Questions

1. Which logic gate is represented by each of the following truth tables?

   **(a)**

   [1]

   | Input A | Input B | Output |
   |---------|---------|--------|
   | 0 | 0 | 1 |
   | 0 | 1 | 1 |
   | 1 | 0 | 1 |
   | 1 | 1 | 0 |

→

**(b)** [1]

| Input A | Input B | Output |
|---------|---------|--------|
| 0 | 0 | 0 |
| 0 | 1 | 1 |
| 1 | 0 | 1 |
| 1 | 1 | 1 |

2. Complete a truth table for the following networks.

**(a)** [2]

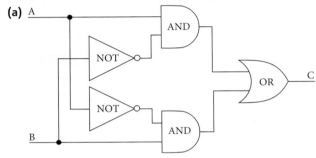

**(b)** [4]

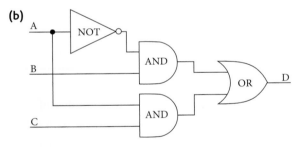

3. Design logic circuits using two-input gates for the following logical statements. Show your working before you draw the table and check your network by producing a truth table.

(a) The boiler (B) will be **on**, if EITHER the timer (C) is **on** AND the temperature sensor (T) is **off**, OR the timer (C) is **off** AND the frost sensor (F) is **on**. [11]

(b) The wheelchair propulsion motor (M) is **on**, if the power switch (P) is **on** AND EITHER the forward switch (F) is **on** AND the reverse switch (R) is **off** OR the forward switch (F) is **off** AND the reverse switch (R) is **on**. [10]

# Appendix A – Paper 3 scenario

In this question you are asked to read about an existing manual, paper-based stock control system in a large garage. It is the intention that a computer-based semi-automatic stock control system is introduced as a replacement. You will be given a full description of both the present manual method and the intended new computerised scheme.

## Description of the existing system

When a customer comes into the garage to buy a spare part for his car, the salesman asks a clerk to go to a filing cabinet where he or she would be able to locate the appropriate files containing all the necessary part details. The information stored on these paper files includes:

- part number;
- part description;
- price of the part;
- number of items in stock;
- minimum re-order level;
- details of the suppliers;
- location of spare part in the warehouse.

The salesman then goes to the warehouse to locate the part. The customer pays for the item and the salesman makes out an invoice and gives one copy to the customer and a second copy is given to a filing clerk. At the end of the day, the clerk processes all the invoices, records the money taken and updates the number of each item in stock. The clerk fills out and sends off the order forms for any items which are running low in number. All transactions are currently carried out on paper and stored in files in several large filing cabinets.

## Description of the proposed computer-based system

The intention is to replace all the paperwork by introducing a computer-based database, which contains all the information described above, but automatically prints out new orders at the end of the day.

A systems analyst is to be employed to review the existing manual method. The analyst will be responsible for drawing up an action plan for the new computer-based system. This will then be designed, tested and implemented. All the necessary documentation will also be produced together with a full evaluation of the system performance 6 months after its introduction.

In the new system, when a customer asks for a part, the salesman pulls up the following information on a computer screen:

---

### SELECTAPART SYSTEM V2.2

Please select from the following options:

- Interior
- Engine
- Gearbox and transmission
- Brakes
- Suspension
- Electric equipment

---

Once a selection is made, a number of spare parts are listed on the screen together with a diagram of the part. The required part is then identified and the salesman *clicks* on the diagram using a mouse and all the information about the selected part is displayed on the screen.

The salesman then locates the spare part, which is now identified with a barcode (which is the same as the part number). When sold, the barcode is read by a barcode reader and the number in stock is automatically checked and updated on the database. The value of the daily takings is also automatically updated.

When the minimum stock level for a part is reached, an order is automatically printed out together with the name and address of the supplier. When new stock arrives the barcodes are read and the database automatically updated.

*Scenario and text taken from Question 1 Cambridge IGCSE Computer Studies 0420/03 Specimen Paper 3 2011*

# Answers to SAQs

## Chapter 1

### SAQ 1
a  A word processor.
b  A DTP program.

### SAQ 2
A relational database application would be appropriate because records of three different sorts of things are needed, linked by relationships.

### SAQ 3
You might think that a poster can only be printed, but a modern poster might be an electronic one, used on a large LCD screen with speakers. So the answer is presentation application (to cater for the sound).

### SAQ 4
You need to customise your word processor by creating a macro that can be called up every time you want to delete multiple new lines. Rather than write your own macro, use the word processor's 'Find and Replace' facility

## Chapter 2

### SAQ 1
Shirt type (football, tennis, basketball, etc.), price in dollars, size (M, L, XL, etc.).

### SAQ 2
a  The verification method cannot detect this error because the transposed characters 5 and 0 result in $5 \times 3 + 0 \times 1 = 15$, compared to the correct value $0 \times 3 + 5 \times 1 = 5$. The difference is 10, so it still gives result modulo 10 as 0.

b  The verification method can detect this error because the incorrect character 7 does not give result modulo 10 of 0.
c  The verification method can detect this error because the calculated check digit of 5 does not match the received check digit of 0.

### SAQ 3
If the field's data type were text/string, it would be accepted as a string but might still fail a format check. If the data type were integer, it would fail the type check because 78.123 is a real number.

### SAQ 4
a  `CapitalLookup[6, 1]`.
b  Kabul.

## Chapter 3

### SAQ 1
The limited speed of thinking and typing of the human operator.

### SAQ 2
a  Look at the design of the entire keyboard: is all the detail included (length, width, height and required number of each type of timber)? Also look for extra things such as method of payment.
b  Details such as the address for delivery need characters to be typed in. The alphabet could feature on the concept keyboard. Does this make the keyboard confused or is there plenty of space? If the business has a customer file then the address will be on it and access to the file can be via a button on the concept keyboard. (There are problems with this that you could consider, such as a new customer or different address.)

## SAQ 3

An automatic data capture method is using the phone's camera to read a QR Code or other two-dimensional barcode containing a URL or other address, or a phone number. The phone may also be able to receive data stored on another phone or on a computer via a Bluetooth connection.

## SAQ 4

There is no 'right' answer. You could argue that a mechanical mouse would be sensible because it is connected to the computer and hence is not going to go missing. However, in the dusty conditions of a timber yard, it might well become clogged up with sawdust. It would be used for many things but basically for defining the position on the screen at which the user wants the cursor to be. A scroll wheel can be used to move through the customer file quickly; a button can be used to select a particular customer, and so on.

## SAQ 5

a  A mechanical mouse is unreliable because of the environment in which it is used; an optical mouse is mechanically more reliable but needs a visually textured surface beneath it; it is also susceptible to vandalism and the firm 'loses' them.

b  The standard advantages and disadvantages in the text are relevant, especially because they are less vulnerable to vandalism or theft than a mouse, but still likely to become clogged with sawdust.

## SAQ 6

There are many appropriate responses. One would be to control the positioning of a circular saw when it is cutting the timber. This can then be done from a distance, which is safer, and also allows for finer adjustments to be made.

## SAQ 7

Touchscreens are difficult to vandalise compared with something like a mouse. They can be made reasonably weatherproof so can be in the open air, on a station platform, for example. They need no computer knowledge to be able to operate them.

A disadvantage is that it is difficult to point precisely using a stylus, which can easily get lost or damaged.

## SAQ 8

It can be viewed on a screen, emailed, edited, digitally archived, projected, used as wallpaper on a computer, etc.

## SAQ 9

A timber yard might use webcams to monitor vehicles entering and leaving and to monitor the buildings remotely at night.

## SAQ 10

Speech-to-text conversion may improve speed and ease of data entry for office workers. It can also open up jobs to disabled people. The difficulty of using voice entry of data in a potentially noisy environment can make it unsuitable; not all data lends itself to this form of entry; and there are issues over reliability.

## SAQ 11

a  OCR software compares the pixel patterns in the bitmap of a scanned document with its stored bitmaps of characters and whenever a character is matched, the computer stores it. It is used for the input of data from existing paper documents, because it is much quicker than retyping them.

b  OMR software recognises simple marks in specific positions on the bitmap of a scanned image of a paper form. It is used for capturing data from multiple-choice questionnaires, as it is faster and more accurate than transcribing answers by hand.

c  MICR software recognises strings of characters printed in magnetic ink from magnetic scans. It is used to read account numbers and sort codes on cheques, because it can read characters accurately even if they have been obscured for the human reader by visible marks and printing in magnetic ink is harder to forge.

## SAQ 12

Thermometers cannot be used for control; they provide visual output for a human. The system would use a temperature sensor. The sensor would not make any decisions; this would be done by a computer. The heater would be controlled by the computer using an actuator such as a relay. The sensor is electrical but has an insulating cover that protects it from the water.

## SAQ 13

**a**  A dot matrix printer has pins that tap an inked ribbon against paper. It is used in industrial environments where noise is less important and multiple copies are required.

**b**  An inkjet printer squirts minute droplets of ink from one or more jets on to paper. A high-quality version is used for printing photographs as it can achieve high-resolution printing with a wide range of colours.

**c**  A laser printer uses a laser to scan the surface of a drum leaving the required image as a pattern of electric charge which picks up toner particles and deposits them onto paper where they are baked on by heated rollers. It is used for producing business documents because of its high speed and low cost of toner per copy.

**d**  A plotter draws graphics with a pen or cutter. This is used for making precision drawings or cut-outs of vector graphics as it is the only sort of printer that moves a pen or cutter in direct response to a vector graphic file.

## SAQ 14

**a**  A school computer has 3 **gigabytes** of memory.

**b**  A byte is a unit of computer **internal memory** or **backing storage** and it consists of **eight** bits.

## SAQ 15

16 bits, 1.5 MB, 2048 KB, 1.2 GB, 1 terabyte.

## SAQ 16

When the user or a program issues a command to open a specific file in a specific folder, the file system uses the relevant directory file to look up the logical address of the file. The disk drive's electronics uses the logical address to calculate the physical address of the start of the file on the disk.

## SAQ 17

No. They can only be written to once. So every time a backup was needed a new disk would have to be used. This would incur the expense of buying the disks and managing their storage, as it would be tempting to keep them rather than shred them after a reasonable time.

## SAQ 18

A netbook with solid-state storage would be more robust and possibly provide faster access than the hard disk equivalent.

# Chapter 4

## SAQ 1

When the computer is switched back on, part of the operating system's job is to look around to see what is connected to the computer. If it finds more memory, it will assume it is for use and allocate it as available. It will also see the new disk, find the software to control it (the driver) and offer to format it if blank.

## SAQ 2

Computer X needs an operating system that supports real-time process control, in order to receive and store data from multiple sensors and send control signals to actuators frequently and at regular intervals. It must also support network operation, since the sensors and actuators are likely to be connected to a network rather than each directly connected to a port on the computer and Computer X needs to be connected to Computer Y for data download.

Computer Y needs a batch operating system also with network operation, since it must efficiently process downloaded files of previously collected data without any need for user input.

## SAQ 3

The printer signals to the PC that the transmission failed. The PC re-sends the data. If the checksum agrees this time, then the printer prints the photo. If the checksum is wrong again, it is re-sent again. This is repeated for a fixed number of times by the operating system before it gives up.

Senine doesn't need to do anything – retransmissions are under the control of the operating system. It is only when the maximum number of repeats has been reached that Senine is informed by an error message that transmission failed. Senine might consider changing the WLAN access point's channel and transmission power or moving the printer closer to the PC and retrying.

# Chapter 5

### SAQ 1

A bank may print monthly bank statements as a batch process.

A business may invoice their customers once a month. Only then are the totals calculated.

### SAQ 2

Dedicated sound and graphics cards have their own processor and relieve the main processor of the intensive load associated with sound and graphics.

### SAQ 3

Video files (such as MPEG, WMV, AVI, MOV, MP4, FLV and H.264) are very large. If you are editing video, you have a lot of raw data to work with. Typically, you need several hundred gigabytes of backing storage – even 2 or 3 terabytes is now affordable. A school or college may have a file server of 20–30 terabytes or more in the video-editing suite.

# Chapter 6

### SAQ 1

The feasibility study and the requirements specification must be agreed before moving on to the next stage. Any reasons for disagreement have to be sorted out and the documents revised until the client agrees their content. If they can't be agreed, then the project would be terminated.

### SAQ 2

Development is quicker because several modules can be developed in parallel by different programmers. In testing, it is easier for the programmer who coded the module to fix any errors.

### SAQ 3

The rewritten code would need annotation to explain how it worked. The technical documentation would need amending to explain how data is passed to the following module. The user documentation would need amending to show the change to the user interface.

### SAQ 4

Deployment, rollout, adoption. Alternatively switchover, conversion, transfer.

### SAQ 5

Direct changeover.

### SAQ 6

Direct changeover.

### SAQ 7

**a** The support staff will have looked at the technical documentation (and possibly the original requirements specification) to check whether the system was designed to do what the user tried.

**b** The problem can be addressed in two ways depending on what the user was trying to do. If it is not generally useful, then the bug report will be closed. A known error log will be kept so that if any other users try the same thing, it is not re-investigated. If the user was trying to do something that is generally useful, it will be added to the list of functionality changes (enhancements) to be made to the system. The change will need to be developed, tested, and implemented at some point during a maintenance period.

# Chapter 7

### SAQ 1

A broadband data transfer rate of 5.6 Mbps is $5,600,000 \div 56,000 = 100$ times the maximum rate of a dial-up connection.

### SAQ 2

You can be sure that the transaction is secure if the web browser shows a closed padlock symbol and the URL starts https://.

### SAQ 3

EFT stands for electronic funds transfer.
POS stands for point of sale.
ATM stands for automatic teller machine.
PIN stands for personal identification number.

## SAQ 4

Supermarkets do not like being paid in cash because cash is bulky and difficult to trace if stolen. It is also relatively expensive to handle because it must be stored and transported under conditions of high security.

## SAQ 5

The benefit to banks of the increasing use of EFT is that these transactions are easier and cheaper to process than cash or cheque transactions.

## SAQ 6

The advantages of simulations are that they are usually cheaper than constructing prototypes and safer because they enable trainees to gain experience of a situation without putting anyone at risk.

## SAQ 7

Movement sensors ignore small animals in two ways. Some sensors respond in proportion to the size of the intruder and only raise the alarm if the intruder is over a certain size. They usually have a sensitivity control to adjust this. Other sensors only cover the region above waist height.

## SAQ 8

To make computerised meteorological measurements, you need a temperature sensor, a pressure sensor, an anemometer, a rain gauge, a humidity sensor and a light sensor. You would mount these sensors on a roof or some other point where the sensors will not be shielded from the weather conditions.

## SAQ 9

A temperature sensor and a light sensor.

## SAQ 10

The times of day for data sampling and the overall length of time over which sampling will occur.

## SAQ 11

A doctor who uses a medical expert system may be more accurate and faster in diagnosing less common illnesses from a set of symptoms. It may also be possible to make some parts of the expert system available to patients to act as a triage or screening process, so that only patients who really need to see the doctor do so.

## SAQ 12

Iron ore can be detected by using a magnetometer to look for local anomalies in the Earth's magnetic field over a region of its surface. The correlation between such data and the likely presence of the ore can be recorded in the expert system's rule base. Iron ore also can be detected by chemical tests on rock samples obtained by digging or drilling.

## SAQ 13

To find information about a character in a Shakespeare play, I would enter the name of the character, the word 'Shakespeare' and the name of the play in quotes. For example, Prospero Shakespeare "The Tempest"

# Chapter 8

## SAQ 1

Essential hardware requirements for working at home as a salesperson are a telephone, a computer and an Internet or private WAN connection.

## SAQ 2

Regularly look away from the screen. Regularly blink to moisten their surfaces. Looking away from the screen also relaxes eye muscles, but this is not recommended for racing drivers, real or virtual!

## SAQ 3

Data privacy means not having an organisation's or individual's information disclosed to others. Data security refers to not only maintaining the privacy of data, but also ensuring that they are not lost or corrupted.

## SAQ 4

First, restart your computer. If you suspect that a virus has infected your computer, disconnect it from the Internet. Use anti-virus software to run a full scan on your computer. If necessary, download up-to-date anti-virus software onto a USB drive and run it on your computer from the USB drive. Alternatively, perform a System Restore to a restore point, perform a complete restoration from a system image, or reinstall your operating system and applications and restore your data from a backup copy.

# Chapter 9

### SAQ 1
Use standard symbols. Place inputs on the left, processes in the middle and outputs on the right.

### SAQ 2
Understand the problem, devise a solution, document the solution, test the solution.

### SAQ 3
If we don't set clear limits to the facilities that the solution will provide, we may end up doing far more than we need to in the solution. We are limiting ourselves to a sensible solution.

# Chapter 10

### SAQ 1
It is quicker and easier to write complex programs in a high-level language. Such programs are also easier to debug and are portable between different operating systems and processors.

### SAQ 2
Source code is written in a high-level language or assembly language and is not directly executable, although a high-level language program can be executed by an interpreter program. A compiler or assembler program converts source code into object code, machine code that is executable.

### SAQ 3
An assembler translates a low-level assembly language program into machine code – a compiler translates a high-level program into machine code. An assembler translates one assembly language instruction into one machine code instruction – a compiler translates one high-level program statement into many machine code instructions.

### SAQ 4
It is better to use a low-level language (assembly language, or possibly machine language) rather than a high-level language where it is important that the machine code program fits into limited storage space, requires limited RAM as workspace or runs rapidly, or where the program needs to interact directly with the hardware or operate in real-time.

### SAQ 5
The most obvious loop to use is a `FOR ...TO... NEXT` loop but all the types of loop are available:

```
FOR Count ← 1 TO 10000
    PRINT Count
NEXT
```

Or:

```
Count ← 1
WHILE Count <= 10000
    DO
        PRINT Count
        Count ← Count + 1
ENDWHILE
```

Or:

```
Count ← 1
REPEAT
    PRINT Count
    Count ← Count + 1
UNTIL Count > 10000
```

### SAQ 6

```
IF Total >= 40
    THEN
        WRITE "Pass"
    ELSE
        WRITE "Fail"
ENDIF
```

# Chapter 11

### SAQ 1
A NAND gate is a combination of an AND gate followed by a NOT gate. A NOR gate is a combination of an OR gate followed by a NOT gate.

# Glossary

## A

**Access rights** Permissions given to a user to control access to files.

**Actuator** Device used by a computer to move machinery in a control system.

**Adware** Software that displays adverts on the user's computer.

**Algorithm** A sequence of steps to solve a problem.

**Alphanumeric string** A string of alphabetic letters and numerals only, such as a name, phone number or product code.

**Analogue data** Real-world data that smoothly model even small changes, such as output from a temperature sensor.

**Analogue-to-digital converter (ADC)** Device that changes analogue data to digital data so that they can be processed by a computer system.

**Anti-virus software** Software that identifies computer viruses and deals with them by not allowing them access to files or by erasing them. It usually protects against other forms of malware.

**Application software** Programs that allow people to use the computer to perform a specific task.

**Array** Data structure that stores items of a single type that can be referred to by one or more indices or subscripts.

**Artificial intelligence** The facility within some expert systems that enables them to modify their knowledge and rule bases so that they can learn from experience.

**Assembler** Software which is used to translate the instructions written in an assembly language into the computer's machine code.

**Assembly language** A low-level language which uses short words and abbreviations as mnemonics for machine code instructions.

**Attribute** A specific type of data representing a particular characteristic of each data record. Also known as a field or column.

**Authoring package** See Multimedia authoring program and Web authoring program.

**Automated system** A system that carries out control tasks with limited interactivity.

**Automated teller machine (ATM)** A 'cash point' machine used to withdraw cash or manage a bank account, on the street or in a shopping centre.

**Automatic data capture** The use of automated devices and methods for data input without human intervention.

**Automatic stock control system** A computerised system that records sales and deliveries and automatically reorders fresh stock.

**Auxiliary storage** See Backing storage.

## B

**Backing storage** Long-term, non-volatile storage for programs and data.

**Backup** Term applied to a copy of a data file, stored separately from the computer's main backing storage (preferably at another site in case of fire, theft or natural disaster), that can be used to restore the file if data are lost.

**Barcode** A machine-readable series of black and white lines representing an ID code.

**Barcode reader** A combination of optical or infrared scanner and software used to read barcodes – can be fixed or hand-held.

**Batch operating system** An operating system that manages a succession of batch jobs.

**Batch processing system** A system in which data are prepared as a batch job at a convenient, later, time without any interaction between the user and the running program and its data.

**Bespoke software** Software written to suit the needs of a particular client.

**Biometric data** Data captured about a person's physical or behavioural characteristics. They can be stored in a database and used for authentication of someone's claimed identity or as the sole means of identification.

**Bit** A single binary digit, which can take the value 0 or 1.

**Bit stream** A series of bits over time. A live broadcast is distributed as a stream. A stream may be captured from an input device and stored as a file and later 'streamed' for distribution.

**Bitmap graphic** A digital representation of an image in which the colour of each pixel in an array is mapped to a number stored in a file.

**Block (of data)** A sequence of bytes of a standard length that is transmitted and stored as a unit.

**Blog** Short for 'web log', a website with occasional entries, like a diary.

**Bluetooth** A trademark indicating that a product conforms with a widely-used WPAN protocol.

**Boolean data type** A data type that accepts input representing just two alternatives e.g. True/False.

**Broadband** A high data transfer rate or high-speed connection to the Internet.

**Buffer** An area of memory used for the temporary storage of data.

**Bus network** A network in which the devices are all connected to a common cable.

**Byte** A group of eight bits, used as a unit of memory and backing storage.

## C

**Central processing unit (CPU)** The main processor or processing chip of a computer, which manipulates the data.

**Changeover** The process of installing and commissioning a new system to replace an old system.

**Character check** A validation check that a string of characters does not contain invalid characters or symbols.

**Checksum** A summary value that is calculated from a block of data.

**Chip and PIN** The UK name for an international standard for the use of smart cards to improve the security of debit and credit card transactions.

**Circuit** An assembly of electronic components, logic gates or communication channels.

**Client** A computer or application program that uses a service provided by a server.

**Codec** Compression and decompression software that compresses (saves space) the stream of transmitted data and decompresses (recovers the data from) the stream of received data compressed by the sender.

**Combinatorial logic circuit** A logic circuit without feedback from output to input, whose one or more outputs depend only on their current inputs. Also known as a combinational logic circuit.

**Command line interface (CLI)** An interface between the computer and the user in which a screen displays text without graphics and the user can only input commands with a keyboard.

**Compiler** Software that translates an entire program written in a high-level language into a computer's machine code.

**Computer** An automatic, programmable, electronic data processing device.

**Computer-aided design (CAD)** The process of using a computer to design an item.

**Computer-aided engineering (CAE)** The process of using computer simulation to check the design of a structure before construction or manufacture.

**Computer-aided manufacture (CAM)** The process of using a computer to control the automatic manufacture of an item.

**Computer-assisted learning (CAL)** The process of using computers to learn at a self-paced rate from presentations, often with computer-based assessment questions and feedback of results.

**Computer-based learning** The use of computers for interactive learning activities, including computer-assisted learning and computer-based training.

**Computer-based training (CBT)** Similar to computer-assisted learning, but usually for training in work skills rather than academic learning.

**Conditional statement** A structured statement for controlling selection, which is a decision between alternative routes through the algorithm.

**Consistency check** A validation check that different fields in the same record correspond correctly (for example, title and gender). Also known as a cross field check.

**Control application** Application in which one or more computers are used as part of a control system.

**Control system** One or more computers used to regulate the operation of other devices.

**Cookie** A small text file in which a web browser stores data that enable a web server to recognise the user the next time that their browser requests a web page from the server.

**Corruption** Unwanted changes to data.

**CRT monitor** An older and bulkier type of computer monitor that contains a cathode-ray tube.

**Currency data type** A data type that accepts numerical input and enables appropriate processing, storage and formatting for display as a value of a specific currency (for example, with a dollar symbol and two digits after the decimal point).

**Customised software** Generic software that has been altered to suit the needs of a particular customer.

# D

**Data** The items we give to a computer as its input, which it holds and processes as binary numerical codes.

**Data capture** The process by which data actually enter the computer. It may be manual or automatic.

**Data collection** The process of gathering data, often on paper forms, ready for entry into a computer.

**Data dictionary** A table listing field names, data types, validation and other relevant information for each field in each table of a database. It may be produced in either or both of the analysis and design stages.

**Data glove** An input device containing sensors that detect the movements of the user's hand and fingers. Input data from the glove is processed to reproduce the movements of the user's hand in a VR environment.

**Data goggles** An output device used in a VR system to display stereoscopic 3-D images and, with headphones, deliver stereophonic sound. May also contain motion sensors to enable computer to track motion of the user's head and display appropriate images.

**Data logging** Automatic data capture used to record data automatically for scientific, engineering and statistical purposes, usually at regular intervals of time.

**Data protection act** The name typically given to a law that requires organisations to keep personal data secure and private.

**Data storage** The process of holding data. The term is usually applied to holding data in backing storage or non-volatile internal memory, but sometimes even in volatile internal memory (RAM).

**Data structure** A complex data type that consists of a number of data items of one or more simpler data types.

**Data type** A specification of the type of data to be entered in a particular context, so that an application program can process, store and display the data items appropriately.

**Database** An organised collection of related data that can be accessed by a variety of application programs.

**Database management system (DBMS)** Software that manages a database.

**Dataflow diagram (DFD)** A diagram that shows where data came from, where they are stored, how they are processed and where they go in a system.

**Date/time data type** A data type that accepts input representing a date alone, a time alone or a date and time, and enables processing and storage as a real number in units of days and appropriate formatting for display.

**De-skilling** The effect on workers whose skills are no longer valued because they are performed by new technology.

**Dial-up connection** A slow link to the Internet, based on analogue telephone lines.

**Digital data** Data in binary numerical form, suitable for processing and storage on a computer.

**Digital media sharing website** A Web 2.0 site that enables users to share image, video and sound files.

**Digital-to-analogue converter (DAC)** A device that changes digital data to analogue data so that it can be used to drive a display, loudspeaker or actuator.

**Digitisation** The process of converting analogue data to digital data.

**Direct access file** A file than can be accessed using an algorithm to generate a record's disk address from the record's key value, making access to a randomly chosen record very fast. Also known as a random file.

**Direct access medium** A magnetic disk or optical disk storage medium for which the drive's read/write head can travel straight to the correct track on the surface of the medium, enabling rapid access to files.

**Dot matrix printer** A relatively slow, noisy device that prints characters by pins striking an inked ribbon against paper to make a pattern of relatively large dots.

**Double entry** A verification check in which the data are entered twice, the program compares the two inputs and only accepts them if they match; for example, when setting up or changing a password.

**Drum plotter** A plotter device that uses one or more pens to make marks on paper as it passes over a drum. Many modern drum 'plotters' are actually inkjet printers that spray ink droplets onto the paper.

**Dry run** A run-through in a programmer's mind of an algorithm, a step at a time, to test its performance. A trace table is often used to record the inputs, variables and outputs at each stage.

**DTP (desktop publishing) software** Application software that allows the import of text and graphics and complex layout on the pages of publications such as newsletters and magazines.

# E

**E-commerce** The use of the Internet for commercial activities such as Internet banking and shopping.

**Electronic funds transfer (EFT)** The process by which money is transferred from one bank account to another, by computer.

**Electronic funds transfer at the point of sale (EFTPOS)** The process by which money is transferred at the checkout from a customer's bank account to the shop's bank account, by computer.

**Element** An item in an array of data.

**Email** Electronic mail.

**Embedded object** A file that is incorporated into another file but remains editable in its original application program.

**Encoded data** Data that have been abbreviated to ID or category codes to simplify entry and storage in the computer.

**Encryption** Secret encoding, or scrambling, of data during transmission in order to keep them private. Before reading, the encrypted data must be decrypted.

**Even parity** An even number of ones in a byte, agreed between sender and receiver as part of a parity check.

**Expert system** A computer program that aims to achieve the problem-solving competence of a human expert in a specific task area by using the knowledge and rules of inference gathered from one or more human experts.

**Exporting** Saving a version of a file in a format that can be read by another program. This enables file transfer between applications with different native (standard) file formats.

**Extranet** An intranet that is externally accessible over the Internet by authorised users.

# F

**Feedback** Measurements of the results of a control process fed back as input to optimise control under varying conditions.

**Field** A part of a record that holds data of a specific type about one characteristic of the subject of the record.

**File** A collection of related data.

**File directory** An index of the contents of each drive or folder that enables the operating system's file manager to locate files or sub-directories for sub-folders on a storage drive.

**File maintenance** Processing of a file that is not part of routine transaction processing and involves inserting, updating and deleting records.

**File manager** Software in an operating system that enables the user to navigate folders and sub-folders, and list, open, move, copy and print files.

**Fingerprint reader** A combination of fingerprint scanner and software that captures the print of a finger placed on it and identifies features for comparison with one or more database records.

**Firewall** Software, possibly with separate hardware, that blocks unwanted communication with a computer or LAN, through a WAN, especially the Internet; it stops viruses and unauthorised access to the system.

**Firmware** Software stored in non-volatile memory, such as a simple operating system or control program for an automated system.

**Flatbed plotter** A plotter device that uses one or more pens to draw lines on a sheet of paper lying on a flat surface.

**Folder** A virtual container for files, provided by the operating system's file manager and used to organise files on backing storage.

**Format check** A validation check that a string of characters has the required pattern or 'format'. Also known as a picture check.

**Formatting of data for display** Settings of the properties of an object, such as the font name, style and size of some text, the alignment of a paragraph or the margins of a section of a word-processed document.

# G

**Gantt chart** A diagram used for project management that shows project tasks and their dependencies in the form of a calendar.

**Gateway** Hardware and software that allow communication between different types of network.

**Generic application software** Software that enables a user to carry out a variety of similar tasks. Examples are word processing, spreadsheet and database application programs. Off-the-shelf software is not necessarily generic.

**Graphical object** 1. An object in a GUI, such as a text box in a DTP program. 2. In a vector graphics file, part of a drawing whose numerical properties are stored, and can be edited, separately.

**Graphical user interface (GUI)** A user interface that uses windows to display application programs, icons to represent commands and files, menus to give access to lists of commands and a pointer to select menu options and draw, select or move objects. Hence, sometimes called a WIMP interface.

**Graphics tablet** An input device consisting of a large, smooth surface containing sensors that produce signals representing the touch of a stylus. Used as a pointing device for drawing and editing graphics.

# H

**Hacking** Unauthorised access to a computer system.

**Handshaking** The process by which two devices negotiate the protocol (rules) they will use to communicate for the rest of the session, or signal their readiness to send or receive data.

**Hard disk** A non-removable, rigid, magnetic disk medium. It is currently the dominant storage medium for computers from laptops upwards.

**Hard disk drive (HDD)** A magnetic storage device that spins one or more hard disks and controls access to the surfaces through read/write heads.

**Hardware** The physical parts of a computer system.

**Head-mounted display (HMD)** A helmet-like version of data goggles.

**Headphones** A sound output device, consisting of miniature loudspeakers, worn over the user's ears, for personal listening.

**High-level language** A programming language most similar to a human language or mathematical notation and therefore easiest for a person to code.

**Hub** Central node of a star network or sub-network to which each node (computer or network-enabled device) is connected. Data transmitted by one node are re-broadcast to all the other nodes.

**Hyperlink** Text or image on a web page or other document that acts as an automatic reference, allowing the user to navigate to another point in a long page or to another resource. When the user clicks on the hyperlink, the web browser or other application program displays the target resource.

## I

**Immediate access store (IAS)** See Internal memory.

**Importing** Bringing into the user's work the whole of another data file, often from a different application program.

**Index** An integer value that enables a programmer to refer to an element in an array.

**Inference engine** Part of an expert system that processes the user's problem using the contents of the knowledge and rule bases.

**Information** The result of processing data to give them context and meaning and make them understandable.

**Information retrieval software** Application programs for searching for information as whole documents, within documents and about documents, in databases and in the Web.

**Inkjet printer** A device that prints precise characters and images on paper by spraying tiny droplets of ink.

**Input device** Equipment used to put data into the computer.

**Installation** The process of unpacking software files and copying them onto a computer's internal storage device.

**Instant messaging (IM)** An Internet service that enables users to exchange text messages in real-time.

**Instruction set** The instructions for all the operations that a family of processors performs. It can be thought of as the language in which machine code programs are written for that family of processors.

**Integer** A number (numeric) data type consisting of a whole number that is positive, negative, or zero.

**Integer data type** A numeric data type consisting of a whole number that is positive, negative, or zero.

**Integrated development environment (IDE)** A single application program for writing, compiling and debugging program code.

**Integrity** The completeness and correctness of data during processing, storage, copying and transmission.

**Interactive system** A computer system that provides immediate feedback to the user so that they can influence processing.

**Interactivity** Opportunities for someone using a website to interact with and change what is displayed.

**Internal memory** Electronic device that holds the instructions and data for one or more programs that the processor is currently running. Access is extremely rapid. There are two sorts: RAM and ROM. Also known as Main memory.

**Internet** A global WAN to which organisations and individuals can gain access through an ISP. It consists of many interconnected networks and contains servers that provide a variety of services, only one of which is the World Wide Web.

**Internet service provider (ISP)** A company that provides customers with a connection to the Internet for a subscription.

**Interpreter** A translation program that translates statements of a high-level language program, usually one statement at a time, and executes them on the target processor but does not create machine code.

**Interrupt** A signal sent from a peripheral device (hardware) or program event (software) to the processor to indicate that the sender needs attention.

**Intranet** Web-based services on a LAN.

**Iris scanner** A specialised camera, often using IR illumination, that can capture an image of the iris in a person's eye.

**Iteration** The process of repeating a sequence of steps.

## J

**Joystick** An input device consisting of a lever connected to sensors, used for steering in automated control of an aircraft or vehicle or as a pointing device in simulations and games.

## K

**Key (field)** See Record key.

**Knowledge base** The store of facts to which an expert system's inference engine applies the rules in its rule base to solve a problem.

## L

**Laser printer** A high-speed device that prints precise characters and images on paper by using a laser to modify the electrostatic charge pattern that attracts toner particles to a drum, transfers the particles to a sheet of paper and fuses them on with heated rollers.

**LCD monitor** A computer monitor that uses a liquid-crystal display.

**LED** Light-emitting diode. It is used as an output device to provide illumination and also as an indicator.

**Length check** A validation check that the number of input characters in a string is within specified limits.

**Library file** A set of program modules that can be re-used in new programs.

**Limit check** A validation check that a numerical, currency or date/time data item lies within a single minimum or maximum limit.

**Local area network (LAN)** A number of computers or other suitably enabled devices on a single site, connected by cables or short-range wireless links.

**Logic circuit** An electronic circuit in which the output of a logic gate forms an input to one or more other gates for further processing.

**Logic gate** A relatively simple, digital, electronic circuit that processes two-state signals according to a logical rule. It has one or more inputs and a single output.

**Logic level** One of two voltage signal values for a family of logic gates: high and low. Each logic level is represented by a specified range of 'legal' voltages.

**Loop** Another term for iteration (or repetition), originating from the loop drawn in a program flowchart when control is passed back to an earlier step.

**Loudspeaker** An output device that uses an electromagnet linked to a conical diaphragm to produce audible vibrations of the air from an analogue electrical signal. Its sound output can be heard by many people at once.

## M

**Machine code** A sequence of binary codes representing processor instructions, which is the only form in which a processor can run a computer program. It is written in machine language.

**Machine language** The lowest level of programming language, in which machine code is written. The machine language for a particular family of processor consists of its instruction set.

**Macro** A small piece of program code that can be run by clicking a toolbar button or pressing a keyboard shortcut. Macros are used to customise software.

**Magnetic disk** A revolving-disk, magnetic storage medium to which a suitable drive provides direct access.

**Magnetic ink character recognition (MICR)** The use of software to read human-readable numerals and symbols printed in magnetic ink rapidly and reliably from data from a magnetic scanner.

**Magnetic storage device** A backing storage device, known as a drive, that uses a medium consisting of a coating of magnetisable material on a suitable surface. Data are written and read in the medium using an electromagnetic read/write head.

**Magnetic stripe** A strip of magnetic material on various sorts of plastic and paper card that stores machine-readable data about the purpose of the card.

**Magnetic tape** Plastic tape coated with magnetisable material that acts as a serial access backing storage medium. A tape cartridge is a removable medium used for making backup copies of data.

**Mail merge** Combining standard text for a letter or catalogue from one file with name and address or other information from a database file.

**Mainframe computer** An organisation's large, central computer that provides processing power and data storage for many users, who gain access through terminal devices.

**Malware** Malicious, that is harmfully intended, software of all sorts, including but not restricted to, viruses.

**Manual input device** A device (such as a keyboard or mouse) that enables a person to enter data into a computer by hand.

**Memory stick** See USB flash drive.

**Menu** A list of command options.

**Merging files** Combining the contents of two sequential files into a new sequential file.

**MICR** See Magnetic ink character recognition.

**Microcomputer** A term for a desktop-sized computer that has been largely replaced by the term personal computer (PC).

**Microcontroller** An integrated circuit that combines a microprocessor with memory, backing storage and other circuitry to form a computer-on-a-chip.

**Microphone** An input device that converts sound vibrations into an analogue electrical signal.

**Microprocessor** A single integrated circuit or silicon chip that contains many sets of circuitry required by a computer to manipulate its data. The term is usually shortened to processor.

**Modem** A dial-up modem is a device used to modulate a carrier tone on an analogue phone landline with a stream of digital data transmitted by a computer and to demodulate received signals to obtain a digital data stream. Similar devices are used for sending and receiving broadband digital data on a suitably equipped landline, a TV distribution cable or mobile phone network.

**Module** 1. One of a number of sections of program code that provides a sub-solution in a program. 2. One of a set of standardised parts used to construct something such as a logic circuit, computer or virtual learning environment.

**Monitor** An output device that displays information from a computer visually on a screen.

**Monitoring application** Application in which one or more computers are used as part of a monitoring system.

**Multi-access operating system** An operating system that allows multiple users to use the same powerful, central computer through terminals.

**Multimedia** Text, graphics, photographs, sound, animation and video.

**Multimedia authoring program** Application software that enables a user to create output that uses multimedia to produce movie files, often intended for viewing with a web browser.

**Multimedia projector** An output device used for multimedia presentations. Also known as a data projector.

**Multimedia system** A computer system that uses a combination of two or more types of multimedia.

**Multi-tasking operating system** An operating system that can apparently simultaneously run several operating system processes and services, and more than one application program.

**Multi-user system** A system in which many users have apparently simultaneous access to a single computer.

**Musical instrument digital interface (MIDI)** A protocol that has become the industry standard for recording and editing performances on digital musical instruments.

# N

**Network** A number of computers or other suitably enabled devices connected by communications channels provided by cable or wireless. It provides communication between users and allows shared access to resources such as file storage, servers and printers.

**Network operating system** An operating system that manages a computer's, or other suitably enabled device's, communication with a network.

**Network system** A system in which processing occurs independently in two or more computers in more than one location connected to a network, so that they have shared and controlled access to resources such as backing storage and printers.

**Non-volatile** Term applied to data to indicate that when the power is switched off, the data persist and are not lost. Often applied to the memory device, currently flash memory, itself.

**Non-volatile memory** An alternative term for solid-state storage.

**Numeric data type** A data type that accepts input representing a number and enables appropriate processing, storage and formatting for display. There are various sub-types, such as integer and real or decimal.

# O

**Object code** Machine code that a compiler or assembler produces from higher-level source code.

**Objectives** Testable things that a solution should do. A list agreed between the analyst and the client is used after testing to evaluate the success of the solution.

**Odd parity** An odd number of ones in a byte, agreed between sender and receiver as part of a parity check.

**Off-the-shelf software** Software that is standard and readily available. Such software is purchased with no customisation for the purchaser, although it may be customisable. Off-the-shelf software is not necessarily generic.

**Online** A term applied to a computer or a service provided by a computer, meaning that the computer is connected to its network and that it is available on demand by users.

**Operating system (OS)** Software that manages the computer's hardware and all other software. It provides an interface between application programs and the computer's hardware.

**Optical character recognition (OCR)** A process in which software extracts text from the image data of a scanned document.

**Optical disc** A revolving-disc, optical storage medium to which a suitable drive device provides direct access.

**Optical mark form** Printed form used to record optical marks which are then read by OMR software.

**Optical Mark Reading (OMR)** A process in which a combination of optical scanner and software extracts response data from certain positions in the image of a specially prepared data collection form.

**Optical storage device** A backing storage device, known as a drive, that uses an optically-reflective medium. Data are written and read in the medium using a laser.

**Output device** Equipment used to report results to the user or cause something to happen.

# P

**Parity bit** In a parity check, the extra bit added in each byte transmitted to achieve the agreed odd or even number of ones.

**Parity check** A simple data verification check in which an extra bit is added at an agreed position in each byte of data before transmission to make the total number of ones (its parity) odd or even. Reception of a byte with the wrong parity indicates a transmission error.

**Password** A secret code known only to an authorised user of a computer system, folder or file.

**Peer-to-peer (P2P) file-sharing protocol** A protocol for distributing large data files. Instead of downloading a whole file from the original distributor's server, a user joins a swarm of other downloaders' computers to obtain the file piece-meal, downloading from, and uploading to, each other simultaneously.

**Pen drive** See USB flash drive.

**Peripheral devices** Extra equipment connected to the computer, including input devices such as a scanner, output devices such as a printer and backing storage such as an external hard disk drive.

**Permissions** Differing access rights to files, folders or drives given to different users and groups of users, to help maintain privacy and to reduce the risk of data corruption or loss being caused by people.

**Pharming** A hacking attack that intercepts browser requests and redirects them to a fake website where the attacker exposes the user to a phishing attack.

**Phishing** A theft of ID data by deception carried out by sending an email or other sort of message, containing a hyperlink to a fake clone of a legitimate website which directs the user to enter their ID data.

**Picture check** See Format check.

**Pixel** A picture element forming part of an image array that can be processed and stored as a bitmap graphic.

**Plotter** An output device that uses one or more pens to draw curves or lines. This restricts it to line-art, such as shapes stored as vector graphics and simple text characters.

**Podcast** A series of audio or video files that is published on a website and made available as a feed.

**Point of sale (POS)** A checkout (till) at which shop customers pay for their purchases.

**Pointing device** An input device used to point by positioning the cursor in a GUI. For example, a mouse or finger or stylus with a touchscreen.

**Polling** The process carried out by an operating system of periodically interrogating each peripheral device in turn to discover whether it needs the attention of the operating system.

**Prepared data** Data that have been made ready for input, so that they can be input and processed reliably. For example, dates should be in an acceptable format and all required data should be present.

**Presence check** A validation check that essential data items have been entered when the current record is submitted.

**Presentation program/software** An application program that can produce and display a presentation, which is a sequence of multimedia pages known as slides.

**Priority** The importance assigned to a task or message by the user or operating system, which affects its order in a queue for processing.

**Privacy** The state of an organisation or individual not having their information disclosed to others. Maintaining the privacy or confidentiality of data in a computer system involves trying to prevent unauthorised access and accidental or deliberate disclosure by a worker.

**Processor** A silicon 'chip' that carries out the processing in a computer.

**Processor power** The rate at which a processor performs processing, measured in Millions of Instructions Per Second (MIPS) or large numbers of FLoating point Operations Per Second (FLOPS).

**Program** A sequence of instructions, that a programmer must write, to make a computer perform a certain task.

**Program flowchart** A graphical method for representing steps of input, process, decision and output in an algorithm, with arrows showing the order of steps, or flow of control.

**Programming** The process of writing a program.

**Programming language** A language in which a program can be written.

**Protocol** A set of rules for communication.

**Prototype** A partially built solution to a problem so that that area of the solution can be evaluated without reference to the rest of the solution.

**Pseudocode** A method of representing an algorithm's steps like program statements using plain English, mathematical notation and keywords commonly found in high-level languages, without being bound by the strict rules of vocabulary and syntax of any particular programming language.

**Pseudocode keyword** Widely-recognised word used in pseudocode.

**Pseudocode structure** Use of keyword rules (syntax) to implement a program control structure such as iteration or selection.

# R

**Random access memory (RAM)** The main type of internal memory. 'Random' indicates that the processor can access the memory's data in any order needed by the program. This direct, electronic, access gives the processor extremely rapid access to the data. The data stored are volatile, meaning that they are lost when the power is turned off.

**Random file** See Direct access file.

**Range check** A validation check that a numerical, currency or date/time data item lies within minimum and maximum limits.

**Read-only memory (ROM)** This type of internal memory can only be read from, but, like RAM, ROM also provides extremely rapid, 'random' access to its data for the processor. The data stored are non-volatile, meaning that they are not lost when the power is turned off.

**Real data** Data supplied by a project's client for testing purposes, as opposed to test data.

**Real-time operating system** An operating system that supports one or more real-time application programs.

**Real-time process control operating system** An operating system that supports application programs for real-time control of industrial processes.

**Real-time program** A program that processes input and produces output within a guaranteed maximum time.

**Real-time transaction processing operating system** An operating system that supports application programs for real-time processing of transactions, such as seat bookings.

**Record** A set of data representing characteristics of an individual person, object or transaction. It is often displayed as a row of data in a table.

**Record key** A field containing unique values that identify records within a table or file.

**Relational database** A database that stores records in one or more tables. Records in one table can refer to records in another table to avoid redundant storage of data.

**Reliability** Term applied to data to indicate how much of the time they are available, often expressed as a percentage.

**Rendering** In CAD and other forms of 3-D CGI, the processor-intensive process of adding coloured, textured and shaded surfaces to the wire-frame model of a drawing.

**Repetitive strain injury (RSI)** An injury caused by the constant use of certain muscles, mainly in the fingers or wrists, as a result of typing for long periods of time.

**Requirements specification** A list of the needs of a project's client, usually written as a description of what the client wants the new system to do, together with any requirements for specific hardware or software.

**Re-skilled** Description of a worker with skills that are no longer valued, who has learned news skills to improve their employability.

**Resolution** Quantity representing the detail in an image, expressed as the number of pixels per centimetre or inch used to capture or display it.

**Retina scanner** A specialised camera, often using IR illumination, that can capture an image of the retina in a person's eye.

**Ring network** A network in which segments of cable join devices in a ring and data are transmitted from one device to the next in a consistent direction.

**Robot** A machine that can repeatedly carry out a task under the control of a computer.

**Robotics** The study, design and use of robots in automated industrial processes.

**Router** An automated network switching device that remembers the network addresses of the attached computers or other network-enabled devices and can forward data to the correct one. It is often used with a broadband modem to prevent LAN traffic from being sent to the Internet.

**RSS feed** A standardised format for automatic publication of the text of a blog or news service, to which a user can subscribe.

**Rule base** The store of rules that an expert system's inference engine applies to the facts in its knowledge base to solve a problem.

## S

**Scanner** Unless otherwise specified, an optical type of device that creates a digital photograph of a paper document by mechanically scanning the illuminated surface of the document with a single row of hundreds or thousands of light sensors.

**Scope** The limits of the facilities that a solution will provide.

**Search engine** A web application that uses search criteria supplied by the user, to search its index for Internet resources.

**Security** Maintaining the privacy and integrity of data and protecting them against loss.

**Semi-skilled** Term applied to a job whose skills are of intermediate level and can be learned in a few weeks with only limited training.

**Sensor** A device that produces an electrical signal in response to a physical or chemical stimulus.

**Sequential file** Set of stored data containing records sorted into the order (sequence) of their record key values.

**Sequential logic circuit** An arrangement of logic gates connected with feedback from output to input and having one or more outputs whose values depend on the history as well as the current values of their inputs.

**Serial access medium** A storage medium in which data items are written, and must be read, one after another, from the physical start of the medium.

**Serial file** Set of stored data containing records in no particular order other than the chronological order in which they were created.

**Server** A combination of computer and software that provides a service to other, client, computers.

**Simulator** VR hardware and software that provides feedback to the user that closely resembles a real-life experience, such as flying an aircraft.

**Single-user system** A computer system that only one person at a time can use.

**Skilled** Term applied to a job whose skills are of high level and can only be learned over a long period of time with extensive training.

**Smart card** A microcontroller with external contact pads embedded in a plastic card which provides enhanced security for debit and credit card payments and withdrawals from ATMs and other applications.

**Smart card reader** An input device that communicates with a smart card's chip and uses cryptographic techniques to check that the card is authentic and has not expired. It may also accept the input of the PIN and check it against encrypted data stored on the card to authenticate the card's user.

**Smartphone** A mobile phone that has a more flexible operating system than a standard mobile phone and can run more advanced application programs.

**Social networking website** A Web 2.0 site that allows a user to customise a website with personal information, multimedia files and blog entries; communicate by email, chat rooms and private IM conversations; make friends, submit comments to friends' websites and invite friends or the public to events.

**Software** A collective term for computer programs and related data files.

**Solid-state storage device** Backing storage made from integrated circuits or chips. The chip is the medium and little separate drive electronics are required to read from, and write to, it. The currently predominant technology is flash memory, which holds data that are non-volatile but can also be erased and rewritten in large blocks. Also known as non-volatile memory.

**Source code** The high-level language code or assembly code that a compiler or assembler, respectively, can convert to object code.

**Spreadsheet program** An application program that stores data items in a grid of cells and performs user-written calculations on them. It is used to perform reliable and re-usable calculations, including mathematical modelling.

**Spyware** Malware that secretly collects data from a computer.

**Star network** A network in which separate segments of cable or wireless links join devices to a central node that receives data and re-transmits them to some or all of the other devices.

**Statement** 1. In a program written in a high-level programming language, this is a procedural step. 2. In banking this is a list of transactions in a specified period of time.

**Stepwise refinement** The process employed in top-down design of successively breaking down the solution to a problem or task into a number of steps that can be considered as separate sub-solutions or sub-tasks, until we reach sufficiently simple steps.

**Storage medium** The physical material in which a device stores data.

**String data type** A data type that accepts input consisting of a sequence of characters and enables appropriate processing, storage and formatting for display.

**Structure diagram** A diagram that documents top-down design by showing a problem broken down into simpler steps at each level of the structure.

**Sub-directory** A file directory that is listed within another directory and provides an index of the contents of a sub-folder.

**Sub-folder** A folder within another folder displayed by a file manager in a GUI.

**Supercomputer** The most powerful type of computer, its extremely fast processing speeds make it useful for applications requiring large amounts of calculation, such as weather forecasting.

**Switch** Similar to a hub, a central node of a star network or sub-network to which each node (computer or network-enabled device) is connected. Unlike a hub, data transmitted by one node are only re-transmitted to other nodes that are addressed, rather than to all devices. This helps to avoid data collisions on busy networks.

**System flowchart** A diagram that uses symbols to represent the hardware used for input, storage and output and each stage of processing performed by the user or software. Arrows between symbols represent the flow of either data or control.

**System life cycle** The successive processes of analysing, designing, building, testing, documenting, implementing (changing over) and maintaining a system, which may in time be repeated.

**System software** This consists of an operating system and tools with which to do house-keeping and monitoring tasks, such as disk defragmentation and task management.

**Systems analysis** Investigation of all aspects of the operation of a complex system in order to improve its efficiency and of the client's requirements for its replacement. It uses a number of fact-finding methods and methods of representing the results.

**Systems analyst** A person responsible for carrying out a feasibility study and systems analysis and possibly for recommending hardware and software, planning a new system, including its development, implementation (changeover) and maintenance and evaluation of the new system.

# T

**Tagging** A method of indexing the contents of a website to make them easier to find. The person publishing a media file or blog entry associates one or more with each item. Such keywords are known as tags or labels.

**Technical documentation** Information about how a solution was built and is intended to operate to enable (a) a technician to carry out hardware or file maintenance or (b) a designer-programmer to update it to meet changed requirements.

**Teleworker** A person who works away from their organisation's site, including at home, communicating using a computer and telephone.

**Terminal** A device consisting of input devices such as a keyboard and output devices such as a monitor, but without any local backing storage or significant processing power. It simply sends the user's input to a central computer and returns output from the computer to the user.

**Terminator** A device used at each end of a bus network cable to absorb signals so that they are not reflected back into the network and cause data corruption.

**Test data** Specially prepared data to test that a part of a system is working. Normal, extreme, boundary and abnormal values need to be chosen to test input validation and conditional processing.

**Test plan** A list of proposed tests to test specific parts of a solution, using three types of data (normal, extreme and abnormal) for input validation and any conditional processing.

**Test strategy** A specification of aspects of a solution that require testing, for example navigation or reports. For bespoke software written in modules, this may include unit testing of each module, followed by integration testing of the complete system. A thorough strategy also specifies by whom, where and when testing will be performed.

**Text data type** See String data type.

**Top-down design** The strategy of using step-wise refinement to simplify the solution to a problem or task. This involves successively breaking down the solution into a number of steps that can be considered as separate sub-solutions or sub-tasks, until we reach sufficiently simple steps.

**Topology (network)** The pattern of connections between devices in a network, for example star, ring or bus.

**Touchscreen** A display screen that provides input as well as output. The screen has sensors that produce signals representing the touch of a stylus or finger so that it can act as a pointing device.

**Trace table** A table that shows the inputs and variables at each stage when testing an algorithm with a dry run.

**Transaction processing** Processing of an operation, such as a seat booking, retail sale or banking payment, in which the user provides input, a file or database is updated and the user receives a response.

**Trojan horse** Malware that seems to be, or is bundled with, useful and desirable software in order to deceive a user into installing it.

**Truth table** A table written to show the output of a logic gate or circuit for all possible combinations of inputs.

# U

**Uniform Resource Locator (URL)** A unique address for each resource on the Internet.

**Updating** The file maintenance process of altering an existing record; for example, when a person changes their name, address or telephone number. Also known as amending.

**USB flash drive** A solid-state storage device that behaves like a tiny, removable HDD with a built-in USB plug. It uses flash memory chips as the storage medium. The device is also known as a memory stick or pen drive.

**User credentials** The combination of username and secret password that gives a user access to a computer system.

**User documentation** Information about what a system does and how to use it, to assist users of the system. Often called the user guide or user manual.

**User interface** Hardware and software through which a user provides input to a computer or receives information from it. Also known as a human–computer interface (HCI).

**Username** An ID code given to an authorised user of a system. It is not necessarily secret.

# V

**Validation** Checking carried out by a computer system to make sure that only data that follow rules set by a user or programmer are accepted as input. This ensures that data are valid, that is, within the limits of what a user might sensibly or reasonably enter.

**Variable** A uniquely named location in memory in which a single data item can be held while a program is running. By definition, the program can change the value held, although a constant variable's value is set when the program is compiled, but is not varied when the program runs.

**Vector graphic** A digital representation of an image in which the properties of each separate drawn graphical object, such as the centre co-ordinates, radius, line thickness and colour of a circle, are stored as numbers in a file. Graphical objects can be edited separately.

**Verification** Checking for accuracy when data are copied into a computer system from paper documents or from another computer. Valid data may still be incorrect, so verification is a useful further step.

**Video-conferencing** A communication system in which participants in different locations can receive a video stream as well as an audio stream from each other.

**Virtual reality (VR)** A system that presents to the user computer-generated stereoscopic 3-D visual imagery and stereophonic sound of a simulated environment.

**Virtual reality headset** See Head-mounted display

**Virtual reality suit** A device consisting of a set of clothes containing sensors that detect the movements of the user's limbs. Input data from the suit is processed to reproduce the user's movements in a virtual environment.

**Virus** A piece of program code within a data or program file that copies itself and infects other files in the same or another computer. Sometimes used loosely to mean all forms of malware.

**Virus scanner** See Anti-virus software.

**Visual check** A verification check in which an operator reads through a whole record's data on the display screen, comparing each item with the original document to check for and correct any errors.

**Voice over Internet Protocol (VoIP)** A set of communication rules that enables streams of voice data to be exchanged over the Internet rather than over communication circuits maintained by telephone companies.

**Volatile** Term applied to data to indicate that when the power is switched off, the data are lost. Often applied to the memory device, currently RAM, itself.

# W

**Walk-through** In CAD, a VR tour of a design for a real-world environment through which the user has the impression of moving near ground level. The aerial version of such a tour is known as a fly-through.

**Waterfall model** Process of working sequentially through the stages of the system life cycle.

**Web 2.0** Term used to describe to cumulative changes in the ways the Web is used to aid interoperability, user-centred design and collaboration. For example, a social networking site allows an account holder to contribute their own user-generated content to the site via a form viewed in a web browser.

**Web authoring program** An application program that allows a user to generate markup and scripting code for a web page automatically.

**Web browser** An application program that enables a user to interactively access information in the form of text and other media from remote web servers.

**Web pages** An HTML or similar data file that can be stored as a resource on a web server and accessed with a web browser. It may consist of text and multimedia content and contain hyperlinks for navigating to other resources.

**Webcam** An input device consisting of a digital video camera without recording facilities that can feed its data stream to a computer to provide live video while communicating over a broadband Internet connection.

**Website** A collection of web pages stored within a single folder on a web server.

**Wide area network (WAN)** A network that extends beyond the single-site scale of a LAN. It uses links such as telephone lines, fibre-optic cables, and terrestrial and satellite microwave radio links to connect computers.

**Wi-Fi** Commonly used to mean any sort of WLAN. Wi-Fi is actually a trademark indicating that a product conforms with certain widely used international WLAN standards.

**Wiki** A type of Web 2.0 site that allows one or more contributors to create and edit a set of interlinked web pages.

**Window** A rectangular region of the screen in which a running program, document or dialogue box is usually displayed by a multi-tasking operating system with a GUI. It also usually receives input from a pointing device.

**Wireless local area network (WLAN)** A LAN that uses radio waves rather than cables to transmit data between computers or other network-enabled devices.

**Wireless personal area network (WPAN)** Devices within the immediate area of the user, such as a keyboard, mouse, printer, mobile phone, camera or headset, connected to a computer without cables using a short-range wireless technology. Bluetooth is currently the dominant technology. When Wi-Fi is used as the wireless technology, it is known as a Wi-Fi PAN.

**Word processing** A type of application program mainly for creating, editing and formatting documents containing text and graphics.

**Word processor** A word processing application program.

**World Wide Web (WWW)** All the interlinked web pages stored on web servers connected to the Internet.

**Worm** A type of self-replicating malware. It differs from a virus in that it does not need to embed itself within another file and may be able to send copies of itself through a network without any action by a user.

# Index

off-the-shelf software, 24
office automation applications, 165–6
OMR (optical mark reading), 56, 61
online banking, 171
online shopping, 171, 203–4
opcodes, 256
optical storage devices, 82, 84–5
OR gates, 274–6
OS (operating systems), 45, 92
    file management, 101–2
    functions of, 93
    loading, 92–3
    peripheral device control, 102–4
    types of, 94–8
    user interface, 99–101
output design, 129
output devices, 45, 71. *See also* VR
    (virtual reality), I/O devices

palmtops, 48
parallel running, 142
parity bits, 36–7
parity checks, 36–7
patient monitoring equipment, 179
patient records systems, 161–2
payroll systems, 168
PCs (personal computers), 47
PDAs (personal digital assistants), 48
peer-to-peer (P2P) file-sharing
    protocols, 235
pen drives, 86
perfective maintenance, 144
personnel records systems, 167
PERT (Project Evaluation and Review
    Technique) charts, 126
pharming, 231
phased changeover, 142
phishing, 230–1
photo printers, 74
picture check, 34
pilot changeover, 142
PIN (personal identification
    number), 64–5, 169–71, 208,
    226–7. *See also* chip and PIN
PIR (passive infrared) technology, 69
pixelation, 16

pixels, 16, 57
planning, 125–7
plotters, 75
podcasts, 235
polling, 102
POS (Point of sale), 51, 62, 166
POST (power-on self-test), 93
presence check, 34
presentation programs, 20–1
pressure sensors, 68
printers, 72–5
privacy of data, 221–2
processing design, 131–2
processors, 45
productivity software, 3
program flowcharts, 244–5
programming languages, 256–60
programs, 255–6
prototypes, 129
pseudocode, 260
    arithmetic operators, 260
    assignments, 260
    conditions, 261
    input/output, 260
    logical expressions, 261
    producing algorithms, 265–6
    repetition, 261–2
    selection, 264–5
    testing, 266–70
    totalling, 261

RAM (random access memory),
    79–80
range check, 33
raster graphics, 16
re-skilling, 218
real-time operating systems, 96–8
record keys, 38
reed switches, 67
referential integrity, 9
relational databases, 9
remote controls, 59–60
requirements specification, 124–5
retina scanners, 66
RFID (radio-frequency identification)
    tag readers, 62–3

RIAs (rich Internet applications), 114
ring networks, 110
robots, 192. *See also* industrial robots
ROM (read-only memory), 79–80
RSS feeds, 235
RSS narrators, 235

satnavs (satellite navigation devices),
    190–2
scanners, 56
screen readers, 76
scripting languages
    multimedia authoring programs, 20
    web pages, 13
search engines, 14–16, 206–7
seat booking systems, 159–60
sensors, 66–71. *See also* actuators
sequential files, 38
sequential logic circuits, 274
serial files, 38
servers, 10
simulation software, 173–4
    architectural simulations, 176–7
    virtual reality, 177–8
    *See also* CAD; CAE; weather-
        forecasting systems
smart card readers, 64–5, 170, 226
smartphones, 48, 155
social networking websites, 232–3
software, 2, 45
software packages, 2
software selection, in system
    design, 127
solderless breadboard, 281
solenoids, 76
solid-state storage devices, 82, 86
source code, 257
spam, 232
speakers. *See* loudspeakers
speech recognition software, 58–9
spreadsheets, 7–8
    for simple simulations, 174
spyware, 230
star networks, 110–11
statements, 258
stepwise refinement, 241

# Acknowledgements

We would like to thank the following for permission to reproduce images:

Cover: Frank Muckenheim / Westend61 / Corbis

Unnumbered, page 3 © 2011 Corel, © 2011 Microsoft, © 2011 Adobe, © 2011 Quark; 1.7 Skype; 1.11 © Google; 1.15 Michael H Ramage; 1.18 Reproduced with the permission of Omega Engineering, Inc, Stamford, CT 06907 USA, www.omega.com; 1.19a Supplied by OMRON Healthcare; 1.20 BunsenTech; 2.1a Oticon Agil miniRITE; 2.02 Access - IT; 3.2 iStock / 300dpi; 3.3 Andy Lauwers / Rex Features; 3.4 IBM; 3.4b Godfried Edelman / iStock; 3.5a Chas Spradbery / Alamy; 3.5b Ton Kinsbergen / Science Photo Library; 3.5c Hugh Threlfall / Alamy; 3.7 Shutterstock / Stocklite; 3.9 Created by NASA; 3.10 Shutterstock / gabor2100; 3.10b www.kinesis.com; 3.10c Shutterstock / carroteater; 3.12a Shutterstock / Bojan Pavlukovic; 3.12b Shutterstock / Oleksiy Mark; 3.13a swinner; 3.13b Gregory Badon; 3.14 RTimages / Alamy; 3.15 Eyebyte / Alamy; 3.16 Shutterstock / daseaford; 3.16b ColourBlind Images; 3.17 Bluudaisy / Alamy; 3.18 Anthony Hatley / Alamy; 3.19 Art Director & TRIP / Alamy; 3.20 Thinkstock; 3.22 iStock / © Finecollection; 3.23 iStock / Suprijono Suharjoto; 3.24 BrazilPhotos.com / Alamy; 3.25 ICP / Alamy; 3.26 iStock / kokopopsdave; 3.30 Vartanov Anatoly; 3.31 Image provided by Tagsys; 3.33 Corbis Premium RF / Alamy; 3.34a Shutterstock / Dr_Flash; 3.35 iStock / Becart; 3.36a Bromba GmbH; 3.38b André Karwath; 3.40 Shutterstock / Gertjan Hooijer; 3.41 Brando Workshop; 3.42 PHOTOTAKE / Alamy; 3.43 © EUMETSAT 2011; 3.44 www.remotemonitoringsystems.ca; 3.45 Image provided by Futurlec; 3.46b Shutterstock / litvis; 3.46b GraphicHead / iStock; 3.47 cambpix / Alamy; 3.48a iStock / Kjschraa; 3.48b iStock / Greg Nicholas; 3.48c Ted Foxx / Alamy; 3.53a Ton Kinsbergen / Science Photo Library; 3.53b Hewlett Packard; 3.54 Shutterstock / ene; 3.55a growing image; 3.56 Shutterstock / Lucian Conman; 3.58 Shutterstock / Yury Kosourov; 3.59 Shutterstock / Maryunin Yury Vasilevich; 3.60 Rapid Electronics (www.rapidonline.com); 3.61a www.vuzix.com; 3.61b Humanware S.r.l. - Pisa - Italy; 3.63a iStock / Bedo; 3.63b Shutterstock / Bragin Alexey; 3.65 Shutterstock / Rimantas Abromas; 3.66 iStock / jacus; 3.67 Shutterstock / Chudo-Yudo; 3.68 Shutterstock / Serg64; 4.1 Ed Thelen / Computer History Museum; 4.5 Southbank Centre 2011; 4.6 iStockphoto / Thinkstock; 4.7 Shutterstock / Christopher Parypa; 5.2 BBC Proms; 5.7 Shutterstock / PozitivStudija; 6.7 Stock Connection Distribution / Alamy; 6.12 iStockphoto / Thinkstock; 6.14 iStock / track 5; 6.15 Gary Doak / Alamy; 7.4 Ian Howard / Geekcorps; 7.5 Screenshot of Calma Interactive learning package for music developed at the University of Huddersfield by Michael Clarke, Julia Bowder and James Saunders, 1997–2000; 7.6 Dave Pape, University of Buffalo; 7.8 Stephen Coburn; 7.9 Chris Howes / Wild Places Photography / Alamy; 7.10 Drugs.com; 7.11 Fancy / Alamy; 7.17 ElsvanderGun / iStock; 7.19 Andrew Howe; 7.20 Monkey Business Images; 7.22 USGS; 7.25 Autodesk; 7.26 ObieOberholzer; 7.27 Produced using the building EXODUS software by FSEG, University of Greenwich; 7.28 imagebroker / Alamy; 7.30 Steve Snowden (StevieS) / iStock; 7.31 iStock / Parema; 7.32a transport picture library / paul ridsdale / Alamy; 7.32b Iosoft Ltd; unnumbered, page 182 imac / Alamy; 7.33 Shutterstock / PozitivStudija; 7.36 Duane Branch / Alamy; 7.38a Shutterstock / Arthur Synenko; 7.38b Microchip; 7.40 Shutterstock / Photoseeker; 7.42 Hugh Threlfall / Alamy; 7.45 Shutterstock / Rezachka; 7.46 iStock / Ricardo Azoury; 7.47 Shutterstock / Bobo Ling; 7.50 NHS Direct; 7.51 Sudheer Sakthan / Shutterstock; 7.53 Phattanapon Rhienmora; 7.54 Sibelius® 6 screenshot reproduced with permission from Avid; 7.55 steinbergnorthamerica.com; 7.56 Steve Twist; 7.59 © Google; 7.60 © Google; 7.61 Stuart White; 8.1 iStock / Karen Harrison; 8.2 iStock / Ugur Bariskan; 8.3 iStock / Andres Balcazar; 8.6 iStock / Peepo; 8.7 AVG; 10.6 Shutterstock / Irina Fischer; 11.10 Inductiveload; 11.13 www.logiccircuit.org; 11.14 scitoys.com.

While every effort has been made, it is not always possible to identify the sources of all images used, or to trace all copyright holders. If any omissions are brought to our attention we will be happy to include the appropriate acknowledgement on reprinting.